Social Science Research

A Cross Section of Journal Articles for Discussion and Evaluation

Third Edition

Turner C. Lomand

Editor

Pyrczak Publishing

P.O. Box 39731 • Los Angeles, CA 90039

Although the author and publisher have made every effort to ensure the accuracy and completeness of information contained in this book, we assume no responsibility for errors, inaccuracies, omissions, or any inconsistency herein. Any slights of people, places, or organizations are unintentional.

Project director: Monica Lopez.

Scanning and editorial services provided by Kiblena Peace.

Copyeditors: Brenda Koplin and Sharon Young.

Proofreaders: Elaine Parks, Cheryl Alcorn, and Randall R. Bruce.

Cover design by Robert Kibler and Larry Nichols.

Printed in the United States of America by McNaughton and Gunn, Inc.

ISBN 1-884585-36-1

Table of Contents

Continued →

Introduction to the Third Edition

Students who are learning how to read research can practice their skills on the articles in this book. They were selected because they are clearly written, employ straightforward research designs, deal with interesting topics, and, as a group, illustrate a variety of methodological techniques.

The articles represent a cross section of social science research. Although sociology, social work, social psychology, and criminal justice are most heavily represented, works from other disciplines are also included.

Learning How to Read Research

Social science students, instructors, researchers, and practitioners all read far more research than they conduct. The ability to read research well is clearly a useful skill, but it is not a skill most people acquire naturally. It needs to be learned. Like most learned skills, one gets better through instruction and practice. A classroom teacher can provide instruction, but learning to read research well also requires practice. Structured practice is exactly what this collection of articles and the associated questions provide.

Evaluating Research

All the research articles in this collection make a contribution to the advancement of knowledge in their fields. However, none of them are examples of perfect research. Perfect research eludes researchers for three primary reasons.

First, there is no perfect way to sample. Some groups such as successful criminals are difficult to locate. Even if they can be located, some of the people a researcher wants to include in a sample are unwilling or unable to participate. In addition, due to time and budgetary limitations, many researchers make do with samples of convenience such as the students in the classes they teach.

Second, there is no perfect way to measure the key variables of interest to social scientists. For example, if a researcher conducts interviews using a tape recorder, he or she can review the material as often as needed to obtain accurate transcripts and reliable interpretations. However, the presence of an audiotape recorder may influence what the respondents are willing to tell the researcher. Using alternatives such as taking notes or relying on the interviewer's memory are likely to lead to an incomplete record. In short, researchers often have to select among imperfect ways to measure the variables of interest.

Finally, interpreting and drawing implications from data involves subjectivity. Trained researchers may have honest differences of opinion on how to do this for a given set of data.

For the reasons stated above, important decisions in the social sciences should be based on the *body of relevant research* in which different researchers used different methods to sample, measure, and interpret research. The last two articles in this collection illustrate how a body of research may be examined quantitatively (through meta-analysis) or qualitatively (through a traditional review of literature). In both methods, more emphasis should be placed on research that is judged to be methodologically stronger. Hence, it is important to be able to judge the quality of individual research reports.

Reading Statistics

Most of the articles in this book employ relatively simple statistical procedures. There are exceptions, however. It is almost certain that every reader will encounter some statistical techniques with which he or she is not familiar. This happens not just to students but to professionals as well. Unless directed differently by an instructor, in these situations students should focus on the author's *interpretation* of the statistics in the narrative of the report.

The Appendix

For most students, primary instruction in reading research articles comes from a classroom instructor. Appendix A may help in that instruction. It contains an excellent article that explains the purpose of each part of a standard research article: heading, abstract, introduction, method, results, discussion, and conclusion.

Factual and Discussion Questions

The Factual Questions appearing at the end of each article address major points of the article, particularly methodological issues. These questions can be answered directly from the article itself. The lines in each article are numbered, which should help in documenting answers. These questions should help students recognize the types of information in research articles that are substantively important and should be noticed.

The Questions for Discussion draw attention to methodological issues on which there may be honest differences of opinion. There are no right or wrong answers to these questions. However, you should be prepared to provide reasons for your answers if they are discussed in class.

Evaluation Criteria

At the end of each article are eleven very basic evaluation criteria that require quality ratings. These may also be used as the basis for classroom discussions. Depending upon the objectives for your research methods class, some instructors may require students to apply a more detailed set of criteria when evaluating the articles.

New to the Third Edition

While some of the articles from the Second Edition have been retained, most of the articles in the Third Edition are new. On the average, the articles in the Third Edition are somewhat shorter than those in the Second. The decision to place more emphasis on shorter articles was based on feedback from users of the Second Edition.

The previous two editions contained only factual questions, which were tailored to each article, and a standard set of evaluation questions that were the same for all articles. The Questions for Discussion, which focus on the unique aspects of the article that need evaluation, are new to this edition.

Acknowledgment

Robert F. Szafran pioneered this reader in the social sciences. In his capacity as editor of the First Edition, he established many structural elements that guided the development of this edition. His contribution is greatly appreciated.

Feedback

I welcome your feedback on this collection and am especially interested in receiving suggestions that can be used to improve the next edition of this book. You can write to me care of the publisher using the address on the title page of this book or by e-mailing messages to me via PyrPublish@hotmail.com

Turner C. Lomand
Editor

Article 1

College Students' Responses to Content-Specific Advisories Regarding Television and Movies

C. Mo Bahk
University of Cincinnati

ABSTRACT. Extending Ingold's research on adult viewers' responses to mature content advisories, this study examined the likelihood of viewing television programs and of viewing theatrical movies with general and content-specific advisories. The results show that among the 63 undergraduate men, viewing likelihood was increased significantly with the provision of all types of mature content advisories, whereas among the 122 undergraduate women viewing interest increased with the "sexuality" advisory but decreased with the "violence" advisory.

From *Psychological Reports*, *87*, 111–114. Copyright © 2000 by Psychological Reports. Reprinted with permission.

Researchers have been concerned with influences of advisory warnings and ratings on television and movie audiences (e.g., Austin, 1980; Bahk, 1998; Cantor & Harrison, 1997; Herman & Leyens, 1977;
5 Ingold, 1997, 1999; Sneegas & Plank, 1998; Wurtzel & Surlin, 1978). Ingold (1999) reported that about 27% of his 568 mail survey respondents replied either "more likely" (11%) or "less likely" (16%) to watch television programs and movies with an announcement that they
10 contain "mature subject matter." In particular, respondents aged 18–34 years indicated the most interest in viewing programs with such advisories (18% of them replying "more likely"). The present study was done to replicate and extend Ingold's study (1999).
15 Although television and movie guides use similar descriptive terms such as sexuality, violence, and language, there appear to be differences in explicitness between movie and television portrayals of such content. For example, while there are many instances of
20 contextually implied sexual intercourse and verbal references to intercourse on television, scenes of actual intercourse are rarely shown on network and basic cable channels (Greenberg, Stanley, Siemicki, Heeter, Soderman, & Linsangan, 1993). Thus, similar adviso-
25 ries might elicit different responses for theatrical movies than for television programs. Further, viewers' responses would also be different when they are provided with advisories to specific content, e.g., sexuality, violence, and coarse language, rather than general advi-
30 sory warnings, e.g., "mature subject matter," as used in

Ingold's study (1999). Bahk (1998) found that college students' viewing interest was significantly increased when they were informed of the presence of "sexual content" in R-rated movies, although the effect was
35 found only for women. Men indicated about the same level of interest in both sexual and nonsexual films when they were rated "R". Cantor and Harrison (1997), on the other hand, reported that one of their stimulus movies whose description suggested sexual content
40 produced significantly higher interest for the men than for the women. These rather inconsistent findings also need to be clarified.

Method

A total of 185 students (122 women and 63 men) enrolled in undergraduate courses at a Midwestern uni-
45 versity participated in the study. Their mean age was 21.1 yr. ($SD = 2.5$). Participants were given randomly one of two versions of the questionnaire that contained items measuring responses to advisories about either television programs or theatrical movies. To assure
50 their answers would be kept anonymous and confidential, participants were asked not to write their names on any of the pages. They were also told not to hand their booklet directly to the researcher when finished but to put it in a large cardboard box at the back of the room.
55 The responses to advisories were measured in the same manner as used by Ingold (1999), except that the questions were asked about both general and content-specific advisories, separately for television programs and for theatrical movies. Thus, the participants
60 were first asked either, "Movie guides in newspapers sometimes indicate that some movies shown at theaters contain mature subject matter. When you see such information about a movie, are you more or less likely to watch the movie?" or "Television programs sometimes
65 have announcements that they contain mature subject matter. When you see such an announcement, are you more or less likely to watch the program?" Three response choices were provided: "more likely," "neither more nor less likely," and "less likely." Then, partici-
70 pants were asked, "When the movie guide [television program announcement] specifically relates to each of the following mature content categories, are you more or less likely to watch the movie?" The three response

Table 1

Likelihood of Viewing Television Programs and Movies with Mature Content Advisories

Medium	Advisory			
	Mature Subject Matter	Sexuality	Violence	Language
Television				
Men ($n = .32\ddagger$)[a]				
M	.34‡	.63‡	.56‡	.19*
SD	.48	.50	.50	.44
m/n/l[b]	11/21/0	20/12/0	18/14/0	6/26/0
Women ($n = 58$)				
M	.22‡	.40‡	−.17*	−.03
SD	.46	.49	.60	.42
m/n/l	14/43/1	23/35/0	6/36/16	4/48/6
Movies				
Men ($n = 31$)				
M	.32†	.45‡	.29*	.26*
SD	.54	.57	.64	.51
m/n/l	11/19/1	15/15/1	12/16/3	9/21/1
Women ($n = 64$)				
M	.22†	.20†	−.34‡	.02
SD	.52	.59	.60	.49
m/n/l	17/44/3	19/39/6	4/34/26	8/49/7

[a]Independent t tests indicated significant differences between men and women in Sexuality ($t_{88} = 2.11$, $p < .05$), Violence ($t_{88} = 5.90$, $p < .001$), and Language ($t_{88} = 2.46$, $p < .05$) for television programs, and in Violence ($t_{93} = 4.74$, $p < .001$) and Language ($t_{93} = 2.23$, $p < .05$) for movies. [b]Raw frequencies: m = "more likely to watch," n = "neither more nor less likely to watch," and l = "less likely to watch." *$p < .05$, †$p < .01$, ‡$p < .001$ (two-tailed).

options were used again for each of the three mature content categories: Sexuality, Violence, and Language.

Results

A viewing likelihood index was computed by giving a value "1" to the response "more likely to watch," "0" to "neither more nor less likely to watch," and "−1" to "less likely to watch" and averaging the responses so that positive numbers indicate favorable inclinations and, also, the larger the number, the stronger the inclination (minimum = −1, maximum = 1). The index score in each cell was statistically tested against the theoretical midpoint (0) by using a one-sample t test. The results show that both male and female students on an average tend to report an increase in their viewing interest in television programs ($M = .34$; $t_{31} = 4.03$, $p < .001$ for men and $M = .22$; $t_{57} = 3.71$, $p < .001$ for women) and in theatrical movies ($M = .32$; $t_{30} = 3.32$, $p < .01$ and $M = .22$; $t_{63} = 3.38$, $p < .01$) when they are accompanied by general "mature content" advisories. As for content-specific advisories, differential patterns of responses were found for men and women. Whereas the men generally indicated an increased interest in television programs and movies with any of the three content-specific advisories, women's interest increased only with the "sexuality" advisory ($M = .40$; $t_{57} = 6.12$, $p < .001$ for television and $M = .20$; $t_{63} = 2.73$, $p < .01$ for movies). Female students also indicated a significant decrease in their interest in viewing television programs ($M = -.17$; $t_{57} = -2.20$, $p < .05$) and movies ($M = -.34$; $t_{63} = -4.61$, $p < .001$) with the "violence" advisory.

The increase in viewing interest in programs and movies with "mature subject matter" appears to be much higher in this study than reported by respondents aged 18–34 years in Ingold's mail survey (1999), which had a return rate of 51%. In the present study, however, being assured of the anonymity and confidentiality of their responses, all 185 participants provided their responses for the analysis, whereas it is possible that some of Ingold's respondents who would say "more likely to watch" might not have returned their survey or might have provided socially acceptable responses, which he discusses as a potential limitation. It is interesting to find in the present study that the women's viewing interest increased when they were informed of the presence of sexual content in a television program or a movie, which supports Bahk's previous finding (1998). In contrast, women's viewing interest decreased significantly about programs and movies with violent content. The results suggest that women may be less likely to watch a television show or a theatrical movie if they know it contains an advisable amount of violence. It is notable that these findings were consistent for both television and movies.

References

Austin, B. A. (1980) The influence of the MPAA's film-rating system on motion picture attendance: a pilot study. *The Journal of Psychology, 106,* 91–99.

Bahk, C. M. (1998) Descriptions of sexual content and ratings of movie preference. *Psychological Reports, 82,* 367–370.

Cantor, J., & Harrison, K. (1997) Ratings and advisories for television programming. In *National television violence study.* Vol. 1. Thousand Oaks, CA: Sage. Pp. 361–410.

Greenberg, B. S., Stanley, C., Siemicki, M., Heeter, C., Soderman, A., & Linsangan, R. (1993) Sex content on soaps and prime-time television series most viewed by adolescents. In B. S. Greenberg, J. D. Brown, & N. Buerkel-Rothfuss (Eds.), *Media, sex and the adolescent.* Cresskill, NJ: Hampton. Pp. 29–44.

Herman, G., & Leyens, J. (1977) Rating films on TV. *Journal of Communication, 27,* 48–53.

Ingold, C. H. (1997) Responses to televised depictions of intimacy. *Psychological Reports, 80,* 97–98.

Ingold, C. H. (1999) Television audience's responses to "mature subject matter" advisories. *Psychological Reports, 85,* 243–245.

Sneegas, J. E., & Plank, T. A. (1998) Gender differences in pre-adolescent reactance to age-categorized television advisory labels. *Journal of Broadcasting & Electronic Media, 42,* 423–434.

Wurtzel, A., & Surlin, S. (1978) Viewer attitudes toward television advisory warnings. *Journal of Broadcasting, 22,* 19–31.

Exercise for Article 1

Factual Questions

1. How did the researcher determine which one of the two questionnaires (television or theatrical) each participant would receive? random

2. What were the three mature content categories? sexuality, violence, language

3. When a participant said "less likely to watch," what score did he or she receive?   – 1

4. How many of the women stated that they were more likely to watch a television program if the advisory said it contained mature subject matter? 14

5. Was the difference between men and women regarding sexuality television advisories statistically significant? w

6. Which mean in Table 1 is closest to zero? Women regarding language content in movies

Questions for Discussion

7. The researcher used undergraduates as participants in this study. Does this limit the generalizability of the results? Explain. Yes only college students aged 18–25* took the survey

8. Did the researcher take adequate measures to assure participants that their responses would remain anonymous? yes

9. The researcher mentions the possibility of participants giving "socially acceptable responses" in studies on this topic. Do you think that this is an important issue? Explain. (See lines 114–115.)

no

10. If you were to conduct another study on the same topic, what changes in the research methodology would you make, if any? none other than even out the disparity in gender

Quality Ratings

Directions: Indicate your level of agreement with each of the following statements by circling a number from 5 for strongly agree (SA) to 1 for strongly disagree (SD). If you believe an item is not applicable to this research article, leave it blank. Be prepared to explain your ratings.

A. The introduction establishes the importance of the study.
   SA   5   (4)   3   2   1   SD

B. The literature review establishes the context for the study.
   SA   5   (4)   3   2   1   SD

C. The research purpose, question, or hypothesis is clearly stated.
   SA   (5)   4   3   2   1   SD

D. The method of sampling is sound.
   SA   5   4   (3)   2   1   SD

E. Relevant demographics (for example, age, gender, and ethnicity) are described.
   SA   5   (4)   3   2   1   SD

F. Measurement procedures are adequate.
   SA   (5)   4   3   2   1   SD

G. All procedures have been described in sufficient detail to permit a replication of the study.
   SA   (5)   4   3   2   1   SD

H. The participants have been adequately protected from potential harm.
   SA   (5)   4   3   2   1   SD

I. The results are clearly described.
   SA   (5)   4   3   2   1   SD

J. The discussion/conclusion is appropriate.
   SA   5   (4)   3   2   1   SD

K. Despite any flaws, the report is worthy of publication.
   SA   5   (4)   3   2   1   SD

Article 2

Implications of Racial Diversity in the Supervisor-Subordinate Relationship

Sandy Jeanquart-Barone
Murray State University

ABSTRACT. This study addresses the impact of race on the supervisor-subordinate relationship. The purpose is to examine this relationship with minority subordinates reporting to both majority and minority group members. Using the subordinates needs framework identified by Baird and Kram (1983), 5 areas were addressed: supervisory support, developmental opportunities, procedural justice, acceptance or assimilation, and discrimination. The results indicated that African American subordinates with White supervisors experience less supervisory support, developmental opportunities, procedural justice, assimilation, and more discrimination than African American subordinates with African American supervisors.

From *Journal of Applied Social Psychology*, *26*, 935–944. Copyright © 1996 by V. H. Winston & Son, Inc. Reprinted with permission.

The supervisor-subordinate relationship is the fundamental building block of the organization. A smooth working relationship without unnecessary tension between the supervisor and the subordinate is critical to the organization since most of the initiatives and activities are taken at that level to achieve the organization's goals. The perceived attitudes and behaviors of the supervisor influence the attitudes and behaviors of the subordinates and vice versa. The effort expended on the job and the subordinate's performance and satisfaction with work are also influenced by the attitudes and behaviors of the supervisor (Klimoski & Hayes, 1980). Despite the importance of the supervisor-subordinate relationship, little research focuses exclusively on this relationship when the subordinate is an African American, with the exception of Tsui and O'Reilly (1989). This issue will become more and more important given the expected increase of minorities in the work force as predicted by Johnston and Packer (1987).

The importance of addressing the impact of race on the supervisor-subordinate relationship is not only important because of the increasing numbers of minorities in organizations, but more so because supervisors differing in race have greater propensity for poor relations (Shuter, 1982; Tsui & O'Reilly, 1989). The purpose of this study is to examine the supervisor-subordinate relationship for African Americans reporting to Whites as compared to African Americans reporting to African Americans. Examining these different effects will allow organizations to identify the specific areas of the supervisor-subordinate relationship that are prone to be problematic when subordinates differ in race from their supervisors. By identifying these areas, interventions can be taken to allow virtually all employees a positive relationship with their supervisor.

Framework

The projected demographic changes can be expected to lead to an increase in the level of tension experienced by minority subordinates in organizations since the dynamics of interactions between members differing in race are shown to be different from interactions among members of the same race (Shuter, 1982). People who differ in race have different socialization patterns, come from different backgrounds, possess different values (Foeman & Pressley, 1987), and quite possibly differ in their social interaction mode. These factors are likely to contribute to difficulties, especially between the supervisor and the subordinate (Dalton, 1959; Thompson, 1960) due to misperceptions and personal prejudices.

In the supervisor-subordinate relationship, as in any relationship, both parties bring their own needs into the situation. Several needs of the subordinate were identified by Baird and Kram (1983). These needs include the career support of the supervisor, developmental opportunities, accurate performance appraisals (procedural justice), and acceptance or assimilation into the majority work group of the organization. A final variable not included in the work of Baird and Kram, but which has been found to be of concern to women and minorities, is shelter from discriminatory treatment from the subordinate's supervisor. Considerable research has shown that discrimination would be an issue for a minority subordinate. Using the variables that Baird and Kram found to be pertinent in a healthy supervisor-subordinate relationship, this study examined these five variables (supervisory support, developmental opportunities, procedural justice, assimilation, and discrimination) when supervisors and subordinates are both similar and dissimilar in terms of race.

Supervisory support refers to both the amount of

career guidance and information and the number of challenging work assignments that promote development. Using the work of Jones (1986) and Alderfer, Alderfer, Tucker, and Tucker (1980), it can be expected that African American subordinates will receive less support from their White supervisors. Jones found only 15% of the African Americans in his sample experienced a supportive climate, while Alderfer et al. found that African American employees do not receive as much important career information as do their White counterparts. While this research examined the experiences of African Americans reporting to Whites, research addressing African Americans reporting to African Americans is virtually nonexistent. However, when the supervisor is African American and has most likely had similar organizational experiences, the African American supervisor as opposed to the White supervisor may be more sensitized to the needs of the African American subordinate. Given this sensitivity, it could be expected that African Americans reporting to African Americans will experience higher levels of supervisory support than African Americans reporting to Whites.

Developmental opportunities are measured by the extent to which supervisors provide their subordinates with opportunities to improve skills and abilities through self-improvement seminars and challenging assignments. The work of Ilgen and Youtz (1986), Alderfer et al. (1980), and Nixon (1985) suggests that minorities in organizations receive fewer opportunities for training and development that prepare them for additional responsibilities. Again, this research is based on examining situations in which African Americans report to Whites. However, the African American supervisor may make extra efforts to ensure that African American subordinates are given opportunities for further development. Based on this, it can be expected that African Americans reporting to Whites will experience significantly fewer developmental opportunities than African Americans reporting to African Americans.

Procedural justice refers to the perceived fairness in the allocation of organizational rewards. While research examining procedural justice is limited, we can look at how supervisors evaluate the performance of subordinates. Kraiger and Ford (1985) in their meta-analysis, and more recently Greenhaus, Parasuraman, and Wormley (1990), found that the race of the rater and ratee did indeed influence performance evaluations. More specifically, it was found that African American employees were rated less favorably, especially when their rater was White. When this happens, it is quite likely that African American subordinates will perceive the appraisal process as unfair since the supervisor's evaluation is perceived as being inaccurate. Given these studies, it can be expected that African Americans reporting to Whites will perceive lower levels of procedural justice than African Americans reporting to African Americans.

Assimilation refers to the socialization or the acceptance of an individual into the informal networks of an organization (Teske & Nelson, 1974). Using the attraction-similarity paradigm, we can examine the dynamics of race in the assimilation process. The attraction-similarity paradigm suggests that people tend to be drawn to those who are similar to them in terms of demographic characteristics, activities, or attitudes (Byrne, Clore, & Worchel, 1966). Since the majority group in organizations is usually Whites, and since there are obvious differences between African Americans and Whites, it can be expected that African Americans as compared to Whites would experience more difficulties in being accepted by majority group members. Tsui and O'Reilly (1989) found that the more dissimilar the supervisor and subordinates are in terms of race and gender, the less effective the supervisor perceives the subordinate to be and the less the supervisor is attracted to the subordinate. These perceptions and attitudes are likely to contribute to distancing, aloofness, and related problems in the supervisor-subordinate relationship. Based on the above discussion, it is expected that African Americans reporting to Whites will experience significantly lower levels of assimilation than African Americans reporting to African Americans.

Discrimination is defined as making a distinction in favor of or against a person on the basis of the group, class, or category to which the individual belongs, rather than on actual merit (Webster, 1989). Biased perceptions and discriminatory treatment are most influenced by stereotypes held by individuals. Common stereotypes of African Americans include: "African Americans are trying to use Whites," "African Americans will always welcome and appreciate inclusion in White society," "All African Americans are alike in their attitudes and behaviors," and "African Americans are lazy and prefer not to work." These stereotypes portray African Americans in a negative light. While stereotypes abound for Whites as well, African Americans are more likely to be stifled by stereotypes than Whites, due in part to the greater number of Whites in the upper levels of organizations. Fernandez (1987) has shown that racist stereotypes are often carried into the organization, resulting in discriminatory treatment. Based on this discussion, it is suggested that African Americans reporting to Whites will experience significantly higher levels of discrimination than African Americans reporting to African Americans.

In sum, it is expected that African Americans reporting to African Americans will experience higher levels of supervisory support, developmental opportunities, procedural justice, assimilation, and lower levels of discrimination than African Americans reporting to Whites.

Table 1
Means, Standard Deviations, Reliabilities, and Source of Measures

Variable	Source of measure	Maximum possible	Number of items	M	SD	Cronbach's α	Split-half reliability
Supervisory support	Greenhaus, Parasuraman, & Wormley (1990)	5	9	2.30	1.01	.95	.92
Developmental opportunities	Developed for study	5	3	2.69	1.05	.88	.80
Procedural justice	Folger & Konovsky (1989)	5	26	2.15	0.82	.94	.83
Assimilation	Hood (1989)	7	10	2.98	1.18	.84	.81
Discrimination	Adapted from ISR[a]	5	7	3.29	0.93	.89	.83

[a]ISR is the Institute for Social Research, the University of Michigan, Ann Arbor, 1973.

Method

Subjects

The population for this study was a national minority organization for federal government employees. This sample was selected due to its minority population. The cover letter of the questionnaire was written on the organization's letterhead and signed by the top executive. The survey ensured confidentiality to the respondents and was accompanied by a postage-paid envelope pre-addressed to the researcher. Of the 1,400 questionnaires that were sent, 163 were returned and 146 of those were from African American respondents. Due to the low response rate (12%), the demographic data of the respondents were compared to the demographic data of the population. Since no significant differences were apparent, subsequent analyses were run. According to King and Miles (1992), it is not uncommon for minorities to be less responsive to surveys than Whites. In fact, one respondent to the survey indicated that he/she filled out several surveys in the work place and nothing was done with the information. For many individuals when this happens, any surveys that are subsequently sent are perceived as a waste of time. Despite the response rate, this study is important since it is one of the first to examine the supervisory relationships of minorities using a national sample.

The sample was composed only of African American employees, 26% of whom were clerks, 23% were postal carriers, 9% were general managers, and the remaining 42% held various other positions, including consultant, therapy technician, data technician, superintendent, nurse, and so on. Forty percent of the respondents were females. Thirty-nine percent of the respondents were between the ages of 41 and 50, with 29% being younger, and 32% being older. Forty-five percent of the respondents had attended some college, while 30% had at least a bachelor's degree. Thirty-one percent of the respondents had been employed by their organization between 19 and 25 years, and 46% were with the organization less than 19 years. Seventy-six (52%) of the respondents had an African American supervisor, and 70 (48%) respondents reported to a White supervisor.

Variables and Measures

Single-item questions tapped the demographic variables of gender, race, age, education, tenure in the job and organization, and race of supervisor. The measure and reliabilities for supervisory support, developmental opportunities, procedural justice, assimilation, and discrimination are provided in Table 1.

Data Analysis

The purpose of this study is to compare the relationship between African American subordinates reporting to African American supervisors and African American subordinates reporting to White supervisors. In order to achieve this objective, t tests were used to determine if there were significant differences in supervisory support, developmental opportunities, procedural justice, assimilation, and discrimination for African Americans reporting to African Americans and African Americans reporting to Whites.

Results

The means and standard deviations are also shown in Table 1. As can be seen, the supervisory support and the procedural justice experienced by the respondents are relatively low. Discrimination is moderately high at 3.29.

The results of the t tests are reported in Table 2. As can be seen, African Americans reporting to Whites experience significantly lower levels of supervisory support, fewer developmental opportunities, less procedural justice, and less assimilation and higher levels of discrimination than African Americans reporting to African Americans. The implications of this study will now be addressed.

Discussion

This study is one of the first to empirically contrast the relationship between African American subordinates reporting to African American supervisors and African American subordinates reporting to White supervisors. The results suggest that African American subordinates with White supervisors experience less supervisory support, fewer developmental opportunities, less procedural justice, less assimilation, and higher levels of discrimination. These results clearly

Table 2
Results of t Tests for Blacks Reporting to Blacks and Blacks Reporting to Whites

Variable	M		t value	$p <$
	Blacks reporting to Blacks[a]	Blacks reporting to Whites[b]		
Supervisory support	2.51	2.08	2.54	.005
Development opportunities	2.84	2.57	1.61	.05
Procedural justice	2.42	1.91	3.70	.0001
Assimilation	3.13	2.79	1.74	.04
Discrimination	3.13	3.50	−2.45	.005

[a]$n = 76.$ [b]$n = 70.$

265 indicate that supervisors are going to have to learn to better manage their subordinates who differ from them in terms of race.

The findings also have strong implications for organizations, especially in the context of the changing 270 demographics of the work force. Organizations will have to have formal interventions to improve the relationships between supervisors and subordinates who differ in race if the organization wants to achieve high levels of productivity. Several suggestions are provided 275 below.

One key intervention can occur in awareness training programs. These programs are similar to sensitivity training in that the program allows people to get in touch with their stereotypes and false assumptions 280 about members of other races. Once they become aware of their stereotypes, the next step is the discovery of how these stereotypes influence their behaviors and decisions that result in subtle discrimination. The purpose is to encourage discussion and self-285 development to allow people to struggle with their prejudices in a safe environment. The goal of this technique is to change the attitudes of managers and to help them understand the dynamics of race.

While training is important, it is often not enough. 290 Xerox found that training was a start, but unless something else was done to reinforce the newly acquired behavior, the old behavior continued to occur. It was only when Xerox tied their efforts at managing a diversified work force to the performance appraisal 295 system that managers took the program seriously (Sessa, 1992). It was after this that Xerox noticed changes in the ways that minority employees were being managed.

A third intervention can occur with the organiza-300 tion's socialization process. A formal mentoring program for organizational members will help in the assimilation process as all members learn both the formal and the informal systems. This can also be expected to help the supervisor-subordinate relationship since su-305 pervisors perceive subordinates with mentors as more competent than subordinates without mentors (Kram, 1985).

While the above three interventions are generalized approaches, organization specific strategies are still

310 required and should entail communicating with minorities in the organization. For instance, conduct an anonymous survey. Examine responses and identify areas that seem especially problematic for minority group members as well as majority group members. 315 When these variables are identified and eliminated, all members benefit. Another aspect is to examine the turnover rate for specific groups of individuals. Exit interviews can then be conducted to identify processes or people that are racially biased.

320 The goal of this study was to compare the experiences of African American subordinates with White supervisors to African American subordinates with African American supervisors. Future research may also wish to examine the interaction of race and gen-325 der, as well as to look at how the cross-race supervisor-subordinate relationship can be altered by the presence of a mentor. While further research in this area is necessary, the results from this exploratory study suggest that the relationship between African American subor-330 dinates and their White supervisors requires improvements. These improvements can increase the competitive advantage of organizations, as well as productivity.

References

Alderfer, C. P., Alderfer, C. J., Tucker, L., & Tucker, R. (1980). Diagnosing race relations in management. *Journal of Applied Behavior Science, 27,* 135–166.

Baird, L. & Kram, K. E. (1983). Career dynamics: Managing the superior/subordinate relationship. *Organizational Dynamics, 11,* 46–64.

Byrne, D., Clore, G. L., Jr., & Worchel, P. (1966). The effect of economic similarity-dissimilarity as determinants of attraction. *Journal of Personality and Social Psychology, 51,* 1167–1170.

Dalton, M. (1959). *Men who manage.* New York, NY: John Wiley & Sons.

Fernandez, J. P. (1987). *Survival in the corporate fishbowl.* Lexington, MA: Lexington.

Foeman, A. K. & Pressley, G. (1987). Ethnic culture and corporate culture: Using Black style in organizations. *Communication Quarterly, 35,* 101–118.

Folger, R. & Konovsky, M. (1989). Effects of procedural justice and distributive justice on reactions to pay raise decisions. *Academy of Management Journal, 32,* 115–130.

Greenhaus, J. H., Parasuraman, S., & Wormley, W. M. (1990). Effects of race on organizational experiences, job performance evaluations, and career outcomes. *Academy of Management Journal, 33,* 64–86.

Hood, J. (1989). *Acculturation and assimilation as applied to the business organization.* Unpublished doctoral dissertation, University of Colorado at Boulder.

Ilgen, D. R. & Youtz, M. A. (1986). Factors affecting the evaluation and development of minorities in organizations. In K. Rowl & G. Ferris (Eds.), *Research in personnel and human resource management: A research annual* (pp. 307–337). Greenwich, CT: JAI.

Johnston, W. B. & Packer, A. E. (1987). *Workforce 2000.* Indianapolis, IN: Hudson Institute.

Jones, E. (1986). Black managers: The dream deferred. *Harvard Business Review, 64,* 84–93.

King, W. C. & Miles, E. W. (1992, August). *Questionnaire design, organizational diversity, and response rate: Does random distribution alone guarantee equal representation?* Presented at the 1992 National Academy of Management Meeting, Las Vegas, NV.

Klimoski, R. J. & Hayes, M. J. (1980). Leader behavior and subordinate motivation. *Personnel Psychology, 33*, 543–564.

Kraiger, K. & Ford, J. (1986). A meta-analysis of ratee race effects in performance ratings. *Journal of Applied Psychology, 70*, 56–65.

Kram, K. E. (1985). *Mentoring at work: Developmental relationships in organizational life.* Glenview, IL: Scott Foresman & Co.

Nixon, R. (1985). *Black managers in corporate America: Alienation or integration.* Washington, DC: National Urban League.

Sessa, V. I. (1992). Managing diversity at the Xerox Corporation: Balanced workforce goals and caucus groups. In Susan E. Jackson (Ed.), *Diversity in the workplace* (pp. 37–64). New York, NY: Guilford.

Shuter, R. (1982). Interaction of American Blacks and Whites in interracial and intraracial dyads. *Journal of Social Psychology, 117*, 45–52.

Teske, R. H. C. & Nelson, B. H. (1974). Acculturation and assimilation: A clarification. *American Ethnologist, 1*, 351–367.

Thompson, J. D. (1960). Organizational management of conflict. *Administrative Science Quarterly, 4*, 389–409.

Tsui, A. & O'Reilly, C. A. (1989). Beyond simple demographic effects: The importance of relational demography in superior-subordinate dyads. *Academy of Management Journal, 32*, 402–423.

Webster's encyclopedic unabridged dictionary of the English language (1989). New York, NY: Portland House.

Address correspondence to: Sandy Jeanquart-Barone, Department of Management and Marketing, Murray State University, Murray, KY 42071.

Exercise for Article 2

Factual Questions

1. What is the dictionary (Webster) definition of *discrimination* cited in this article?

2. How many questionnaires were sent out? How many were returned?

3. Was the sample confined to one area of the nation?

4. What was the value of the split-half reliability coefficient for the measure of discrimination?

5. What was the mean on supervisory support of Blacks reporting to Blacks? What was the mean on supervisory support of Blacks reporting to Whites?

6. Was the difference between the two means that you reported in response to question 5 statistically significant? If yes, at what probability level?

Questions for Discussion

7. Given that the cover letter was written on the organization's letterhead and signed by the top executive, would you have expected a higher rate of return? Explain.

8. Would it have been of interest to you to see the results analyzed separately for some of the demographic groups (e.g., separately for males and fe-males)? Explain. (See lines 210–226 for the demographics collected in this study.)

9. Would you be willing to generalize the results of this study to employees who do *not* work for the federal government? Explain.

10. If you were to conduct another study on the same general topic, what changes in the research methodology, if any, would you make?

11. This research report is relatively short. If the journal had enough space to give the author a few additional pages in which to report on this research, on which aspects of the research would you like to have more information, if any?

Quality Ratings

Directions: Indicate your level of agreement with each of the following statements by circling a number from 5 for strongly agree (SA) to 1 for strongly disagree (SD). If you believe an item is not applicable to this research article, leave it blank. Be prepared to explain your ratings.

A. The introduction establishes the importance of the study.

SA   5   4   3   2   1   SD

B. The literature review establishes the context for the study.

SA   5   4   3   2   1   SD

C. The research purpose, question, or hypothesis is clearly stated.

SA   5   4   3   2   1   SD

D. The method of sampling is sound.

SA   5   4   3   2   1   SD

E. Relevant demographics (for example, age, gender, and ethnicity) are described.

SA   5   4   3   2   1   SD

F. Measurement procedures are adequate.

SA   5   4   3   2   1   SD

G. All procedures have been described in sufficient detail to permit a replication of the study.

SA   5   4   3   2   1   SD

H. The participants have been adequately protected from potential harm.

SA   5   4   3   2   1   SD

I. The results are clearly described.

SA   5   4   3   2   1   SD

J. The discussion/conclusion is appropriate.

SA   5   4   3   2   1   SD

K. Despite any flaws, the report is worthy of publication.

           SA   5   4   3   2   1   SD

Article 3

Homelessness in a Small Southern City

Linda A. Mooney
East Carolina University

Kevin R. Ousley
East Carolina University

ABSTRACT. With recent predictions of the increase in the numbers of homeless, there has been a renewed interest in estimating homeless populations in a variety of locations. While a considerable amount of research has been conducted on homelessness in urban areas, less research has been directed toward estimating and describing the numbers of homeless in rural or nonurban areas. Further, several methodological issues surrounding the definitions of urban, nonurban, and rural (Toomey, First, Greenlee, and Cummins 1993) have made comparisons between these locations difficult. Despite methodological confusion and the consensus that few comprehensive studies of nonurban and rural homelessness exist (Lawrence 1995; Toomey et al. 1993; NCH 1997a; Fitchen 1992), researchers have been quick to conclude that rural and nonurban homelessness are demographically different than urban homelessness. The present research fills the gap in the homeless literature by collecting data on the homeless in a nonurban location, and comparing the results to representative urban and rural samples. A discussion of homelessness within the context of recent welfare reform follows the presentation of results.

From *Electronic Journal of Sociology*, 5, May 2000. Copyright © by Linda A. Mooney and Kevin R. Ousley. Reprinted with permission.

Introduction

The study of homelessness has become "old hat" (Hopper 1998; Wright, Rubin and Devine 1998; Hambrick and Johnson 1998). Once the target of a flurry of research activity, by the early 1990s the significance of homelessness as a major social problem had considerably diminished. For example, in 1985, 32 separate bills relating to homelessness were introduced in the U.S. Congress; by 1992, politicians were all but silent on the topic—a topic soon to be dubbed as "last decade's issue" (Wright et al. 1998:2). Further evidence is gleaned from the news media's coverage of "the homeless problem." In the fall of 1988, the *New York Times* carried over 50 articles on homelessness; in the fall of 1992, 25; and by the fall of 1998, 10. (Hsiao 1999).

Of the many reasons homelessness has faded from the public's consciousness, one stands out—the tendency to view the problem as temporary (Hambrick and Johnson 1998; Wright et al. 1998). Such a belief led to quick fixes in which the day-to-day needs of the homeless became the focus of attention (e.g., food, shelter) rather than addressing structural constraints (e.g., lack of affordable housing) or individual deficiencies (e.g., alcoholism) (*Priority Home!* 1994; Wright et al 1998; *America* 1999).[1] Thus, few significant changes in the causes of homelessness have been initiated and, with the signing of the 1996 welfare reform bill, the numbers of homeless are likely to increase dramatically over the next several years (NCH 1997; Willis 1997a; Applewhite 1997; Stanfield 1997; U.S. Conference of Mayors 1998; Wright et al. 1998).

Such predictions have led to a renewed interest in homelessness and a return to empirical documentation of the numbers and characteristics of the homeless to better develop policy directives. Estimates of the numbers of homeless and their characteristics have significantly changed over the years. Much of the variation in estimates is a result of definitional problems, that is, what constitutes homelessness (cf. Toomey et al. 1993). Estimates also vary with the political persuasion of those involved—activist, for example, versus government official. It is not surprising that calculations vary considerably, from a low of 300,000 to a high of several million (Barak 1991; National Law Center on Homelessness and Poverty 1996; NCH 1998; Wright et al. 1998).

While there is little agreement over the number of homeless, there is some consensus that they are a heterogeneous population, at least in urban areas where the bulk of research has been conducted (Rossi 1989; Barak 1991; Snow and Anderson 1993; Jencks 1994; NAEH 1998; Reganick 1997; NCH 1999). There is also evidence that the rural homeless are different from their urban counterparts, more often female, intact-families, white, and currently working. They also have lower rates of chronic substance abuse and mental illness, and are disproportionately Native Americans and migrant workers (First, Rife and Toomey 1994; NCH 1999; NRHA 1996; Vissing 1996; U.S. Department of Agriculture 1996; Butler 1997).

Considering the relatively few studies on rural homelessness, there is a remarkable lack of agreement as to what constitutes a "rural area" (Hewitt 1989: Toomey et al. 1993). Despite the implied dichotomy of a rural-urban designation, "the distribution of people and the density and form of living arrangements exist on a continuum" (Toomey et al. 1998: 25). The U.S.

Census Bureau defines rural areas as incorporated locations that have a population of less than 2,500 residents, and unincorporated less densely populated areas.
Urbanized areas are places with a population greater
than 50,000. Any area with a population between 2,500
and 50,000 is simply considered a nonurban location
(Hewitt 1989; Toomey et al. 1993; *Statistical Abstract
of The United States* 1998).

Despite these relatively unambiguous definitions, in
studies of rural homelessness the distinctions have become muddied. Butler defines small towns as *cities*
which are "not incorporated...but have populations of
more than 2,500" (1997: 430); Vissing speaks of "urbanized rural areas" (1996:10); Segal investigates "two
contiguous small towns" (1989:28); and Fitchen refers
to "small towns and the open countryside" (1992:173).

Of even greater concern, many investigators appear
willing to draw definitive conclusions about the differences between these ill-defined, inadequately researched areas. For example, Lawrence (1995:298)
states that "...homelessness in the countryside is qualitatively different from homelessness in the city."
Similarly, Vissing (1996:12) concludes that
"[H]omeless people in small towns are much more like
those in rural areas than those in cities...." Alterna-
tively, Dahl, Harris and Gladden comment that comparisons of rural data from North Dakota to several
urban samples suggest that "...the origin of homelessness, demographics, and medical problems of urban
and rural homeless are quite similar" (1992:2).

The present research thus fills a gap in the homeless
literature by: 1) providing a picture of homelessness in
a clearly defined nonurban location, and 2) comparing
the results to both urban and rural samples of homeless.
The two studies selected for comparison have each
been hailed as the leading research in their respective
locations. First, Toomey and Rice's (1990) *Homelessness in Rural Ohio* has been called the "largest and
most comprehensive study of homelessness in rural
America" (Dahl et al. 1992). Although almost a decade
old, the results of this study still serve as the foundation
for present-day discussions on rural homelessness (cf.
Wright et al. 1998: 182-184).

Similarly, Burt and Cohen's (1989; 1990) investigation of homelessness in a national sample of twenty
urban areas with populations over 100,000, has been
described as the "most comprehensive study of its
kind" (Jencks 1994:10) as well as the "most methodologically sound" (Toomey et al. 1993: 23). As recently
as 1998, the Urban Institute described this data set as
the "most recent nationwide study of the urban homeless" available (Urban Institute 1999).[2]

Methodological variations in sampling techniques,
however, should be noted. Burt and Cohen's (1989;
1990) respondents were from homeless shelters and/or
soup kitchens, while the rural data included people
staying in shelters, inexpensive hotels and motels, or
other unique transient locations (First et al. 1990;

1994). The use of nonshelter sources of the homeless is
common in rural areas where there are fewer shelters
and thus fewer visible homeless (Aron and Fitchen
1996; NCH 1997; Wright et al. 1998; NCH 1998).

The present investigation uses shelter residences
only—the common denominator between the two other
data sets.[3] Although the rural data's inclusion of nonshelter residents may make data comparisons more
difficult, Shlay and Rossi (1992) state that the majority
of studies on the homeless use shelter residents as a
criteria for inclusion, and Jencks (1993:13) concludes
that "...the rate of shelter use is about the same in
smaller communities as in big cities." Further, respondents were asked if they knew other homeless people
who did not stay at the shelter. Ninety-seven percent of
the respondents said no. Nonetheless, estimates of the
homeless from shelter populations may *underestimate*
the numbers of the homeless and, thus, skew the resulting demographics.

Methodology

Situated on the coastal plains of North Carolina,[4]
Southern City had a population of 46,000 and a land
area of 18.1 square miles at the time the survey was
conducted. Serving as the regional center for com-
merce, health care, and education, Southern City is
surrounded by several smaller communities with
populations ranging from just over 5,000 to just less
than 500. Dominated by agriculture in general, and
tobacco and cotton production in particular, Southern
City is the county seat—the county having a population
of 108,000 with an unemployment rate of 5.5 in 1992.

Southern City's homeless shelter was established in
1988 as a response to citizen complaints of a number of
people "hanging around in the streets." The shelter
operates as a nonprofit organization, supported by a
variety of church-affiliated groups and volunteers from
the community. Although small grants through the
Federal Emergency Management Agency and United
Way provide the bulk of the over $100,000 operating
budget, much of the food provided to the residents
comes from contributions by the U.S. Department of
Agriculture and donations from local churches, restaurants, and private individuals. Nonfood items such as
bedding and clothes are exchanged with other facilities
such as the County Family Violence Shelter.

The shelter is located in an abandoned elementary
school, built in the 1950s and located in an inner-city
Black residential neighborhood. The "gymtorium"
serves as the center of the facility. It is here that residents sleep in a barracks-like setting with access to
bathrooms and showers, and limited access to a cafeteria. There are no admitting restrictions, although "troublemakers" are required to leave the shelter for the
night.[5] Facilities are sex-segregated with women and
children sleeping on the stage behind a cloth barrier.
The facility also contains an office and sleeping quar-
ters for the full-time director and two part-time assis-

11

Table 1
Characteristics of Homeless by Location

Year of Study:	URBAN Burt and Cohen 1987	SOUTHERN CITY 1992	RURAL First et al. 1990
Age			
Percent 18-30	30	34	52 (18-29)
Percent 31-50	51	57	40 (30-49)
Percent 51-65	16	9	5 (50-59)
Percent over 65	3	0	3 (60+)
Mean Age	n/a	36	32
Marital Status			
% Never Married	55	44	32
% Married/Living Together	10	15	28
% Divorced/Separated/Widowed	34	41	39
Education			
Percent 0-11 years	48	40	43
Percent H.S. Graduate or Equivalent	32	29	57 (H.S.+)
Percent Some Post H.S.	14	25	
Percent College Graduate or More	6	6	
Percent H.S. Graduate or More	52	60	57
Sex			
Percent male	81	75	49
Percent female	19	25	51
Race			
Percent Black	41	54	10
Percent White	46	29	85
Percent Hispanic	10	17	2
Percent Other	3	0	2
Percent Nonwhite	54	71	14

Note: Numbers do not necessarily sum to 100 due to rounding error and/or missing data.

tants. The shelter is open from 6:00 P.M. to 6:00 A.M.

Interviews of shelter residents took place in February and March of 1992, and were conducted by senior and graduate sociology students who had undergone several hours of faculty-led sessions on interviewing techniques. All interviews were conducted at the shelter between 7:00 and 10:00 in the evening and were, with the participants' permission, tape recorded. Each of the seven students was assigned ten of the seventy beds (although not necessarily occupied) located in the shelter and were responsible for interviewing residents in those beds over the course of a six-week period. The days on which the interviews were conducted were determined by shelter activities (i.e., no interviews took place on, for example, "clinic night" or "church night"). Hispanic residents were interviewed with the help of an interpreter. Forty-one residents were interviewed in total.

In addition to asking homeless-specific questions, standard demographic data were recorded (sex, race, age, number of children, marital status, education, and employment). Following Wright (1986: 228-229), percentage differences of ten or more were considered meaningful.

Results

Table 1 reports demographic data from Southern City, as well as from the rural and urban samples. As in previous studies of the homeless, the majority of shelter residents were male—75 percent. The percentage of males and females is significantly different from that of the rural sample, but varies little from the urban data.

Females have traditionally made up a larger proportion of the shelter population than other homeless populations, for example, the soup kitchen population. Most research suggests that the overrepresentation of women in shelters is due to their need to care for dependent children (Vissing 1996; Burt and Cohen 1989; 1990; Butler 1997). While just over half the respondents reported having children (57.1%), females (77.8%) compared to males (52.0%) were more likely to report so and to have their children with them at the shelter.

Southern City homeless shelter residents were predominantly nonwhite (71%), a number significantly higher than the percentage of nonwhites in the urban or rural samples. While approximately 34 percent of the county population is nonwhite, the disproportionately high rate of nonwhites in the Southern City sam-

Table 2
Characteristics of Homeless by Location

		URBAN Burt and Cohen	SOUTHERN CITY	RURAL First et al.
Year of Data Collection:		1987	1992	1990
Time Homeless?[a]				
Percent < 3 months		21	52	50 (49 days or less)
Percent 4-12 months		33	33	89 (1 year or less)
Percent over 1 year		46	15	6 (2 years or more)
Mean days		1170	141	221
Work for Pay Previous Month?		25	34	31
Income Maintenance				
Percent yes (any form)		20	48	n/a
Percent Mentioning:				
SSI		4	13	11
GA		5	27	38
AFDC		12	n/a	n/a
SS/Pension		n/a	7	3
Causes of Homelessness (self-report)?[b]				
Economics	75	(unemployed)	43	55
Chronic Disability	13	(poor health)	21	7
Personal Crisis	33	(alcohol/drugs)	26	36
	21	(suicide attempt)		
	43	(psychologically distressed)		
	66	(institutionalized)		
N =		1,704	41	919

[a] The urban and Southern City homeless were asked, "How long have you been homeless?" First, et al. (1994) asked, "When was the last time you had a home or a permanent place to stay?"

[b] Burt and Cohen (1989) asked respondents a series of questions about: 1) employment for pay in the last month, 2) self-reported health as excellent, very good, good, fair or poor, 3) suicide attempts: "Was there ever a time in your life when you felt so bad that you tried to kill yourself?" 4) alcohol and drug involvement, 5) psychological distress as measured by a score of 16 or above on the CES-D scale, and 5) whether or not respondents had ever been institutionalized in a prison/jail, detoxification center, or mental hospital. Answers to these questions, although not dealing directly with the causes of homelessness, are conditions that could "impair their ability to become self-sufficient" (Burt and Cohen, 1990, p. 31).

ple may be an artifact of the time of year in which the interviews were conducted—in the winter months. Of
230 the 71 percent nonwhite residents, 54 percent were African American and 17 percent Hispanics. Hispanics were more likely than any other racial/ethnic group to report being "farm laborers" (83%). Farm labor, like construction, the second most frequently reported work
235 category, is seasonal and may have been responsible for the inflated number.

Consistent with both the urban and rural samples, the average age of shelter respondents was 36, with a median value of 34. As Rossi (1990:957) states,
240 "...today's homeless are surprisingly young; virtually all recent studies of the homeless report median ages in the low to middle 30s." Somewhat surprisingly, however, younger respondents were not more likely to report being first-time shelter residents.

245 Southern City shelter residents were less likely to never be married (44%) than their urban counterparts (55%), but more likely than rural respondents (32%). As Barak (1991:36) notes, the percentage of married people among the urban homeless is lower than that
250 among the rural homeless. However, Southern City and

urban data in other marital categories are comparable. Respectively, Southern City and the urban data indicate that 15 percent and 10 percent of the respondents were married or living together, and 41 percent and 34 per-
255 cent of the respondents were divorced, separated, or widowed.

Over half the Southern City respondents reported graduating from high school or higher levels of education (60%), which is similar to the urban and rural
260 samples. Educational levels varied little by sex, but were substantively interesting by race/ethnicity. Forty percent of the nonwhite respondents reported having less than a high school degree compared to 67 percent of the white respondents. Thus, in the present sample,
265 minority shelter residents were better educated than their white counterparts.

Of the variables of interest, length of time homeless was the most difficult to compare across samples given differences in measurement intervals. Some respon-
270 dents initially explained being unsure how long they had been homeless, reporting moving in and out of relatives' and friends' homes and abandoned houses. When asked how long he had been homeless, one 39-

year-old white male responded, "Off and on. I would
275   say approximately, you know, maybe a year and a
half...two years...maybe three." (#7)

Table 2 continues the analysis of characteristics of
urban, nonurban, and rural respondents. Southern City
residents most often reported being homeless three
280   months or less (52%), followed by four to twelve
months (33%), and more than 12 months (15%). Burt
and Cohen's (1989; 1990) research found that the modal interval was over a year (46%) while 89 percent of
the rural respondents report being homeless for a year
285   or less. Mean days homeless indicate that time homeless is significantly greater in urban areas (1170 days),
followed by rural (221 days) and nonurban areas (141
days).

Respondents in the rural and Southern City samples
290   were asked whether they had worked for pay in the
previous month. While rural and Southern City respondents varied little in the percent responding yes, 31 and
34 percent, respectively, urban homeless respondents
reported that 25 percent were "presently working."
295   Income maintenance was measured by whether or
not a respondent, at the time of the survey, was receiving Aid to Families with Dependent Children
(AFDC), General Assistance (GA), Supplemental Security Income (SSI), or Social Security (SS)/pension. A
300   slightly higher than might be expected proportion of
Southern City shelter residents received income maintenance benefits—48 percent—over twice the number
receiving such benefits in the urban sample. However,
when asked the type of benefit received, respondents in
305   the nonurban and rural samples were most likely to
mention General Assistance over any other type of
benefit.

Finally, respondents were asked, "What do you
think caused your homelessness?"[6] Categories included
310   *chronic disability* (mental and physical illness, substance abuse, institutionalization); *personal crisis* (divorce, runaway/throwaway, family conflicts, death of
spouse); and *economic conditions* (loss of employment,
lack of sufficient funds, eviction, and/or no transporta-
315   tion). Consistent with other research (cf. Momeni
1990:79), the modal category for the nonurban and
rural samples is economic conditions (43% and 55%,
respectively). As one 30-year-old Black female responded (#15):

320   The reason I'm in this place is because I do not have a
job. It is simply that. You have to have money to pay for
those things and most people are staying here because
they don't have a job. If you had a job you could stay and
save up money. No one wants to stay. The only people
325   who have to stay here, some of the people like, have alcohol problems or something like that, and they can't
work but I don't have any of those problems. There is no
reason why I should not be able to work and get out of
this shelter—none.

330   Chronic disability variables were the least likely to
be mentioned in both the nonurban and rural samples.

However, an examination of responses from the urban
sample indicates that a fairly high proportion of respondents reported being in poor health (13%) and
335   receiving some form of institutionalized treatment at
least once in their life (66%).

Discussion

The results, although reaffirming the heterogeneity
of the homeless population and the need for consistent
measurement techniques, also suggest that, contrary to
340   Vissing (1996), Lawrence (1995) and Dahl et al.
(1992), the characteristics of the nonurban homeless
reflect those of both comparison samples. The homeless in Southern City were predominantly nonwhite
males, with an average age of 36. Most were never
345   married; almost half did not graduate from high school
and, on the average, had been homeless for four to five
months. A third had worked for pay in the month prior
to the survey, and almost half were receiving some
kind of income maintenance.
350   The above portrait bears a remarkable similarity to
Burt and Cohen's (1989:36) description of urban respondents:

...homeless persons in cities with a population of 100,000
over....are male... the majority are nonwhite...between 30
355   and 51 years of age...[A]lmost half have not graduated
from high school...

Southern City homeless were also disproportionately Black, young, single males. However, similarities
between Southern City homeless and First et al.'s
360   (1990; 1994) rural sample also exist. Nonurban and
rural homeless were less likely to be homeless for over
a year, the mean days for rural and Southern City samples being 141 and 221 respectively. The mean number
of days of homelessness for the urban sample was
365   1,170.

Further, the distribution of income maintenance
between the rural and Southern City samples are similar—General Assistance being the most common form
of aid in both samples. While comparisons of self-
370   reported causes of homelessness are difficult given
differences in the interview formats, educational levels
appear analogous for all three groups with a range of
only 52 to 60 percent completing high school and/or
with some post-high school experience.
375   It is possible, however, that the variations in the
characteristics of the homeless may, in part, be an artifact of variations in the three sampling designs. For
example, Southern City homeless were exclusively
from shelters. Some research suggests that women are
380   more likely to seek refuge in shelters and, thus, the
Southern City estimates of the number of homeless
females may be exaggerated (Toomey et al. 1993). On
the other hand, Vissing (1996) and First et al. (1994)
suggest that homeless rural families, the highest pro-
385   portion of which are headed by females, are more
likely to stay with friends and family than in shelters,
which would suggest that the Southern City sample

underestimated the number of homeless females. Given that 75% of the sample were men, the second interpretation appears more likely.

Additionally, as noted earlier, the proportion of nonwhites was considerably higher than that in the urban or rural samples. It was suggested that the months in which the interviews took place—February and March—may have impacted the number of African Americans and Hispanics who were disproportionately migrant workers. State statistics support this contention. North Carolina farm worker service providers estimate that between 15 and 50 percent of all migrant workers spend at least some time in a shelter, most frequently in the winter months (North Carolina Consolidated Plan 1996). Further, the number of the homeless in Southern City could be overestimated and/or "urbanized" as the homeless migrate south from the harsh winters of the northern states (Jencks 1994:1).

The shelter has grown considerably since the data were collected. As if in preparation for what lies ahead, the staff has more than doubled. Consistent with national trends, there have been rumblings of funding cutbacks and moving the shelter to a different, i.e., less visible, location. The National Law Center on Homelessness and Poverty recently published a report, *Out of Sight, Out of Mind?*, which documents similar efforts to conceal the homeless through the relocation of shelters, nightly "sweeps," and forcible removal from high visibility areas (Nieves 1998; Hsiao 1998; *America* 1999).

Such trends reflect a general movement toward what Hooper (1998) calls "remoralizing" the poor and, by extension, the homeless. The implication that the poor and homeless are somehow accomplices in their own circumstances, that poverty is symptomatic of individual deficiency, is implicit in the Personal Responsibility and Work Opportunity Reconciliation Act of 1996, which subordinates need to merit. Ironically, many of the same people who have been denied welfare assistance are now homeless and, once again, are being penalized for their poverty. For example, New York City officials have declared that shelters are a form of public assistance and, therefore, shelter residents must meet the requirements of all public assistance recipients including workfare (Bernstein 1999:1).

The effects of welfare reform are, and will continue to be, disproportionately felt in rural areas where homelessness is most closely linked to poverty and there are fewer shelters and other services to compensate for the loss of welfare benefits (Aron and Fitchen 1996; Butler 1997; NCH 1998; Wright et al. 1998). In Wisconsin, a largely rural state, a 75 percent reduction in welfare recipients has resulted in a three-fold increase in the homeless population (DeParle 1999; Willis 1997a; Stanfield 1997); and in Maine, a five-year limit on welfare benefits has increased homelessness in a state "where welfare has kept many [of the

respondents] one step away from life on the streets" (Butler 1997: 432).

Thus, while government officials, as indicated by the policies they initiate, pursue the path of least resistance by blaming the victim, homeless advocates continue to call for structural alterations, most notably the reduction of poverty and an adequate supply of low-income housing (Wright et al. 1998: 210). Ultimately, homelessness is a problem of poverty and in areas where poverty rates are the highest, often nonurban areas, homelessness will continue to increase, particularly with the removal of the safety net of public assistance. The need to count and classify, describe and define, hence remains paramount in identifying the causes of homelessness in the hopes of developing public policies that work.

References

America. 1999. "More Homeless, More Hungry." *America* 180 (3): 3.

Applewhite, Steven Lozano. 1997. "Homeless Veterans: Perspectives on Social Services Use. *Social Work 42* (1): 19-31.

Aron, Laudan Y. and Janet M. Fitchen. 1996. "Rural Homelessness: A Synopsis" in *Homelessness in America* 1996. National Coalition for the Homeless. Washington, D.C.: Oryx Press.

Barak, Gregg. 1991. *Gimme Shelter* N.Y: Praeger.

Bernstein, Nina. 1998. "New York City Plans to Extend Workfare to Homeless Shelters." *New York Times* (February 20): 1.

Burt, Martha and Barbara E. Cohen. 1989. *America's Homeless: Numbers, Characteristics, and Programs that Serve Them."* Washington, D.C.: The Urban Institute Press.

Burt, Martha and Barbara E. Cohen. 1990. "A Sociodemographic Profile of the Service-Using Homeless: Findings from a National Survey. " Pp. 17-38 in *Homelessness in the United States—Data and Issues,* edited by Jamshid Momeni. N.Y.: Praeger.

Butler, Sandra Sue. 1997. "Homelessness Among AFDC Families in a Rural State: It Is Bound to get worse." *Affilia* 12 (4): 427- 441.

Dahl, Sherlyn, Helen Harris and Joanne Gladden. 1992. "Homelessness: A Rural Perspective." *Prairie Rose* (August):1-6. First, Richard, John Rife, and Barbara Toomey. 1994. "Homelessness in Rural Areas: Causes, Patterns, and Trends." *Social Work* 39 (1): 97-108.

DeParle, Jason. 1999. "Wisconsin Welfare Overhaul Justifies Hope and Some Fear. " *New York Times* (January 15): A1.

Department of Health and Human Services. 1998. "National Survey of Homeless Assistance Providers and Clients." HHS Homepage. <http://www.dhhs.gov>

First, Richard, John Rife, and Beverly Toomey. 1994. "Homelessness in Rural Areas: Causes, Patterns and Trends." *Social Work* 39 (1): 97-108.

First, Richard, Beverly Toomey and J. Rife. 1990. *Homelessness in Rural Ohio.* Columbus, Ohio: Ohio State University.

Fitchen, Janet M. 1991. "On the Edge of Homelessness: Rural Poverty and Housing Insecurity." *Rural Sociology* 57 (2) 173-193.

Hambrick, Ralph S. and Gary Johnson. 1998. "The Future of Homelessness." *Society 35 (6): 28-38.*

Hewitt, M. 1989. "Defining 'Rural' Areas: Impact on health care policy and research." Washington, D.C.: Community for Creative Nonviolence.

Hopper, Kim. 1998. "Housing the Homeless." *Social Policy* 28 (3): 64-67.

Hsiao, Andrew. 1998. "The Disappeared." *The Village Voice* 43 (49): 32-33.

Jencks, Christopher. 1994. *The Homeless.* Cambridge, MA: Harvard University Press.

Lawrence, Mark. 1995. "Rural Homelessness: A Geography without a Geography. *Journal of Rural Studies* 11 (3): 297-301.

Momeni, Jamshid. 1990. "No Place to Go: A National Picture of Homelessness in America." Pp. 165-183 in *Homelessness in the United States—Data and Issues,* edited by Jamshid Momeni. N.Y.: Praeger.

NAEH (National Alliance to End Homelessness). 1998. "Facts about Homelessness." National Alliance to End Homelessness, 1518 K Street, NW, Washington, D.C., 20005 <http://www.naeh.org>

NCH (National Coalition for the Homeless). 1999. "Who is Homeless?: Fact Sheet No. 3." February. 1012 14th Street, NW. Suite 600. Washington, D.C. 20005. 202/73775-6444.

_____.1998. "How Many Homeless: Fact Sheet No. 2." May. 1012 14th Street NW. Suite 600. Washington, D.C. 20005. 202/73775-6444.

_____. 1997a. "Rural Homelessness: Fact Sheet Number 13." October. 1012 14th Street, NW. Suite 600. Washington, D.C. 20005. 202/73775-6444.

_____. 1997b. "Homelessness in America: Unabated and Increasing." 1012 14th Street, NW. Suite 600. Washington, D.C. 20005. 202/73775-6444.

National Law Center on Homelessness and Poverty. 1996. "Mean Sweeps: A Report on Anti-Homeless Laws, Litigation and Alternatives in 50 United States Cities." National Law Center on Homelessness and Poverty. 918 F Street, NW, Washington, DC 20004. 202/638-2535.

National Rural Health Association. 1996. "The Rural Homeless: America's Lost Population." Kansas City: NRHA #PU0896-42.

Nieves, Evelyn. 1998. "Homelessness Tests San Francisco's Ideals." *New York Times* (November 13): A1.

North Carolina Consolidated Plan. 1996. "Housing Needs Assessment: Homeless Needs, Facilities and Services." November. Washington, D.C.: U.S. Department of Housing and Urban Development. Office of Community Planning and Development. <http:www.state.nc.us/commerce/commasst/plan>

Oreskes, Michael and Robin Toner. 1989. "The Homeless at the Heart of Poverty and Policy." *New York Times* (January 29).

Priority Home! 1994. "The Federal Plan to Break the Cycle of Homelessness." Interagency Council on the Homeless. Washington, D.C.: Government Printing Office.

Reganick, Karol A. 1997. "Prognosis for Homeless Children and Adolescents." *Childhood Education* 73 (3): 133-136.

Rossi, Peter H. 1989. *Down and Out in America: The Origins of Homelessness.* Chicago, Il.: University of Chicago Press.

Shinn, Marybeth. 1997. "Family Homelessness: State or Trait?" *American Journal of Community Psychology* 25(6): 755-770.

Shlay, Anne B. and Peter Rossi. 1992. "Social Science Research and Contemporary Studies on Homelessness." *Annual Review of Sociology* 18: 129-160.

Snow, David and Leon Anderson. 1993. *Down on Their Luck: A Study of Homeless Street People.* Berkeley: California University Press.

Snow David, Susan Baker, Leon Anderson, and Michael Martin. 1986. "The Myth of Pervasive Mental Illness Among the Homeless." *Social Problems* 33 (5): 407-423.

Sosin, Michael. 1992. "Homeless and Vulnerable Meal Program Users: A Comparison Study." *Social Problems* 39 (2): 170-188.

Stanfield, Rochelle. 1997. "HUD Choice May Face Old Problems." *National Journal* 28 (3): 120-122.

Statistical Abstract of the United States, 118th edition. 1998. Washington, DC: Government Printing Office.

Toomey, Beverly, Richard First, Richard Greenlee and Linda Cummings. 1993. "Counting the Rural Homeless Population: Methodological Dilemmas." *Social Work Research and Abstracts 29(4):23-27.*

U.S. Conference of Mayors. 1998. "A Status Report on Hunger and Homelessness in American Cities." U.S. Conference of Mayors. <http://www.usmayors.org/uscm/>

U.S. Department of Agriculture, Rural Economic and Community Development. 1996. "Rural Homelessness: Focusing on the Needs of the Rural Homeless." U. S. Department of Agriculture, Rural Housing Service, Rural Economic and Community Development, 14th St. and Independence Ave. SW. Washington, DC 20250-1533.

Urban Institute. 1998. "Homelessness: Ten Basic Questions Answered." <http://www.urban.org/news/ factsheet/homelessFS.html>

Vissing, Yvonne M. 1996 *Out of Sight, Out of Mind.* Lexington: University of Kentucky Press.

Willis, Laurie. 1997a. "Grim Forecast for Needy." *News and Observer.* December 5: B1.

Willis, Laurie. 1997b. "Conference to Focus on Homeless." *News and Observer.* December 4: B7.

Wright, James D., Beth A. Rubin and Joel A. Devine. 1998. *Beside the Golden Door.* New York: Aldine.

Wright, S. E. 1986. *Social Science Statistics.* Newton, MA: Allyn and Bacon, Inc.

Note: This paper was presented at the annual meetings of the Southern Sociological Society in Chattanooga, TN, on April 2, 1993.

Acknowledgments: The authors gratefully acknowledge the valuable assistance of Jon Beckert, Brian Crisp, Michael Dalecki, Donna Evans, Bonnie Haswell, Michelle Hilhorst, Sarah Poulos, Christine Ransdell, Lisa Tripp, and Amy Whitcher.

Address correspondence to: Linda A. Mooney, Department of Sociology, East Carolina University, Greenville, NC 27858. E-mail: mooneyl@mail.ecu.edu

Endnotes

[1] Obviously, any given individual's homelessness has multiple causes. Nonetheless, the debate over causality most often has been framed as one between structural versus individualistic variables or what Shinn (1997) calls "states versus traits." Wright et al. (1998) proposes an intermediate and theoretically sound position: "defects and dislocations of structure...create a population at risk of homelessness; defects of persons determine who within the at-risk population actually becomes homeless" (p. 9).

[2] A more recent survey, the 1996 National Survey of Homeless Assistance Providers and Clients, was modeled after the Burt and Cohen (1989) study. Its emphasis, however, unlike its predecessor, is on the providers of homeless assistance and the clients they serve (Department of Health and Human Services 1998).

[3] Southern City does not have a soup kitchen or any other assisting services, with the exception of the Salvation Army, which, if called by the police, accompany the homeless person to the shelter.

[4] According to the North Carolina Consolidated Plan (1996), homelessness in the state varies by geographical region. The most populated area of the state, the Piedmont, has the highest rate of homeless, followed by the coastal plains and the mountains. Statistics from 1994, those that most closely approximate the study date, indicate that North Carolina had 187 emergency shelters with a sleeping capacity of 4,271 in 64 of the state's 100 counties. As in other states, homelessness in North Carolina is predicted to grow with a 1997 estimate of over 500,000 North Carolinians on the verge of homelessness (Willis 1997b).

[5] Several city police were interviewed, as was the police attorney, in reference to police policy concerning the homeless. Police indicated that on any given night, the shelter was the location of an estimated 90 to 100 percent of the homeless in the city limits. Police, when coming upon a homeless person, drive the person to the shelter if so desired, or simply make sure that the person "moves along" since there is a policy of "no sleeping" in public parks at night, or in alleys, streets, or sidewalks. Additionally, the shelter director and staff members were interviewed concerning shelter policy and history.

[6] Burt and Cohen did not ask for self-reported causes of homelessness. They did, however, ask about employment, health concerns, institutionalization (prison/jail, mental hospital, drug/alcohol treatment facility), psychological distress, and attempted suicide.

Exercise for Article 3

Factual Questions

1. Estimates of the number of homeless nationally vary from a low of 300,000 to a high of how many?

2. Who conducted the interviews?

   senior + graduate sociology students

3. Were the interviews conducted in the shelters?

   at the shelter

4. In Southern City, what percentage of the homeless were males?

   75%

5. According to the researchers, of the variables of interest, which one was the most difficult to compare across samples?

   length of time homeless

6. Did a higher percentage of Southern City *or* urban respondents receive income maintenance benefits?

Southern City

Questions for Discussion

7. In your opinion, is it reasonably valid to compare the results of a study in which only respondents in shelters/soup kitchens were interviewed with results of a study in which other groups were also included, such as respondents in inexpensive motels? Explain. (See lines 119–143.)

8. Would it be interesting to know why Southern City and not some other city was chosen as the site for the survey? *Yes, but they mentioned why*

9. If you had been conducting this study, are there any other questions you would have asked the homeless? Explain. *Why do you think you homeless?* *p.91* *147-164*

10. The researchers are critical of "government officials." In your opinion, is it acceptable for researchers to voice such opinions? Explain. (See lines 448–458.) *no. Researchers must be objective.*

11. In light of the information in this article, do you believe that more research on the homeless is needed? *Yes*

Quality Ratings

Directions: Indicate your level of agreement with each of the following statements by circling a number from 5 for strongly agree (SA) to 1 for strongly disagree (SD). If you believe an item is not applicable to this research article, leave it blank. Be prepared to explain your ratings.

A. The introduction establishes the importance of the study.

   SA   5   (4)   3   2   1   SD

B. The literature review establishes the context for the study.

   SA   5   (4)   3   2   1   SD

C. The research purpose, question, or hypothesis is clearly stated.

   SA   5   (4)   3   2   1   SD

D. The method of sampling is sound.

   SA   5   (4)   3   2   1   SD

E. Relevant demographics (for example, age, gender, and ethnicity) are described.

   SA   (5)   4   3   2   1   SD

F. Measurement procedures are adequate.

   SA   (5)   4   3   2   1   SD

G. All procedures have been described in sufficient detail to permit a replication of the study.

   SA   (5)   4   3   2   1   SD

H. The participants have been adequately protected from potential harm.

   SA   5   (4)   3   2   1   SD

I. The results are clearly described.

   SA   (5)   4   3   2   1   SD

J. The discussion/conclusion is appropriate.

   SA   5   (4)   3   2   1   SD

K. Despite any flaws, the report is worthy of publication.

   SA   5   (4)   3   2   1   SD

Article 4

The Blessing As a Rite of Passage in Adolescence

Christopher A. Bjornsen
Longwood College

ABSTRACT. Central to the transition from adolescence to early adulthood is the transformation that takes place in the parent-child relationship, heretofore studied as emotional autonomy, psychological separation, and separation-individuation. Blos (1985) suggested that individuation perhaps necessarily includes the confirmation of the child's adult status by the same-sex parent, called "the blessing." Of the 281 late adolescents in the present study, 71.5% indicated they had received some type of blessing from a parent and described the event as meaningful. Males were more likely to receive a blessing regarding instrumental traits, while females were more likely to receive a blessing regarding overall maturity, pubertal changes, or a specific rite of passage. These results offer support for Blos's position regarding the importance of this event to the young adult.

From *Adolescence*, *35*, 357–363. Copyright © 2000 by Libra Publishers, Inc. Reprinted with permission.

Psychosocial development during preadolescence, early adolescence, and middle adolescence has received much attention over the past decade. Less research has focused on the transition to early adulthood in the 18- to 25-year-old population. Central to this transition is the transformation that takes place in the parent-child relationship and the impact upon the youth's psychosocial maturity, investigated as emotional autonomy, psychological separation, and separation-individuation (Delaney, 1996; Fuhrman & Holmbeck, 1995; Grotevant & Cooper, 1986; Hoffman, 1984; Mather & Winston, 1998; McClanahan & Holmbeck, 1992; Paladino Schultheiss & Blustein, 1994; Ryan & Lynch, 1989; Steinberg & Silverberg, 1986; White, Speiseman, & Costos, 1983). Blos (1985) suggested that an important aspect of the maturation process is "the blessing." According to Blos, the blessing is the father's acknowledgment and acceptance of the son's adult status and, more important, his adult masculinity. The present study expanded on Blos's treatment of the father-son relationship to include the mother-daughter relationship.

Blos (1985) supported the traditional interpretation of the initial, childhood resolution of the Oedipal conflict. However, he offered a different view of the crucial task of adolescence. Blos argued that the adolescent male must indeed address feelings toward his mother during this phase of development, but the resolution or transformation of such feelings has a different likelihood of resolution since they are closer to the surface. Put another way, the adolescent male is relatively conscious of his need for female companionship, and acts in ways that help him meet this need. In "normal" development, the male is forced to confront any troublesome issues he may have with the opposite sex, such as issues with his mother, in order to move on to a more satisfying, less anxious state.

On the other hand, there remains the issue of identification with the father, which brought to a close the Oedipal phase. Blos argued that feelings are involved—having firm roots in early childhood development—that do not simply disappear of their own accord once the male reaches a certain age, and are not resolved merely as a by-product of the male's resolution of son-mother issues. It was Blos's contention that a transformation of the son-father relationship may be a more important developmental issue than that which occurs between son and mother. The question is, how is the son's identification with the father, an identification that served him well during late childhood and early adolescence, transformed into a "representation" that allows the son to leave childhood and adolescent attachments to the father behind, and thus progress into adult emotional (or psychosexual) status? According to Blos, an event that has an important effect on the son's ability to make this transition is the conferring of the father's blessing, which serves to acknowledge the son's masculine identity. To restate this idea, the blessing is the father's message that "you are a man, my son." Blos stated: "At the termination of adolescence, a new stage in the life of the growing son appears, when the father's affirmation of the manhood attained by his son, conveyed in what we might call the father's blessings of the youth's impatient appropriation of adult prerogatives and entitlements, reaches a critical urgency" (p. 11).

Blos proposed that the blessing is "one component of the son-father relationship that needs to be settled before childhood can be brought to a natural termination" (p. 12). The implication is that not receiving a parental blessing may be associated with problematic

Table 1
Blessing Received and Wanted (by Gender)

| | Received | | | | Wanted | | | |
| | Male | | Female | | Male | | Female | |
	n	%	n	%	n	%	n	%
Rite of Passage	17	22.1	33	26.6	–	–	2	7.1
Pubertal Growth	4	5.2	12	9.7	1	5.9	2	7.1
Respect	10	13.0	25	20.2	8	47.1	14	50.0
Decision-making	29	37.7	33	26.6	7	41.2	9	32.1
Skills	8	10.4	10	8.1	–	–	1	3.6
Finances	8	10.4	4	3.2	1	5.9	–	–
Always Treated	1	1.3	7	5.6	–	–	–	–

development during early adulthood. This possibility was investigated in the present study using self-reports of attitudes toward interpersonal violence.

Method

Participants

Students at one rural open-admission public college, two small private colleges, and one large urban public university in the mid and south Atlantic regions of the United States voluntarily participated in this research. Completed questionnaires were obtained from 108 males and 173 females (mean age = 22.18 years).

Materials

Questionnaires included items on the blessing, as well as items related to late adolescent development. Respondents were asked to answer the following questions with regard to their same-sex parent: (1) "Was there a time when your parent did something or said something to you that meant that you were 'all grown up' or had reached maturity?" (2) "Was there a time when you *wanted* your parent to do something or say something to you that meant that you were 'all grown up' or had reached maturity?"

Respondents also completed the 20-item Attitudes Toward Violence Scale (Huesmann & Guerra, 1997), which asks respondents to evaluate whether or not specific and general types of physical and verbal violence are acceptable. Items are summed to generate a global score indicating attitude toward violence.

Coding and Scoring

Open-ended responses to the blessing items were coded using the following categories: (1) rite of passage (e.g., my parent told me I was all grown up: when I turned 18, moved out of the house, started college, got a job, got a car, got married, graduated); (2) puberty indicated maturity (e.g., experienced first menstruation, started shaving my legs, started dating, told me about sex, acknowledged I had completed puberty); (3) respect for adolescent (told me/other people how grown up/responsible I was, treated me like an adult, trusted me on a regular basis, recognized me as a peer, parent said how proud he/she was of me); (4) recognized decision-making ability (told me I could/had to make my own decisions, gave me adult privileges,

trusted my judgment/decision-making, stopped worrying about me); (5) recognized specific skills (household finances, adult chores, allowed use of expensive items, allowed to stay home alone); (6) financial responsibility (got paid for doing chores, expected me to pay for my things/mistakes); (7) always treated me as grown up (throughout my life I have been treated with respect, like an adult).

Responses to the blessing questions were coded primarily by the author. A random subset of responses was scored by another trained coder. Cronbach's alpha coefficients were computed for both questions; alpha was .80 for the first question and .90 for the second question. Responses to items on the Attitudes Toward Violence Scale were scored according to the procedures described by Huesmann and Guerra (1997).

Results

Blessing Responses

The late adolescents in this study were significantly more likely to state that they had received a parental blessing than to state that they had not (χ^2= 52.103, *df* = 1, *p* < .001). Males (*n* = 77, 71.3%) and females (*n* = 124, 71.7%) were equally as likely to have received a blessing from a parent. As shown in Table 1, males were more likely than females to have received a blessing regarding decision-making abilities, specific skills, and financial responsibilities. Females were more likely than males to have received a blessing from a parent regarding a rite of passage, pubertal changes, and increased respect (a message that communicated, succinctly or over time, that the child was "all grown up"). Based on these findings, responses were further analyzed by collapsing blessings into two categories: rite of passage/overall maturity and decisions/skills. Chi-square analysis indicated that females were significantly more likely to have received a blessing regarding rite of passage/overall maturity, while males were more likely to have received a blessing regarding decisions/skills (χ^2 = 6.695, *df* = 1, *p* = .010).

Of those who stated they did not receive a blessing, females (*n* = 28, 57.1%) were slightly more likely than males (*n* = 17, 54.8%) to wish that a parent had provided a blessing during their lifetime, although this difference was not statistically significant ($\chi^2 = .094$, *df* = 1, *p* = .759). Both females and males predominantly wished a parent had acknowledged (1) their "grown up" status (respect) or (2) their decision-making abilities. Further, females were more likely than males to wish that a parent had said or done something related to a rite of passage, pubertal changes, respect, and skills. Males were more likely than females to wish that a parent had said or done something related to their decision-making abilities and financial responsibilities.

Attitudes Toward Violence

Subjects' attitudes toward violence were not significantly related to whether or not they had received a blessing ($t = -.270$, *df* = 277, *p* = .787). In addition, attitudes toward violence were not significantly related to whether or not they would have liked to receive a blessing from a parent ($t = -1.816$, *df* = 77, *p* = .073).

Discussion

These data provide partial support for Blos's assertion that receiving a blessing from the same-sex parent toward the end of adolescence may be an important aspect of the transition to adulthood. Most of the participants in the present study did in fact receive some type of blessing. In addition, 45 of the 80 who did not receive a blessing stated that they wanted to receive one while they were growing up. In total, 87.5% either received or wanted to receive a parent's blessing during adolescence. Although not discussed here, they wrote sensitive and powerful accounts of the blessing they received, or wanted to receive, as their adolescent years came to a close.

Blos's description of the blessing noted "the youth's impatient appropriation of adult prerogatives and entitlements." The data supported this notion, as the majority of males and females stated that they received or wanted to receive a blessing regarding their own decision-making abilities or that conveyed recognition of, and respect for, their grown-up status. Further, the results suggest that, when a blessing is given, males are more likely than females to be acknowledged for instrumental traits, while females are more likely than males to be recognized for their sexual development, for having successfully experienced a rite of passage, and for overall maturity (garnering respect).

Of special note here is that when the adolescents did not receive a blessing, they reported being more concerned with recognition of their instrumentality than with sexual development or a rite of passage. It is hypothesized that acknowledgment of sexual maturity may be sought more in the context of the peer group than within the family, yet if there is parental recognition, it is perceived as important (and is more likely to occur between mother and daughter).

Attitudes toward violence were not related to the parental blessing. It may be that self-esteem or interpersonal skills are more strongly associated with this aspect of the parent-adolescent relationship, as compared with attitudes. Finally, it should be noted that the sample consisted of college students, and caution should be exercised in generalizing the findings to others.

References

Blos, P. (1985). *Son and father: Before and beyond the Oedipus complex.* New York: The Free Press.

Delaney, M. E. (1996). Across the transition to adolescence: Qualities of parent/adolescent relationships and adjustment. *Journal of Early Adolescence, 16*(3), 274-300.

Fuhrman, T., & Holmbeck, G. N. (1995). A contextual-moderator analysis of emotional autonomy and adjustment in adolescence. *Child Development, 66,* 793-811.

Grotevant, H. D., & Cooper, C. R. (1986). Individuation in family relationships. *Human Development, 29,* 82-100.

Hoffman, J. A. (1984). Psychological separation of late adolescents from their parents. *Journal of Counseling Psychology, 31,* 170-178.

Huesmann, L. R., & Guerra, N. G. (1997). Children's normative beliefs about aggression and aggressive behavior. *Journal of Personality and Social Psychology, 72*(2), 408-419.

Mather, P. C., & Winston, R. B. (1998). Autonomy development of traditional-aged students: Themes and processes. *Journal of College Student Development, 39*(1), 33-50.

McClanahan, G., & Holmbeck, G. N. (1992). Separation-individuation, family functioning, and psychological adjustment in college students: A construct validity study of the Separation-Individuation Test of Adolescence. *Journal of Personality Assessment, 59*(3), 468-485.

Paladino Schultheiss, D. E. P., & Blustein, D. L. (1994). Role of adolescent-parent relationships in college student development and adjustment. *Journal of Counseling Psychology, 41*(2), 248-255.

Ryan, R. M., & Lynch, J. H. (1989). Emotional autonomy versus attachment: Revisiting the vicissitudes of adolescence and young adulthood. *Child Development, 60,* 340-356.

Steinberg, L., & Silverberg, S. (1986). The vicissitudes of autonomy in adolescence. *Child Development, 57,* 841-851.

White, K. M., Speiseman, J. C., & Costos, D. (1983). Young adults and their parents: Individuation to mutuality. In H. D. Grotevant & C. R. Cooper (Eds.), *Adolescent development in the family: New direction in developmental psychology* (pp. 61-76). San Francisco: Jossey-Bass.

Address correspondence to: Christopher Bjornsen, Department of Psychology, Longwood College, 201 High Street, Farmville, VA 23909. E-mail: cbjornse@longwood.lwc.edu

Exercise for Article 4

Factual Questions

1. This study expanded on Blos's treatment of the father-son relationship to include what?

    attitudes toward violence

2. According to Blos, the father's blessing "serves to acknowledge" what?

    masculine identity

3. Of the females who received a blessing, what percentage of the blessings were related to finances?

    3.2%

4. Of the males who received a blessing, how many of the blessings indicated that they were "always treated" that way?

5. What percentage of the males received a blessing?

    71.3%

6. The researcher hypothesizes that the acknowledgment of sexual maturity may be sought more in the context of the peer group than in what?

Questions for Discussion

7. The researcher notes that students voluntarily participated in this study. Would you be interested in knowing whether any of the students who were approached to be in the study refused to be in it? Explain. (See lines 75–80.)

8. In your opinion, does the researcher provide a strong rationale for measuring attitudes toward violence in this study? Explain.

9. The researcher refers to the sensitive and powerful accounts of the blessings that the students provided. Would samples of these accounts be of interest to you? Explain. (See lines 178–181.)

10. If you were conducting a study on the same topic, what changes, if any, would you make in the research methodology?

Quality Ratings

Directions: Indicate your level of agreement with each of the following statements by circling a number from 5 for strongly agree (SA) to 1 for strongly disagree (SD). If you believe an item is not applicable to this research article, leave it blank. Be prepared to explain your ratings.

A. The introduction establishes the importance of the study.

SA   5   (4)   3   2   1   SD

B. The literature review establishes the context for the study.

SA   5   (4)   3   2   1   SD

C. The research purpose, question, or hypothesis is clearly stated.

SA   (5)   4   3   2   1   SD

D. The method of sampling is sound.

SA   5   4   3   (2)   1   SD

E. Relevant demographics (for example, age, gender, and ethnicity) are described.

SA   5   4   3   (2)   1   SD

F. Measurement procedures are adequate.

SA   (5)   4   3   2   1   SD

G. All procedures have been described in sufficient detail to permit a replication of the study.

SA   5   (4)   3   2   1   SD

H. The participants have been adequately protected from potential harm.

SA   5   (4)   3   2   1   SD

I. The results are clearly described.

SA   5   4   (3)   2   1   SD

J. The discussion/conclusion is appropriate.

SA   5   (4)   3   2   1   SD

K. Despite any flaws, the report is worthy of publication.

SA   5   4   (3)   2   1   SD

Article 5

Most Working Women Deny Gender Discrimination in Their Pay

Lydia Saad
The Gallup Poll

EDITOR'S NOTE: The material in lines 1 through 56 appears at the beginning of each issue of *The Gallup Poll Monthly*. It describes general issues in the conduct and interpretation of the telephone surveys reported in the journal. The report on the survey on working women's views on pay discrimination begins with line 57.

From *The Gallup Poll Monthly* (Number 413: February 2000), 35–36. Copyright © 2000 by The Gallup Poll. Reprinted with permission. All rights reserved.

The Gallup Poll gathers public opinion data primarily through surveys conducted by telephone, which are designed to provide representative samples of adults living in the continental United States.

5 The standard methods used to conduct telephone surveys and the sampling tolerances for interpreting results collected by telephone are detailed below.

Design of the Sample for Telephone Surveys

The samples of telephone numbers used in telephone interview surveys are based on a random digit
10 stratified probability design. The sampling procedure involves stratifying the continental U.S. into 4 time zones and 3 city size strata within each time zone to yield a total of 12 unique strata.

In order to avoid possible bias if only listed tele-
15 phone numbers are used, the Gallup Poll uses a random digit procedure designed to provide representation of both listed and unlisted (including not-yet-listed) numbers. Samples are drawn within each stratum only from "active blocks," where an "active block" is defined as
20 100 contiguous telephone numbers containing three or more residential telephone listings. By eliminating nonworking blocks of numbers from the sample, the likelihood that any sampled telephone number will be associated with a residence increases from only 20%
25 (where numbers are sampled from all banks) to approximately 55%. Since most banks of telephone numbers are either substantially filled (i.e., assigned) or empty, this practical efficiency is purchased at a negligible cost in terms of possible coverage bias.

30 The sample of telephone numbers drawn by this method is designed to produce, with proper adjustments for differential sampling rates, an unbiased random sample of telephone households in the continental United States.

35 The standard size for national Gallup Poll telephone surveys is 1,000 interviews. More interviews are conducted in specific instances where greater survey accuracy is desired. Fewer interviews are conducted in specific instances where speed in collecting data and
40 reporting the results is required.

Telephone Survey Weighting Procedures

After the survey data have been collected and processed, each respondent is assigned a weight so that the demographic characteristics of the total weighted sample of respondents matches the latest U.S. Census Bu-
45 reau estimates of the demographic characteristics of the adult population living in households with access to a telephone.

The procedures described above are designed to produce samples approximating the adult civilian
50 population (18 and older) living in private households (that is, excluding those in prisons, hospitals, hotels, religious and educational institutions and those living on reservations or military bases), with access to a telephone. Survey percentages may be applied to Cen-
55 sus estimates of the size of these populations to project percentages into numbers of people.

The Report on Pay Discrimination

A new Gallup Poll finds that 30 percent of working women in the U.S. believe they are paid less than they would be if they were a man, while more than two in
60 three, 70 percent, do not. On the other hand, with just 13 percent saying women at their workplace get paid less than men who perform the same job, working men are even less likely to perceive that women are victims of gender discrimination in their pay.

65 "Pay equity," a longtime goal of the feminist movement, resurfaced in the news a few weeks ago when President Clinton proposed increased federal funding for programs aimed at closing the wage gap between working men and women in this country.
70 Clinton did so touting statistics showing that the average salary for full-time working women is only 75 cents on the dollar of what full-time working men earn.

The Gallup survey, conducted January 25-26, asked respondents about their employment status. Roughly
75 two-thirds of men and just under half of women indi-

cated they are employed full time. Among these groups, only slight differences in attitudes about women's pay were found along age, educational status, income and other dimensions. The largest difference
80 among full-time employed women is seen by education. Those with a college degree are less likely to feel discriminated against in this way than are women with less formal education, by a 22 percent to 35 percent margin.

Clinton's Plan

85 Critics of President Clinton's initiative say that the "75 cents" indicator is misleading, and cite other statistics showing that men and women of equal educational and work experience are actually virtually equal when it comes to pay. Nevertheless, Gallup finds the
90 American people widely supportive of Clinton's proposal to spend $27 million on additional pay equity efforts. Seventy-nine percent favor the proposed spending, including 70 percent of men and 86 percent of women. Just 18 percent are opposed to the plan.

Table 1
Question: As you may know, President Clinton has proposed that Congress allocate $27 million to increase enforcement of equal pay laws relating to women in the workplace. Do you favor or oppose this proposal?

	Favor	Oppose	No Opinion
2000 Jan 25-26	79%	18	3

Table 2
Question: Which of the following best describes your current situation—employed full time, employed part time, retired, a homemaker, a student, unemployed but looking for work, or unemployed and not looking for work?

	Men	Women
Employed full time	65%	45
Employed part time	5%	12
Retired	19%	20
Homemaker	0%	15
Student	5%	4
Unemployed, looking for work	3%	2
Unemployed, not looking for work	1%	2
Disabled (vol.)	2%	*
No answer	*	*

* Less than 0.5%

Methodology

95 The results are based on telephone interviews with a randomly selected national sample of 1,044 adults, 18 years and older, conducted January 25–26, 2000. For results based on this sample, one can say with 95 percent confidence that the maximum error attributable to
100 sampling and other random effects is plus or minus 3 percentage points. In addition to sampling error, question wording and practical difficulties in conducting surveys can introduce error or bias into the findings of public opinion polls.

Table 3
[Based on – 265 – Women employed full time; ± 7 Pct Pts]
Question: Do you personally feel that because you are a woman, you get paid less than a man would in your same job, or is this not the case?

	Yes, get paid less	No, not the case	No opinion
2000 Jan 25–26	30%	70	0

Table 4
[Based on – 331 – Men employed full time; ± 6 Pct Pts]
Question: From what you know or just your impression—do women at your workplace get paid less than men who do the same job, or is this not the case?

	Yes, get paid less	No, not the case	No opinion
2000 Jan 25–26	13%	78	9

Exercise for Article 5

Factual Questions

1. The 12 strata are based on which two variables?

2. What is done to avoid a possible bias if only listed telephone numbers are used?

3. What is the standard sample size for Gallup telephone surveys?

4. What is the purpose of assigning "weights" to the respondents?

5. For the full sample of 1,044 respondents used in this poll, how many percentage points should be allowed for sampling and other random effects (based on 95% confidence)?

6. What percentage of the women were homemakers?

7. A separate question was asked of men who were employed full time. What percentage of these men had no opinion on the question?

Questions for Discussion

8. This poll was conducted via telephone. In your opinion, are there advantages to polling via tele-

phone over polling via direct face-to-face interviews? Explain.

9. This poll was conducted via telephone. In your opinion, are there disadvantages to polling via telephone over polling via direct face-to-face interviews? Explain.

10. The researcher uses procedures to approximate the adult civilian population, excluding certain groups. Do you think that the exclusions affect the validity of the poll? (See lines 48–54.)

11. The researcher notes that question wording can introduce error or bias into the findings of public opinion polls. Do you think that the wording of the four questions used in this poll is adequate? Explain. (See lines 101–104.)

Quality Ratings

Directions: Indicate your level of agreement with each of the following statements by circling a number from 5 for strongly agree (SA) to 1 for strongly disagree (SD). If you believe an item is not applicable to this research article, leave it blank. Be prepared to explain your ratings.

A. The introduction establishes the importance of the study.

SA   5   4   3   2   1   SD

B. The literature review establishes the context for the study.

SA   5   4   3   2   1   SD

C. The research purpose, question, or hypothesis is clearly stated.

SA   5   4   3   2   1   SD

D. The method of sampling is sound.

SA   5   4   3   2   1   SD

E. Relevant demographics (for example, age, gender, and ethnicity) are described.

SA   5   4   3   2   1   SD

F. Measurement procedures are adequate.

SA   5   4   3   2   1   SD

G. All procedures have been described in sufficient detail to permit a replication of the study.

SA   5   4   3   2   1   SD

H. The participants have been adequately protected from potential harm.

SA   5   4   3   2   1   SD

I. The results are clearly described.

SA   5   4   3   2   1   SD

J. The discussion/conclusion is appropriate.

SA   5   4   3   2   1   SD

K. Despite any flaws, the report is worthy of publication.

SA   5   4   3   2   1   SD

Article 6

Client Gender as a Process Variable in Marriage and Family Therapy: Are Women Clients Interrupted More Than Men Clients?

Ronald Jay Werner-Wilson
Colorado State University

Sharon J. Price
The University of Georgia

Toni S. Zimmerman
Colorado State University

Megan J. Murphy
Colorado State University

ABSTRACT. Influenced by language and therapeutic discourse as well as the feminist critique of marriage and family therapy, the authors conducted research to evaluate conversational power in marriage and family therapy. Research on interruptions has received the most empirical attention, so the authors examined videotaped therapy sessions to see if women clients were interrupted more than men clients. This strategy integrated scholarship on gender and conversation into research on marriage and family therapy process. Multivariate analysis of variance was used to examine the different treatment of women and men clients; gender of therapist was used as a control variable. Results indicated that marriage and family doctoral students interrupted women clients three times more than men clients.

From *Journal of Family Psychology*, *11*, 373–377. Copyright © 1997 by the American Psychological Association, Inc. Reprinted with permission.

We conducted research to evaluate conversational power in marriage and family therapy. This research was influenced by two themes: language and therapeutic discourse as well as the feminist critique of mar-
5 riage and family therapy. Empirical research has demonstrated that men and women use different conversational tactics in cross-gender interactions. Women, for example, frequently ask questions and follow-up on topics introduced by men; these tactics support conver-
10 sation (Fishman, 1983). Men, on the other hand, are more likely to interrupt women and are more likely to successfully introduce a new topic of conversation; these are power tactics (Fishman, 1983). Research on interruptions has received the most empirical attention,
15 so we examined videotaped therapy sessions to see if women clients were interrupted more than men clients. This strategy integrated scholarship on gender and conversation into research on marriage and family therapy process.

Relevant Literature
Conversation: The Currency of Therapy

20 From a social constructionist perspective, discourse defines social organization: The therapeutic system is a linguistic system that features the social construction of meaning between the client or clients and the therapist (Anderson & Goolishian, 1988). The therapist is prin-
25 cipally responsible for the organization of therapeutic discourse, so she or he uses conversation to facilitate change (Anderson & Goolishian, 1988) or to maintain the status quo in a relationship (Avis, 1988; Davis, 1984; Goldner, 1988; Hare-Mustin, 1987, 1994).

30 Research on conversational strategies has supported the premise that therapists fundamentally shape therapeutic process. Viaro and Leonard (1983) examined videotaped therapy sessions in order to identify therapeutic rules. They suggested that the therapeutic setting
35 provides therapists with conversational prerogatives (i.e., direct conversation, interrupt client) and identified four clinical implications: (a) therapists govern the process and organization of therapy, (b) therapists' prerogatives influence the rights of family members,
40 (c) therapists maintain the central role in therapy, and (d) therapists are the source for all therapeutic rules (Viaro & Leonard, 1983). The present study examined the use of interruptions, a conversational prerogative.

Gender, Conversation, and Power

A linguistic approach to studying therapy is en-
45 hanced by an understanding of gender (Hare-Mustin, 1994; Hoffman, 1990). Therapeutic conversation features both competition for influence by each family member as well as negotiation for power between men and women (Avis, 1988; Davis, 1984; Goldner, 1988;
50 Hare-Mustin, 1987). Men and women use different conversational strategies and receive different treatment in cross-gender dialogue. Because therapy is conversation, these differences may influence therapeutic process. Women are more likely to be interrupted in
55 conversation than men (Smith-Lovin & Brody, 1989;

West & Zimmerman, 1983), so their efforts to participate in therapy may be disrupted.

An interruption is a power tactic, an overlap of speech that is disruptive or intrusive (West & Zimmerman, 1983; Zimmerman & West, 1975); it has been referred to as a small insult that establishes and maintains power differences (West & Zimmerman, 1983). Interruptions by men are rated as more appropriate than interruptions by women (Hawkins, 1988), and women are more likely to be interrupted in cross-gender conversations than in same-gender conversations (West & Zimmerman, 1983; Zimmerman & West, 1975). Responding to the explanation that men interrupt women because women talk more, West and Zimmerman found the same results when they controlled for amount of talk. Power, according to a review of research on interruptions, is the most important predictor of an interruption (Orcutt & Harvey, 1985; see also Kollock, Blumstein, & Schwartz, 1985). Gender is a diffuse status characteristic that influences power, which, in turn, influences interruptions (Orcutt & Harvey, 1985).

Purpose

If women and men therapy clients are treated differently—a possibility because gender influences conversation—clinicians could perpetuate inequality rather than serve as agents for change. We examined family therapy process to evaluate the use of interruptions by therapists, who have the prerogative to influence participants' rights (Viaro & Leonard, 1983), to see if women and men clients were treated differently. We used gender of therapist as an interaction effect because some research on individual counseling suggests that gender of therapist influences therapy. For example, research shows that a therapist's perception of therapy is influenced by gender of client: Men therapists report more problems than women therapists working with women clients, and men therapists are more likely than women therapists to describe clients negatively (see Nelson, 1993, for a thorough review of the literature).

Method

Participants

The sample for this study consisted of clients and therapists at a nonprofit marriage and family therapy clinic at a major southern university. All therapists in this study were doctoral students in a marriage and family therapy program accredited by the American Association for Marriage and Family Therapy. Five women and seven men therapists contributed cases. This sample included 41 couples or families that included both an adult woman and man who attended a first session at the marriage and family therapy clinic. Participants were videotaped during their initial therapy session.

Procedures

Initial therapy sessions influence client expectations and lay the foundation for subsequent treatment. We examined the first therapy session to control for treatment duration. Therapy sessions have predictable stages (e.g., social, engagement, information collection, intervention, closure), so we examined multiple time points in the session. Three 5-min. segments were coded for every client from early, middle, and later stages in the session: (a) 10- to 15-min. segment, (b) 25- to 30-min. segment, and (c) 40- to 45-min. segment. Two senior-level undergraduate students, a man and a woman, who were naïve to the purpose of this research, coded videotapes from the first therapy session.

Coder training. Coders learned the coding scheme by practicing on tapes not featured in the sample until they achieved 80% agreement. The principal investigator in this study coded every fourth tape to determine criterion reliability. The coders maintained high interrater reliability (intraclass correlations were .96; based on Shrout & Fleiss, 1979).

Coding scheme. The transcripts were arranged with codes adjacent to each spoken turn to promote reliability by eliminating the need for coders to memorize codes: The coders viewed the video with the transcript and circled the appropriate code as they occurred during each speaking turn. A distinct set of codes was printed next to each speaker (e.g., therapist, woman client, man client), but each set of codes featured the same possible codes. For example, the therapist could interrupt either the woman or man client. Similarly, each client could interrupt either her or his partner or the therapist. In addition to enhancing reliability, this coding arrangement disguised the nature of the research project, because coders identified conversational strategies used by each speaker, not just the therapist.

Dependent Measure: Interruptions

Interruptions were distinguished from other forms of overlap such as supportive statements, which represent active listening skills. Statements that tailed off in tone or volume were not coded as interruptions because they represented invitations for reply.

It is possible that people who talk more are interrupted more, so we developed two measures to control for amount of client participation. First, we constructed a variable from the ratio of interruptions made by the therapist to the number of speaking turns taken by the client. Second, we constructed a variable from the ratio of interruptions made by the therapist to the number of words spoken by the client. These ratios provided standardized measures to examine therapist interruptions.

Results

We conducted multivariate analysis of variance (MANOVA) to examine the main effect and interaction effect of client gender and therapist gender on three measures of the dependent variable. We examined interaction effects because gender-linked conversational strategies might influence how therapists interact with clients. In addition, gender of therapist might influence the therapeutic process (Nelson, 1993). The mean values and standard deviations for therapist and client behaviors are presented in Table 1.

Table 1
Mean Values of Therapist and Client Behaviors by Gender of Client

| | Gender of client | | | |
| | Man ($n = 41$) | | Woman ($n = 41$) | |
Group	M	SD	M	SD
Therapist				
Interruptions	0.87	1.45	2.37	2.73
Interruptions (no. of client turns)	0.03	0.05	0.09	0.09
Interruptions (no. of client words)	0.0011	0.0017	0.0028	0.0026
Client				
No. of turns	22.80	15.68	25.90	13.01
No. of words	600.17	512.69	822.02	544.45

There was a significant difference for gender of client on all measures of interruption, including measures that controlled for number of turns and number of words (see Table 2). Neither gender of therapist nor the interaction of Gender of Client x Gender of Therapist was significant (see Table 2). Overall, marriage and family therapy doctoral students interrupted women clients three times more than men clients.

Table 2
Multivariate Analysis of Variance for Therapist Behaviors: Interruption (N = 82)

Dependent Variable	Source	$F(1, 78)$
Interruption	Client Gender	9.10*
	Therapist Gender	0.15
	Client Gender × Therapist Gender	0.39
Interruption (client turns)	Client Gender	8.96*
	Therapist Gender	0.03
	Client Gender × Therapist Gender	0.20
Interruption (client words)	Client Gender	9.59*
	Therapist Gender	0.01
	Client Gender × Therapist Gender	0.10

*$p < .01$.

Discussion

Previous research on gender as a process issue in marriage and family therapy has identified differences between men and women therapists as well as between men and women clients, but these differences do not seem to influence interruptions. Gender of therapist did not affect interruptions directed toward clients in this study. This finding is consistent with recent research that suggests that modality (i.e., marital vs. family therapy) influences therapy process but gender of therapist does not (Werner-Wilson, 1995; Werner-Wilson, Price, & Zimmerman, 1996). Although gender of therapist does not influence therapy, results from this study provide additional information about the influence of client gender on the therapeutic process: Women clients are more likely to be interrupted than men clients. This finding suggests an ongoing need to consider the influence of gender as a process variable in marriage and family therapy.

Interruptions are power tactics that are influenced by gender in a variety of settings, including marriage and family therapy with student therapists. Although they are power tactics, interruptions may not reflect deliberate action by the therapist to exert power over the client. For example, therapists may block communication attempts by women clients in order to engage men clients who are often reluctant to engage in therapy. Although the effort to engage a reluctant client is meritorious, it should not occur at the expense of another participant. Interruptions may also reflect socialization: Therapists may interrupt women clients more because it is a common feature of conversation.

The findings from this study support what feminist scholars have recommended: (a) Research should incorporate gender themes and power analysis, (b) therapists should pay careful attention to their position in therapy, and (c) therapists should consider larger social forces (e.g., conversational conventions, power) and individual needs in therapy.

References

Anderson, H. & Goolishian, H. A. (1988). Human systems as linguistic systems: Preliminary and evolving ideas about the implications for clinical theory. *Family Process, 27,* 371–394.

Avis, J. M. (1988). Deepening awareness: A private study guide to feminism and family therapy. *Journal of Psychotherapy and the Family, 33,* 15–46.

Davis, K. (1984). The process of problem and (re)formulation in psychotherapy. *Sociology of Health and Illness, 8,* 44–74.

Fishman, P. M. (1983). Interaction: The work women do. In B. Thorne, C. Kramarae, & N. Henley (Eds.), *Language, gender and society* (pp. 89–101). Rowley, MA: Newbury House.

Goldner, V. (1988). Generation and gender: Normative and covert hierarchies. *Family Process, 27,* 17–31.

Hare-Mustin, R. T. (1987). The problem of gender in family therapy theory. *Family Process, 26,* 15–33.

Hare-Mustin, R. T. (1994). Discourses in the mirrored room: A postmodern analysis of therapy. *Family Process, 33,* 19–35.

Hawkins, K. (1988). Interruptions in task-oriented conversations: Effects of violations of expectations by males and females. *Women's Studies in Communication, 11,* 1–20.

Hoffman, L. (1990). Constructing realities: An art of lenses. *Family Process, 29,* 1–12.

Kollock, P., Blumstein, P., & Schwartz, P. (1985). Sex and power in interaction: Conversational privileges and duties. *American Sociological Review, 50,* 34–46.

Nelson, M. L. (1993). A current perspective on gender differences: Implications for research in counseling. *Journal of Counseling Psychology, 40,* 200–209.

Orcutt, J. D. & Harvey, L. K. (1985). Deviance, rule-breaking and male dominance in conversation. *Symbolic Interaction, 8,* 15–46.

Shrout, P. E. & Fleiss, J. L. (1979). Intraclass correlations: Uses in assessing rater reliability. *Psychological Bulletin, 2,* 420–428.

Smith-Lovin, L. & Brody, C. (1989). Interruptions in group discussions: The effects of gender and group composition. *American Sociological Review, 54,* 424–435.

Viaro, M. & Leonard, P. (1983). Getting and giving information: Analysis of a family-interview strategy. *Family Process, 22*, 27–42.

Werner-Wilson, R. J. (1995, November). *Client gender and the working alliance.* Paper presented at the American Association for Marriage and Family Therapy Annual Meeting, Baltimore, MD.

Werner-Wilson, R. J., Price, S. J., & Zimmerman, T S. (1996). *Is therapeutic topic influenced by gender in marriage and family therapy?* Manuscript submitted for publication.

West, C. & Zimmerman, D. H. (1983). Small insults: A study of interruptions in cross-sex conversations between unacquainted persons. In B. Thorne, C. Kramarae, & N. Henley (Eds.), *Language, gender and society* (pp. 103–117). Rowley, MA: Newbury House.

Zimmerman, D. H. & West, C. (1975). Sex-roles, interruptions and silences in conversation. In B. Thorne & N. Henley (Eds.), *Language and sex: Difference and dominance* (pp. 105–129). Rowley, MA: Newbury House.

Note: This research was funded, in part, by a grant from Platinum Mortgage Company, Jonesboro, Georgia.

About the authors: Ronald Jay Werner-Wilson, Toni S. Zimmerman, and Megan J. Murphy, Department of Human Development and Family Studies, Colorado State University; Sharon J. Price, Department of Child and Family Development, The University of Georgia. Megan J. Murphy is now at Department of Child and Family Development, The University of Georgia.

Address correspondence to: Ronald Jay Werner-Wilson, Department of Human Development and Family Studies, Colorado State University, Fort Collins, CO 80523. Electronic mail may be sent via the Internet to rjwilson@lamar.colostate.edu

Exercise for Article 6

Factual Questions

1. What has been referred to as "a small insult that establishes and maintains power differences"?

2. How many of the therapists were women? How many were men?

3. The coders learned the coding scheme by practicing on tapes not used in the study until they reached what percentage of agreement?

4. Were statements that tailed off in tone or volume coded as interruptions? If yes, why? If no, why not?

5. What was the mean number of times that women were interrupted (without considering number of turns speaking or number of client words)?

6. When the researchers controlled for number of client words, was there still a significant difference in terms of number of therapist interruptions? If yes, at what probability level?

Questions for Discussion

7. Would you be interested in knowing more about the selection of the 41 cases and why they were attending therapy? Explain.

8. Do you think it was a good idea to control for treatment duration by examining only initial therapy sessions? Explain. (See lines 108–111.)

9. Do you think it was a good idea to keep the undergraduates who coded the videotapes naïve regarding the purpose of the study? Explain. (See lines 118–121.)

10. The researchers did not find a significant "Gender of Client × Gender of Therapist" interaction. In other words, both male and female therapists were equally likely to interrupt female clients more often than male clients. (See lines 171–173 and Table 2.) Does this result surprise you? Explain.

11. To what population(s), if any, would you be willing to generalize the results of this study?

12. If you were going to conduct another study on this topic, what changes in the research methodology would you make, if any?

Quality Ratings

Directions: Indicate your level of agreement with each of the following statements by circling a number from 5 for strongly agree (SA) to 1 for strongly disagree (SD). If you believe an item is not applicable to this research article, leave it blank. Be prepared to explain your ratings.

A. The introduction establishes the importance of the study.

SA   5   4   3   2   1   SD

B. The literature review establishes the context for the study.

SA   5   4   3   2   1   SD

C. The research purpose, question, or hypothesis is clearly stated.

SA   5   4   3   2   1   SD

D. The method of sampling is sound.

SA   5   4   3   2   1   SD

E. Relevant demographics (for example, age, gender, and ethnicity) are described.

SA   5   4   3   2   1   SD

F. Measurement procedures are adequate.

SA   5   4   3   2   1   SD

G. All procedures have been described in sufficient detail to permit a replication of the study.

SA   5   4   3   2   1   SD

H. The participants have been adequately protected
from potential harm.

SA   5   4   3   2   1   SD

I. The results are clearly described.

SA   5   4   3   2   1   SD

J. The discussion/conclusion is appropriate.

SA   5   4   3   2   1   SD

K. Despite any flaws, the report is worthy of publication.

SA   5   4   3   2   1   SD

Article 7

An Unobtrusive Measure of Racial Behavior in a University Cafeteria

Stewart Page
University of Windsor
Windsor, Ontario, Canada

ABSTRACT. Observational data were gathered from a large university cafeteria for a period of 22 days, in l-hour periods per day, over one semester. Observations were made of the frequency with which Black and White cashiers were selected. Chi-square analyses showed a significant association between a cashier's being Black and increased likelihood that she would not be selected. Some comments and comparisons are made with other research using similar measures.

Reprinted with permission from *Journal of Applied Social Psychology*, Vol. *27*, No. 24, 2172–2176. Copyright © 1997 V. H. Winston & Son, Inc., 360 South Ocean Boulevard, Palm Beach, FL 33480. All rights reserved.

The study of interracial behavior has long-standing familiarity to social and community psychologists, as well described in the classic writings of Kenneth Clark, Gordon Allport, Thomas Pettigrew, and others. Allport's (1958) *The Nature of Prejudice,* for example, remains one of the most frequently cited books on the issue, both within and without the discipline of psychology (Pettigrew, 1988). The dramatic effects of race as a variable in research have been demonstrated, for example, in a variety of situations assessing social influence and stigmatization. Many such studies have used some form of Bogardus' (1931, 1959) notion of *social distance* (social intimacy) measures of racial acceptance.

Observational and experimental studies of race have undoubtedly declined somewhat in recent times, while more pragmatic and biopolitical aspects such as equal opportunity, affirmative action, ethnic and cultural diversity, and so on have become more prominent. These issues are important, yet many aspects of interracial behavior remain incompletely understood.

One such aspect involves behavior in open situations; that is, those without racial demand characteristics or obligations (Orne, 1962). Moreover, the factor of race may also function differently at varying levels of awareness and in accordance with the extent of reactivity in measures used to observe it (e.g., Webb, Campbell, Schwartz, & Sechrest, 1966). For example, in a study which has now become a classic, Weitz (1972) administered a questionnaire assessing White-Black racial attitudes to a university population. For many of her subjects who had expressed egalitarian attitudes, Weitz nevertheless found that these same individuals showed subtly, rejecting nonverbal behaviors when later placed in a laboratory situation requiring cooperative work alongside a Black individual. From a psychoanalytic perspective, Weitz referred to these results as supporting a *repressed-affect model* of racial behavior. In this view, racial behavior assessed reactively, such as with questionnaires or interviews, is typically egalitarian, yet may show "leakage," that is, negative aspects, when assessed nonreactively and unobtrusively. Similarly, in a series of studies (e.g., Page, 1995; Page & Day, 1990), we have found frequently that publicly advertised rental accommodation is likely to be described privately (thus unobservably) as "already rented" when landlords receive telephone inquiries from persons alleging to have some type of stigmatizing characteristic.

Although their study was not concerned directly with race, Hechtman and Rosenthal (1991) found, as another example of such leakage, that teachers showed more nonverbal warmth toward pupils for whom the teaching task was stereotypically gender appropriate (e.g., vocabulary items for girls; mechanical items for boys), as compared to when they taught a task which was gender inappropriate. Lott (1987), also in a nonracial context, similarly found that men did not show unfavorable attitudes toward women on paper-and-pencil measures. They did, however, in unobtrusively observed work situations, show subtle avoidance behaviors, more negative statements, and increased social distance specifically toward female coworkers. In a racial context, Taylor (1979) found that teachers' nonverbal behaviors varied subtly according to the race (White vs. Black) of their pupils in an unobtrusively observed teaching situation.

A long-standing difficulty in many studies remains that of generalization from laboratory-based research. The present study examined some aspects of racial behavior using a nonlaboratory (cafeteria) setting, whose essential functions are those of dining and socialization. Such settings generally carry no outward prescriptions or expectations regarding race, based on the tacit assumption that this factor indeed "does not

exist." The cafeteria setting is also one in which many behaviors, performed with little awareness or at low levels of intensity, may be unobtrusively observed. The speculative hypothesis was explored that a pre-
80 dominantly White population of customers, consisting mostly of undergraduate students, might select a White cashier more frequently than a Black cashier.

Method

Participants

During a recent semester, observations were made of a university population in a large public cafeteria at
85 the University of Windsor over a period of 22 (nonconsecutive) weekdays, excluding Fridays. A daily 1-hour observation period, from approximately noon until approximately 1:00 P.M. each day, was used.

Procedure

The spatial arrangement of the cafeteria was such
90 that once food items are collected and before entering the main eating area, customers must select a cashier from (usually) three choices during peak lunchtime hours throughout the academic year. Cashiers for the current period of observation were three females, lo-
95 cated at the end of three separate pathways, one of which must be selected by exiting customers. Distances to each cashier, from locations occupied by customers after selecting all food items, are approximately equal. In the eating area directly beyond the cashiers is a
100 counter area, containing a straight row of individual seats. A vertical partition attached to the front edge of the counter partially obscures the occupants of these seats from view. From one end of the counter, the activities of each cashier can be observed reliably and
105 unobtrusively.

Throughout the above time period, one of the three cashiers was Black; the remaining two were White. On the campus, as typical of Ontario universities generally, Black students form a distinct and visible minority
110 group.

A daily record was kept of the number of (non-Black) customers paying for food at each cashier. For consistency, observations were made only when three cashiers, at separate locations, were on duty. In-
115 dividual cashiers varied nonsystematically in their location from day to day. Cases in which a single person paid for one or more companions' food were counted as representing only a single customer. Cases where individuals only requested change or approached a
120 cashier for reasons other than paying for food were excluded. In general, therefore, a "unit" of observation was recorded and signaled, in most cases, when a cashier was observed extending her hand to return change. No subjective judgments or ratings were thus
125 required; data (Table 1) were gathered solely in the form of frequency counts.

Results and Discussion

Results, in terms of frequency of cashier selection,

are shown in Table 1. A goodness-of-fit (χ^2) analysis of the frequency data showed a significant tendency for
130 customers to select less frequently a cashier who was Black, $\chi^2(2, N = 9,713) = 6.57, p < .038$.

In order to evaluate further the possibility that a directional or spatial bias played some role in cashier selection, some additional data (covering 19 days;
135 non-Fridays) were gathered, during a different semester. For these data, all three cashiers were White. There was no significant location preference in selection, $\chi^2(2, N = 8,015) = 2.44, p < .296$.

In interpreting such results, one must exercise cau-
140 tion in view of certain limitations. One cannot know precisely what percentage of customers might have been included more than once over the total time period, nor does one have complete information about other factors in a university population which are ger-
145 mane to the issue of race. Moreover, populations such as the one observed in the present study consider themselves (and are considered) highly accepting, aware, and sensitive to matters concerning race, as congruent with commonly prevailing values and norms within a
150 North American university campus.

Table 1
Frequency of Cashier Selection by Race

Cashier	Frequency of selection
1 (White cashier)	3,320
2 (White cashier)	3,271
3 (Black cashier)	3,122
Cashier selection: Three White cashiers	
1	2,659
2	2,622
3	2,734

Yet there remain other, more abstract issues, still largely unresolved by social and community psychologists. One concerns Kelman's (1958) early distinctions between levels of attitude internalization, and between
155 the emotional, evaluative, and behavioral components of attitudes. Another concerns the unreliable, indeed sometimes disturbing, relationship between racial attitudes and racial behavior (Pettigrew, 1988). Another concerns the related issue of congruence between be-
160 haviors elicited under reactive conditions, in which they may be detected, and those which may be observed nonreactively and which may be performed at low levels of awareness. In this light, one is reminded of recent videotaped demonstrations on the ABC net-
165 work program *Prime Time Live,* in which Black "pseudoclients" were given false information about job availability, higher prices for used cars, and less accommodating service in stores. One is also reminded of LaPiere's (1934) classic study in which restaurateurs
170 indicated by telephone that Chinese couples would not be served, yet most such couples were served when

they actually entered the restaurants.

Again, while the factor of race may become a conspicuous factor in research situations where reactive
175 measures or manipulations are used, its presence and effects in other situations may remain more insidious and ill-defined. Indeed, the present data reflect only frequency counts; that is, simple observations of human behavior. They seem sufficient, however, to illus-
180 trate the myth that race is irrelevant or does not exist in the context of everyday acts and social routines. Further research on the repressed affect model of racial behavior therefore seems clearly warranted.

References
Allport, G. (1958). *The nature of prejudice.* Garden City, NY: Doubleday Anchor Books.
Bogardus, E. (1931). *Fundamentals of social psychology.* New York, NY: Century Press.
Bogardus, E. (1959). *Social distance.* Yellow Springs, OH: Antioch.
Hechtman, S., & Rosenthal, R. (1991). Teacher gender and nonverbal behavior in the teaching of gender-stereotyped materials. *Journal of Applied Social Psychology, 21,* 446-459.
Kelman, H. (1958). Compliance, identification, and internalization: Three processes of attitude change. *Journal of Conflict Resolution, 2,* 51-60.
LaPiere, R. (1934). Attitudes versus actions. *Social Forces, 13,* 230-237.
Lott, B. (1987). Sexist discrimination as distancing behavior: A laboratory demonstration. *Psychology of Women Quarterly, 11,* 47-59.
Orne, M. (1962). On the social psychology of the psychological experiment: With particular reference to demand characteristics and their implications. *American Psychologist, 17,* 776-783.
Page, S. (1995). Effects of the mental illness label in 1993: Acceptance and rejection in the community. *Journal of Health and Social Behavior, 7,* 61-69.
Page, S., & Day, D. (1990). Acceptance of the "mentally ill" in Canadian society: Reality and illusion. *Canadian Journal of Community Mental Health, 9,* 51-61.
Pettigrew, T. (1988). The ultimate attribution error. In E. Aronson (Ed.), *The social animal* (pp. 325-344). New York, NY: W. H. Freeman.
Taylor, M. (1979). Race, sex, and the expression of self-fulfilling prophecies in a laboratory teaching situation. *Journal of Personality and Social Psychology, 37,* 897-912.
Webb, E., Campbell, D., Schwartz, R., & Sechrest, L. (1966). *Unobtrusive measures.* New York, NY: Rand-McNally.
Weitz, S. (1972). Attitude, voice, and behavior: A repressed affect model of interracial interaction. *Journal of Personality and Social Psychology, 24,* 14-21.

Address correspondence to: Stewart Page, Department of Psychology, University of Windsor, 401 Sunset, Windsor, Ontario N9B 3P4, Canada.

Exercise for Article 7

Factual Questions

1. What is the "speculative hypothesis" that was explored in this study?

2. The observations were made during which hour of the day?

3. Did the individual cashiers work in the same station (location) every day?

4. What was the "unit" of observation?

5. The first number 1 White cashier was selected how many more times than the Black cashier?

6. Was the first chi square test statistically significant at the .05 level (i.e., with a probability of .05 *or less*)? Explain.

7. What is the first limitation mentioned by the researcher?

Questions for Discussion

8. The researcher suggests that questionnaires and interviews assess racial behavior *reactively*. What do you think this term means? Is it a good idea to use questionnaires and interviews for this purpose? Explain. (See lines 39–43.)

9. The researcher points out that this is a *nonlaboratory* study. In your opinion, is this important? Explain. (See lines 68–78.)

10. Would it be informative to have a larger number of White and Black cashiers in a future study on this topic? Explain.

11. In your opinion, does this study *prove* that there is racial discrimination? Explain.

Quality Ratings

Directions: Indicate your level of agreement with each of the following statements by circling a number from 5 for strongly agree (SA) to 1 for strongly disagree (SD). If you believe an item is not applicable to this research article, leave it blank. Be prepared to explain your ratings.

A. The introduction establishes the importance of the study.

SA 5 4 3 2 1 SD

B. The literature review establishes the context for the study.

SA 5 4 3 2 1 SD

C. The research purpose, question, or hypothesis is clearly stated.

SA 5 4 3 2 1 SD

D. The method of sampling is sound.

SA 5 4 3 2 1 SD

E. Relevant demographics (for example, age, gender, and ethnicity) are described.

SA 5 4 3 2 1 SD

F. Measurement procedures are adequate.

SA 5 4 3 2 1 SD

G. All procedures have been described in sufficient detail to permit a replication of the study.

SA   5   4   3   2   1   SD

H. The participants have been adequately protected from potential harm.

SA   5   4   3   2   1   SD

I. The results are clearly described.

SA   5   4   3   2   1   SD

J. The discussion/conclusion is appropriate.

SA   5   4   3   2   1   SD

K. Despite any flaws, the report is worthy of publication.

SA   5   4   3   2   1   SD

Article 8

Crime Stories as Television News: A Content Analysis of National, Big City, and Small Town Newscasts

Brendan Maguire
Western Illinois University

Diane Sandage
Western Illinois University

Georgie Ann Weatherby
Gonzaga University

ABSTRACT. The present paper is a five-week content analysis of crime stories reported on television news. The sample consists of three nightly newscasts available on a rural, Midwestern cable system. Included are nightly newscasts from a national network, a big city television station, and a small town channel. Findings from this exploratory study show that these three sources of television news differ substantially in their coverage of crime stories.

From *Journal of Criminal Justice and Popular Culture*, 7, 1-14. Copyright © 1999 by School of Criminal Justice, University of Albany: www.albany.edu/scj/jcjpc/

In 1945 George Gallup asked survey respondents if they had *ever* seen a television in operation. Only 19 percent said that they had (Gallup, 1972:551). Things have changed dramatically. Today, about 250,000 tele-
5 visions are built each day worldwide and in the United States there are two television sets per household (Macionis, 1997:135; Steinberg, 1985:85). In the average household, the television set is on nearly eight hours a day and, except for sleeping or working, watching tele-
10 vision is the most time-consuming behavior of Americans (Perkinson, 1996; Steinberg, 1985:85). The point is that television has become a primary agent of socialization in American society, rivaling, if not superseding, the importance of the family, religion, and
15 schools.

One reason television has become so influential is that it is the main source of information about the world. In a 1995 poll, for example, Americans were asked to indicate *all* the sources from which they got
20 their news and information. Seventy-eight percent answered "nightly national news" (the most frequent source) and seventy-five percent reported "local television news" (Gallup Jr., 1996:117–118). A good share of this information deals with crime and criminals. As
25 we shall presently see, however, there are noteworthy differences in crime reporting among national, big city, and small town television newscasts.

Television News and Crime Reporting

Media coverage of crime and justice is as old as printing (Surette, 1998:53). Historically, newspapers
30 commonly carried stories about crime and criminals. The same was true of the radio when it became a dominant information medium. And today, millions of Americans watch television news on a daily basis and these broadcasts regularly feature crime stories (Bailey
35 and Hale, 1998; Barak, 1994; Graber, 1980; Katz, 1986; Surette, 1998; Warr, 1995). Crime news is one of the most frequent subject areas of television news, claiming 10 to 20 percent of total news air time (Dominick, 1978; Graber, 1980). A recent examination
40 of the local news at Chicago's three major network stations found that local news devoted 15 to 17 percent of noncommercial time to crime stories (Johnson, 1998). Crime was the number one content area of these Chicago television newscasts, followed by health and
45 medicine at 11 to 13 percent. Moreover, the present research has found that local news programs most often begin with a crime story.

Why is crime such a popular subject in television newscasts? There are several reasons (Katz, 1986).
50 First, crime news is relatively cheap and readily accessible. Crime stories are routine and reporters rely on regular sources such as police officials (Chermak, 1995b). Second, providing information about crime can be seen as serving a useful purpose. Viewers are
55 alerted to dangers that they may face and are generally kept apprised of the boundaries of acceptable behavior. Third, and perhaps most pivotal, crime stories are able to capture viewer attention. Surveys repeatedly show that Americans judge crime to be a serious problem in
60 society and are usually interested in this topic. As recently as May 1997, poll respondents identified crime as the number one problem facing the United States (Maguire and Pastore, 1997:114). However, because most people do not personally know criminals, they
65 rely on media portrayals for intimate details.

It is clear that television newscasts are a major source of information concerning crime in the United States. There is reason to believe that ordinary citizens tend to accept crime news uncritically. For example, 64

70 percent of American adults think that the press "accurately reflects how much crime there is" (Maguire and Pastore, 1996:222). Social scientists are more skeptical of the accuracy of crime reporting. Some have even argued that the media creates the social reality of crime
75 (Barak, 1993), or at the very least, exercises significant power over the interpretation of that reality (Gans, 1980). Unfortunately, researchers have consistently found that crime reporting on television is distorted in key respects (Barrile, 1986; Chermak, 1995a, 1994;
80 Dominick, 1978; Kappeler, Blumberg, & Potter, 1996; Sheley and Ashkins, 1981; Tunnell, 1998). One of the greatest distortions is that television news coverage of crime exaggerates the prevalence of violent interpersonal crime, while it underplays the extent of white-
85 collar crime. Researchers agree that this pattern exists in the media in general, and in television programming (news and entertainment) in particular. What is missing, however, is a targeted investigation of levels of television newscasts. Do all newscasts follow the pat-
90 tern of accentuating violent crime? The present project, an exploratory study, provides a preliminary answer to this question by presenting findings from a five-week content analysis of television news crime reporting at the national, big city, and small town levels.

Data and Methods

95 Data for this study were obtained between September 23, 1997 and November 24, 1997. Between these dates, five weeks of selected television newscasts were sampled. An every-other-week schedule was adopted in order to minimize the chances of repeat crime stories
100 dominating the reports examined.

The television newscasts that were analyzed were selected from options offered on a Tele-Communications Incorporation (TCI) cable system operating in west-central Illinois. The sample includes national, big
105 city, and small town newscasts. The NBC nightly news was chosen because it was (and is) the highest rated evening news broadcast. Chicago's WGN (9:00 P.M.) news was examined as representative of big city news (Chicago is the third largest city in the United States,
110 with a city population of about three million). It might be argued that because WGN is a "superstation," it is not like most big city stations. However, with regard to television news, WGN is on record as stating that the goal of its coverage "is to serve local audiences" (Kirk,
115 1998:2). In any event, WGN was the only big city newscast shown on the cable system used in the study. The (6:00 P.M.) newscast of WGEM of Quincy, Illinois, was chosen as representative of small town television news (Quincy's population is just under 40,000).
120 WGEM was selected because it is the highest-rated small town news program offered on the aforementioned cable system. Plainly, it would have been preferable had the cable system included at least two representatives of each level of newscast, yet the selection

125 of NBC, WGN, and WGEM was adequate for this exploratory work.

One newscast per day/per channel was videotaped. This means that in theory, five weeks of taping should have yielded a total of 105 programs, 35 each for NBC,
130 WGN, and WGEM. However, in seven instances major league baseball or professional football preempted the NBC and WGEM newscasts (WGEM is an NBC affiliate that presents local news immediately after conclusion of the national news). Hence, the sample contains
135 28 NBC programs and 28 WGEM programs. Thirty-four WGN newscasts were taped. The one missing WGN newscast resulted because a Chicago Bulls game went well beyond the scheduled time and the videocassette recorder was programmed for the regular time
140 (the researchers were out of town and unable to respond to this development).

Content analysis is a research method for "analyzing the symbolic content of any communication" (Singleton, Straits, Straits, & McAllister, 1988:347). The
145 main enterprise of content analysis is coding. In the present project over 1,200 news stories (90 newscasts) were coded. The first step in the coding operation was to identify crime stories as contrasted from all other news stories. Each crime story was then transferred to a
150 special videotape so that these stories could more conveniently be the subject of detailed content analysis. The crime stories were then coded for *type of crime*: "interpersonal violence," "white-collar crime," "drug offense," or "other." Each of these content categories
155 was defined in reference to the description or depiction of specific recording units. The interpersonal violence category included stories on bodily harm or threat of bodily harm. Mainly, this consisted of homicide, rape, assault (and/or battery), and robbery. The white-collar
160 crime category included crimes committed by a person in the course of his or her high status occupation or crimes committed in the interest of corporations or government agencies. The third content area, drug offense, consisted of stories that treated the growing,
165 selling, purchasing, or using of drugs. Finally, the "other" category included all the crime stories that did not fit into any of the three previous categories.

The coding was divided between two principle coders. Approximately 10 percent of the overall sample of
170 news stories and about 20 percent of the 246 crime stories were double-coded for "reproducibility reliability" (Krippendorf, 1980:130-154; Weber, 1990:17). Intercoder reliability scores ranged from .98 for identification of a crime story to .91 for type of crime story.
175 Problematic cases were reviewed and judged by three coders.

Results

Perhaps the most important finding from this study is that newscasts do not follow a uniform pattern in their coverage of crime stories. Significant differences were found between national (NBC), big city (WGN of
180

Chicago), and small town (WGEM of Quincy, IL) television news programs. To begin with, in our sample we found that crime was not given an equal amount of coverage. On average, WGN newscasts broadcast about three times as many crime stories as NBC, and about five times as many as WGEM. The average frequency of crime stories per newscast was as follows: 1.67 for NBC; 4.88 for WGN; and 0.97 for WGEM. It is worth noting that the WGN 9:00 P.M. News is a 60-minute program, while the NBC and WGEM newscasts are 30 minutes in length. Even taking this into account, WGN had the highest rate of crime story coverage. In drawing out further distinctions between level of newscast, it will now be useful to detail the types of crime most often reported.

National Newscasts (NBC)

As noted earlier, existing research shows that the reporting of crime on television news, like other media outlets, focuses especially on interpersonal violence. With regard to NBC, the present data support this finding. Table 1 shows that crime stories covered in our sample of national newscasts most frequently featured violent offenses. Fifty-five percent of NBC crime stories highlighted violent crimes. The two crime stories most frequently reported on NBC were the Louise Woodward "nanny" case and the Marv Albert sexual assault case. Both these cases were exceptional and sensational, and they were frequently "framed" (and reframed) in the sense meant by Peter Manning (1998). Manning argues that the media commonly show an image, for example, an image of a particular crime, and then show the image again (reframe it) in another context (e.g., a crime story might be shown at the various stages of arrest, trial, and sentencing). This was certainly the case with regard to the Woodward and Albert stories.

Table 1
Type of Crime Reported by NBC (N = 47)

VIOLENCE (26 = 55%): Nanny case (5); Marv Albert sexual assault case (4); Oklahoma City bombing (3); Pearl, Miss. killings (2); robbery; bicyclist kills motorist; convicted rapist pardoned; terrorist plot foiled but could have killed hundreds; assault weapons & street killings; man with AIDS has sex with numerous women; Rabin assassination; Atlanta bombings; terrorism in Egypt; 11-year-old boy shoots motorists; skinhead kills a black for being black; terrorism in Germany.

DRUG OFFENSES (4 = 9%): Mexican drug cartel; heroin use in U.S.; Olympians use of illegal drugs; heroin use in Plano, Texas.

WHITE-COLLAR CRIMES (11 = 23%): IRS illegal tactics (2); federal government cover-up; federal government corruption; Chrysler loses lawsuit regarding defective vans; FBI unit head convicted of obstruction of justice; nursing home neglect; Whitewater crimes; mortgage scams; real estate scams; fraudulent telemarketers.

OTHER (6 = 13%): Nuclear theft; programs for deterring juvenile crime; Iraq's germ warfare research; home repair swindles; Internet information on poison bombs; credit card fraud from stealing discarded junk mail.

Table 2
Type of Crime Reported by WGN (N = 166)

VIOLENCE (108 = 65%): Marv Albert sexual assault case (7); nanny case (6); hit & run case (6); reckless homicide (6); kidnapping (4); beating death of elderly woman by daughter (3); triple shooting/double murder (3); baby abandoned in garbage can (3); mob hit man on trial (3); bank robbery (3); Unabomber (3); husband hires man to murder wife (2); felony drunk driving by school bus driver (2); stabbing death of elderly woman (2); Oklahoma City bombing (2); Jon Benet Ramsey killing (2); armed robbery (2); sexual assault (2); gang warfare leads to shooting of a cop (2); football homecoming murder (2); attempted murder (2); serial rapist (2); convicted murderers ask not to be executed (2); child abuse & neglect (2); robbery and seven killings at fast food restaurant (2); car jacking with victim shot; woman killed in her own home; armored car robbery; convicted criminals released on basis of new DNA evidence; terrorism in Egypt; Ennis Cosby killing; robbery led to killing; hate crime in which Hispanic student beaten by black students; two-year-old severely beaten for bed wetting; family assaulted in their own home; man stabbed then kills perpetrator; young girl shot and killed; murder of millionaire; reward offered for killer; sudden infant deaths may be killings; suspect shot by cop after car chase; felony stalking; arrest of man wanted for murder; man suspected of killing wife; retrospective on Tylenol killings; women motorists hit train while fleeing from men; D.C. gunman fires shots at random; woman assaulted by football players; Pearl, Miss. killings; aggravated assault; shooting near a school; two older boys drop younger boy from window of building; charges of terrorism dropped; wife tortured, beaten, & raped by husband; murder mystery; retrospective on Susan Smith case; stabbing; man with AIDS has sex with numerous women.

DRUG OFFENSES (8 = 5%): Mexican drug lord case; drunk driving; residents shut down crackhouse; drug bust of 31 individuals; news conference on DUI; drug dealer involved in car crash; routine traffic stop leads to drug bust; hostage & robbery case involving drug dealers.

WHITE-COLLAR CRIMES (16 = 10%): Illegal campaign fund raising (2); money missing from funds raised for Girl X (2); six companies involved in counterfeit clothes; company fraud regarding furs; IRS illegal tactics; alderman on trial for racketeering; possible consumer fraud by cable television companies; state legislators implicated in cash for grants; obstruction of justice charges; ADM price-fixing case; city council member resigns amidst charges of shady financial dealings; Microsoft versus U.S. Department of Justice; elections fraud; former state representative & tollway chief indicted for illegal financial gain.

OTHER (34 = 20%): Elaborate burglary ring (5); reckless driving in Loop (4); bootleg tapes & videos (3); reckless boat driving (2); school vandalism (2); counterfeiting ring; arson; illegal immigrant story; man flashes teenage girl; baby-food scam; cell phone cloning; half-brother of Jesse Jackson sent to prison; truck smashes into building; crime investigation of bus driver; electrical blackout intentionally caused; theft of ATM cards; school burglary; pedophiles on the Internet; reckless driving; White House intruder; program to foil car theft; gambling raid; stolen car.

The nanny case centered on a 19-year-old woman from England charged with shaking to death the baby of two medical doctors. Marv Albert, a famous sports broadcaster, was charged with biting a woman with whom he was sexually involved. One of the many alle-

gations to emerge in this case was that Albert enjoyed wearing women's underwear. The point is that attention focused on the Woodward and Albert stories not just because the acts involved interpersonal violence,
225 but because there were sensational aspects to the cases.

Other violent and sensational crimes reported by NBC included stories on the Oklahoma City bombing; a multiple killing case in Pearl, Mississippi, in which a male adolescent murdered his mother and two school-
230 mates; and a hate crime in Denver in which a white male skinhead killed a black man for being black. The Oklahoma City, Pearl, and Denver stories were three of the most serious, and most violent, crimes covered by NBC during the five-week sample.
235 As noted earlier, the research literature suggests that the media tend to give little attention to white-collar crime. Importantly, this was not found to be the case with regard to NBC newscasts. In fact, 23 percent of all NBC crime reports focused on white-collar of-
240 fenses. These stories included such diverse topics as Whitewater offenses; illegal tactics of the Internal Revenue Service; government "cover-ups" and "pay-outs"; unsafe consumer products; and various corporate scams.

Big City Newscasts (WGN)

245 The crime stories reported on WGN were even more likely to describe violent offenses than was the case with the national news. As seen in Table 2, 65 percent of all WGN crime reports described interpersonal violence. Many of these reports highlighted na-
250 tional stories. The nanny trial, Marv Albert's case, and the Oklahoma City bombing are three examples of this. However, a majority of WGN violent crime stories referred to behavior that occurred in the greater Chicago area. Illustrations of local violent offenses in-
255 cluded the stabbing death of an elderly woman by a man intent on stealing the victim's car; sexual assault involving one female victim and four male offenders at a local college; seven killings at a suburban fast food restaurant; the beating death of an elderly woman by
260 her daughter; the severe beating of a two-year-old for bedwetting; and perhaps the most sensational story of all involved the torture, beating, and raping of a woman. In this case, a 24-year-old man assaulted his wife for several days. He whipped her, cutting her skin
265 open, and then forced her to soak in a tub of salt water. She was eventually rescued when someone at the apartment door became suspicious.

WGN featured a considerably smaller percentage of white-collar crimes than was the case with NBC. Only
270 10 percent of WGN crime stories highlighted white-collar offenses. Furthermore, the WGN sample contained only eight drug crime stories (5 percent), a lower percentage of such stories than what was found for NBC (9 percent) or WGEM (33 percent).

Small Town Newscasts (WGEM)

275 The pattern found with WGEM newscasts differed substantially from the sample of national and big city newscasts. Only 30 percent of all crime stories reported on WGEM dealt with violence. Table 3 identifies 10 violent offenses. The killing of a four-year-old boy, the
280 robbery of a convenience store, and an altercation leading to a nondeadly shooting were perhaps the three most serious and violent crimes reported (actually, the first story pertained to a Peoria, Illinois, case and was one of only two crime stories set outside the WGEM
285 viewing audience).

Table 3
Type of Crime Reported by WGEM (N=33)

VIOLENCE (10 = 30%): Possible suicide (2); motorist shot; girl assists boy in occult-related suicide attempt; four-year-old boy killed by man; aggravated assault charges; possible suicide; robbery; altercation leads to nonfatal shooting of a college football player; man arrested for stalking of ex-girlfriend; sheriff's deputy charged with battery.

DRUG OFFENSES (11 = 33%): community efforts to combat underage drinking (2); arrest for possession of controlled substances (2); arrest for marijuana possession (2); two women sentenced for drug charges; drunk driving laws; pharmacist charged with illegal dispensing of narcotics; drug dealing; smuggling drugs into prison.

WHITE-COLLAR CRIMES (0).

OTHER (12 = 36%): Theft of explosives (2); check-cashing fraud (2); delinquent child support payments; child pornography on the Internet; arson investigation; illegal tree cutting; property damage done by inmates; illegal disposal of leaves; program to fight auto theft; program to fight scams against the elderly.

Previous research indicates that 8 percent of crime stories reported on big city news telecasts featured drug offenses (Chermak, 1997:696). Comparable results were found in the present study for national and big
290 city newscasts, but not for the small town WGEM news. While violent crime was a far more frequent topic on NBC and WGN than on WGEM, the reverse pattern was found for drug offenses. As shown in Table 3, 33 percent of WGEM crime stories pertained to
295 drugs, whereas the percentages for NBC and WGN were 9 percent and 5 percent, respectively. Though WGEM showed a high rate of drug stories, the offenses reported were typically less serious than the drug crimes covered by NBC or WGN. For example, several
300 of the WGEM drug cases dealt with marijuana or drinking and driving. On the other hand, NBC profiled a Mexican drug cartel and WGN described a drug bust in which 31 people were arrested. The point is, the drug stories on WGEM generally focused on relatively
305 minor offenses.

Finally, an examination of the content category "Other" suggests that NBC and WGN might share a news selection strategy quite different from the strategy used at WGEM. NBC covered stories involving nu-
310 clear theft, germ warfare, and the manufacture of poi-

son bombs, and WGN broadcast stories on an elaborate burglary ring, a man flashing a teenage girl, and a White House intruder. These were spectacular stories. WGEM, on the contrary, highlighted stories on delin-
315 quent child support payments and the illegal disposal of leaves. These reports were fairly mundane, at least in comparison to the NBC and WGN stories just cited. This raises an interesting question: Does the size of the news organization and its audience influence not just
320 the type of crime story reported, but the affective nature or function of the reports? That is, are crime stories picked not just in terms of the seriousness of the offense, but for what the story has to offer to the audience?

Discussion and Conclusion
325   This study advances several noteworthy findings. Some of these points support previous research findings, while others challenge or add to the existing literature. First, while all newscasts featured crime as a staple topic, news programs varied in their attention to
330 crime. Our sample of big city newscasts had the highest rate of crime reports, while national and small town newscasts paid less attention to crime stories. Second, in support of previous research, this project found that a high percentage of crime stories focused on interper-
335 sonal violence. This pattern was clearly less pronounced for small town news, however. Third, except for WGEM, the small town station, there was little coverage of drug offenses. This is perhaps odd because drug offenders make up an increasingly high percent-
340 age of new arrestees. In Illinois, for example, drug arrests have tripled between 1983 and 1996 (Smith, 1998). Fourth, although researchers have typically found that "news in general pays little attention to white-collar crime" (Tunnell, 1998:114), there was
345 considerable emphasis on white-collar crime in the national news sample. However, noting yet another difference in level of newscast, white-collar crime stories were not a frequent topic in big city newscasts, and there was no coverage of white-collar crime in the
350 sample of small town newscasts. Fifth, contrary to some popular thoughts and selected published research (e.g., Cooper, 1996), we found no evidence that television news exaggerated African-American involvement in crime. Most of the sample news reports did not offer
355 any information about the race of the offender, but for those stories that did identify the race of the offender, the results were as follows: NBC (three of 16 offenders were African American); WGN (23 of 56 were African American); and WGEM (zero of three were African
360 American).
    The final finding, which is overarching in scope, is that level of newscast appeared to manifest a distinctive news strategy with regard to crime reports. Research has shown that there are important strategic differences between newspaper and television news cov-
365 erage of crime (Chermak,1995b; Sheley and Ash-

kins,1981), but here we were concerned with differences related to the level of television news. NBC and WGN show a marked preference for violent types of
370 crime, while WGEM was much less likely to report on violent crimes and much more likely to highlight drug offenses. In the remainder of this paper, we offer a speculative but informed explanation for these findings.
375   As was noted earlier, all forms of media news, including TV newscasts, take an interest in crime. Kenneth Tunnell (1992) refers to this phenomenon as the "commodification of crime." Crime is such a recurring story line on television newscasts because viewers are
380 interested in crime, and crime stories are inexpensive to deliver. One reason explaining the low expense is that police authorities are more than willing to supply up-to-date information on crimes. Crime control is widely seen, by both the police and the public, as the main job
385 function of the police. From the perspective of the police, media crime reports dramatize why communities need police protection (although there is a danger in that some viewers might conclude that there is too much crime and that the police are to be blamed for
390 this). It is worth noting that the police do not provide television news personnel with information on all types of crime. Typically, the most serious crimes (e.g., interpersonal violence) receive the most attention. Perhaps this meets the needs of newscasters who may be-
395 lieve that these stories are most likely to grab the interest of viewers. Taking these general observations as an overview, perhaps some light can be shed on the differential strategies of the three newscasts sampled in this study.
400   Each of the news programs has a mandate to cover a specified area. For NBC the area of coverage is the world, although most attention is focused on the United States. The main area of coverage for WGN is the city of Chicago and its surrounding suburbs, and WGEM is
405 primarily concerned with events happening in Quincy, Illinois, and the general rural viewing area of the WGEM station. An important consideration here is the Federal Communications Commission's (FCC) "localism doctrine," which has traditionally required stations
410 (as part of the licensing process) to meet the needs and interests of the communities in which they broadcast. Even though the localism doctrine has been relaxed in recent decades, it remains a concern of broadcasters. In fact, one study showed that between 1976 and 1992
415 newscasts increased their attention to local news (Slattery, Hakenen, and Doremus, 1996). This may help explain, in part, why NBC and WGN are far more likely than WGEM to air crime stories that are violent and sensational. If crime reporting focuses on the most
420 serious crimes taking place in the coverage area, NBC and WGN probably have a daily surplus of violent offenses to choose from. WGEM has a more limited selection. This could be one reason why drug offenses (e.g., marijuana possession) received so much more

425 coverage on WGEM than on either NBC or WGN. In a small town, a charge of marijuana possession might be the most serious offense on which to report. At the same time, this is not a complete explanation for the differences noted above. After all, it is always possible
430 for a television newscast to broaden its scope. This is something that WGN frequently did. Similarly, WGEM could have easily reported crimes taking place in St. Louis or Chicago (interestingly, this station routinely presented sports stories concerning teams from
435 St. Louis and Chicago). With regard to crime, however, WGEM seldom reported stories about crimes that occurred elsewhere.

It seems likely that area focus is not a total explanation for differential crime reporting. There may be
440 strategic differences among the newscasts. While it is probably the case that hard news, high ratings, and community service (defined broadly) would be a concern for each of the newscasts, the priorities may vary. Arguably, NBC, WGN, and WGEM may define their
445 fundamental missions differently. Although an oversimplification, perhaps NBC and WGN newscasts were interested mainly in hard (serious) news stories and segments that promoted high ratings. Indeed, recent research shows that viewers are particularly attentive to
450 television news messages that provoke anger and fear (Newhagen, 1998). Clearly, anger and fear are common emotional reactions to violent crime stories. But research also suggests that when fear messages are too pronounced, viewers are likely to "tune out" (Strong
455 and Dubas, 1993). This presents a problem for small town stations. While big city viewers can temper their personal fear by disassociating themselves from what is reported to happen in "bad" areas, small town viewers are likely to identify themselves closely with the news
460 of the community. Accordingly, small town newscasts might be more interested in promoting positive, community-oriented news.

In sum, despite sample limitations (future research should extend the analysis to other national, big city,
465 and small town newscasts), the present study offers preliminary evidence that television crime news varies significantly by level of newscast. This general conclusion is a point not found in the present literature, which tends to lump all levels of television news together.
470 Researchers have been critical of the media for misrepresenting the actual facts of crime; researchers too need to be careful about their representation of media reports. One size does not fit all.

References

Bailey, F. & Hale, D. (1998). *Popular culture, crime and justice*. Belmont, CA: West/Wadsworth.

Barak, G. (1994). Media, society, and criminology. In G. Barak (Ed.) *Media, process, and the social construction of crime* (pp. 3-45). New York: Garland.

Barak, G. (1993). Media, crime, and justice: A case for constitutive criminology. *Humanity & Society, 17*: 272-296.

Barrile, L. (1986). Television's 'Bogeyclass?': Status, motives and violence in crime drama characters. *Sociological Viewpoints, 2*: 39-56.

Chermak, S. (1997). The presentation of drugs in the news media: The new sources involved in the construction of social problems. *Justice Quarterly, 14*: 687-718.

Chermak, S. (1995a). Crime in the news media: A refined understanding of how crimes become news. In G. Barak (Ed.) *Media, process, and the social construction of crime* (pp. 95-129). New York: Garland.

Chermak, S. (1995b). *Victims in the news: Crime and the American news media*. Boulder: Westview.

Chermak, S. (1994). Body count news: How crime is presented in the news media. *Justice Quarterly 11*: 561-582.

Cooper, T. (1996). Racism, hoaxes, epistemology, and news as a form of knowledge: The Stuart case as fraud or norm? *Howard Journal of Communications, 7*: 75-95.

Dominick, J. (1978). Crime and law enforcement in the mass media. In C. Winick (Ed.) *Deviance and mass society*, (pp. 105-128). Beverly Hills: Sage.

Gallup, G., Jr. (1996). *The Gallup poll: Public opinion 1995*, Wilmington, DE: Scholarly Resources Inc.

Gallup, G. (1972). *The Gallup poll: Public opinion 1935-1971*. New York: Random.

Gans, H. (1980). *Deciding what's news: A study of CBS Evening News, NBC Nightly News, Newsweek and Time*. New York: Vintage Books.

Graber, D. (1980). *Crime news and the public*. New York: Praeger.

Johnson, S. (1998). A newscast is a newscast is a newscast... *Chicago Tribune*, January 20, Section 2, pp. 1, 4.

Kappeler, V., Blumberg, M., & Potter, G. (1996). *The mythology of crime and criminal justice*. Prospect Heights, IL: Waveland.

Katz, J. (1986). What makes crime 'news'? In R. Collins (Ed.) *Media, culture, and society: A critical reader* (pp. 47-75). Thousand Oaks, CA: Sage.

Kirk, J. (1998). Local focus aside, TV execs closely watch scandal. *Chicago Tribune*, October 7, Section 3, p. 2.

Krippendorff, K. (1980). *Content analysis: An introduction to its methodology*. Beverly Hills: Sage.

Macionis, J. (1997). *Sociology*. Upper Saddle River, NJ: Prentice-Hall.

Maguire, K. & Pastore, A. (1997). *Sourcebook of Criminal Justice Statistics—1996*. Washington, DC: U.S. Department of Justice.

Maguire, K. & Pastore, A. (1996). *Sourcebook of Criminal Justice Statistics—1995*. Washington, DC: U.S. Department of Justice.

Manning, P. (1998). Media loops. In F. Bailey & D. Hale (Eds.) *Popular culture, crime and justice* (pp. 25-39). Belmont, CA: West/Wadsworth.

Newhagen, J. (1998). TV news images that induce anger, fear, and disgust: Effects on approach-avoidance and memory. *Journal of Broadcasting & Electronic Media 42*: 265-276.

Perkinson, H. (1996). *Getting better: Television & moral progress*. New Brunswick, NJ: Transaction.

Sheley, J. & Ashkins, C. (1981). Crime, crime news, and crime views. *Public Opinion Quarterly 45*, 492-506.

Singleton, R., Jr., Straits, B., Straits, M., & McAllister, R. (1988). *Approaches to social research*. New York: Oxford.

Slattery, K., Hakanen, E., & Doremus, M. (1996). The expression of localism: Local TV news coverage in the new video marketplace. *Journal of Broadcasting & Electronic Media 40*: 403-413.

Smith, N. (1998). Drug offenders crowd Illinois' criminal justice system. *The Compiler 17*: 8-9.

Steinberg, C. (1985). *TV facts*. New York: Facts on File.

Strong, J. & Dubas, K. (1993). The optimal level of fear-arousal in advertising: An empirical study. *Journal of Current Issues and Research in Advertising 15*: 93-99.

Surette, R. (1998). *Media, crime, and criminal justice: Images and realities*. Belmont, CA: West/Wadsworth.

Tunnell, K. (1992). Film at eleven: Recent developments in the commodification of crime. *Sociological Spectrum 12*: 293-313.

Tunnell, K. (1998). Reflections on crime, criminals, and control in newsmagazine television programs. In F. Bailey & D. Hale (Eds.) *Popular culture, crime and justice* (pp. 111-122). Belmont, CA: West/Wadsworth.

Warr, M. (1995). Public perceptions of crime and punishment. In J. Sheley (Ed.) *Criminology: A contemporary handbook* (pp. 15-31). Belmont, CA: Wadsworth.

Weber, R. (1990). *Basic content analysis*. Newbury Park, CA: Sage.

Exercise for Article 8

Factual Questions

1. According to the literature review, previous researchers have found that what type of crime is

underreported in television news?

2. Why was NBC nightly news chosen for this study?

3. According to the researchers, what is the "main enterprise" of content analysis?

4. What percentage of the 246 crime news stories was double–coded to determine reliability?

5. What percentage of the crimes reported by WGN related to violence?

6. For what type of crime is there an increasingly large number of arrestees yet little coverage of it on the big city and national news?

7. The researchers reach the general conclusion that television crime news varies significantly by level of newscast. According to the researchers, has this been previously reported in the literature?

Questions for Discussion

8. Have the researchers convinced you of their point that television has become a primary agent of socialization in American society? (See lines 11–15.)

9. The researchers refer to their research as "exploratory." Do you agree that it is? Why? Why not? (See lines 90–94 and 122–126.)

10. The researchers report intercoder reliability coefficients of .91 and .98. In your opinion, are these adequate? Explain. (See lines 173–174.)

11. In the first paragraph under the heading "Results," the researchers discuss what is "perhaps the most important finding" of the study. Are you surprised by this finding? Explain.

12. The researchers suggest that future research should extend the analysis to additional television stations. Do you think this is an important suggestion? Explain.

Quality Ratings

Directions: Indicate your level of agreement with each of the following statements by circling a number from 5 for strongly agree (SA) to 1 for strongly disagree (SD). If you believe an item is not applicable to this research article, leave it blank. Be prepared to explain your ratings.

A. The introduction establishes the importance of the study.

SA   5   4   3   2   1   SD

B. The literature review establishes the context for the study.

SA   5   4   3   2   1   SD

C. The research purpose, question, or hypothesis is clearly stated.

SA   5   4   3   2   1   SD

D. The method of sampling is sound.

SA   5   4   3   2   1   SD

E. Relevant demographics (for example, age, gender, and ethnicity) are described.

SA   5   4   3   2   1   SD

F. Measurement procedures are adequate.

SA   5   4   3   2   1   SD

G. All procedures have been described in sufficient detail to permit a replication of the study.

SA   5   4   3   2   1   SD

H. The participants have been adequately protected from potential harm.

SA   5   4   3   2   1   SD

I. The results are clearly described.

SA   5   4   3   2   1   SD

J. The discussion/conclusion is appropriate.

SA   5   4   3   2   1   SD

K. Despite any flaws, the report is worthy of publication.

SA   5   4   3   2   1   SD

Article 9

Poverty As We Know It:
Media Portrayals of the Poor

Rosalee A. Clawson
Purdue University

Rakuya Trice
Indiana University

Introduction

On the campaign trail during the 1992 presidential election, Bill Clinton's stump speech included a pledge to "end welfare as we know it" to the delight of most audiences. Two years later during the 1994 congres-
5 sional election, one of the most popular planks of the Republicans' Contract with America was the "Personal Responsibility Act," which called for a major overhaul of the welfare system. The election of this Republican Congress initiated a great deal of legislative activity and
10 presidential maneuvering on the issue of welfare reform. The culmination of those efforts occurred in August of 1996 when President Clinton signed into law sweeping welfare reform legislation. By ending the federal guarantee of support for the poor and turning
15 control of welfare programs over to the states, this legislation reversed 6 decades of social policy and begot a new era of welfare politics. Throughout this period of intense political activity, the media focused a significant amount of attention on poverty and welfare reform.
20 In this research, we analyze media portrayals of the poor during this time when welfare reform was high on the nation's agenda. We investigate whether the media perpetuate inaccurate and stereotypical images of the poor. Specifically, we examine the photographs that
25 accompany stories on poverty in five U.S. news magazines between January 1, 1993, and December 31, 1998.

Portrayals of the Poor

In a study of news magazines between 1988 and 1992, Gilens (1996a) investigated the accuracy of the
30 media in their portrayals of the poor. Gilens (1996a) found that poverty was disproportionately portrayed as a "black" problem. Blacks make up less than one-third of the poor, but the media would lead citizens to believe that two out of every three poor people are black.
35 Moreover, Gilens (1996a) found that the "deserving" poor, especially the black deserving poor, were underrepresented in news magazines. For example, the black elderly poor and black working poor were rarely por-

trayed. In addition, Gilens examined media depictions
40 of the poor between 1950 and 1992 and found that blacks were "comparatively absent from media coverage of poverty during times of heightened sympathy for the poor" (1999, p. 132). In this research, we pick up where Gilens left off by analyzing media portrayals of
45 the demographics of poverty between 1993 and 1998.

In addition, we extend Gilens's work by investigating whether common stereotypical traits or behaviors associated with the poor are portrayed in the media. In our society, citizens believe poor people have many
50 undesirable qualities that violate mainstream American ideals. For example, many citizens say people are poor due to their own "lack of effort" and "loose morals and drunkenness" (Kluegel and Smith 1986, p. 79). A majority of Americans believe that "most people who re-
55 ceive welfare benefits are taking advantage of the system" (Ladd 1993, p. 86). Another piece of conventional wisdom is that poor mothers on public assistance have additional babies to receive greater welfare benefits. People also believe that poor families are much
60 larger than middle-class families (Sidel 1996).

Several media studies have found such stereotypical representations of poverty (Golding and Middleton 1982; Martindale 1996). The media often describe the underclass in behavioral terms as criminals, alcoholics,
65 and drug addicts, and the underclass is linked with pathological behavior in urban areas (Gans 1995). Parisi's (1998) in-depth analysis of a *Washington Post* series on poverty demonstrated that the media perpetuate stereotypes of the poor as lazy, sexually irresponsi-
70 ble, and criminally deviant. Coughlin (1989) discussed the media's emphasis on "welfare queens" – a phrase that invokes images of poor women living the high life by defrauding and taking advantage of the welfare system. These studies focused on how the poor were de-
75 scribed in the text of news stories; in this study, we analyze whether stereotypical traits of the poor are presented in magazine photographs.

Why is it important to study the visual images surrounding the issue of poverty? The visual representa-
80 tion of a political issue is an integral part of the definition of that issue.[1] Visual images (along with metaphors, exemplars, and catch phrases) define and il-

Table 1
Representations of Poverty by Magazine, 1993-98

	Business Week	Newsweek	New York Times Magazine	Time	U.S. News & World Report	Total
Number of Stories	18	13	8	13	22	74
Number of Pictures	21	24	18	30	56	149
Number of Poor People	40	64	35	78	140	357

lustrate particular issue frames (Gamson and Lasch 1983). For example, Nelson and Kinder (1996) demon-
85 strate that visual frames have a significant impact on public attitudes toward affirmative action. People and events that appear in photographs accompanying news stories are not simply indicative of isolated individuals and occurrences; rather, the photographs are symbolic
90 of "the whole mosaic" (Epstein 1973, p. 5). The pictures provide texture, drama, and detail, and they illustrate the implicit, the latent, the "taken for granted," and the "goes without saying." Furthermore, scholars should pay attention to visual images because journal-
95 ists and editors perceive them to be a central part of a news story. In his classic study of how journalists select stories, Gans argues that magazine "editors consider still pictures as important as text" (1979, p. 159).

Research Design

In this research, we test the hypothesis that the me-
100 dia portray poor people inaccurately and stereotypi-cally. The data were collected by examining every story on the topics of poverty, welfare, and the poor between January 1, 1993, and December 31, 1998, in five news magazines: *Business Week, Newsweek, New York Times*
105 *Magazine, Time,* and *U.S. News & World Report.*[2] We used the *Reader's Guide to Periodical Literature* to locate the stories and to identify other cross-referenced topics (e.g., income inequality). Seventy-four stories were identified as relevant for a total of 149 pictures of
110 357 poor people.[3] See Table 1 for the distribution of stories, pictures, and people by magazine.

The photographs were analyzed in two ways. First, we scrutinized each picture as a whole. For those pictures that included a mother with children, we noted the
115 size and race of the family. Second, we examined the demographic characteristics of each poor individual in the pictures. For coding race, we departed from Gilens's coding procedure. Gilens (1996a, 1999) coded whether the poor person was black, nonblack, or unde-
120 terminable. In contrast, we used a more detailed classi-fication scheme and coded whether the poor person was white, black, Hispanic, Asian American, or undeter-minable.

We coded each person's gender (male or female),
125 age (young: under 18; middle-aged: 18–64; or old: 65 and over), residence (urban or rural), and work status (working/job training or not working).[4] We also ana-lyzed whether each individual was depicted in stereo-typical ways, such as pregnant, engaging in criminal

130 behavior, taking or selling drugs, drinking alcohol, smoking cigarettes, or wearing expensive clothing or jewelry.[5] For many of our variables, we were able to compare the portrayal of poverty in news magazines to the reality of poverty as measured by the Current
135 Population Survey (CPS) conducted by the U.S. Census Bureau or as reported by the U.S. House of Represen-tatives Committee on Ways and Means.[6]

Research Findings

Many citizens greatly overestimate the number of black people among the poor (Gilens 1996a). Do news
140 magazines perpetuate and reinforce that belief? Ac-cording to the 1996 CPS, African-Americans make up 27 percent of the poor, but these five magazines would lead citizens to believe that blacks are 49 percent of the poor ($p < .001$; see Table 2). Whites, on the other hand,
145 are depicted as 33 percent of the poor, when they really make up 45 percent of those in poverty ($p < .001$). There were no magazine portrayals of Asian Americans in poverty, and Hispanics were underrepresented by 5 percent.

150 This underrepresentation of poor Hispanics and Asian Americans may be part of a larger phenomenon in which these groups are ignored by the media in gen-eral. For example, Hispanics and Asian Americans are rarely found in mass media advertising (Bowen and
155 Schmid 1997; Wilkes and Valencia 1989). Similarly, Dixon (1998) documented the invisibility of Hispanics in local news; however, there is evidence that in par-ticular regions, Hispanics are represented in accordance with their proportion in the population (Greenberg and
160 Brand 1998; Turk et al. 1989). Unlike blacks, Asian Americans are associated with intelligence, not welfare dependency (Gilbert and Hixon 1991; Gilens 1999). Thus, their absence may reflect a positive stereotype, but a stereotype nonetheless. Clearly these comments
165 regarding Hispanics and Asian Americans are specula-tive. Further research is needed on media representa-tions of these two groups.

Focusing on just the three magazines Gilens in-cluded in his study (i.e., *Newsweek, Time,* and *U.S.*
170 *News & World Report*), whites make up 33 percent, blacks make up 45 percent, and Hispanics are 22 per-cent of the magazine poor (see Table 2). In comparison, Gilens (1996a) found that 62 percent of the poor were African American in these magazines between 1988
175 and 1992. Although at first glance our statistics may suggest that the magazines have become less likely to

Table 2
The Percent of True Poor and the Percent of Magazine Poor by Race, 1993-1998

	Whites	African Americans	Hispanics	Asian Americans
True Poor	45	27	24	4
Magazine Poor	33***	49***	19*	0**
Poor in *Newsweek, Time,* and *U.S. News & World Report*	33***	45***	22	0**

Source: "March Current Population Survey" (U.S. Bureau of the Census, 1996)

Note: We conducted difference of proportion tests in which the proportion observed in the magazine is compared to the true proportion as reported by the Current Population Survey for each racial category (Blalock, 1979). A statistically significant result indicates that the magazine portrayal of a particular racial group is not representative of the true poor. Due to rounding, the percentages may sum to more than 100 percent. The sample size is 347 for the analysis based on all five magazines. The sample size is 272 for the analysis based on *Newsweek, Time,* and *U.S. News & World Report.*
*p < .05.
**p < .01.
***p < .001.

put a black face on poverty, we hesitate to draw that conclusion given the coding difference mentioned earlier. Recall that Gilens coded whether the poor person 180 was black, nonblack, or undeterminable. Since Gilens (1996a) reports a higher percentage of poor people for which race was not identified (12 percent compared to our 4 percent), it seems likely that many of the poor people we coded as Hispanic, Gilens would have coded 185 as undeterminable. If we treat Hispanics in that fashion and therefore exclude them from our analysis, blacks make up 58 percent of the poor and whites make up 42 percent -- figures that mirror Gilens's data quite closely. Regardless of the exact proportion, it is clear 190 these news magazines continue to race code the issue of poverty.[7]

Table 3
The Percent of AFDC Parents and the Percent of Magazine Adult Poor by Race, 1993-1998

	Whites	African Americans	Hispanics	Native Americans, Asian Americans, and Other
AFDC Parents	36	37	21	7
Magazine Adult poor	34	48**	18	0***

Source: *Overview of Entitlement Programs* (U.S. House of Representatives, Committee on Ways and Means, 1998)

Note: *N* = 159.
**p<.01.
***p<.001.

Since we are examining portrayals of the poor during a period of intense debate over welfare reform, perhaps the racial characteristics of the magazine poor 195 mirror welfare recipients more closely than they represent poor people in general. The House Ways and Means Committee provides the racial breakdown for parents on Aid to Families with Dependent Children (AFDC). Therefore, in Table 3 we compare the racial 200 composition of AFDC parents to the magazine portrayal of poor adults. Indeed, the portrayal of poor whites and Hispanics matches more closely the true racial characteristics of welfare recipients; however, blacks are still heavily overrepresented (48 percent) 205 among the magazine poor. Moreover, blacks make up 52 percent of the poor adults who are portrayed in stories that focus specifically on welfare (rather than on poverty in general).

Gilens (1996a, 1999) found that blacks were even 210 more prominent in stories on poverty topics that were not very popular with the public. Between 1993 and 1998, there were several stories on unpopular issues, such as welfare reform and pregnancy, public housing, and welfare and the cycle of dependency.[8] We examined the proportion of blacks among the poor in these 215 stories and found that it jumped to 63 percent, whereas whites made up only 19 percent and Hispanics were 18 percent. In contrast, blacks were associated less often with sympathetic topics. In stories on welfare reform 220 and children, welfare recipients and day care, and job training, 46 percent of the poor were black, while 32 percent were white and 22 percent were Hispanic.[9] We also analyzed two stories that focused on various "myths" surrounding welfare reform. Ironically, 16 of 225 the 22 poor people depicted in these two stories were black.

The news magazines exaggerated the feminization of poverty by about 14 percent. According to the CPS, 62 percent of the adult poor are women, whereas 76 230 percent of the magazine poor are women (*N* = 161).[10] Again, though, since most of these stories discuss pov-

erty specifically in the context of welfare reform, it is important to compare the magazine poor to people on welfare. The vast majority of adult AFDC recipients are
235 female, so the predominance of women among the poor is fairly accurate (U.S. House of Representatives, Committee on Ways and Means 1998).

In terms of the age of the poor people, we found that children were overrepresented among the magazine
240 poor (see Table 4).[11] Children are usually thought of as a fairly deserving group of poor people (Cook and Barrett 1992); however, the large proportion of black children among the magazine poor may undermine that belief. In Iyengar's (1990) experimental research on
245 attributions of responsibility for poverty, subjects indicated that black children should take responsibility for their own plight, whereas white children were not expected to solve their own problems.

Table 4
The Percent of True Poor and the Percent of Magazine Poor by Age, 1993-1998

	Under 18	18-64	65 and Over
True Poor	40	51	9
Magazine Poor	53***	43**	4**

Source: "March Current Population Survey" (U.S. Bureau of the Census, 1996)

Note: $N = 347$.
**$p < .01$.
***$p < .001$.

In contrast, the elderly, who are the most sympathetic
250 group of poor people, were rarely portrayed. Most people believe the elderly really need their benefits and that they use them wisely (Cook and Barrett 1992). Iyengar (1990) found that people thought society should aid (both black and white) poor elderly widows.
255 This sympathetic group makes up 9 percent of the true poor, but only 4 percent of the magazine poor (see Table 4).

We also examined whether poor people were portrayed in urban or rural settings. The magazine depictions
260 implied that poverty is almost completely an urban problem. Ninety-six percent of the poor were shown in urban areas.[12] According to the CPS, most poor people (77 percent) do reside in metropolitan areas; however, the magazine portrayals greatly exaggerate
265 the true proportion ($p < .001$).[13] According to Gans (1995), the urban underclass is often linked with various pathologies and antisocial behavior. Thus, this emphasis on the urban poor does not promote a positive image of those in poverty.
270 The media leave the impression that most poor people do not work: only 30 percent of poor adults were shown working or participating in job training pro-

grams ($N = 198$). In reality, 50 percent of the poor work in full- or part-time jobs, according to the CPS ($p < $
275 $.001$).[14] When we focus solely on those stories that specifically discuss welfare, 35 percent of the poor are shown either working or in job training. According to the House Ways and Means Committee, 23 percent of AFDC recipients worked or participated in education or
280 job training programs in 1995. These photographs reflect the emphasis of many contemporary welfare reformers, liberal and conservative, on "workfare" rather than welfare. Since many citizens support work requirements for welfare recipients (Weaver, Shapiro, and
285 Jacobs 1995), these images are positive ones. Not surprisingly, whites were more likely to be shown in these pictures than blacks.

Next, we analyzed the extent to which the news magazines relied on stereotypical traits in their depictions
290 of the poor. We examined whether the media perpetuate the notion that women on welfare have lots of children. When a mother was portrayed with her children in these magazines, the average family size was 2.80. This is virtually identical to the figure of 2.78 reported
295 by the House Ways and Means Committee for the average AFDC family size in 1996. In the magazines, the representation of poor women and their children differed by race. The average family size for whites was 2.44, whereas the average size for blacks
300 was 3.05 and 2.92 for Hispanics. Although these differences are not statistically significant, the direction suggests that citizens received a less flattering view of poor minority families. The Ways and Means Committee does not report the true figure by race; however, the
305 U.S. Census Bureau (1995) provides data on the average number of children ever had (rather than the average number of children currently receiving benefits) by AFDC mothers by race.[15] These data show that black AFDC women have only slightly (and nonsignificantly)
310 more children than white AFDC women. Hispanic AFDC mothers, on the other hand, do have more children than non-Hispanic AFDC women.

To our surprise, the media did not overly emphasize other stereotypical characteristics associated with the
315 poor. Of the 357 people coded, only three were shown engaging in criminal behavior, and another three were shown with drugs. No alcoholics were presented, and only one person was smoking a cigarette. However, of those seven stereotypical portrayals, only the person
320 smoking was white—the others were either black or Hispanic. Only one poor woman was pregnant, so the media were not providing images suggesting that poor women simply have babies to obtain larger welfare checks. Again, though, this stereotypical portrayal is of
325 a Hispanic woman. We also examined whether the media presented images consistent with the "welfare queen" stereotype. We felt that poor people who were shown wearing expensive jewelry or clothing would fit this stereotype. Thirty-nine individuals were shown
330 with flashy jewelry or fancy clothes; blacks and His-

panics were somewhat more likely to be portrayed this way than whites.

In sum, the magazines often portrayed an inaccurate picture of the demographic characteristics of poor people. These magazines overrepresented the black, urban, and nonworking poor. Blacks were especially prominent in stories on unpopular poverty topics, and black women were portrayed with the most children. Other stereotypical traits linked with poor people were not common in the magazine portrayals. Nevertheless, in those instances when the media depicted poor people with stereotypical characteristics, they tended to be black or Hispanic. The most sympathetic group of poor people, the elderly, was underrepresented among the magazine poor. The media were most accurate in mirroring the predominance of women among welfare recipients.

Discussion

These portrayals of poverty are important because they have an impact on public opinion. A variety of experimental research demonstrates that negative images of blacks influence public opinion (Gilliam et al. 1996; Iyengar 1990; Johnson et al. 1997; Mendelberg 1997; Peffley, Shields, and Williams 1996). Furthermore, white citizens' stereotypical beliefs about blacks decrease their support for welfare (Gilens 1995, 1996b).

In turn, public opinion has an impact on public policy (Page and Shapiro 1983). Thus, if attitudes on poverty-related issues are driven by inaccurate and stereotypical portrayals of the poor, then the policies favored by the public (and political elites) may not adequately address the true problems of poverty. Furthermore, these inaccurate portrayals of the racial characteristics of the poor may prime the white public to favor political candidates who make racially coded arguments a linchpin of their campaign strategies. When these candidates are elected, they favor welfare (and other) policies that are in keeping with their racialized rhetoric.

It is possible that the text of these stories on poverty contains data describing the true demographic characteristics of the poor. It is unclear what impact a story that dispels stereotypes in its text but perpetuates stereotypes in its photographs would have on public opinion. Graber's research on television suggests that audiovisual themes are more memorable than verbal information (Graber 1990, 1991). Although news magazines are a very different medium than television, it is certainly possible that magazine photos capture the audience's attention in the same way as television visuals. Psychological research suggests that vivid images of particular cases are more memorable and influential than dry statistical data (Fischhoff and Bar-Hillel 1984). Indeed, Hamill, Wilson, and Nisbett's (1980) experimental research shows that a vivid, detailed description of a poor woman on welfare has a larger im-

pact on subjects' opinions about welfare recipients than statistical information about women on welfare.

Gilens (1996a, 1999) investigated several explanations for why blacks are overrepresented among the poor and concluded that, at least in part, it is due to journalists' stereotypes. Gilens's research received considerable attention from media elites, including being the lead topic of discussion on CNN's *Reliable Sources* on August 24, 1997. Unfortunately, our data illustrate that journalists and editors have continued the practice of race coding the issue of poverty even after it was brought to their attention.

We must also point out that this race coding of poverty in news magazines is not an isolated incident; rather, the racial bias reported here is a widespread phenomenon. For example, Clawson and Kegler (in press) conducted a comparable analysis on the portrayal of poverty in introductory textbooks on American government and found that blacks were disproportionately represented. In addition, several scholars have documented the negative images of blacks in news coverage of crime (Delgado 1994; Dixon 1998; Entman 1990, 1992, 1994; Johnson 1987). And it does not end there: whether it is children's programs, "reality-based" programs, sitcoms, or advertising, blacks are often portrayed in a stereotypical fashion (Graves 1996; Humphrey and Schuman 1984; Oliver 1994; Poindexter and Stroman 1981). These images are pervasive in our society.

Conclusion

In conclusion, blacks were disproportionately portrayed among magazine portrayals of the poor between 1993 and 1998. Blacks were especially overrepresented in negative stories on poverty and in those instances when the poor were presented with stereotypical traits. In addition, the "deserving" poor were underrepresented in the magazines. Overall, the photographic images of poor people in these five news magazines do not capture the reality of poverty; instead, they provide a stereotypical and inaccurate picture of poverty which results in negative beliefs about the poor, antipathy toward blacks, and a lack of support for welfare programs.

References

Blalock, Hubert M., Jr. 1979. *Social Statistics*. 2d ed. New York: McGraw-Hill.

Bowen, Lawrence, and Jill Schmid. 1997. "Minority Presence and Portrayal in Mainstream Magazine Advertising: An Update." *Journalism and Mass Communication Quarterly* 74(1):134–46.

Clawson, Rosalee A., and Elizabeth R. Kegler. In press. "The 'Race Coding' of Poverty in American Government Textbooks." *Howard Journal of Communications*.

Cook, Fay Lomax, and Edith Barrett. 1992. *Support for the American Welfare State*. New York: Columbia University Press.

Coughlin, Richard M. 1989. "Welfare Myths and Stereotypes." In *Reforming Welfare: Lessons, Limits, and Choices*, ed. Richard M. Coughlin. Albuquerque: University of New Mexico.

Delgado, Richard. 1994. "Rodrigo's Eighth Chronicle: Black Crime, White Fears—on the Social Construction of Threat." *Virginia Law Review* 80:503-48.

Dixon, Travis L. 1998. "Race and Crime on Local Television News." Paper presented at the annual meeting of the National Communication Association, New York.

Entman, Robert M. 1990. "Modern Racism and the Images of Blacks in Local Television News." *Critical Studies in Mass Communication* 7:332-45.

1992. "Blacks in the News: Television, Modern Racism and Cultural Change." *Journalism Quarterly* 69(2):341-61.

1994. "Representation and Reality in the Portrayal of Blacks on Network Television News." *Journalism Quarterly* 71(3):509-20.

1995. "Television, Democratic Theory and the Visual Construction of Poverty." *Research in Political Sociology* 7:139-59.

Epstein, Edward Jay. 1973. *News from Nowhere*. New York: Random House.

Fischhoff, Baruch B., and Maya Bar-Hillel. 1984. "Diagnosticity and the Base Rate Effect." *Memory and Cognition* 12:402-10.

Gamson, William A., and Kathryn E. Lasch. 1983. "The Political Culture of Social Welfare Policy." In *Evaluating the Welfare State*, ed. Shimon E. Spiro and Ephraim Yuchtman-Yaar. New York: Academic Press.

Gans, Herbert J. 1979. *Deciding What's News*. New York: Pantheon Books.

1995. *The War against the Poor*. New York: Basic Books.

Gilbert, Daniel T., and J. Gregory Hixon. 1991. "The Trouble of Thinking: Activation and Application of Stereotypic Beliefs." *Journal of Personality and Social Psychology* 60(4):509-17

Gilens, Martin. 1995. "Racial Attitudes and Oppositions to Welfare." *Journal of Politics* 57(4):994-1014.

1996a. "Race and Poverty in America." *Public Opinion Quarterly* 60(4):515-41.

1996b. "'Race Coding' and White Opposition to Welfare." *American Political Science Review* 90(3):593—604.

1999. *Why Americans Hate Welfare*. Chicago: University of Chicago Press.

Gilliam, Franklin D., Jr., Shanto Iyengar, Adam Simon, and Oliver Wright. 1996. "Crime in Black and White." *Harvard International Journal of Press/Politics* 1(3):6-23.

Golding, Peter, and Sue Middleton. 1982. *Images of Welfare*. Oxford: Martin Robertson.

Graber, Doris A. 1990. "Seeing Is Remembering: How Visuals Contribute to Learning from Television News." *Journal of Communication* 40:134-55.

1991. "What You See Is What You Get." Paper presented at the annual meeting of the American Political Science Association, Washington, DC.

Graves, Sherryl Browne. 1996. "Diversity on Television." In *Tuning In to Young Viewers*, ed. Tannis M. MacBeth. Thousand Oaks, CA: Sage Publications.

Greenberg, Bradley S., and Jeffrey E. Brand. 1998. "U.S. Minorities and the News." In *Cultural Diversity and the U.S. Media*, ed. Yahya R. Kamalipour and Theres Carilli. Albany, NY: SUNY Press.

Hamill, Ruth, Timothy DeCamp Wilson, and Richard E. Nisbett. 1980. "Insensitivity to Sample Bias: Generalizing from Atypical Cases." *Journal of Personality and Social Psychology* 39:578-89.

Humphrey, Ronald, and Howard Schuman. 1984. "The Portrayal of Blacks in Magazine Advertisements: 1950-1982." *Public Opinion Quarterly* 48:551-63.

Iyengar, Shanto. 1990. "Framing Responsibility for Political Issues: The Case of Poverty." *Political Behavior* 12(1):19-40.

Johnson, James D., Mike S. Adams, William Hall, and Leslie Ashburn. 1997. "Race, Media, and Violence: Differential Racial Effects of Exposure to Violent News Stories." *Basic and Applied Social Psychology* 19(1):81-90.

Johnson, Kirk A. 1987. "Black and White in Boston." *Columbia Journalism Review* 26 (May/June): 50-52

Kluegel, James R., and Eliot R. Smith. 1986. *Beliefs about Inequality*. New York: Aldine de Gruyter.

Ladd, Everett Carll, ed. 1993. "Public Opinion and Demographic Report: Reforming Welfare." *Public Perspective* 4(6):86-87.

Martindale, Carolyn. 1996. "Newspaper Stereotypes of African Americans." In *Images That Injure*, ed. Paul Martin Lester. Westport, CT: Praeger.

Mendelberg, Tali. 1997. "Executing Hortons." *Public Opinion Quarterly* 61(1):134-57.

Nelson, Thomas E., and Donald R. Kinder. 1996. "Issue Frames and Group-Centrism in American Public Opinion." *Journal of Politics* 58(4):1055-78.

Oliver, Mary Beth. 1994. "Portrayals of Crime, Race, and Aggression in 'Reality-Based' Police Shows: A Content Analysis." *Journal of Broadcasting and Electronic Media* 38(2):179-92.

Page, Benjamin I., and Robert Y. Shapiro. 1983. "Effects of Public Opinion on Policy." *American Political Science Review* 77:175-90.

Parisi, Peter. 1998. "A Sort of Compassion: The *Washington Post* Explains the 'Crisis in Urban America.'" *Howard Journal of Communications* 9:187-203.

Peffley, Mark, Todd Shields, and Bruce Williams. 1996. "The Intersection of Race and Crime in Television News Stories: An Experimental Study." *Political Communication* 13:309-27.

Poindexter, Paula M., and Carolyn A. Stroman. 1981. "Blacks and Television: A Review of the Research Literature." *Journal of Broadcasting* 25:103-22.

Sidel, Ruth. 1996. *Keeping Women and Children Last*. New York: Penguin Books.

Turk, Judy VanSlyke, Jim Richstad, Robert L. Bryson, Jr., and Sammye M. Johnson. 1989. "Hispanic Americans in the News in Two Southwestern Cities." *Journalism Quarterly* 66(1):107-13.

U.S. Bureau of the Census. 1995. "Statistical Brief: Mothers Who Receive AFDC Payments—Fertility and Socioeconomic Characteristics." *Census Bureau Web Page*. http://www.census.gov

1996. "March Current Population Survey." *Census Bureau Web Page*. http://www.census.gov/ftp/pub/income/histpov

U.S. House of Representatives, Committee on Ways and Means. 1998. *Overview of Entitlement Programs*. Washington, DC: U.S. Government Printing Office.

Weaver, R. Kent, Robert Y. Shapiro, and Lawrence R. Jacobs. 1995. "The Polls—Trends: Welfare." *Public Opinion Quarterly* 59(4):606-27.

Wilkes, Robert E., and Humberto Valencia. 1989. "Hispanics and Blacks in Television Commercials." *Journal of Advertising* 18(1):19-25.

Acknowledgments: We would like to thank the Purdue University MARC/AIM Summer Research Program for providing summer support for Rakuya Trice, the Purdue Research Foundation for providing a Summer Faculty Grant for Rosalee Clawson, and the Purdue University Library Scholars Grant Program. We greatly appreciate the efforts of Jill Clawson and Chris Salisbury, who were instrumental in obtaining information from the Census Bureau Web site. We would also like to thank the editor and anonymous reviewers for their helpful comments.

Endnotes

[1] See Entman (1995) for a discussion of how poverty is implicitly linked to other issues such as crime, drugs, and gangs through visual images on television news.

[2] Taken as a whole, these five magazines have a circulation of over 12 million: *Business Week* reaches 1,000,000 people; the *New York Times Magazine* has a circulation of 1,650,179; *Newsweek* has an audience of 3,100,000; *U.S. News & World Report* has a distribution of 2,351,313; and *Time* has the largest readership with 4,083,105 subscribers.

[3] There were several stories on poverty we did not include in our sample because: (1) the story did not include any pictures; (2) the story was an editorial or opinion column that only included a picture of the author; (3) the story was found to be irrelevant to our research topic (e.g., one story was cross-listed as income inequality and poor, but actually focused on Democratic and Republican party efforts to win working-class votes); (4) the pictures in the story did not pertain to contemporary poverty in the United States; (5) the story itself was missing from its bound volume ($n = 6$); or (6) the story was in a magazine that was at the binders ($n = 1$).

[4] A "Do Not Know" category was included for these variables.

[5] To ensure the integrity of our data, we conducted a test of intercoder reliability. A second person, who was unaware of the hypotheses, coded a subset of our sample of photographs. Across the variables of interest, there was an average intercoder reliability of .90.

[6] Although we are analyzing media portrayals of poverty between 1993 and 1998, for ease of presentation we use CPS data from March 1996 or Ways and Means Committee data from 1996 to establish the true characteristics of the poor. The 1996 data represent a reasonable midpoint. Moreover, the relevant numbers do not vary much across the time period of interest; in

no instance would the minor fluctuations change the substantive or statistical interpretation of our results.

[7] Unfortunately, we faced a trade-off between providing a more detailed analysis of the racial portrayal of the poor and making exact comparisons with Gilens's research.

[8] These stories on unpopular issues included 75 poor individuals.

[9] These stories on sympathetic topics included 100 poor individuals.

[10] There was no race by gender interaction.

[11] There was no race by age interaction.

[12] Please note these statistics are based on a reduced sample size ($N = 205$), because many (43 percent) of the poor individuals were coded as "Don't Know" for their residency. In many cases it was difficult to ascertain whether the setting was a rural or urban one, so we decided to err on the conservative side and code only the unambiguous settings.

[13] There was no race by residence interaction.

[14] The data on the working poor from the Current Population Survey include people who are 16 and over, whereas the data on the magazine working poor include people who are 13 and over.

[15] These data are from the Survey of Income and Program Participation conducted between June and September of 1993 (U.S. Bureau of the Census 1995).

Exercise for Article 9

Factual Questions

1. According to the researchers, the visual representation of a political issue is an "integral" part of what?

2. A person was coded as being "young" if he or she appeared to be what age?

3. According to the CPS, African Americans make up what percentage of the poor?

4. For Hispanics, was the difference between the percentage of "True Poor" Hispanics and "Magazine Poor" Hispanics statistically significant?

5. According to the researchers, who constitutes the most sympathetic group of poor people?

6. When mothers were portrayed with their children in the magazines (without regard to race), was there a substantial difference between the average family size in the magazines and the figure cited by Congress? Explain.

7. Were any alcoholics represented in the magazines?

Questions for Discussion

8. The five magazines are listed in lines 104–105. Would you be interested in knowing the basis for their selection (i.e., how and why they were selected)?

9. Each person in a photograph was coded as either being white, black, Hispanic, Asian American or undeterminable. In addition, they were also coded for other characteristics such as their age. In your opinion, might it be difficult to make some of these judgments? Explain. (See Endnote 5 at the end of the article.)

10. Does it surprise you that the researchers found it difficult to ascertain whether the setting in a photograph was rural or urban? Explain. (See Endnote 12.)

11. In Endnote 3, the researchers note that some stories on poverty were omitted for a variety of reasons. In your opinion, could these omissions have affected the validity of the study? Explain.

12. The researchers mentioned that they were surprised by some of the findings. Were you surprised by any of them? (See lines 313–332.) Explain.

Quality Ratings

Directions: Indicate your level of agreement with each of the following statements by circling a number from 5 for strongly agree (SA) to 1 for strongly disagree (SD). If you believe an item is not applicable to this research article, leave it blank. Be prepared to explain your ratings.

A. The introduction establishes the importance of the study.

SA   5   4   3   2   1   SD

B. The literature review establishes the context for the study.

SA   5   4   3   2   1   SD

C. The research purpose, question, or hypothesis is clearly stated.

SA   5   4   3   2   1   SD

D. The method of sampling is sound.

SA   5   4   3   2   1   SD

E. Relevant demographics (for example, age, gender, and ethnicity) are described.

SA   5   4   3   2   1   SD

F. Measurement procedures are adequate.

   SA   5   4   3   2   1   SD

G. All procedures have been described in sufficient detail to permit a replication of the study.

   SA   5   4   3   2   1   SD

H. The participants have been adequately protected from potential harm.

   SA   5   4   3   2   1   SD

I. The results are clearly described.

   SA   5   4   3   2   1   SD

J. The discussion/conclusion is appropriate.

   SA   5   4   3   2   1   SD

K. Despite any flaws, the report is worthy of publication.

   SA   5   4   3   2   1   SD

Article 10

The Role of Peer Conformity in the Decision to Ride with an Intoxicated Driver

Jack L. Powell
University of Hartford

Aaron D. Drucker
University of Hartford

ABSTRACT. Forty university students participated in a study in which they were faced with the decision of whether to enter an automobile with an apparently intoxicated driver or not. Participants were randomly assigned to one of four conditions: Driver with one beer, intoxicated driver, intoxicated driver and confederate who enters the car, and intoxicated driver and confederate who refuses to enter the car. Students' decisions whether to enter the car and their concern about the driver's drinking were assessed. Results revealed that participants consistently chose to enter the car in all conditions except when the confederate refused. Condition had no effect on participants' reported concern.

From *Journal of Alcohol and Drug Education, 43,* 1–7. Copyright © 1997 by the American Alcohol and Drug Information Foundation. Reprinted with permission.

The dangers involved with driving while under the influence of alcohol are well documented. It is estimated that alcohol plays a role in 40% to 50% of all vehicle fatalities (McGinnis & Foege, 1993). Young
5 drivers (16 to 24 years of age) are especially vulnerable to these dangers. Over half of all traffic fatalities occur among drivers between the ages of 15 and 24 years of age, and over half of the fatalities in this age group involve alcohol. This makes drinking and driving the
10 leading cause of death among adolescents (Furby & Beyth-Marom, 1990; Kenkel, 1993).

Most of the research on drinking and driving has focused on policies intended to reduce drinking and driving (Kenkel, 1993). Much less research has been
15 conducted on the factors that can influence an individual's decision to drive while intoxicated. Several researchers have investigated the personality and psychosocial characteristics of the driver and have found some variables that significantly distinguish
20 between individuals arrested for driving intoxicated from others (Donovan, Marlatt, & Salzberg, 1983; Jonah, 1990; Miller & Windle, 1990).

But few researchers have investigated an equally important and related question: What are the immediate
25 situational factors influencing the decision of individuals to drive while intoxicated or to ride with an intoxicated driver? Laboratory research has found that individuals are very conforming to the opinions of peers (Asch, 1955) and obedient to the requests of
30 authority figures (Milgram, 1970). This research has also revealed that individuals are much more resistant to pressures to comply when even just one other person around them is also noncompliant. Thus, the present study investigated the role of conformity in college
35 students' decisions to ride with an intoxicated driver. It is hypothesized that the presence of either a conforming or a nonconforming confederate would produce important differences in individuals' decisions to enter a car with an intoxicated driver.

Method

Participants and Cover Story

40 Forty (16 male and 24 female) undergraduate students signed up for an experiment described as investigating cognitive maps and spatial relationships. The written description stated that participants would be blindfolded and driven around in a car for approxi-
45 mately five minutes, but would not be taken out of the university campus. Participants were instructed to meet the experimenter at a specific location on campus, and each participant signed up for a specific evening time slot. There was no mention of alcohol.

Procedure

50 When participants arrived at the experimental location, they were greeted by the experimenter and given a consent form for their participation. In the confederate conditions, the confederate, too, was given the slip in the presence of the participant. When the driver ar-
55 rived, the experimenter went over to the car, opened the door for the participant (and confederate), and instructed them to enter the car. The experimenter then left momentarily with the excuse that he needed something from his bag which was about twenty feet
60 away. About thirty seconds later, the experimenter returned to the car and stopped the experiment. Participants were then debriefed. They were asked how they felt, whether they were nervous or scared, and whether they thought the driver was intoxicated.

Design

65 Participants were randomly assigned to one of four conditions. In the unintoxicated driver condition, the driver appeared sober when he arrived in his car, but

Table 1
Number of Participants who Entered or Refused to Enter Car and who Expressed and did not Express Concern in Each Condition

Driver Condition	Confederate Condition	Entered Car	Refused to Enter	Not Concerned	Expressed Concern
One Beer	None	9	1	5	5
Intoxicated	None	10	0	4	6
Intoxicated	Complies	10	0	4	6
Intoxicated	Refuses	1	9	2	8

had a fake beer in his hand (i.e., water in a real beer bottle). There was no confederate present.

70   In the three intoxicated driver conditions, the driver drove up appearing intoxicated: He jammed on the brakes, so the car stopped suddenly; the music was loud; and the driver had slightly slurred speech. Inside the car there were four empty beer bottles in the front
75   seat and one fake beer in his hand. In the intoxicated-driver/no-confederate condition, no confederate was present. In the intoxicated-driver/complying-confederate condition, the confederate entered the car without saying a word. In the intoxicated-driver/non-com-
80   plying-confederate condition, the confederate just said to the participant that he felt the driver had a little too much to drink, and that he was not going to enter the car.

Results

A two-way chi-square test was performed on the
85   relationship between the four conditions and whether or not the participant entered the car. The results of this test were significant, χ^2 ($df = 3, n = 40$) = 30.40, $p <$ .001. Participants were less likely to enter the car when the driver was intoxicated and the confederate did not
90   comply (one of ten entered the car) than when the driver was not intoxicated (nine of ten entered), or when the driver was intoxicated with no confederate (ten of ten entered), or when the driver was intoxicated and the confederate complied (ten of ten entered). See
95   Table 1.

A second chi-square test revealed no significant relationship between condition and concern, χ^2 ($df = 3,$ $n = 40$) = 2.03, $p >$ .10. Participants were categorized as concerned if they made any mention of being ner-
100   vous or scared during the debriefing. Twenty-five of the forty participants (62.5%) expressed some concern. Chi-square tests were also calculated to determine whether there were significant differences between males and females in their decision to enter the car, or
105   in their expressed concerns about the driver. Both tests revealed no significant differences (p's > .10).

Finally, a chi-square test revealed a significant relationship between an individual's concern and his or her decision whether to enter the car, χ^2 ($df = 1, n = 40$)
110   = 4.30, $p <$ .05. Of the 30 participants who entered the car, 16 (53%) expressed concern; of the ten participants who refused to enter the car, nine (90%) expressed concern.

Discussion

Almost all participants (96%) entered the car when
115   the driver was not intoxicated (one beer), when the driver was intoxicated and there was no confederate, and when the driver was intoxicated and the confederate entered the car. Only when the driver was intoxicated and the confederate refused to enter the car
120   did the majority of participants then refuse (90% refused).

This is not to say, however, that the behavior of the confederate increased the concerns of the participants. The results suggest that individuals were just as con-
125   cerned in the other conditions. Instead, the presence of the noncomplying confederate made the participant much more comfortable to refuse to enter the car. Even though many participants knew they should not enter in the other conditions, it took the presence of an ally for
130   them to conform.

It is also important to note that not one of the participants attempted to stop the confederate from entering the car, or to stop the driver from driving, or to encourage the experimenter to intervene. Previous
135   studies have found anywhere from 39% of college students (Mills & McCarty, 1983; Rabow, Hernandez, & Watts, 1986) to 68% of college students (Hernandez, Newcomb, & Rabow, 1995) reporting intervening in an intoxicated driving intervention. Perhaps participants in
140   the present study did not interpret the situation as dangerous, or perhaps they were hesitant to intervene because they did not know the persons involved. The first of these explanations could be tested in future studies by adding a noninvolved spectator and having this per-
145   son judge how drunk the driver was and how dangerous the situation appeared to be.

Before proceeding further in drawing conclusions from this study, it is important to note the potential limitations of the study, or at least some of the features
150   of the design which may be responsible for some of the results and which can be investigated in future studies. The most obvious limitation is the lack of power and generalizability due to the small sample size. It is possible that with more participants, significant relation-
155   ships may have been found between, for example, condition and concern. Also, a larger sample size would have allowed more investigations of individual differences between those participants who agree and those who don't agree to ride with the driver. For ex-

160 ample, future studies could test more participants and ask them more questions, including the participants' age, self-esteem, and drinking behaviors and attitudes.

An additional feature of this design which may have influenced the results is how the participants'
165 concern was determined. It is likely that in any design, the very act of asking participants if they are concerned can make them concerned. The present study attempted to minimize this possibility by having the experimenter ask participants informally and in person immediately
170 after the experiment. Unfortunately, a potential drawback to this method is the increased chance of the experimenter inadvertently influencing the participants' responses. Future studies may attempt to ascertain participants' concern through a standardized question-
175 naire, perhaps measuring their degree of concern on a scale rather than just concerned or not concerned.

Further studies should be conducted in this area to discover other factors involved in the decision to ride with an intoxicated driver. For example, the driver,
180 experimenter, and confederate all were male in the present study. Whether decisions are affected by the gender of the person in any of these roles would be an interesting area for additional research. Also, the level of intoxication or the perceived degree of
185 dangerousness could be made more extreme. This is a difficult manipulation, however, without compromising the realism of the study. Finally, it would be interesting to explore the possibility that many participants may have felt some concern because the driver had been
190 drinking, but rode along anyway because they had been assured that the driver and car would stay on campus. Would the level of compliance have changed dramatically if participants had been told they would be riding with this driver on an interstate highway at high
195 speeds?

Some of these variables have, in fact, been investigated, especially their abilities to predict intervention in drunk driving situations (Newcomb, Rabow, Monto, & Hernandez, 1991; Rabow, Newcomb, Monto, &
200 Hernandez, 1990). These investigations have typically not been experimental studies, however, but have been paper-and-pencil surveys which have less external validity than the present study. It is hoped that this study will prompt future investigators to employ more inno-
205 vative and real-world experiments in this area. Any studies that help us better understand the factors that lead people to participate in these dangerous behaviors may also help us design better prevention strategies to see that they don't.

References

Asch, S. (1955). Opinions and Social Pressure. *Scientific American, 93,* 31-35.

Donovan, D. M., Marlatt, G. A., & Salzberg, P. M. (1983). Drinking behavior, personality factors and high-risk driving: A review and theoretical formulation. *Journal of Studies on Alcohol, 44,* 395-428.

Furby, L., & Beyth-Marom, R. (1990). *Risk taking in adolescence: A decision-making perspective.* Washington, DC: Carnegie Council on Adolescent Development.

Hernandez, A. C. R., Newcomb, M. D., & Rabow, J. (1995). Types of drunk-driving intervention: Prevalence, success, and gender. *Journal of Studies on Alcohol, 56,* 408-413.

Jonah, B. A. (1990). Psychosocial characteristics of impaired drivers: An integrated review in relation to problem behavior theory. In R. J. Wilson and R. E. Mann (Eds.), *Drinking and driving: Advances in research and prevention* (pp. 13–41). New York: Guilford.

Kenkel, D. S. (1993). Drinking, driving, and deterrence; The effectiveness and social costs of alternative policies. *Journal of Law and Economics, 36,* 877-905.

McGinnes, J. M., & Foege, W. H. (1993). Actual causes of death in the United States. *Journal of the American Medical Association, 270,* 2207-2211.

Milgram, S. (1970). *Obedience to authority.* New York: Harper & Row.

Miller, B. A., & Windle, M. (1990). Alcoholism, problem drinking, and driving while impaired. In R. J. Wilson and R. E. Mann (Eds.), *Drinking and driving: Advances in research and prevention* (pp. 68-95). New York: Guilford.

Mills, K.C., & McCarty, D. (1983). A data-based alcohol abuse prevention program in a university setting. *Journal of Alcohol and Drug Education, 28(2),* 15-27.

Newcomb, M. D., Rabow, J., Monto, M., & Hernandez, A.C.R. (1991). Informal drunk driving intervention: Psychosocial correlates among young adult women and men. *Journal of Applied Social Psychology, 21,* 1988-2006.

Rabow, J., Hernandez, A. C. R., & Watts, R.K. (1986). College students to intervene in drunk driving situations. *Sociology and Social Research, 70,* 224-225.

Rabow, J., Newcomb, M. D., Monto, M. A., & Hernandez, A. C. R. (1990). Altruism in drunk driving situations: Personal and situational factors in intervention. *Social Psychology Quarterly, 53,* 199-213.

Address correspondence to: Jack L. Powell, Department of Psychology, University of Hartford, West Hartford, CT 06117.

Note: Aaron D. Drucker is now a doctoral student at the California School of Professional Psychology.

Acknowledgment: Special thanks to Brian Georgi and Adam Raider for their help in the project.

Exercise for Article 10

Factual Questions

1. Did the participants know they were signing up for a study on drinking and driving? Explain.

2. Was the confederate given a consent form?

3. What was the basis for assigning the participants to the four conditions?

4. Did the driver have a fake beer in his hand in all four conditions?

5. How many of the ten participants refused to enter the car in the condition where the confederate refused to enter the car?

6. The relationship between whether the participants entered the car and the four experimental conditions was statistically significant at what probability level?

7. According to the researchers, what would be the problem with making the driver's degree of intoxication more extreme in future studies?

Questions for Discussion

8. The researchers used undergraduates as participants in this study. Does this limit the generalizability of the results? Explain.

9. What is your opinion on the ethics of using confederates in social science research?

10. Do you agree that telling participants that the driver and car would stay on campus (as opposed to going on an interstate highway) might have influenced the results of this study? Explain. (See lines 187–195.)

11. The researchers imply that this study is innovative and real-world. Do you agree? Explain. (See lines 203–205.)

12. If you were to conduct another study on the same topic, what changes in the research methodology would you make, if any?

Quality Ratings

Directions: Indicate your level of agreement with each of the following statements by circling a number from 5 for strongly agree (SA) to 1 for strongly disagree (SD). If you believe an item is not applicable to this research article, leave it blank. Be prepared to explain your ratings.

A. The introduction establishes the importance of the study.

   SA   5   4   3   2   1   SD

B. The literature review establishes the context for the study.

   SA   5   4   3   2   1   SD

C. The research purpose, question, or hypothesis is clearly stated.

   SA   5   4   3   2   1   SD

D. The method of sampling is sound.

   SA   5   4   3   2   1   SD

E. Relevant demographics (for example, age, gender, and ethnicity) are described.

   SA   5   4   3   2   1   SD

F. Measurement procedures are adequate.

   SA   5   4   3   2   1   SD

G. All procedures have been described in sufficient detail to permit a replication of the study.

   SA   5   4   3   2   1   SD

H. The participants have been adequately protected from potential harm.

   SA   5   4   3   2   1   SD

I. The results are clearly described.

   SA   5   4   3   2   1   SD

J. The discussion/conclusion is appropriate.

   SA   5   4   3   2   1   SD

K. Despite any flaws, the report is worthy of publication.

   SA   5   4   3   2   1   SD

Article 11

A Novel Social Situation
and Loneliness

Glen E. Getz
John Carroll University

ABSTRACT. Although social isolation has been shown to have a negative long-term influence on feelings of loneliness, there has been no systematic investigation of situational influences on loneliness. The purpose of this study was to compare scores on the UCLA Loneliness Scale, the loneliness which people feel prior to performing a novel task, with those on the same scale after engaging in the task. Thirty-one college freshmen were divided into those working alone (*n* = 14) and those working in a group (*n* = 17). Those who performed the novel task within a group felt significantly less lonely after than prior to performing the task and reported less loneliness than the students who performed the same task in isolation. An important implication of this study is that group interaction may *directly* and *immediately* reduce the amount of loneliness individuals feel.

From *Psychological Reports*, *86*, 947–950. Copyright © 2000 by Psychological Reports. Reprinted with permission.

Loneliness has been defined as the feeling of being alone and alienated or disconnected from positive persons, places, or things (Woodward & Kalyan-Masih, 1990). Studies indicate that adolescents, especially
5 college students, may experience severe loneliness (Cheek & Busch, 1981; Roscoe & Skomski, 1989; Damsteegt, 1992), but that most people experience at least moderate loneliness at some point in late adolescence. In a study of 1,696 students, Roscoe and Skom-
10 ski (1989) reported that lonely and nonlonely adolescents differed mainly in their involvement in organized groups. Nonlonely adolescents were more aware of services at their school, belonged to social groups, belonged to professional groups, and when lonely they
15 sought out others with whom to talk. They also showed that lonely and nonlonely adolescents differed in their strategies for dealing with loneliness. Lonely adolescents reported that their strategies for dealing with loneliness were to withdraw into solitary activities,
20 e.g., reading, listening to music, sleeping, while nonlonely adolescents made deliberate efforts to find and interact with others. Damsteegt's (1992) study indicated that loneliness is particularly prevalent among college students. By having students fill out question-
25 naires, he showed that there is a strong correlation between loneliness and the presence of social provisions

in students' lives. Particularly, social integration had the strongest negative correlation with loneliness, while alienation and isolation are the cognitive set of social
30 provisions that have the strongest positive correlation with feelings of loneliness. Thus, social isolation seems to be most strongly related to feelings of loneliness reported in college samples.

Other findings have also indicated that social situa-
35 tions contribute to the amount of loneliness that one feels over time. Cheek and Busch (1981) showed that freshmen in college report a decline in loneliness from the first week to the last week of classes. In addition, Xie (1997) reported that both Chinese and American
40 freshmen students scored higher on loneliness than did sophomores. These studies support the idea that the process of habituation to a novel social situation decreases the amount of loneliness a person feels. To date, however, no research has been undertaken to ex-
45 amine the direct and immediate effect of group participation on feelings of loneliness.

This study placed individuals into small groups in an attempt to reduce loneliness already being felt. Because it is unethical to manipulate loneliness systemati-
50 cally (Russell, Peplau, & Cutrona, 1980), this experiment investigated whether a manipulated situation could decrease reported loneliness in an everyday situation for college freshmen. The purpose of the present study was to compare the loneliness individuals
55 report prior to and after performing a task within a group or in isolation. It was hypothesized that those who performed a task within a group would report less loneliness than prior to performing the task. Also, it was hypothesized that this group would report less
60 loneliness after the task than those who performed the same task in isolation.

Method

Participants

Thirty-one college freshmen (13 women and 18 men), with the average age of 18.7, from a private midwestern university were divided into two groups:
65 those working on a task alone (*n* = 14) and those working on a task within a group of three or four people (*n* = 17). To prevent participants from signing up with a friend, university instructors passed out sign-up

sheets in introductory psychology courses that contained one time slot per experimental time frame. The participants were given experimental credit that contributed to a course requirement.

Measure

The Revised UCLA Loneliness Scale detects variations in loneliness which occur in everyday life (Russell, et al., 1980) and is widely used to quantify loneliness. This scale was divided in half to measure loneliness pretask and posttask. Items 2, 3, 4, 6, 9, 10, 11, 13, 18, and 19 from the revised scale were on the pretask questionnaire, while Items 1, 5, 7, 8, 12, 14, 15, 16, 17, and 20 were on the posttask questionnaire. While this procedure is unusual and, to the knowledge of this researcher, has not been done before with this scale, an equal number of positively and negatively worded items constituted both formats. For example Items 3 ("There is no one I can turn to") and 19 ("There are people I can talk to") were on the pretask questionnaire, while 7 ("I am no longer close to anyone") and 20 ("There are people I can turn to") were on the posttask scale. Also, a pilot study with 10 similar respondents indicated a significant correlation of .93 between the split-scale scores. This scale was one of several questionnaires administered to the participants before and after the task. The other questionnaires only served the purpose of reducing demand characteristics.

Procedure

Upon arrival, participants sat in individual rooms and completed a series of questionnaires, including the pretask UCLA Loneliness Scale. Then, the participants in the Alone Condition worked on completing a 100-piece puzzle of the United States for 15 min. in the room in isolation. Participants in the Group Condition sat with other participants in a larger room and completed an icebreaker task, which included introducing themselves, naming their hometowns, and discussing why they chose to attend the university. Following the icebreaker, they worked on assembling the puzzle together for 15 min. or until the puzzle was completed. After completing the task, participants in both conditions completed a second set of questionnaires, including the posttask UCLA Loneliness Scale, in the original room by themselves.

Results

A Spearman Brown split-half equal-lengths test was conducted to assess further the reliability of scale scores and yielded a correlation of .92 which indicated high reliability.

A 2 (Condition: Alone vs. Group) x 2 (Trial: Pretask vs. Posttask) mixed analysis of variance with repeated measures on the second variable was conducted to analyze the effects of the two conditions for the pretask and the posttask scores on the UCLA Loneliness Scale. An alpha level of .05 was used for all statistical tests. The main effect of condition was statistically significant ($F_{1,30} = 14.34$) and was qualified by a significant interaction between condition and trial ($F_{2,67} = 20$), indicating that the pattern of performance on the test varied for the different groups.

There was no significant difference between the pretask scores in the Alone vs. Group Condition ($t = 1.91$). Yet, the posttask scores in the Group Condition were significantly lower than the posttask scores in the Alone Condition ($t = 9.98$). In addition, the Group Condition's posttask scores were significantly less than the pretask scores ($t = 8.79$); however, there was no significant difference in the Alone Condition for the pretask vs. posttask scores ($t = 1.65$; see Table 1).

Table 1
Scores for Alone and Group Conditions Across Trials on the UCLA Loneliness Scale

		Condition[a]	
		Alone	Group[c]
Pretask	M	15.3	15.9
	SD	2.7	2.0
Posttask[b]	M	16.0	13.3
	SD	3.3	1.4

Note. Scores could range from 10–40 for all conditions; higher scores indicate more loneliness reported. [a]The main effect of Condition was statistically significant ($p = .05$). [b]The posttask scores in the Group Condition were statistically lower than the posttask scores in the Alone Condition ($p = .05$). [c]The Group Condition's posttask mean score was significantly lower than the mean pretask score ($p = .05$).

Discussion

Results indicate that those who performed a task within a group reported themselves to feel less lonely than they felt prior to performing the task and reported to feel less lonely after the task than those who performed the same task alone. This suggests that working in a group for as little as 15 min. decreased the amount of loneliness felt. These results relate to previous research, which suggests that group activities decrease loneliness. Rokach (1996) studied how to cope with and reduce the pain of loneliness. She showed that social interaction and increased activity are the best coping strategies to deal with loneliness. Olds, Schwartz, and Webster (1996) theorized that when people help one another accomplish a given task, they create a fertile context in which relationships can develop. The current study, however, is the first controlled experiment placing individuals into a manipulated situation to reduce the feelings of loneliness of everyday life. Thus, the implication of this study, in light of the previous research, suggests that group involvement is an important factor in reducing the feeling of everyday loneliness immediately for college students. Researchers might attempt to assess what other type of social interactions reduce the amount of loneliness in different populations and how long the affect lasts. In addition, how the size of the group affects the people's feeling of loneliness could be examined.

References

CHEEK, J. M., & BUSCH, C. M. (1981) The influence of shyness on loneliness in a new situation. *Personality and Social Psychology Bulletin, 7,* 572–577.

DAMSTEEGT, D. (1992) Loneliness, social provisions and attitude. *College Student Journal, 26,* 135–139.

OLDS, J., SCHWARTZ, R. S., & WEBSTER, H. (1996) *Overcoming loneliness in everyday life.* Secaucus, NJ: Carol Group.

ROKACH, A. (1996) The subjectivity of loneliness and coping with it. *Psychological Reports, 79,* 475–481.

ROSCOE, B., & SKOMSKI, G. G. (1989) Loneliness among late adolescents. *Adolescence, 24,* 947–955.

RUSSELL, D., PEPLAU, L. A., & CUTRONA, C. E. (1980) The revised UCLA Loneliness Scale: Concurrent and discriminant validity evidence. *Journal of Personality and Social Psychology, 39,* 472–480.

WOODWARD, J. C., & KALYAN-MASIH, V. (1990) Loneliness, coping strategies and cognitive style of the gifted rural adolescent. *Adolescence, 25,* 977–988.

XIE, X. (1997) Scores on loneliness of Chinese and American college students. *Psychological Reports, 81,* 317–318.

Address correspondence to: Glen E. Getz, Department of Psychiatry, University of Cincinnati Medical Center, 231 Bethesda Ave., P.O. Box 670559, Cincinnati, OH 45267-0559.
E-mail: getzg@email.uc.edu

Exercise for Article 11

Factual Questions

1. According to the researcher, to date no research has been undertaken to examine what?

2. How many items from the Revised UCLA Loneliness Scale were on the pretask questionnaire?

3. The researcher states that the loneliness scale was only one of several questionnaires. He states that the other questionnaires served what purpose?

4. Were the posttask means for the two groups significantly different?

5. What was the value of the pretask mean for those in the Alone Condition? What was the corresponding mean for those in the Group Condition?

6. For those in the Group Condition, by how many points did the mean loneliness score decrease from pretask to posttask?

7. Is this study experimental or nonexperimental?

Questions for Discussion

8. The researcher reports that "social integration had the strongest negative correlation with loneliness." What is a negative correlation? How does it differ from a positive correlation? (See lines 27–28.)

9. The researcher states that the students were divided into two groups. Would it be of interest to know whether they were divided at random? Explain. (See lines 62–64.)

10. The researcher reports reliability coefficients of .93 and .92. In your opinion, are these sufficiently high? Explain. (See lines 89–91 and 111–114.)

11. Table 1 includes standard deviations. Are they an important part of this research report? Explain.

12. Do you believe that this topic is worthy of additional research? Why? Why not?

Quality Ratings

Directions: Indicate your level of agreement with each of the following statements by circling a number from 5 for strongly agree (SA) to 1 for strongly disagree (SD). If you believe an item is not applicable to this research article, leave it blank. Be prepared to explain your ratings.

A. The introduction establishes the importance of the study.

   SA   5   4   3   2   1   SD

B. The literature review establishes the context for the study.

   SA   5   4   3   2   1   SD

C. The research purpose, question, or hypothesis is clearly stated.

   SA   5   4   3   2   1   SD

D. The method of sampling is sound.

   SA   5   4   3   2   1   SD

E. Relevant demographics (for example, age, gender, and ethnicity) are described.

   SA   5   4   3   2   1   SD

F. Measurement procedures are adequate.

   SA   5   4   3   2   1   SD

G. All procedures have been described in sufficient detail to permit a replication of the study.

   SA   5   4   3   2   1   SD

H. The participants have been adequately protected from potential harm.

   SA   5   4   3   2   1   SD

I. The results are clearly described.

   SA   5   4   3   2   1   SD

J. The discussion/conclusion is appropriate.

   SA   5   4   3   2   1   SD

K. Despite any flaws, the report is worthy of publication.

   SA   5   4   3   2   1   SD

Article 12

Evocation of Freedom and Compliance:
The "But You Are Free of..." Technique

Nicolas Guéguen
South-Brittany University

Alexandre Pascual
University of Bordeaux

ABSTRACT. Many investigations have shown that the semantic characteristics of a request could lead to more compliance. A feeling of freedom is also a factor favoring compliance to numerous types of requests. An experiment was carried out, in which the evocation of freedom was formulated verbally, following a demand for money made by confederates. Results show that the verbal incentive used (demand for money + "but you are free to accept or to refuse") increased the rate of subjects' compliance as well as the average amount of granted gifts. The semantic activation of the feeling of freedom is discussed within the framework of numerous paradigms of research on compliance.

From *Current Research in Social Psychology*. Sponsored by the Center for the Study of Group Processes at the University of Iowa at http://www.uiowa.edu/~grpproc/crisp/crisp.html Copyright © 2000 by the authors. Reprinted with permission.

Introduction

Research on helping behavior has traditionally emphasized the characteristics of the donor, the beneficiary, and the context. Some research, however, concerns the linguistic aspect of the requests for help. Thus,
5 Cialdini and Schroeder (1976) showed that the addition of the sentence "even a penny will help" leads the solicited people to give more to a humanitarian organization. This sentence also increased the rate of donors. Numerous replications of this technique (Reeves, Ma-
10 colini and Martin 1987; Reeves and Saucer 1993) give evidence of its efficiency on compliance behavior. By manipulating the semantic contents of the request, Enzle and Harvey (1982) showed that an indirect negation request (e.g., You will help me, won't you?) elicited
15 greater helping than either a direct negation (e.g., Won't you help me?) or a control form (e.g., Will you help me?).

In the same way, Howard (1990) had demonstrated that asking someone how he feels improves compliance
20 with a helping request made immediately after the subject's response. Another procedure that improves compliance to a request is the "that's-not-all technique" (Burger 1986). When applying this technique, the requester presents a recipient with a first request at a
25 certain price but does not allow the subject the instant opportunity to decline or to accept the offer. As the

subject considers the price, the requester then improves the deal by including an extra product or by lowering the price of the offer. In Burger's first experiment,
30 people approaching a bake sale table were told that the price of a cupcake was $0.75. At this moment, the seller was interrupted by a second seller who needs help. The first seller then asked the subject to "wait a second." Then after a brief exchange between the two
35 salesmen (5–10 seconds), the first seller returned to the client and announced to him that the offer also included two cookies. Results showed that 73.0% of the subjects in this "that's-not-all condition" bought the cupcake with the two cookies package whereas 40.0% bought
40 this package when the complete offer was made at the same price.

Another factor facilitating compliance to requests, but which does not proceed from the semantic characteristics of the request, is the feeling of freedom of the
45 subject. This feeling of freedom would be one of the main factors predisposing to the compliance (Kiesler 1971). Now, we cannot keep count of research on the compliance without pressure, which gives evidence of the efficiency of techniques facilitating the activation
50 of this feeling of freedom: foot-in-the-door (Freedman and Fraser 1966), door-in-the-face (Cialdini, Vincent, Lewis, Catalan, Wheeler and Lee Darby 1975), lowball (Cialdini, Cacioppo, Bassett and Miller 1978) or also the technique of the lure (Joule, Gouilloux and
55 Weber 1989). Surprisingly, experimental research concerning this feeling of freedom has compared some situations where the subject's freedom was reduced, comparatively, to a situation of free choice (Beaman, Svanum, Manlove and Hampton 1974; Chartrand,
60 Pinckert and Burger 1999). According to the reactance theory of Brehm (1966), this feeling of loss of freedom comes along with a drastic fall of compliance. Few studies were made on conditions favoring a feeling of increased freedom in the decision of the subject, nota-
65 bly by means of the semantic characteristics of the requests. With the benefit of hindsight, we realize that the effect of sentences such as "it is up to you to see," "up to you to choose," "but you are free of..." which are generally expressed to punctuate the end of a re-
70 quest in the case of the techniques of compliance without pressure, were never the object of a direct investi-

gation. This is the objective fixed by the experiment presented below.

Hypothesis

Accounting for the persuasive effects contained in the semantic properties of requests, shown by the various research quoted above, we could expect that the direct semantic evocation of the freedom of subject's decision facilitates the request's compliance.

Method

Subjects

Forty men and 40 women (age range 30-50 years old), alone, were chosen at random in the street. Forty people were assigned at random to the experimental group (20 men and 20 women), and 40 were assigned to the control group (20 men and 20 women).

Procedure

Four people, 2 men and 2 women (average age 20-22 years old), played the role of confederates in this experiment. They were dressed neatly and in a traditional way for young people of this age (jeans/sneakers/T-shirt). The experiment took place in a mall during particularly sunny spring days. A confederate approached a subject taken at random after counting the passage of a definite number of pedestrians in a defined zone. If the subject was a child or a teenager or an old man or a group, the confederate took the person coming just after so that she corresponded to the expected profile. In the control condition, the confederate approached the subject by saying to him or her politely: "Sorry Madam/Sir, would you have some coins to take the bus, please?" In experimental condition, the confederate formulated with the same tone the following request: "Sorry Madam/Sir, would you have some coins to take the bus, please? But you are free to accept or to refuse." The confederate then estimated if the subject agreed or not to his request. In the case of a positive answer, the confederate waited for the subject to give him the money. He estimated the amount and then gave back the sum to the subject and proceeded to completely debrief the subject.

Results

On all measures employed in this study, no differences were found between male and female subjects. This is also true with the differences between the four confederates of this experiment. So, data was aggregated. In the control condition, 10.0% of solicited people accepted the request of the confederates, whereas 47.5% accepted in the experimental condition. The comparison of these two rates gives evidence of a significant difference [χ^2 (1, 80) = 13.73, $p < .001$]. The evocation of the freedom of subject's decision leads to favor the request compliance. When we consider the mean amount of the gifts granted by the people having accepted the request in each of the groups, we observe that it is FF 3.25 (US $ 0.48) in the control condition

versus FF 7.05 (US $ 1.04) in the experimental condition. Here also, this difference is significant [$t(21)$ = 3.03, $p < .01$, two-tailed] and this is in spite of a weak compliance rate in the control group (4 persons over 40). The evocation of freedom favored the generosity of solicited people and the average amount of the granted gifts corresponds to the price of a bus ticket at the time of the experiment (FF 6.80 or US $ 1.00).

Discussion

We observe that the semantic evocation of freedom in the content of the request increases the probability of compliance, but also favors the implication of the subject, as this one grants twice as much money to the requester. This experiment confirms that we can obtain more compliance in a request directly by manipulating its verbal contents. This goes along the same lines of numerous previous works as those concerning the technique of "even a penny will help" (Cialdini and Schroeder 1976; Reeves, Macolini and Martin 1987; Reeves and Saucer 1993), that of the "foot-in-the-mouth" (Howard 1990) or that of "that's not all" (Burger 1986; Pollock, Smith, Knowles and Bruce 1998). The results of this experiment seem to show that we can add to this set of techniques the one of "but you are free of..."

Why is there such efficiency with this technique? Naturally, it is not the additional verbal contents which explains our results, but rather what the contents of it activates among the subjects. In this stage of the evaluation, four explanations can be proposed. First, it is possible that the verbal evocation of the freedom contained in the request really activates the feeling of freedom for the subject. Now, numerous researches show that the increase of this feeling of freedom acts as a facilitator of commitment towards the expected behavior (Kiesler 1971; Cialdini 1993). Second, perhaps this evocation of freedom leads the subject to feel socially more involved towards the demand for help formulated by the confederate. Now, this norm of social responsibility, when activated, makes a powerful facilitator for spontaneous help by others and of compliance to requests (Berkowitz and Daniels 1963; Harris 1972). Furthermore, the activation of this norm improves compliance with the request but also the degree of implication of subject (Guéguen and Fisher-Lokou 1999). Third, the evocation of the freedom in the contents of the request would limit the weight of external causes to compliance, and favors the activation of internal causes. Now, in compliance without pressure, notably within the framework of the paradigm of the foot-in-the-door, when requests strengthen the weight of external factors to compliance, less further compliance is obtained (Zuckerman, Lazzaro and Waldgeir 1979). Conversely, more compliance is noticed when the attribution of internal causes is favored (Gorassini and Olson 1995). Finally, it is also possible that the evoked freedom causes a guilty feeling from the subject if he or she does not answer to the request. We have known for a long time now that guilt favors helping behavior (Konecni 1972) and certain classic paradigms of the compliance without pressure, as the door-in-the-face, see their results interpreted in this way (O'Keffe and Gigge 1997)

Naturally, these interpretations appear for the moment premature and the effect of the "but you are free of..." technique still remains to be confirmed, and more factors explaining its efficiency require further research. Nevertheless, because more compliance was obtained in the experimental group, the research reported here demonstrates the effectiveness of this technique based on the simple evocation of freedom.

References

Beaman, A., S. Svanum, S. Manlove, and C. Hampton (1974). "An attribution theory explanation of the foot-in-the-door effects." *Personality-and-Social-Psychology-Bulletin*, 1:122-123.

Berkowitz, L. and L. Daniels (1963). "Responsibility and dependency." *Journal of Abnormal Social Psychology*, 66:429-436.

Brehm, P. (1966). *A theory of psychological reactance.* New-York : Academic Press.

Burger, J. (1986). "Increasing compliance by improving the deal: the that's-not-all technique." *Journal of Personality and Social Psychology*, 51:277-283.

Chartrand, T., S. Pinckert, and J. Burger (1999). "When manipulation backfires: the effects of time delay and requester on the foot-in-the-door technique." *Journal of Applied Social Psychology*, 29:211-221.

Cialdini, R. (1993). *Influence.* New-York: HarperCollins.

Cialdini, R., J. Cacioppo, R. Bassett and J. Miller (1978). "Low-ball procedure for producing compliance: commitment then cost." *Journal of Personality and Social Psychology*, 36:463-476.

Cialdini, R. and D. Schroeder (1976). "Increasing compliance by legitimizing paltry contributions: when even a penny will help." *Journal of Personality and Social Psychology*, 34:599-604.

Cialdini, R., J. Vincent, S. Lewis, J. Catalan, D. Wheeler and B. Lee Darby (1975). "Reciprocal concessions procedure for inducing compliance : the door-in-the-face technique." *Journal of Personality and Social Psychology*, 31:206-215.

Enzle, M. and M. Harvey (1982). "Rhetorical request for help." *Social Psychology Quarterly*, 45:172-176.

Freedman, J. and S. Fraser (1966). "Compliance without pressure: the foot-in-the-door technique." *Journal of Personality and Social Psychology*, 4:195-202.

Gorassini, D. and J. Olson (1995). "Does self-perception change explain the foot-in-the door effect?" *Journal of Personality and Social Psychology*, 69:91-105.

Guéguen, N. and J. Fisher-Lokou (1999). "Sequential request strategy: effect on donor generosity." *The Journal of Social Psychology*, 139:669-671.

Harris, M. (1972). "The effects of performing one altruistic act on the likelihood of performing another." *The Journal of Social Psychology*, 88:65-73.

Howard, D. (1990). "The influence of verbal responses to common greetings on compliance behavior: the foot-in-the-mouth effect." *Journal of Applied Social Psychology*, 20:1,185-1,196.

Joule, R-V., F. Gouilloux, and F. Weber (1989). "The lure: a new compliance procedure." *The Journal of Social Psychology*, 129:741-749.

Kiesler, C. (1971). *The psychology of commitment.* New York: Academic Press.

Konecni, V. (1972). "Some effects of guilt on compliance: a field replication." *Journal of Personality and Social Psychology*, 23:30-32.

O'Keefe, D. and M. Figge (1997). "A guilt-based explanation of the door-in-the-face influence strategy." *Human Communication Research*, 24:64-81.

Pollock, C., S. Smith, E. Knowles, and H. Bruce (1998). "Mindfulness limits compliance with the that's-not-all technique." *Personality and Social Psychology Bulletin*, 24:1,153-1,157.

Reeves, R., R. Macolini, and R. Martin (1987). "Legitimizing paltry contributions: on-the-spot vs. mail-in-requests." *Journal of Applied Social Psychology*, 17:731-738.

Reeves, R. and P. Saucer (1993). "A test of commitment in legitimizing paltry contributions." *Journal of Social Behavior and Personality*, 8:537-544.

Zuckerman, M., M. Lazzaro and D. Waldgeir (1979). "Undermining effects of the foot-in-the-door technique with extrinsic rewards." *Journal of Applied Social Psychology*, 9:292-296.

About the Authors: Nicolas Guéguen is currently assistant professor in social psychology at the South-Brittany University in France. His e-mail address is nicolas.gueguen@iu-vannes.fr Alexandre Pascual is a student in doctoral dissertation at the University of Bordeaux 2 in France. His e-mail address is alpascual@iFrance.com

Exercise for Article 12

Factual Questions

1. According to the researchers, has the effect of "but you are free of..." to punctuate the end of a request ever been the object of direct investigation?

2. What was the sample size?

3. In the control condition, what did the confederates say when they approached the subjects?

4. What percentage of the subjects in the control condition accepted the request of the confederates?

5. Was the mean amount of money given by the subjects in the experimental group significantly larger than the mean amount given by those in the control group?

6. What value of p is associated with the significance test referred to in question 5?

7. What is the final (i.e., fourth) possible explanation for the results that is offered by the researchers?

Questions for Discussion

8. In the table of contents for this book, this report is classified as an example of experimental research. Do you agree with this classification? Explain.

9. The age and clothes of the confederates are described in lines 84–88. Do you think the results should be generalized to individuals at other ages and with other types of clothes? Explain.

10. Does the fact that subjects were assigned at random to experimental and control conditions affect the validity of this study?

11. What do you think the researchers mean when they say the confederates "proceeded to completely debrief the subject." (See lines 105–107.)

12. This research report is shorter than most. In your opinion, is this a weakness? If yes, what other types of information would you like to see included in this report?

Quality Ratings

Directions: Indicate your level of agreement with each of the following statements by circling a number from 5 for strongly agree (SA) to 1 for strongly disagree (SD). If you believe an item is not applicable to this research article, leave it blank. Be prepared to explain your ratings.

A. The introduction establishes the importance of the study.

SA   5   4   3   2   1   SD

B. The literature review establishes the context for the study.

SA   5   4   3   2   1   SD

C. The research purpose, question, or hypothesis is clearly stated.

SA   5   4   3   2   1   SD

D. The method of sampling is sound.

SA   5   4   3   2   1   SD

E. Relevant demographics (for example, age, gender, and ethnicity) are described.

SA   5   4   3   2   1   SD

F. Measurement procedures are adequate.

SA   5   4   3   2   1   SD

G. All procedures have been described in sufficient detail to permit a replication of the study.

SA   5   4   3   2   1   SD

H. The participants have been adequately protected from potential harm.

SA   5   4   3   2   1   SD

I. The results are clearly described.

SA   5   4   3   2   1   SD

J. The discussion/conclusion is appropriate.

SA   5   4   3   2   1   SD

K. Despite any flaws, the report is worthy of publication.

SA   5   4   3   2   1   SD

Article 13

The Effects of Sexual Orientation in the Courtroom: A Double Standard

Jennifer M. Hill
Hartwick College

ABSTRACT. Homonegativity is a term that many psychologists use to describe irrational fear of homosexuality. Due to a growing number of male rapes in the United States and the unchecked levels of homonegativity, it is hypothesized that homosexuals will be treated differently from heterosexuals in sexual assault trials. Four conditions were examined controlling for the gender and sexuality of both the defendant and the victim, and a sexual assault trial text was created controlling for factors known to affect juror's decisions. Seventy-two participants were divided among the four conditions. This research supports the hypothesis with highly significant results. Future research is suggested.

From *Journal of Homosexuality, 39, (2)* 93–111. Copyright © 2000 by The Haworth Press, Inc. All rights reserved. Reprinted with permission.

Men convicted of raping men were decapitated and then burned in front of the Town Hall in Renaissance Florence (Ruggiero, 1985). Homosexuality was unacceptable and punished with the harshest severity under
5 very strict laws. Although times have changed since Renaissance Florence, the occurrence of male rape has not. In fact, eight percent of 141,000 rapes in 1992 were reported by men (Federal Bureau of Investigation, 1995) and, in 1993, the total reported rapes jumped to
10 485,290, of which 43,690 were reported by men (Bureau of Justice Statistics, 1993). From these national statistics, it is obvious that male victims of rape are increasing in number and in need of attention.

However, when was the last time you recall hearing
15 of a male rape victim? Why are so few people willing to admit that male rape is a problem? Perhaps for the same reason the Florentines beheaded and burned convicted offenders: *homophobia.* This is a very general term that is often defined as fear of homosexuality or
20 homosexuals. Homophobia has become such a widely used term that it encompasses any negative attitude, belief, or action directed against homosexuality or the homosexual (Wells & Franken, 1987; Friedman & Downey, 1994) or, more specifically, the anxiety, irra-
25 tional fear, hatred and intolerance associated with being near a homosexual person (Adams, Wright & Lohr, 1996).

In reaction to the general overuse of the term homophobia, Wells and Franken (1987) coined the term *homonega-*
30 *tivity.* Homonegativity is defined on several different levels. It is: insecurity about one's own sexuality, a lack of education about homosexuality, fear that the value of masculine characteristics and the devaluing of feminine characteristics is shifting, strong fundamental religious beliefs, sexual con-
35 servatism and sexual rigidity, and a consciousness or overt awareness of social status (Wells & Franken, 1987).

Does homonegativity differ between genders? Research has both supported and refuted the idea of a gender difference in homonegativity (Kite & Whitley, 1996; Laner &
40 Laner, 1980; Wells & Franken, 1987; Wells, 1991). However, this experimental difference may be apparent because of the various subject pools studied in the cited research. For example, Kite & Whitley (1996) compiled several research reports into a meta-analysis and reported that men high in
45 authoritarianism holding traditional ideals towards gender roles tend to be more homonegative than females, while the subjects that Wells and Franken (1987) studied, who were enrolled in a Human Sexuality course at a university, showed no gender difference in tolerance or acceptance.
50 Laner and Laner (1980) found that the tolerance or intolerance of heterosexuals toward homosexuals was based on how far from "average" the homosexual was. Men who were described as effeminate and women who were described as masculine were disliked more than men and women who
55 were described with gender-average characteristics. The heuristic that has been demonstrated throughout several studies is that women tend to accept and tolerate homosexuality to a greater extent than men.

So what happens when a homosexual is the victim of a
60 violent crime? Is the victim stigmatized for his/her sexual orientation or is he/she able to receive equal treatment in the courtroom? What happens when a homosexual man is accused of sexual assault? Will he be able to receive a fair trial? What if the alleged victim is a heterosexual male, what
65 is the jury going to concentrate on? Will the alleged offender's sexual orientation or the evidence be the concentration of the trial?

As many researchers have proclaimed, and the United States government has acknowledged by creating the Hate
70 Crime Statistic Act of 1990, male rape is not merely an aberration of prison life or traditionally male institutions (i.e., the military or private educational facilities for boys). And fur-

ther, male rape does not victimize only young boys and adolescents (Mezey & King, 1987; Groth & Burgess, 1980; Kaufman, DiVasto, Jackson, Voorhees, & Christy, 1980; Hickson, Davies, Hunt, Weatherburn, McManus & Coxon, 1994). Male rape is a growing problem—as demonstrated by the earlier statistics—that needs attention.

This research will address the controversial issue of homosexuality in the courtroom. With the continual rise in occurrences of male rape, it will not be long before a male victim seeks justice for the crime committed against him. What effects will the sexual orientation of the defendant and that of the victim have on the jury? Will the victim's heterosexuality be the reason that an alleged homosexual defendant is found guilty, or will jury members worry so much about appearing prejudiced that the jury will find an obviously guilty defendant innocent because of his sexual orientation? How are the jurors going to react to the open discussion of sexuality in the courtroom?

The present research will focus on the effects of knowing the sexual orientation of an alleged victim and a defendant in a sexual assault (stranger rape) trial. In order to best isolate this aspect, a thorough investigation of the known aspects of trials that can affect a juror's verdict was performed. For example, alcohol is not mentioned in the case read by the participants of this study because research has shown that when alcohol consumption is involved as a factor in a rape case, stranger or acquaintance, whoever is consuming the alcohol tends to be blamed for the incident. Richardson and Campbell (1982) and Fischer (1995) found that if the victim was intoxicated, more responsibility was attributed to her and her rapist usually was found not guilty of the charges.

Johnson and Jackson (1988) found that when ambiguity of desire for intercourse was present, or the case involved acquaintance rape, the guilty verdicts were few and far between. In other words, in an acquaintance rape, where there is a prior relationship, it is difficult to convince a jury to convict because of the prior relationship, be it sexual or friendship. A stranger rape situation was created to control for any ambiguity.

Willis and Wrightsman (1995) found that the gaze behavior of the victim during testimony (whether eye contact was made with the defendant or not) affected the verdict. Additionally, Alicke and Yurak (1995) found that those accused of acquaintance rape were more likely to be convicted if they were described as dislikable and aggressive, as opposed to likable and unaggressive. For these reasons, the information presented to the participants did not contain any oral or written testimony, only closing arguments of lawyers.

Fischer (1995) summarized several other variables that have been found to affect the verdicts of simulated juries or jurors. A victim of "low" moral character was believed less than a victim of "high" moral character; so, both the victim and the perpetrator are referred to as

being "upstanding citizens." Fischer also discusses the effects of a preset attitude towards rape. If the juror has a preset schema that all women encourage sexual intercourse and rape is a figment of their imagination, the juror will tend to find the defendant innocent. In addition to the preset attitude towards rape, believing in a fair and just world can affect verdicts. People who believe the world is fair and just believe the victims of crimes deserve the punishment because the world is fair and just; therefore, rape victims must deserve what happened to them (Brems & Wagner, 1994; Follingstad, Shillinglaw, DeHart, & Kleinfelter, 1997). Finally, the gender of the juror tends to be a factor. Several studies have concluded that male jurors tend to be more lenient on male defendants, especially in an acquaintance rape trial, than female jurors (Fischer, 1995; Richardson & Campbell, 1982; Grant, Folger, & Hornak, 1995; Johnson & Jackson, 1988). Pre-existing beliefs, believing in a just world, and gender are aspects the participants brought with them to the study and, therefore, were not controlled for.

The four conditions were created for this research in order to vary the sexual orientation and gender of the victim while varying the sexual orientation of the perpetrator, as demonstrated in Table 1. The first condition will act as the control, since it represents the "typical" sexual assault trial involving a heterosexual female victim and a heterosexual male assailant. The remaining three conditions will examine the effect of homonegativity on the perceived level of guilt of the defendant.

It is hypothesized that the fourth condition (a homosexual male assailant and victim) will elicit the lowest average guilt rating because participants will fall back on homosexual stereotypes and assume that homosexual men "do nothing but fornicate all day." The third condition should be the most guilty because it is hypothesized that the participants will identify with the heterosexual male victim and react to the homosexuality of the defendant. Condition two should be less guilty than condition one because the alleged victim is a homosexual female, not a heterosexual female.

Method

Participants

Students enrolled in General Psychology classes at Hartwick College volunteered to participate in this study as partial fulfillment of course requirements. Participants signed up believing the research to be about "Decision Making." A total of 72 students participated (48 females and 23 males). Sixty-five percent reported first-year status, 28% reported second-year status, 6% reported junior and senior status and 1% did not specify.

Materials

The only material used in this study was a text version of a fictitious sexual assault trial in combination with a questionnaire. (See Appendix at the end of this article.) The trial text was self-created and piloted twice on similar populations to ensure the existence of reasonable doubt.

The trial text was designed to ensure ambiguity of the atttacker. The victim never sees the attacker; the entire case

Table 1
Illustration of Conditions in Research

Condition One:	Heterosexual Male Allegedly Assaults Heterosexual Female.
Condition Two:	Heterosexual Male Allegedly Assaults Homosexual Female.
Condition Three:	Homosexual Male Allegedly Assaults Heterosexual Male.
Condition Four:	Homosexual Male Allegedly Assaults Homosexual Male.

is mostly based on voice recognition and the unknown
185 length of absence of the defendant from the popular
nightclub where the assault was reported. There is no
presentation of biological evidence so that there is
doubt as to who the assailant is, and the trial text only
includes the closing arguments of the defense and the
190 prosecution to avoid using actual testimony. The trial
text only contains the facts of the case. Each condition
was presented with almost identical trial texts. The only
variation was the name of the alleged victim in order to
vary gender (Patricia or Patrick Green) and the sexual
195 orientation of the defendant and the alleged victim, as
outlined in Table 1.

The questions immediately following the trial text
asked the participant to rate the defendant's guilt on a
9-point Likert scale ranging from Definitely Guilty (1)
200 to Definitely Not Guilty (9). The participants were then
asked to decide the verdict.

The questionnaire then concentrated on deciphering
the reasons behind the participants' verdict. In addition
to basic demographic questions, participants were asked
205 to rank the importance of 12 factors in their decision
based on a 5-point Likert scale. Two of the 12 factors
were used in the analysis: importance of alleged victim's/defendant's sexuality. The other factors were included as fillers.

Procedure
210 Once all the participants arrived, each was presented
with a packet containing the trial text and questionnaire.
They were asked only to read the top page of instructions, as presented below.

The experiment you are about to take part in is a meas-
215 urement of decision making. For the next twenty minutes,
please imagine yourself as a member of a jury hearing the
following case. Once you turn a page, please do not refer
back to it; this is to encourage the utmost congruence with
an actual criminal trial in respect to evidence and testi-
220 mony.
Please answer all the questions presented to you with
blatant honesty. Your anonymity is guaranteed. Thank
you for your participation.

Participants then received a verbal and emphatic
225 reminder of their right to leave at any time if they felt
their rights had been violated in any way or if the subject matter made them uncomfortable. Due to the sensitivity of the subject matter, they also were informed of
their opportunity to discuss the court case, verdict, or
230 anything they felt was necessary with the experimenter
after the questionnaires had been completed.

The text and questionnaires took approximately 15 minutes to complete. Upon completion, the participants turned
over their questionnaires and were given a debriefing sheet
235 describing homonegativity and how it was being investigated through this study. Important information about the
experimenter also was on the debriefing sheet, should the
students decide at any time that they wanted to talk about the
study or desired more information about the study.

Results
240 The main hypothesis was marginally supported in this
research. As presented in Table 2, a Pearson Chi Square
analysis revealed a marginally significant difference in guilt
rating among the four conditions ($x^2 = 6.725$, $p = .081$). Specifically, more participants found the defendant in condition
245 three guilty than not guilty, whereas the reverse was true for
all the other conditions. In other words, when the victim was
homosexual, the defendant was found guilty less often than
when the victim was heterosexual.

Table 2
Percentage Per Condition Who Found the Defendant Guilty/Not Guilty

Verdict	Condition One[1]	Condition Two	Condition Three	Condition Four
Guilty	37.50	22.22	55.56	20.00
Not Guilty	62.50	77.78	44.44	80.00

[1]In condition one, a heterosexual male allegedly assaults a heterosexual female.

In condition two, a heterosexual male allegedly assaults a homosexual female.

In condition three, a homosexual male allegedly assaults a heterosexual male.

In condition four, a homosexual male allegedly assaults a homosexual male.

Further support for the hypothesis was gathered from a
250 directional one-way ANOVA of the condition by guilt rating
($F_{(3.68)} = 3.19$, $p = .0146$) as demonstrated in Table 3. Specifically, condition three, as expected, was found to elicit the
greatest average guilt rating, significantly higher than conditions four and one.

255 The third analysis was run to determine that there was
actually a difference between the guilt rating for guilty verdicts and not guilty verdicts. This directional test was highly
significant ($t_{(9)} = -6.9432$, $p = .00005$) supporting the assumption that participants who found the defendant guilty
260 rated him as more guilty than those who found him not
guilty.

The average responses to the questions measuring the
importance of specific variables in the final verdict are presented in Table 4 by condition.
265 A directional one-way ANOVA, used to analyze the participants' rating of perceived importance of the sexuality of

Table 3
Average Guilty Rating Presented by Condition

	Condition One[2]		Condition Two		Condition Three		Condition Four	
	M	SD	M	SD	M	SD	M	SD
Guilty Rating[1]	5.13	1.70	4.61	2.09	3.61	2.20	5.45	1.67

[1]The guilty rating is based on a 9-point Likert Scale, 1 being Completely Guilty and 9 being Completely Not Guilty.

[2]In condition one, a heterosexual male allegedly assaults a heterosexual female.

In condition two, a heterosexual male allegedly assaults a homosexual female.

In condition three, a homosexual male allegedly assaults a heterosexual male.

In condition four, a homosexual male allegedly assaults a homosexual male.

the defendant by condition, showed significant results ($F_{(3.66)} = 3.81$, $p = .007$). In other words, the importance of the defendant's sexuality varied significantly with the condition. Specifically, conditions one and two, having heterosexual defendants, rated the importance of the defendant's sexuality as significantly less important than in conditions three and four, having homosexual defendants.

A one-way ANOVA for the rated importance of the sexuality of the alleged victim by the condition was marginally significant ($F_{(3.66)} = 2.71$, $p = 0.52$). This data illustrated that there was a significant difference between condition one, which was very similar to condition two, and conditions three and four. The importance of the victim's sexuality was greatest in conditions three and four, where the defendant was a homosexual male.

Discussion

This research supports the hypothesis that homonegativity affects the guilt rating in sexual assault trials involving homosexuals. Specifically, homosexual males accused of sexually assaulting heterosexual males (condition three) are found more guilty than heterosexual males who assault heterosexual females (condition one) and also more guilty than homosexual males accused of assaulting homosexual males (condition four).

Homonegativity is born from fear and maintained by unfamiliarity with homosexuality. Homonegativity acts in such a way in the courtroom as to deter fair and just verdicts. This research illustrates that it is more acceptable for a homosexual male to sexually assault a homosexual male, but if the homosexual male sexually assaults a heterosexual male, it is a significantly more abhorrent act. Several explanations seem plausible for these results, all of which have their foundation in homonegative thoughts or beliefs.

Perhaps these results are due to the interpretation of the two men with the same sexual orientation participating in consensual sex. This explanation could be likened to the cognition, "He wanted it," the common difficulty faced by female victims in acquaintance rape trials. A homosexual male assaulting a heterosexual male is much more difficult to misconceive as consensual sex because of the differing sexual orientations. Believing the victim in condition four to be a mutually consenting partner, therefore, would justify the signifi-

cant difference from the heterosexual male victim in condition three. However, this explanation is undermined by the careful precautions taken to ensure the case was presented as a *stranger* rape case and not an acquaintance rape case. When there is prior knowledge of the defendant, the victim typically has a difficult time proving that the event was not consensual (Richardson & Campbell, 1982; Fischer, 1995).

A second explanation for the significant difference between the guilt ratings of the defendant in conditions three and four stems from the interpretation of the homosexual male victim as physically suffering less than the heterosexual male victim. Sexual intercourse with a male is a common experience for a homosexual male but not for a heterosexual male. In other words, the heterosexual male victim in condition three could be seen as more of a victim simply because the homosexual male victim has been exposed to male/male sexual experiences and the heterosexual male victim has not.

Also, based on the research done surrounding preset beliefs and the Just World Phenomenon, it is possible that the interaction of homonegative beliefs and believing in a fair and just world lead to the difference in the guilt rating of conditions three and four. Viewing the homosexual victim as deserving the assault because of his chosen lifestyle, or any other homonegative belief, would allow the defendant to be seen as more innocent. In condition three, however, this interaction would not take place because the victim was heterosexual. Any homonegative beliefs would be directed towards the defendant and encourage a greater guilt rating.

Also related to both homonegative beliefs and belief in a just world is belief in homosexual stereotypes such as, "Homosexuals fornicate all the time," and, "It does not matter who it is with, as long as the homosexual male achieves intercourse." Believing these negative stereotypes to be true can taint the juror's verdict. Believing such statements would account for the difference in the guilt ratings between conditions three and four because one would not see anything wrong with the assault against the homosexual male from this thought process.

The final explanation for these results is based on the findings of Rosario, Meyer-Bahlburg, Hunter, Exner, Gwadz, and Keller (1996). They found that the main fuel of homonegativity came from a heterosexual fear of being the object desired by a homosexual. Since the strongest guilt rating was achieved in the condition where a homosexual male assaulted a heterosexual male, it is entirely plausible that the 70 heterosexual participants were inspired to rate the

Table 4

Participants' Average Responses to the Perceived Importance of Possible Variables in the Guilty Verdict by Condition

Importance of[1] ...	Condition One[2]		Condition Two		Condition Three		Condition Four	
	M	*SD*	*M*	*SD*	*M*	*SD*	*M*	*SD*
Reasonable Doubt	1.73	.80	2.44	1.25	1.78	.81	1.90	1.29
Gender of Defendant	3.67	1.11	3.06	1.62	4.11	1.32	4.40	1.05
Gender of Victim	3.67	1.45	3.06	1.59	3.56	1.58	4.15	1.31
Presented Evidence	1.33	.62	1.39	.61	1.50	.71	2.45	1.19
Sexuality of Defendant	3.80	1.26	4.12	1.27	2.78	1.40	3.10	1.33
Sexuality of Victim	4.27	1.16	3.94	1.34	3.16	1.69	3.20	1.20

[1]The averages are based on a Likert Scale of 1 (Very Important) to 5 (Not at all Important).

[2]In condition one, a heterosexual male allegedly assaults a heterosexual female.

In condition two, a heterosexual male allegedly assaults a homosexual female.

In condition three, a homosexual male allegedly assaults a heterosexual male.

In condition four, a homosexual male allegedly assaults a homosexual male.

homosexual defendant who assaulted the heterosexual male because this irrational fear was brought out.

360   The second significant finding was that the scenario depicting the common sexual assault trial (heterosexual male assaulting a heterosexual female) was less guilty than the homosexual male assaulting the heterosexual male. This result implies both the effect of homonega-
365 tivity, as discussed above, and the effect of the gender of the victim. Females, in this study, were treated in stereotypical ways—as second-class citizens. Using the same amount of evidence to convict the homosexual male defendant in condition three, participants found
370 the heterosexual defendant in condition one less guilty. This difference seems to be the result of a combination of factors. First, heterosexual males are being seen as more honest than heterosexual females when placed in the role of victim in a sexual assault trial. The same
375 double standard that has existed for thousands of years is now haunting women in the courtroom when they are the most vulnerable. Second, the importance of the defendant's sexuality seems to affect the outcome. The heterosexual defendant's sexual orientation is rated as
380 less important than the sexual orientation of the homosexual defendant. And the rated importance of the victim's sexuality seems to vary with the sexuality of the defendant. When the defendant was a homosexual, the sexuality of the victim was rated as more important
385 than when the defendant was a heterosexual. In other words, a homosexual in the role of defendant or victim is at a disadvantage in the courtroom.

    More research is needed to determine the effect of homonegativity paired with the victim's gender. For
390 example, why was there no significant difference between the guilt ratings of conditions one and two (heterosexual male defendant and a heterosexual/homosexual female victim) but there was between conditions three and four (homosexual male defendant
395 and a heterosexual/homosexual male victim)? The lack of difference must be related to the gender of the victim, so why are females treated differently when the

eyes of the law should be blind? Perhaps stereotypical thought processes are at work. "There is no such thing as a
400 lesbian. She just has to meet the right man," is a popular misconception that could lead the believer to rate the guilt of the defendant in conditions one and two similarly, since the guilt rating of the defendant in condition one was skewed towards innocence and not guilty. The question that needs to
405 be investigated next from similar research is what happens when the victim is a homosexual female. Why does the guilt rating her attacker receives not differ significantly from any of the other conditions? Is she not regarded as a reliable source of truth because she is homosexual, because she is
410 female, or perhaps a combination of both? Is the Just World Phenomenon at work in this condition as well? Perhaps it is assumed that she deserved to be victimized because she is a lesbian and that is not a socially accepted lifestyle. The interaction of gender with this topic is as important as the in-
415 teraction of homonegativity. More detailed inquiries as to what the participant is thinking when the verdict is made would allow for a better understanding of the reason(s) why there are differences between some conditions and not others in this research.

420   Another important area of further inquiry is investigating how to decrease homonegativity. Research by Wells (1991) has proposed that education is the answer, but Larsen, Reed and Hoffman (1980) found that education in general is not the answer. Although the education offered in the social sci-
425 ences, humanities and fine arts tends to decrease homonegativity, education is not a general "cure-all." Specifically, research should be done in the area of decreasing homonegativity in the courtroom. Homosexuals are not treated equally in sexual assault trials. As the number of males re-
430 porting sexual assault continues to grow day by day, so does the chance of a sexual assault trial between two men grow or the appearance of sexual orientation as a factor in a sexual assault trial.

    This study shows that a homosexual male accused of as-
435 saulting a heterosexual male will not receive a fair trial. This is an obstacle that must be anticipated for the future.

References

Adams, H. E., Wright, L. W., & Lohr, B. (1996). Is homophobia associated with homosexual arousal? *Journal of Abnormal Psychology, 105* (3). 440-445.

Alicke, M. D., & Yurak, T. J. (1995). Perpetrator personality and judgements of acquaintance rape. *Journal of Applied Social Psychology, 25* (21). 1900-1921.

Brems, C., & Wagner, P. (1994). Blame of victim and perpetrator in rape versus theft. *The Journal of Social Psychology, 134* (3), 363-373.

Bureau of Justice Statistics. (1993). *Criminal Victimization in the United States. 1993.* Washington, DC: United States Government Printing Office.

Federal Bureau of Investigation. (1995). *Highlights from 20 Years of Surveying Crime Victims.* Washington, DC: United States Government Printing Office.

Fischer, G. (1995). Effects of drinking by the victim or offender on verdicts in a simulated trial of an acquaintance rape. *Psychological Reports, 77* (2). 579-586.

Follingstad, D. R., Shillinglaw, R. D., DeHart, D. D., & Kleinfelter, K. J. (1997). The impact of elements of self-defense and objective versus subjective instructions on juror's verdicts for battered women defendants. *Journal of Interpersonal Violence, 12* (5), 729-745.

Friedman, R. C., & Downey, J. I. (1994). Homosexuality. *New England Journal of Medicine, 331* (14), 923-930.

Grant, J. M., Folger, W. A., & Hornak, N. J. (1995). College students' perception of victim responsibility in an acquaintance rape situation. *College Student Journal, 29* (4), 532-535.

Groth, N., & Burgess, A. W., (1980). Male rape: Offenders and victims. *American Journal of Psychiatry, 137* (7), 806-810.

Hickson, F. C. I., Davies, P. M., Hunt, A. J., Weatherburn, P., McManus, T. J., & Coxon, A. P. M. (1994). Gay men as victims of nonconsensual sex. *Archives of Sexual Behavior, 23* (3), 281-294.

Johnson, J. D., & Jackson, L. A. (1988). Assessing the effects of factors that might underlie the differential perception of acquaintance and stranger rape. *Sex Roles, 19* (1-2), 37-46.

Kaufman, A., DiVasto, P., Jackson, R., Voorhees, D., & Christy, J. (1980). Male rape victims: Noninstitutional assault. *American Journal of Psychiatry, 137* (2), 221-224.

Kite, M. E., & Whitley, B. E. (1996). Sex differences in attitudes toward homosexual persons, behaviors, and civil rights: A meta-analysis. *Personality and Social Psychology Bulletin, 22* (4), 336-353.

Laner, M. R., & Laner, R. H. (1980). Sexual preference or personal style? Why lesbians are disliked. *Journal of Homosexuality, 5* (4), 339-356.

Larsen, K. S., Reed, M., & Hoffman, S. (1980). Attitudes toward homosexuality: A Likert-type scale and construct validity. *Journal of Sex Research, 16* (3), 245-257.

Mezey, G., & King, M. (1987). Male victims of sexual assault. *Medical Science Law, 27* (2), 122-124.

Richardson, D., & Campbell, J. L. (1982). Alcohol and rape: The effect of alcohol on attribution of blaming the victim. *Social Psychology Quarterly, 46,* 468-476.

Rosario, M., Meyer-Bahlburg, H. F. L., Hunter, J., Exner, T. M., Gwadz, M., & Keller, A. M. (1996). The psychosexual development of urban lesbian, gay, and bisexual youths. *The Journal of Sex Research, 33* (2), 113-126.

Ruggiero, G. (1985). *The Boundaries of the Eros: Sex Crime and Sexuality in Renaissance Venice.* New York: Oxford University Press.

Wells, J. W. (1991). What makes a difference? Various teaching strategies to reduce homophobia in university students. *Annals of Sex Research, 4,* 229-238.

Wells, J. W., & Franken, M. L. (1987). University students' knowledge about and attitudes toward homosexuality. *Journal of Humanistic Education and Development, 26,* 81-95.

Willis, C. E., & Wrightsman, L. S. (1995). Effects of victim gaze behavior and prior relationship on rape culpability attributions. *Journal of Interpersonal Violence, 10* (3), 367-377.

About the author: Jennifer M. Hill is presently a full-time student pursuing her Ph.D. at CUNY Graduate Center. This study is the product of two years worth of work that culminated in the author's undergraduate thesis.

Acknowledgments: The author would like to thank Dr. Ronald Heyduk, Hartwick College, for helping with the development of the idea and the design for this research. She also would like to thank Dr. Lisa Onorato, Hartwick College, for her help and guidance throughout the research. The topic of homonegativity is little researched, and Dr. Heyduk and Dr. Onorato were of great assistance in all aspects of this study.

Address correspondence to: Jennifer M. Hill, CUNY Graduate Center, Developmental Psychology, 365 Fifth Ave., New York, NY 10016.

Appendix
Script from Condition Four

The experiment you are about to take part in is a measurement of decision making. For the next twenty minutes, please imagine yourself as a member of a jury hearing the following case. Once you turn a page, please do not refer back to it; this is to encourage the utmost congruence with actual criminal trials in respect to evidence and testimony.

You will be presented with a brief summary of the case, the court's instructions on reasonable doubt, the prosecution's final argument, the defense's final argument, the prosecution's rebuttal to the defense, and the defense's rebuttal to the prosecution. Following the arguments are some questions.

Please answer all the questions presented to you with blatant honesty. Your anonymity is guaranteed. Thank you for your participation.

On Friday, February 7, 1997, Michael Smith, age 25, was arrested and charged with the sexual assault of Patrick Green, age 24. The defendant will face criminal charges on April 28, 1997, in the County of Otsego.

The Court's Instructions on Reasonable Doubt

The defendant is presumed innocent until proven, beyond any reasonable doubt, that he is guilty of the crime. If the evidence has not convinced you beyond a reasonable doubt that the defendant is guilty, he must be found not guilty.

Reasonable doubt is present when you have carefully considered all of the evidence presented and you cannot say that you are firmly convinced of the truth of the charge.

If, after a full and impartial consideration of all the evidence, and ignoring all irrelevant information or prejudices, you are firmly convinced of the truth of the charge, you must find the defendant guilty. If you are not firmly convinced on the truth of the charge, you must find the defendant not guilty.

You will now be presented with a text version of the criminal trial, the *People vs. Mr. Michael Smith.*

The Final Argument for the Prosecution—Preliminary

We have proven that, beyond a reasonable doubt, Michael Smith is guilty of sexual assault, an act he committed against Patrick Green on February 7, 1997, at approximately 1 A.M. Mr. Smith committed this crime in the parking lot of the popular dance club, The Orange Peel. Several witnesses have testified that the two men were seen at the club on the same night, but not one has testified to seeing the two together at any one time. In addition, you have heard the testimony of Mr. Green's friends supporting the plaintiff's testimony that aside from that night, he had never seen nor socialized with the defendant, Mr. Smith.

Now, Ladies and Gentlemen, I am going to replay the events of that evening for you. Mr. Green was relaxing with his friends at the club. They were playing pool and socializing. Mr. Green was feeling a little hot and decided to get a breath of fresh air outside. Mr. Smith followed him out and began a conversation with him. The two men walked around the parking lot making "small talk." Mr. Smith said that he was taking his leave of Mr. Green and supposedly walked away. Not two minutes later, Mr. Green was attacked from behind and forced to the ground, where a man forced sexual relations on him.

495   Mr. Green was caught off guard, frightened and shocked. Although he struggled and repeatedly begged the defendant to stop, he was unable to force the defendant off him. No, Ladies and Gentlemen of the Jury, he did not scream more than once, because the first time

500   he attempted to cry out, a blunt object was shoved into his back. Now, I don't know about you, but in a situation like this, I would assume that the object was a gun or a knife, especially when accompanied by the phrase, "Shut up or I will make you shut up."

505   How do we know that this incident occurred, Ladies and Gentlemen? I present to you Mr. Green's nonexistent criminal record. He is an upstanding heterosexual citizen. The physician who examined him later that day has confirmed the fact that he partook in sexual rela-

510   tions with another man, and in the opinion of the physician, whose character has not been questioned, the relations were forced. There were severe lacerations and excessive bleeding that would not have been present in consensual sex.

515   Mr. Smith is the man responsible for this crime. Although Mr. Green was unable to concentrate on the defendant's face for a long period of time, he is able to positively identify the defendant's voice. There should be no doubt in your mind of the guilt of Mr. Smith.

The Final Argument for the
Defense—Preliminary

520   As the prosecution has reviewed, there is a mountain of evidence presented in this case. However, it points only to one fact: Mr. Green was attacked by someone in the early morning of February 7.

None of the evidence presented by the Prosecution
525   pertains to the real facts. There is no evidence that my client sexually assaulted Mr. Green. The two men were seen leaving the club at approximately the same time with the intention of getting a breath of fresh air. They walked, chatted, and parted. My client, Mr. Smith, re-

530   turned to the club and someone attacked Mr. Green. There have been several witnesses who saw Mr. Smith return to the club; several of the witnesses from the club that night have testified to the fact that he was not gone more than twenty minutes.

535   Although Mr. Green would like us to believe that my client viciously sexually assaulted him, the Prosecution has failed to provide adequate evidence of this accusation. The parking lot was dimly lit. My client had already taken his leave of Mr. Green and was inside the

540   club when the attack happened. This entire case is based largely on the alleged recognition of my client's voice. There is no reason that my client, an upstanding homosexual citizen with no criminal record, would have committed this crime.

545   Look at my client. He is a young man, freshly graduated from a university. How can there be any

doubt in your mind of his innocence? My client is the real victim of this trial. He is an innocent man who is victimized by falsified charges.

The Final Argument for the
Prosecution—Final

550   I would like to take this time to review the evidence presented in this case, as my colleague has suggested that there is not enough to convict Mr. Smith for sexually assaulting Mr. Green.

Not one witness can testify to the time lapse between Mr.
555   Smith leaving the club and returning. The assault on Mr. Green, although a horrible experience that was both unwanted and unwarranted, did not last for a long time. Mr. Smith, in a twenty-minute time frame, had time to walk outside with Mr. Green, chat, pretend to leave, and then attack

560   Mr. Green from behind, force sexual relations upon him and then return to the club. Mr. Green, I reiterate, has testified to recognizing the voice of his attacker as the voice of his acquaintance Mr. Smith. What further evidence is needed?

Although my colleague would try to convince you that a
565   victim's recognition of the voice is not a legitimate means of identification, I beg you to reconsider. Put yourself in Mr. Green's shoes. Don't you think you would remember a voice heard just moments before? Don't you think you are capable of that memory? Then, please, do not deny Mr. Green that

570   ability to use his owns senses and intelligence in identifying Mr. Smith as his attacker.

Mr. Green has come forward with trust in the American legal system. He is trusting you, Ladies and Gentlemen of the Jury, to help him find justice for the heinous crime

575   committed against him. The defendant, Mr. Michael Smith, is guilty of sexual assault, and I suggest the strongest penalty available for this charge. Thank you.

The Final Argument for the
Defense—Final

As stated earlier, Ladies and Gentlemen, the only evidence presented to you in this courtroom points to the fact
580   that Mr. Green was attacked in a dimly lit area of the parking lot of this popular club. What you must decide is whether or not this vicious assault was performed by my client.

My client was not in the parking lot at the time of the attack. He had returned to the club and was socializing with
585   his friends while someone else, who is free and roaming the streets of our county, attacked Mr. Green. The Prosecution has not offered one ounce of biological evidence because the samples that were found at the scene had been tampered with and were contaminated.

590   Again, I appeal to your sense of honesty and your insight. Why would my client, an upstanding homosexual citizen, sexually assault Mr. Green? My client has no prior convictions and there is no reason to believe he is a monstrous and cruel man. In addition to which, the time frame is not

595   long enough.

The prosecution has asked you to find him guilty, but the prosecution has failed to present enough evidence to rule out reasonable doubt. You must find my client innocent of these charges because he is. Thank you.

600 Based on the case you have just read, please circle a number on the line below that indicates how innocent or guilty you think the defendant, Mr. Smith, accused of sexually assaulting Mr. Green, is.

605 This should be representative of **how you feel**, independent of what decision you think would be made in an actual jury situation.

Did Mr. Smith sexually assault Mr. Green?

1 Definitely yes
2
3 Probably yes
4
5 Maybe
6
7 Probably no
8
9 Definitely no

The Court's Instructions on Reasonable Doubt

610 Please remember the instructions you [read earlier] about reasonable doubt. The defendant is presumed innocent until proven, beyond any reasonable doubt, that he is guilty of the crime. If the evidence has not convinced you beyond a reasonable doubt that the defendant is guilty, he must be acquitted.

615 Reasonable doubt is present when you have carefully considered all of the evidence presented and you cannot say that you are firmly convinced of the truth of the charge.

If, after a full and impartial consideration of all the evidence, and ignoring all irrelevant information or

620 prejudices, you are firmly convinced of the truth of the charge, you must find the defendant guilty. If you are not firmly convinced of the truth of the charge, you must find the defendant not guilty. Thank you for your attention in this case. Now you will be asked to make a

625 legally binding decision. Do you find Mr. Smith guilty or not guilty of the charges? Please circle one of the answers below.

I find Michael Smith
630   Guilty   Not Guilty
of the charge of sexual assault.

Additional Questions

Please answer all the following questions.

1. What is your sex? M   F

2. What is your major? _____

635 3. What do you think this experiment was about? (Just a sentence or two, please.)

4. For each topic subject matter listed below, please indicate using a 1-5 scale (1 = very important to 5 = not

640 at all), how important each was in your decision.

1   Very Important to My Decision
2
3
4
5   Very Unimportant to My Decision

Eyewitnesses from the club_____

Courts instructions about reasonable doubt_____

Age of the defendant (Mr. Smith)_____

Age of the alleged victim (Mr. Green)_____

645 Gender of the defendant_____

Gender of the alleged victim_____

Presentation of the evidence_____

Sexuality of the defendant_____

Sexuality of the alleged victim_____

650 Upstanding citizenship of the defendant_____

Upstanding citizenship of the alleged victim_____

Lack of biological evidence_____

Sexual orientation_____

655 If you feel comfortable knowing that there is no way to trace this survey to your name, please disclose your sexual orientation below.

I prefer/am attracted to:

660   same sex – both sexes – opposite sex

Exercise for Article 13

Factual Questions

1. Why did the researcher present a "stranger rape" case to the participants?

2. Which condition in Table 1 was the "control condition"?

3. Which condition in Table 1 was hypothesized to produce the lowest average guilt rating?

4. After participants turned in their questionnaires, what were they given?

5. According to Table 2, a homosexual male was least likely to be found guilty when he allegedly attacked what type of person (homosexual *or* heterosexual)?

6. In Table 3, the *lower* the mean, the *higher* the average guilt rating. In which condition was the alleged attacker

found to be more guilty? Is this attacker heterosexual or homosexual?

7. In which condition was the alleged attacker found to be least guilty? Is this attacker heterosexual or homosexual?

Questions for Discussion

8. Experimenters often attempt to simplify situations they are manipulating and observing so that they have a more interpretable result. For example, they ruled out alcohol and stranger rape from the experimental scripts. Do you believe that simplifying experimental situations can also be a disadvantage? Explain.

9. The researcher mentions a stereotype in quotations in her article. Would you be interested in knowing the source of this? (For example, see lines 162–163.) Why? Why not?

10. Do you think it is reasonable to have participants sign up for a study believing that the research is to be about "decision making"? Would it have made a difference if the study had been described as something like "decisions about guilt in relation to sexual orientation"? Explain.

11. Do you think the script for this study is reasonably clear? (See lines 437 to the end.)

12. The researcher does not state whether the participants were assigned at random. Is it important to know whether this was the basis for assignment? Explain.

12. Do the data in this study convince you of the validity of the researcher's statement in the last paragraph. Explain. (See lines 434–436.)

Quality Ratings

Directions: Indicate your level of agreement with each of the following statements by circling a number from 5 for strongly agree (SA) to 1 for strongly disagree (SD). If you believe an item is not applicable to this research article, leave it blank. Be prepared to explain your ratings.

A. The introduction establishes the importance of the study.

SA   5   4   3   2   1   SD

B. The literature review establishes the context for the study.

SA   5   4   3   2   1   SD

C. The research purpose, question, or hypothesis is clearly stated.

SA   5   4   3   2   1   SD

D. The method of sampling is sound.

SA   5   4   3   2   1   SD

E. Relevant demographics (for example, age, gender, and ethnicity) are described.

SA   5   4   3   2   1   SD

F. Measurement procedures are adequate.

SA   5   4   3   2   1   SD

G. All procedures have been described in sufficient detail to permit a replication of the study.

SA   5   4   3   2   1   SD

H. The participants have been adequately protected from potential harm.

SA   5   4   3   2   1   SD

I. The results are clearly described.

SA   5   4   3   2   1   SD

J. The discussion/conclusion is appropriate.

SA   5   4   3   2   1   SD

K. Despite any flaws, the report is worthy of publication.

SA   5   4   3   2   1   SD

Article 14

Criterion-Related Validity of the Marital Disaffection Scale as a Measure of Marital Estrangement

Claudia Flowers
University of North Carolina at Charlotte

Bryan E. Robinson
University of North Carolina at Charlotte

Jane J. Carroll
University of North Carolina at Charlotte

ABSTRACT. The Marital Disaffection Scale was administered, along with measures of positive feelings towards spouse, problem-drinking behavior of spouse, workaholic behavior of spouse, and marital status, to 323 female members of the American Counseling Association. Scores on the Marital Disaffection Scale showed significant inverse correlations ($r = -.94$) with positive feelings towards spouse and ($r_{pb} = -.63$) with marital status. Scores on the Marital Disaffection Scale showed significant positive relationships ($r = .36$) with spouse's problem drinking behavior and ($r = .48$) with workaholic behavior of spouse. The results support the use of the Marital Disaffection Scale as a measure of emotional estrangement in marriage.

From *Psychological Reports*, 86, 1101–1103. Copyright © 2000 by Psychological Reports. Reprinted with permission.

The Marital Disaffection Scale (Kayser, 1996) is a 21-item inventory designed to measure the components of emotional estrangement in marriage by focusing on the experience of apathy and indifference, lack of car-
5   ing, and lack of attachments towards one's partner. Marital disaffection does not mean that a marriage will necessarily break down but simply is a description of the loss of love and affection by one partner for the other (Kayser, 1996). Scoring for each item was an-
10 chored by 1 (Not At All True) and 4 (Very True), and a total index of disaffection was the sum of points across all items—the higher the score the greater the disaffection. Keyser (1996) reported a correlation of .93 ($p <$ .001) between the Marital Disaffection Scale and Sny-
15 der and Regts' scale of disaffection (1982). Scores on the Marital Disaffection Scale correlated inversely with general questions on marital happiness ($r = -.56$) and marital closeness ($r = -.86$). Cronbach coefficient alpha for the 21 items on the Marital Disaffection Scale was
20 .97.

The current study examined the concurrent validity of scores on the Marital Disaffection Scale by correlating Marital Disaffection Scale scores with measures of positive feelings towards spouse, problem-drinking
25 behavior of spouse, and workaholic behavior of spouse.

Positive feeling towards spouse was assessed using the Positive Feelings Questionnaire (O'Leary, Fincham, & Turkewitz, 1983). The Problem Drinking Scale (Vaillant, 1980) assessed problem-drinking behavior of
30 spouse, and scores were hypothesized to be positively related to marital disaffection (Geiss & O'Leary, 1981). The Work Addiction Risk Test (Robinson, 1999) assessed workaholic behavior of spouse, and scores were hypothesized to have a positive relation-
35 ship (Robinson, 1998). The predictive validity of scores on the Marital Disaffection Scale was evaluated by correlating Marital Disaffection Scale scores with marital status (coded as 0 = divorced and 1 = married).

The four tests and a demographic form were mailed
40 to 1,000 randomly selected female members of the American Counseling Association. A total of 323 respondents returned and completed all the tests and demographic form. The participants had a mean age of 47.9 yr. ($SD = 10.4$) ranging from 26 to 89 years. Most
45 participants were currently married (77.6%) and had been on the average 18.2 yr. ($SD = 12.3$). The means, standard deviations, ranges, and indexes of skewness for each of the four tests are reported in Table 1.

Table 1
Descriptive Statistics of Scores from Marital Disaffection Scale, Positive Feelings Questionnaire, Problem Drinking Scale, and Work Addiction Risk Test

Measures	M	SD	Range	Skewness
Marital Disaffection	36.86	15.75	20–81	1.12
Positive Feelings	94.33	24.07	18–119	−1.30
Problem Drinking	0.88	2.12	0–11	2.61
Work Addiction	52.79	12.35	28–94	.51

Pearson product-moment correlation coefficients
50 were calculated between scores on the Marital Disaffection Scale and the Positive Feelings Questionnaire, the Problem Drinking Scale, and the Work Addiction Risk Test. A point-biserial correlation coefficient was calculated for scores on Marital Disaffection and
55 marital status. Statistically significant correlations were found between scores on the Marital Disaffection Scale and all other measures. The Marital Disaffection Scale

had an inverse relationship with the Positive Feelings Questionnaire ($r = -.94$, $p < .001$) and marital status $(r_{pb} = -.63$, $p < .001)$. Scores on the Marital Disaffection Scale had a positive association with those on the Problem Drinking Scale ($r = .36$, $p < .001$) and the Work Addiction Risk Test ($r = .48$, $p < .001$).

Hypothesized relationships of the scores on the Marital Disaffection Scale with other measures were supported in this study. The results further confirm the use of the Marital Disaffection Scale as a measure of emotional estrangement in marriage.

References

GEISS, S. K., & O'LEARY, K. D. (1981) Therapist ratings of frequency and severity of marital problems: Implications for research. *Journal of Marital and Family Therapy, 7,* 515–520.

KAYSER, K. (1996) The marital disaffection scale: An inventory for assessing emotional estrangement in marriage. *The American Journal of Family Therapy, 24,* 83–88.

O'LEARY, K. D., FINCHAM, F., & TURKEWITZ, H. (1983) Assessment of positive feelings toward spouse. *Journal of Consulting and Clinical Psychology, 51,* 949–951.

ROBINSON, B. E. (1998) Spouses of workaholics: Clinical implications for psychotherapy. *Psychotherapy, 35,* 260–268.

ROBINSON, B. E. (1999) The work-addiction risk test: Development of a tentative measure of workaholism. *Perceptual and Motor Skills, 88,* 199–210.

SNYDER, D. K., & REGTS, J. M. (1982) Factor scales for assessing marital disharmony and disaffection. *Journal of Consulting and Clinical Psychology, 50,* 736–743.

VAILLANT, G. E. (1980) Natural history of male psychological health: VIII. Antecedent of alcoholism and orality. *American Journal of Psychiatry, 137,* 181–186.

About the authors: Claudia Flowers is a member of the Department of Educational Administration, Research, and Technology. Bryan E. Robinson and Jane J. Carroll are members of the Department of Counseling, Special Education, and Child Development. All are at the University of North Carolina at Charlotte.

Address correspondence to: Claudia Flowers, Ph.D., Department of Educational Administration, Research and Technology, University of North Carolina at Charlotte, 9201 University City Blvd., Charlotte, NC 28223-0001.

Exercise for Article 14

Factual Questions

1. Does a high score on the Marital Disaffection Scale indicate a greater *or* lesser degree of disaffection?

2. The researchers state that they examine what type of validity for the Marital Disaffection Scale?

3. What percentage of the participants was currently married?

4. What was the average score on the Marital Disaffection Scale?

5. Which correlation coefficient reported in this article represents the strongest relationship?

6. What is the value of the correlation coefficient for the relationship between marital disaffection and problem drinking?

Questions for Discussion

7. Would you be interested in seeing sample items from the Marital Disaffection Scale? Why? Why not?

8. The response rate was 323 out of 1,000. In your opinion, does this limit the validity of the study? Explain.

9. Do you agree with the last sentence in this article? (See lines 66–68.)

10. This article is relatively short. In your opinion, does its shortness limit its usefulness and validity? Explain.

11. If you were going to conduct another study on this topic, what changes in the research methodology would you make, if any?

Quality Ratings

Directions: Indicate your level of agreement with each of the following statements by circling a number from 5 for strongly agree (SA) to 1 for strongly disagree (SD). If you believe an item is not applicable to this research article, leave it blank. Be prepared to explain your ratings.

A. The introduction establishes the importance of the study.

   SA   5   4   3   2   1   SD

B. The literature review establishes the context for the study.

   SA   5   4   3   2   1   SD

C. The research purpose, question, or hypothesis is clearly stated.

   SA   5   4   3   2   1   SD

D. The method of sampling is sound.

   SA   5   4   3   2   1   SD

E. Relevant demographics (for example, age, gender, and ethnicity) are described.

   SA   5   4   3   2   1   SD

F. Measurement procedures are adequate.

   SA   5   4   3   2   1   SD

G. All procedures have been described in sufficient detail to permit a replication of the study.

   SA   5   4   3   2   1   SD

H. The participants have been adequately protected from potential harm.

SA   5   4   3   2   1   SD

I. The results are clearly described.

SA   5   4   3   2   1   SD

J. The discussion/conclusion is appropriate.

SA   5   4   3   2   1   SD

K. Despite any flaws, the report is worthy of publication.

SA   5   4   3   2   1   SD

Article 15

The Moral Justification Scale: Reliability and Validity of a New Measure of Care and Justice Orientations

Linda S. Gump
Psychological HealthCare

Richard C. Baker
California School of
Professional Psychology

Samuel Roll
University of New Mexico

ABSTRACT. Research increasingly suggests that there are limitations to Kohlberg's theory of moral development. Gilligan in particular has observed that Kohlberg's theory considers abstract principled reasoning as the highest level of moral judgment, and penalizes those who focus on the interpersonal ramifications of a moral decision. Gilligan calls these *justice* and *care* orientations. The present paper describes the development of the Moral Justification Scale, an objective measure of the two orientations. The scale consists of six vignettes, of which two are justice oriented, two are care oriented, and two are mixed, incorporating both orientations. Construct validity was evaluated by expert judges and, overall, was high. Cronbach's alpha was .75 for the Care subscale and .64 for the Justice subscale, indicating adequate internal consistency. Split-half reliabilities were as follows: Care, $r = .72$, $p < .01$, and Justice, $r = .60$, $p <.05$. Regarding test-retest reliability (approximately two weeks), $r = .61$, $p < .05$, for Care; $r = .69$, $p < .05$, for Justice. Neither subscale correlated significantly with the Marlowe-Crowne Social Desirability Scale. Thus, the Moral Justification Scale shows promise as an easily administered, objectively scored measure of Gilligan's constructs of care and justice.

From *Adolescence, 35*, 67–76. Copyright © 2000 by Libra Publishers, Inc. Reprinted with permission.

The Work of Kohlberg and Gilligan

Kohlberg (1981, 1985; Kohlberg & Kramer, 1969), using Piaget's theories of cognitive and moral development as a starting point, developed a model of moral development with six stages. Kohlberg's stages are
5   grouped into three progressively higher levels: preconventional, conventional, and postconventional. People at the preconventional level (Stages 1 and 2), primarily children, conceive of rules and social expectations as external to the self. Moral decisions are made based on
10 expectations of reward or punishment. At the conventional level (Stages 3 and 4), people subscribe to a morality of shared norms and values, centering on the needs of the individual and the rules and expectations of others. Interpersonal relationships and concern for

15 others' opinions are crucial (Stage 3). At Stage 4, obeying society's laws becomes central. At the postconventional level (Stages 5 and 6), moral decision-making is based on principled reasoning. Stage 5 revolves around the utilitarian maxim, "the greatest
20 good for the greatest number." At Stage 6, people make decisions based on universal principles of justice, liberty, and equality, even if these violate laws or social norms.

Critics of Kohlberg's model, most notably Gilligan
25 (1982), have pointed out that his system is drawn from a Kantian philosophy that uses abstract principles of justice as the basis of advanced moral reasoning. This penalizes those who focus on the interpersonal ramifications of a moral decision. Gilligan (1981) has argued
30 that Kohlberg's representation of women as fixated at Stage 3, which represents interpersonal morality, is flawed. Women's reasoning, according to Gilligan (1982), is contextual and deeply tied to relationships, and Kohlberg has undervalued the equally valid Aris-
35 totelian moral concerns voiced by women (Vasudev, 1988). Thus, the emphasis on justice as the embodiment of morality appears to have underestimated the impact that interpersonal connectedness can have on moral decision-making.

40 Gilligan set out to test the validity of a care perspective, with the assumption that it is morally equivalent to the justice construct. Gilligan's (1977) response to the apparent bias in Kohlberg's theory toward the male (justice) perspective included an alternative stage
45 sequence for the development of females' moral reasoning. These stages are based on the degree of compassion and connection between self and others, manifested in the peace and harmony in relationships (Brabeck, 1983; Muuss, 1988).

50 Gilligan viewed women as progressing from initial selfishness (first level) to caring primarily for others (second level) and finally to an integration of concern for the needs of both self and others (third level). Her morality of responsibility emphasizes attachments,
55 allows for both self-sacrifice and selfishness, and considers connections with others as primary, while Kohl-

berg's morality of justice emphasizes autonomy, rules, and legalities, and considers the individual as primary. Gilligan and Attanucci (1988) have stressed that nei-
60 ther orientation is superior; rather, care and justice are complementary.

Using measures designed to investigate more interpersonally oriented forms of moral reasoning, a number of studies (Gibbs, Arnold, & Burkhart; 1984; Gilli-
65 gan & Attanucci, 1988; Lyons, 1983; Pratt, Golding, Hunter, & Sampson, 1988; Rothbart, Hanley, & Albert, 1986) have found gender differences, with males primarily focusing on issues of justice and females primarily focusing on interpersonal issues. However,
70 other studies have not found significant differences (Crown & Heatherington, 1989; Friedman, Robinson, & Friedman, 1987; Galotti, 1989; Pratt, Golding, Hunter, & Sampson, 1988; Walker, 1989).

There may also be a degree of ethnocentrism in
75 Kohlberg's theory. Miller and Bersoff (1992), for example, challenged Kohlberg's claim of universality in moral reasoning, having found that Americans focus on justice considerations, while Hindus in India emphasize interpersonal considerations in rendering a moral deci-
80 sion. Snarey (1985) likewise concluded that Kohlberg's model is specific to Western culture.

In short, there is reason to believe that Kohlberg's method of studying moral judgment has certain limitations. Other systems—most of which are based on in-
85 terviews—are cumbersome, and require considerable expertise in administration and scoring. Thus, an easily administered, objectively scored measure of moral judgment, tapping both care and justice orientations, would have several advantages (e.g., it would have a
90 greater chance of avoiding gender and cultural biases). The present paper describes such an instrument—the Moral Justification Scale—and provides data on reliability and validity.

Method

Participants

To recruit participants, sign-up sheets were posted
95 at a large state university in Southern California. The study was described only as an investigation of how people make decisions, in order to provide general information while minimizing self-selection bias. Students received extra credit in psychology classes in
100 return for their participation.

One hundred participants completed the research protocol. Since this was the first phase of research comparing Mexican Americans and Anglo Americans, certain inclusion criteria were employed. Using the
105 Acculturation Rating Scale for Mexican Americans (Cuellar, Harris, & Jasso, 1980), Mexican Americans had to be classified as "very Mexican," "Mexican-oriented bicultural," or "syntonic bicultural," not "Anglo-oriented bicultural" or "very Anglicized."
110 The Anglo American group consisted of white, non-Hispanic individuals whose parents were not im-

migrants. All were European-origin "nonethnics," who Spindler and Spindler (1990) have referred to as the "referent ethniclass" (p. 33) of the United States,
115 namely individuals of Anglo-Saxon or northern European Protestant descent, or who adhere to mainstream cultural practices.

The final sample consisted of 40 Mexican Americans and 40 Anglo Americans (20 females and 20
120 males in each group). Their ages ranged from 18 to 25 years ($M = 18.9$, $SD = 1.3$). A separate sample of 16 students (mean age = 29.1, $SD = 7.4$) was employed to investigate test-retest reliability.

Measures

Moral Justification Scale. The Moral Justification
125 Scale (MJS; Gump, 1994), which is the focus of the present study, consists of six dilemmas presented in the form of vignettes. Two involve justice-oriented situations, two involve care-oriented situations, and two are mixed, combining both orientations. For example, the
130 dilemma dealing with the possible breakup of a couple was classified as having a care orientation, as it primarily involves relational issues (i.e., responsiveness toward another person) rather than issues of individual rights and reciprocity between individuals.
135 This is not to say that a justice mode of moral reasoning cannot be used, only that the essence of the dilemma is highly interpersonal. The other care vignette involves a dating dilemma. The justice dilemmas involve cheating on an exam and denting a car. The
140 mixed dilemmas deal with the desire to shoplift to help a sibling and how to handle a friend's drug problem.

The six vignettes were written to be of interest and importance to college students. Furthermore, the names of all protagonists were common for both Anglo
145 Americans and Mexican Americans (e.g., Ana, Michelle, and Tony). Each vignette can have either a male or female protagonist, allowing for counterbalancing. Participants respond to one care, one justice, and one mixed vignette with a male protagonist and one care,
150 one justice, and one mixed vignette with a female protagonist.

After reading the vignette, participants are asked to take a moment to think about what the protagonist should do. They are presented with eight sentences that
155 have been extracted from the vignette, four of which represent care concerns and four of which represent justice concerns. Each is followed by a ten-point scale, with anchors at 1 (not at all important) and 10 (very important); the participant is asked to indicate the im-
160 portance of the item in making a judgment. An example of a care-oriented item is: "Tony was his closest friend, and Marcus didn't want to hurt him by telling the teacher and getting him into trouble." An example of a justice-oriented item is: "Julie glanced up at the
165 sign on the wall which read: 'Shoplifting is illegal.'" A complete justice-oriented vignette, Denting the Car Dilemma (female version), follows.

Julie, a 16-year-old, is having difficulty making a decision. A few days ago, Julie's younger sister, Susanna, had a minor accident with their parents' car. Susanna only had her learner's permit and wasn't allowed to drive without her parents. She had taken the car out anyway and had driven around the neighborhood while her parents were away for the day. Upon her return, Susanna had accidentally dented the car a little by running into a telephone pole while attempting to park. Julie wasn't sure what she should do about this situation, but was seriously considering telling her parents that it was she who had caused the dent instead of Susanna in order to avoid a great deal of family fighting.

Having been in a lot of trouble recently, Susanna had strained her parents' relationship, as they frequently fought over what to do about her being bad. Julie didn't want to cause further strain on her parents' marriage by telling them about Susanna's latest blunder. On the other hand, she didn't want to have to lie about what happened either, as she felt that lying was wrong. Julie was also concerned about covering up for Susanna in this way. She always tried to set a good example for Susanna and didn't want Susanna to think that she could just break the rules whenever she pleased. Besides, Julie didn't want to damage her positive relationship with her parents—she'd worked hard on being close with them and didn't want to risk hurting them by losing their trust. She also worried about her relationship with Susanna. Julie and Susanna had stood up for one another equally in times of trouble in the past, especially when it came to getting in trouble with their parents.

Julie began to wonder what might happen if she told her parents the truth. She had always believed that her parents were too strict in certain areas, and thought that this would probably be one of those areas. More than likely, she thought, their punishment of Susanna would be quite severe, and she didn't want her little sister to have to suffer. If they thought that she had dented the car instead of Susanna, however, they would probably just laugh about it, as she had her driver's license but was just learning how to drive. Besides, Susanna kept it secret last year when Julie skipped school so that she could go to the beach with friends, and she felt she owed Susanna for this. But Julie also realized that the loss of self-respect she would experience might not be worth going along with the story she and Susanna had made up.

Please take a moment to think about what Julie should do, then turn the page and answer the questions.

If you were to make a decision, think about how important each of these statements would be. On a scale from 1 (not at all important) to 10 (very important), please circle the number [1 2 3 4 5 6 7 8 9 10] that indicates how important you think each of the following ideas were in making your decision.

1. Julie didn't want to cause further strain on her parents' marriage by telling them about Susanna's latest blunder.
2. Julie didn't want to have to lie about what happened, as she felt that lying was wrong.
3. Julie didn't want Susanna to think that she could just break the rules whenever she pleased.
4. Julie didn't want to damage her positive relationship with her parents—she'd worked hard on being close with

them and didn't want to risk hurting them by losing their trust.
5. Julie and Susanna had stood up for one another equally in times of trouble in the past, especially when it came to getting in trouble with their parents.
6. More than likely, Julie thought, her parents' punishment of Susanna would be quite severe, and she didn't want her little sister to have to suffer.
7. Susanna kept it secret last year when Julie skipped school so that she could go to the beach with friends, and Julie felt she owed Susanna for this.
8. Julie realized that the loss of self-respect she would experience might not be worth going along with the story she and Susanna had made up.

The Care subscale score is based on responses to the four care items for the six vignettes. Scores across the 24 items are averaged, and thus range from 1 to 10. The Justice subscale is scored similarly.

Miller Social Intimacy Scale. The Miller Social Intimacy Scale (MSIS; Miller & Lefcourt, 1982) is a 17-item self-report inventory designed to assess the level of social intimacy experienced in marriage or friendships. Respondents are asked to rate, on a ten-point scale, their relationship with a spouse or closest friend. Responses are summed to produce a Total score, as well as scores for two subscales, Frequency and Intensity.

Cronbach alpha coefficients of .91 and .86 were reported by Miller and Lefcourt (1982). Test-retest reliability over a one-month interval ($r = .84$, $p < .001$) and two-month interval ($r = .96$, $p < .001$) reflected stability in scores over time (Miller & Lefcourt, 1982). Convergent validity was demonstrated using the UCLA Loneliness Scale (Russell, Peplau, & Ferguson, 1978), $r = -.65$, $p < .001$, and the Interpersonal Relationship Scale (Guerney, 1977), $r = .71$, $p < .001$.

Marlowe-Crowne Social Desirability Scale. The Marlowe-Crowne Social Desirability Scale (SDS; Crowne & Marlowe, 1960) was developed to control for participants who seek to present themselves in an exaggeratedly favorable or unfavorable light. It consists of 33 items, with true-or-false response categories. Crowne and Marlowe reported internal consistency of .88; the test-retest correlation after one month was .89. Construct validity was established through significant positive correlations with the L and K scales of the MMPI (Crowne & Marlowe, 1960).

Acculturation Rating Scale for Mexican Americans. The Acculturation Rating Scale for Mexican Americans (ARSMA; Cuellar, Harris & Jasso, 1980) is a self-report questionnaire designed to assess level of acculturation in both nonclinical and clinical populations. Each of the 20 items on the scale is assigned a value ranging from 1 (extremely Mexican oriented) to 5 (extremely Anglo oriented). The dimensions assessed are language familiarity and usage, ethnic pride and identity, ethnic interaction, cultural heritage, and generational proximity. Five groups of Mexican Americans are identified according to level of acculturation:

very Mexican, Mexican-oriented bicultural, syntonic bicultural, Anglo-oriented bicultural, and very Anglicized.

A coefficient alpha of .88 was obtained for a nonclinical sample. Concurrent validity was demonstrated using the Behavioral Acculturation Scale (Szapocznik, Scopetta, Kurtines, & Aranalde, 1978), rho = .76, p < .001, and the Biculturalism Inventory (Ramirez, Cox, & Castaneda, 1977), rho = .81, p < .001.

Procedure

In a psychology laboratory on the college campus, participants signed a consent form and completed the MJS, MSIS, SDS, and ARSMA in groups of up to 14. Most took about one hour. Upon finishing, participants were debriefed.

Results

Validity of the Moral Justification Scale

To assess construct validity, the 48 MJS items (six vignettes, each with eight items) were rated by eight judges as to whether they represented the care or justice constructs. Judges were clinical psychologists who had taught graduate courses in ethics or developmental psychology, or doctoral candidates in clinical psychology who had taken courses in these areas. The judges were first provided with a brief summary of Gilligan's concepts of care and justice.

For 35 of the items, there was unanimous agreement by the eight judges that the care and justice constructs were accurately represented. There was agreement by seven of the judges for 10 items. The 3 items for which there was agreement by fewer than seven judges were not included in subsequent calculations of MJS scores.

Concurrent validity was assessed via comparison of Care subscale scores and Miller Social Intimacy Scale scores. The MSIS measures interpersonal intimacy and the Care subscale taps interpersonal considerations in moral judgment. While the underlying constructs overlap, they do so only moderately. Therefore, only a modest correlation was expected and, in fact, found (r = .22, p < .05).

Reliability of the Moral Justification Scale

Internal consistency (Cronbach, 1951), split-half reliability, and test-retest reliability were computed for a separate sample of 16 students. Internal consistency and split-half reliability were based on the first administration only, whereas test-retest reliability was calculated using both administrations.

Internal consistency. Cronbach's alpha was .75 for the Care subscale and .64 for the Justice subscale, indicating adequate internal consistency. Because of counterbalancing, it was possible to calculate Cronbach's alpha by sex of the protagonist in each vignette. Alpha levels were expected to be lower than those for the full subscales and, in fact, ranged from .26 to .71.

It was also possible to calculate Cronbach's alpha based on dilemma content (care, justice, or mixed). Alphas ranged from .31 to .57, reflecting marginally acceptable reliability. Examining dilemma content (care, justice, or mixed) by sex of protagonist (male or female) by subscale (Care versus Justice) produced alphas ranging from −.84 to .47, with a mean of .12.

Split-half reliability. Split-half reliability of the Care and Justice subscales was also examined (exclusion of three items, as previously noted, prevented equal representation of dilemmas in each half). For the Care subscale, r = .72, p < .01 (correlation between halves was .91 using Kuder-Richardson Formula 20). For the Justice subscale, r = .60, p < .05 (.75 using Kuder-Richardson Formula 20).

Test-retest reliability. Approximately two weeks after the first administration, the MJS was readministered to the same 16 participants. Test-retest correlations for the Care subscale (r = .61, p < .05) and the justice subscale (r = .69, p < .05) indicated adequate reliability.

Social Desirability

To evaluate whether the 80 participants responded to the vignettes honestly, they were administered the Marlowe-Crowne Social Desirability Scale. The correlations between the SDS and the Care subscale r = −.19) and the Justice subscale (r = −.17) were not significant. Thus, the MJS did not appear to be influenced by social desirability pressures.

Conclusion

The Moral Justification Scale may be a useful alternative to measures based on Kohlberg's system. For example, in clinical work with delinquent children, for whom the nature and style of moral reasoning are important issues, the MJS can be of special help. Those with the capacity to consider the needs and feelings of others (care-oriented) would be distinguished from those with more of a justice orientation. Separate interventions could then be designed and implemented.

Tracking the progress of different groups would itself be of interest, in order to determine whether outcomes differ. Further, with the current focus on values-related education, the MJS could be used to measure how various educational programs produce changes in care or justice orientations, or both.

In accord with the work of Gilligan (1982), Guisinger and Blatt (1994), and other theorists, cross-cultural studies should be undertaken with the MJS. In particular, it would be interesting to determine whether cultures under stress show declines in levels of moral reasoning.

References

Brabeck, M. (1983). Moral judgment: Theory and research on differences between males and females. *Developmental Review, 3*, 274–291.

Cronbach, L. J. (1951). Coefficient alpha and the internal structure of tests. *Psychometrika, 16*, 297–334.

Crown, J., & Heatherington, L. (1989). The cost of winning? The role of gender in moral reasoning and judgments about competitive athletic encounters.
Journal of Sport and Exercise Psychology, 11, 281–289.

Crowne, D. P., & Marlowe, D. C. (1960). Marlowe-Crowne Social Desirability
Scale. *Journal of Consulting Psychology, 24*, 349–354.

Cuellar, I., Harris, L. C., & Jasso, R. (1980). An acculturation scale for Mexican American normal and clinical populations. *Hispanic Journal of Behavioral Sciences, 2*, 199–217.

Friedman, W. J., Robinson, A. B., & Friedman, B. L. (1987). Sex differences
in moral judgments? A test of Gilligan's theory. *Psychology of Women
Quarterly, 11*, 37–46.

Galotti, K. M. (1989). Gender differences in self-reported moral reasoning: A
review and new evidence. *Journal of Youth and Adolescence, 18*, 475–487.

Gibbs, J. C., Arnold, K. D., & Burkhart, J. E. (1984). Sex differences in the
expression of moral judgment. *Child Development, 55*, 1040–1043.

Gilligan, C. (1977). In a different voice: Women's conceptions of self and
morality. *Harvard Educational Review, 47*, 481–517.

Gilligan, C. (1981). Moral development in college years. In A. Chickering
(Ed.), *The modern American college* (pp. 139–157). San Francisco:
Jossey-Bass.

Gilligan, C. (1982). *In a different voice: Psychological theory and women's
development*. Cambridge, MA: Harvard University Press.

Gilligan, C., & Attanucci, J. (1988). Two moral orientations: Gender differences and similarities. *Merrill-Palmer Quarterly, 34*, 223–237.

Guerney, B. G. (1977). *Relationship enhancement*. San Francisco: Jossey-Bass.

Guisinger, S., & Blatt, S. J. (1994). Individuality and relatedness: Evolution of
a fundamental dialectic. *American Psychologist, 49*, 104–111.

Gump, L. S. (1994). *The relationship of culture and gender to moral decision-
making*. Unpublished doctoral dissertation, California School of Professional
Psychology, San Diego, CA.

Kohlberg, L. (1976). Moral stages and moralization. In T. Lickona (Ed.),
Moral development and behavior (pp. 31–53). New York: Holt, Rinehart
and Winston.

Kohlberg, L. (1981). *The philosophy of moral development: Moral stages and
the idea of justice* (Vol. 1. Essays on moral development). New York: Harper
and Row.

Kohlberg, L. (1985). Resolving moral conflicts within the just community. In
C. G. Harding (Ed.), *Moral dilemmas: Philosophical and psychological
issues in the development of moral reasoning* (pp. 71–97). Chicago: Prece-
dent Publishing.

Kohlberg, L., & Kramer, R. (1969). Continuities and discontinuities in childhood and adult moral development. *Human Development, 12*, 93–120.

Lyons, N. P. (1983). Two perspectives: On self, relationships, and morality.
Harvard Educational Review, 53, 125–145.

Miller, J. G., & Bersoff, D. M. (1992). Culture and moral judgment: How are
conflicts between justice and interpersonal responsibilities resolved? *Journal
of Personality and Social Psychology, 62*, 541–554.

Miller, J. G., Bersoff, D. M., & Harwood, R. L. (1990). Perceptions of social
responsibilities in India and in the United States: Moral imperatives or personal decisions? *Journal of Personality and Social Psychology, 58*, 33–47.

Miller, R. S., & Lefcourt, H. M. (1982). The assessment of social intimacy.
Journal of Personality Adjustment, 46, 514–518.

Muuss, R. E. (1988). Carol Gilligan's theory of sex differences in the development of moral reasoning during adolescence. *Adolescence, 23*, 229–243.

Pratt, M. W., Golding, G., Hunter, W., & Sampson, R. (1988). Sex differences
in adult moral orientations. *Journal of Personality, 56*, 373–391.

Ramirez, M., Cox, B., & Castaneda, A. (1977). *The psychodynamics of biculturalism*. (Study prepared for Organizational Research Programs, Office of
Naval Research, Arlington, Virginia.) Santa Cruz, CA: Systems and Evaluations to Education.

Rothbart, M. K., Hanley, D., & Albert, M. (1986). Gender differences in moral
reasoning. *Sex Roles, 15*, 645–653.

Russell, D., Peplau, L. A., & Ferguson, M. L. (1978). Developing a measure of
loneliness. *Journal of Medicine, 60*, 910–921.

Snarey, J. R. (1985). Cross-cultural universality of social-moral development:
A critical review of Kohlbergian research. *Psychological Bulletin, 97*, 202–
232.

Spindler, G., & Spindler, L. (1990). *The American cultural dialogue and its
transmission*. London: Palmer Press.

Szapocznik, J., Scopetta, M. A., Kurtines, W., & Aranalde, M. A. (1978).
Theory and measurement of acculturation. *International Journal of Psychology, 12*, 113–120.

Vasudev, J. (1988). Sex differences in morality and moral orientation: A discussion of the Gilligan and Attanucci study. *Merrill-Palmer Quarterly, 34*,
239–244.

Walker, L. J. (1989). A longitudinal study of moral reasoning. *Child Development, 60*, 157–166.

Address correspondence to: Linda S. Gump, Ph.D., Clinical Psychologist, Psychological HealthCare, PLLC, 110 West Utica,
Oswego, NY 13126.

Exercise for Article 15

Factual Questions

1. Have all previous researchers found gender differences when using more interpersonally oriented
forms of moral reasoning?

2. The "final sample" consisted of how many students?

3. The Moral Justification Scale consists of how many
vignettes?

4. The Marlowe-Crowne Social Desirability Scale
was developed to control for participants who seek
to do what?

5. The judges were in unanimous agreement on how
many of the 48 items?

6. What was the value of the correlation coefficient
for the relationship between Care subscale scores
and Miller Social Intimacy Scale scores?

7. Was the relationship between the social desirability
scores and the Care subscale scores significant?

Questions for Discussion

8. Do you think it was appropriate to describe the
study as only "an investigation of how people make
decisions"? Explain. (See lines 95–97.)

9. How important is the complete vignette in helping
you understand this study? Would the report be just
as strong if the vignette were omitted? Explain.
(See lines 168–243.)

10. What do you think the researchers mean when they
state that ". . . participants were debriefed"? (See
lines 301–302.)

11. How helpful is it to know the test-retest reliability
of the MJS? Do you think it has adequate reliability? (See lines 355–360.)

12. Has this study convinced you that the MJS is reasonably valid? Explain.

Quality Ratings

Directions: Indicate your level of agreement with each of the following statements by circling a number from 5 for strongly agree (SA) to 1 for strongly disagree (SD). If you believe an item is not applicable to this research article, leave it blank. Be prepared to explain your ratings.

A. The introduction establishes the importance of the study.

        SA   5   4   3   2   1   SD

B. The literature review establishes the context for the study.

        SA   5   4   3   2   1   SD

C. The research purpose, question, or hypothesis is clearly stated.

        SA   5   4   3   2   1   SD

D. The method of sampling is sound.

        SA   5   4   3   2   1   SD

E. Relevant demographics (for example, age, gender, and ethnicity) are described.

        SA   5   4   3   2   1   SD

F. Measurement procedures are adequate.

        SA   5   4   3   2   1   SD

G. All procedures have been described in sufficient detail to permit a replication of the study.

        SA   5   4   3   2   1   SD

H. The participants have been adequately protected from potential harm.

        SA   5   4   3   2   1   SD

I. The results are clearly described.

        SA   5   4   3   2   1   SD

J. The discussion/conclusion is appropriate.

        SA   5   4   3   2   1   SD

K. Despite any flaws, the report is worthy of publication.

        SA   5   4   3   2   1   SD

Article 16

The Myth of Peer Pressure

Michael T. Ungar
Memorial University of Newfoundland

ABSTRACT. The construct of peer pressure was examined as part of a qualitative study of the determinants of mental health for 41 high-risk adolescents. While the concept of peer pressure enables adults to explain youths' troubling behaviors, content analysis of the participants' accounts of their lives revealed peer pressure to be a myth. The youths indicated that adoption of the behavior and appearance of peers was a consciously employed strategy to enhance personal and social power. Association with peers was used to construct and maintain health-promoting identities that challenged the stigmatizing labels given to them by others. Three developmental stages to this process of identity construction were identified. During stage one, vulnerable youths learn to maintain a singular self-definition through interaction with peers. In stage two, youths purposefully use their peer relations to experiment with multiple identities. During stage three, youths collaborate with peers as equal partners in the construction of one or more identities for which they find acceptance.

From *Adolescence*, 35, 167–180. Copyright © 2000 by Libra Publishers, Inc. Reprinted with permission.

The construct of peer pressure was examined as part of a larger study investigating the relationship between the process of empowerment and the mental health of high-risk adolescents (Ungar, 1995). It can be
5 defined as pressure from peers to "do something or to keep from doing something else, no matter if you personally want to or not" (Clasen & Brown, 1985, p. 458), and has been used to explain young people's behavior. In the present research, adolescents' personal
10 accounts were compared with data collected from clinical files, family interviews, and focus groups in order to understand peer group interactions and determine whether peer pressure is actually a part of youth culture.
15 Myths shape thinking and provide a convenient way to organize thoughts and experiences (Berger & Luckmann, 1966; Eagleton, 1983; Maturana & Varela, 1987). While people contribute to the meaning of myths through participation in social discourse, or col-
20 lective conversation, the decision as to which myths become prominent and how they are interpreted depends on who has the most power in that discourse (Foucault, 1961/1965, 1972/1980; Weedon, 1987). It

may be adults, not teens, whose description of events is
25 reflected in the term "peer pressure."

Authoring Identity During Adolescence
Identity is the story people tell about themselves (McAdams, 1985, 1995). The language used to construct that story depends on the interpersonal context (Gergen & Davis, 1985; Maturana & Varela, 1987).
30 Marginalized, high-risk youth compete with their parents, mental health professionals, and the broader community for control of the defining labels that contribute to the construction of self-identity. The outcome may have serious consequences. Tyler, Tyler, Tomma-
35 sello, and Connolly (1992), examining the lives of homeless youths in Bogota, Colombia, and Washington, DC, noted: "When I use the words *street youth, delinquents*, and *alienated kids* to describe these youth, I am also separating them from society by words that
40 become labels. Such labels are often inaccurate, stigmatizing, and damaging not only to the children's self-esteem, but to their survival" (p. 206). Similarly, evaluating a self-esteem program for working-class and underclass girls, Simmons and Parsons (1983) found
45 that class bias inherent in the indicators of healthy functioning inadvertently made the girls devalue their knowledge and competencies: They had lower self-esteem *after* participating in the training. Simmons and Parsons concluded that the girls were shown "psycho-
50 logically unreachable roles and coping skills," which heightened their "awareness of the discrepancies between their own lives and the possible alternatives" (p. 922). They came to view themselves as merely "streetwise" (their label) when exposed to middle-class
55 social norms.
While the relationship between the peer group and misconduct has received considerable attention (see Batcher, 1987; Brown, Clasen, & Eicher, 1986; Brown & Lohr, 1987; Clasen & Brown, 1985; Coleman, 1961;
60 Hurrelmann & Engel, 1992; Matza, 1964; Newman & Newman, 1976; Pearl, Bryan, & Herzog, 1990; Simon, Dent, & Sussman, 1997; Ziervogel, Ahmed, Fisher, & Robertson, 1997), the personal agency of individual members has often been ignored. For example, Pearl,
65 Bryan, and Herzog (1990) studied urban and suburban youths with and without learning disabilities and their response to peer pressure. They reported that females felt less pressured than did males to engage in misconduct, learning disabled youths were more likely to en-

70 gage in misconduct, and urban students (mostly from ethnic minority groups) were more likely than their white suburban counterparts to anticipate negative consequences from peers if they refused to engage in misconduct. However, questions arise with regard to why

75 teens choose to associate with peers who are delinquent and why collectively these peer groups choose antisocial behaviors. Do delinquent urban youths from minority cultural groups have as many options to define themselves as powerful and competent as do their

80 white suburban counterparts? Do learning disabled youths find in delinquent acts the personal competence they lack elsewhere in their lives? Why are females more likely to conform to broader social norms?

Other researchers have taken a more optimistic

85 view of the adolescent peer group. They have found it to be necessary for the accomplishment of developmental tasks and critical for cognitive and emotional growth (Furman & Gavin, 1989; Pombeni, Kirchler & Palmonari, 1990; Selman & Shultz, 1989). Pombeni,

90 Kirchler, and Palmonari (1990) have indicated that adolescents who highly identify with their peer group "not only are more inclined to ask other people, peers as well as friends, parents and other adults, for support, to accept their offers of support, and to talk about their

95 problems, but they also seem to be more often able to resolve their problems than low-identifiers" (p. 366). They emphasized that "street groups, although commonly perceived as often close to deviant groups, such as drug abusers or delinquent cliques, provide an

100 equally important and helpful juvenile subculture as formal groups committed to sports, religious programs or politics. The crucial factor is getting involved with peers, sharing thoughts and feelings with the group, rather than the nature of the group itself" (p. 367). At-

105 tachment to the peer group helps the young person avoid the problem of alienation, even when the identification is with a group of delinquents (Hurrelmann & Engel, 1992; Newman & Newman, 1976). In fact, interventions have successfully used the positive aspects

110 of peer relationships to benefit delinquent youth (Gottfredson, 1987; Kuchuck, 1993).

Further, other research has shown the presumed negative influence of the peer group to be exaggerated. For example, after a meta-analysis of the literature,

115 Bauman and Ennett (1996) concluded that peer influence on drug use is overestimated. They argued that the "strong and consistent correlation between drug use by adolescents and the drug use that they attribute to their friends" (p. 186) can be explained by the selection

120 of friends and the projection by adolescents of personal behaviors onto their peers. Bauman and Ennett hypothesized that the causal relationship is the opposite of that implied by the term peer pressure.

Michell and West (1996) investigated the issues of

125 selection and projection in regard to smoking and peer group influences. They found that 12- to 14-year-olds who did not want to smoke "avoided particular social situations and contexts associated with smoking behavior, or chose non-smoking friends, or, if necessary,

130 dropped friends who started to smoke" (p. 47). They concluded: "Data from this study lead us to reject definitions of peer pressure as one-way and coercive, and assumptions about adolescents as socially incompetent and vulnerable.... We agree that individual choice and

135 motivation need to be put back on the drug use agenda and that social processes other than peer pressure need to be acknowledged. These may have more to do with the way like-minded young people group together as friends and then cooperatively develop a 'style' which

140 may, or may not, include smoking" (p. 47).

The present research sought to provide further empirical support for the notion that adolescents exercise personal power through their associations with peers.

Method

In the course of studying the relationship between

145 the process of empowerment and mental health during adolescence (Ungar, 1995), an important question arose: What role do friends and peer groups play in the lives of teenagers? It was thought that experiences of power in relationships with peers might somehow pro-

150 tect high-risk youth against the impact of biopsychosocial risk factors, such as poverty, the mental illness of one or both parents, physical and sexual abuse, family violence, neglect, intellectual and physical challenges, addictions, and mental disorders (e.g., depression).

155 Some combination of three or more of these risk factors were present in the lives of the participants in this research.

The grounded theory approach and qualitative methods used are well-suited to address the above

160 question, as they take into consideration the complexity of interpersonal dynamics without ignoring context (Handel, 1992; Lincoln & Guba, 1985). Glaser and Strauss's (1967) grounded theory approach, with its emphasis on the inductive generation of theory from

165 data, facilitated the discovery of peer processes. Furthermore, it gave participants a great deal of latitude in their exploration of the concept of peer pressure.

Participants

The participants were 41 high-risk adolescents, ages 13 to 18, who had been in therapy within the last

170 12 months. High risk was determined by the presence of three or more of the previously noted biopsychosocial factors known to jeopardize mental health (for a more complete list of the risk factors that predict poor mental health, see Anthony & Cohler, 1987;

175 Cochran, 1988; Garmezy, 1985; Kramer, 1992; Rolf et al., 1990; and Rutter, 1987). The author and at least two other clinicians (with supervisory experience) had to agree that the adolescent showed such characteristics.

180 Participation in the study was voluntary. A small stipend was paid to all the participants to ensure the inclusion of less altruistic youth (Rich, 1968) and to

emphasize the distinction between this research and therapy.

185 Two groups participated. The first group included 21 white adolescents, 12 females and 9 males, from several small urban centers in southwestern Ontario, Canada. Fourteen came directly from the author's clinical practice (individual, group, and family ther-
190 apy); all had been clients for 12–18 months. Seven were referred by other human service workers. All 21 satisfied the eligibility criteria for subsidized counseling services. Interviews with this group were conducted from December 1992 to December 1993.

195 The second group included 4 females and 16 males from a long-term treatment program in a young offenders, closed-custody facility in eastern Canada. Seventeen were white and three were Native Canadians. All of these adolescents and their families were the
200 author's clients for 4–24 months. Interviews with this group were conducted from September 1995 to March 1997.

Difficulties associated with engaging adolescents in interviews, and the related dearth of qualitative studies
205 with this population, provided the motivation and rationale for recruiting participants from the author's clinical practice. The clinical relationships helped establish trust with the youths and their parents, who acted as gatekeepers. Although this approach is un-
210 common, the clinician and ethnographer/researcher roles can be merged when the boundaries between the two are clear (Daly, 1992; Schatzman & Strauss, 1973; Schein, 1987; Snyder, 1992). In the case of the first group, the distinction between the two roles was obvi-
215 ous, as all interviews were conducted after treatment had ended. Given the closed nature of the youth center, role boundaries were more difficult to maintain with the second group, especially during the first interviews, which were conducted while the participants were in
220 custody. To reduce these boundary problems, half of the first round of interviews and three-quarters of the second interviews were conducted by a research assistant.

No clinical distinction was made between youths
225 who found acceptance in socially desirable ways and those who found acceptance as "delinquents," "troublemakers," "victims," and "patients." Instead, the selection of participants was based on variability in the way these adolescents dealt with the risks they faced
230 (several studies, e.g., Hutchinson, Tess, Gleckman, & Spence, 1992, have shown that there are more similarities than differences between clinical and nonclinical groups of at-risk youths).

Data Collection and Analysis

Each teen participated in two interviews lasting one
235 to one-and-a-half hours. The first interview included open-ended questions, covering issues related to adolescence, mental health, relationships, competencies, coping strategies, and experiences of power and con-

trol. Questions regarding relationships with family,
240 peers, and community included: "Who are the important people who have had an influence in your life, before and now?" "Can you tell me about your relationships with your family? Friends? Other people in your community?" Clinical case files, including family
245 data, were reviewed prior to the interviews to gain a better understanding of participants' histories.

The second interviews were used to ensure that the data were trustworthy (Lincoln & Guba, 1985). Participants were asked to comment on the emerging theory.
250 This process, known as dialogic retrospection, helped guide the analysis of the data so as to best reflect the lived experiences of the participants. It also assisted in theory development.

Findings

Power and the Peer Group

Peer groups were described by participants as fo-
255 rums in which to enhance personal power through the assertion of both an individual and a collective identity. Laura (age 14) emphasized the tolerance peers show toward each other. Though her parents are convinced otherwise, Laura noted that her individuality is not
260 compromised by her relationships with peers: "I'm my own unique person and nobody is like me and nobody will ever be just like me. I don't like it when people are the same. People should have their own identity and know who they are." She asserted that she chooses who
265 she associates with on the basis of which relationships enhance her sense of self. "I just stay with my friends who like me and believe in the way I do things and don't believe in what everyone else says."

When asked specifically about their attire, the ado-
270 lescents focused on the unique ways they express their sense of self through clothing. Patricia, a streetwise 14-year-old who was well-known in her community as a leader among other troubled teens, appeared to conform to her peer group in dress and behavior. Yet, she
275 spoke extensively about how she differs from her peers: "Everybody knows this about me, that I dress for me—nobody else.... Like one day I'll wear nice preppy clothes, then the next I'll wear huge jeans that fall off my butt. Like if I think a big long skirt is neat, and if
280 my friends don't like it, I'll say, 'Don't look at it then.'" Casual observers overlook the subtle differences in this form of personal expression.

Kevin, a 15-year-old "delinquent," saw himself as different from other delinquents because, he said, "I
285 always help my friends out when they have problems, and I give good advice." Stephanie, age 16, who had problems with truancy and violent behavior, insisted she is different from her closest friends because she does not drink, wanting to avoid becoming an alcoholic
290 like her mother and aunts and uncles. In each case, apparent conformity hid the important power these adolescents had within the peer group to be themselves.

Three Developmental Stages of Power

In three stages, adolescents progress toward greater power and self expression in their interactions with peers, family members, and others in the community. Though these stages are sequential, high-risk teens move back and forth between them as they attempt to cope with the multiple problems they face.

During the first developmental stage, high-risk teens are *stuck* with one self-definition. Although some choice may be exercised in the selection of this identity, there are few alternatives from which to choose. The peer group helps to reinforce the one label the individual teen controls. These teens typically include the repeat offender whose only talent is getting into trouble, the suicidal youth who has few other coping strategies, and the youth who sacrifices his or her needs for the needs of others.

The second developmental stage is reached when teens become *chameleons*. They appear to adopt the labels available to them from the different groups of people with whom they interact, including peers. These youths are the ones who do fine in school, but act violently toward themselves or others when at home, or appear confident when in leadership positions, but surprise adults with their lack of self-esteem.

The third developmental stage is achieved when youths experience the control and competence necessary to construct self-definitions of their own choosing, which are *accepted* by peers, family, and community members. These are resilient, self-assured individuals who steadfastly proclaim to the world, "This is who I am. Accept me." They use the peer group to assert unique aspects of their identity. Although they may be gifted at sports or academics, many act out socially (for example, running away from home as a result of physical or sexual abuse).

The following case histories help illustrate these three stages of development.

Being Stuck

Tommy (age 16) has attempted to cope with his circumstances by finding one powerful self-definition and tenaciously holding on to it.

In the presence of adults, Tommy is quiet, withdrawn. He is a strong, good-looking young man who has been in and out of jail and foster homes throughout his adolescence. Tommy's mother has moved the family many times throughout her son's life. She talked of five different men who were the fathers of her eight children; in some cases, she was not quite certain who was the father of which child. Alcoholism, spousal abuse, and child abuse characterize the history of this family. Of his siblings, Tommy most idealizes his 17-year-old brother, Jason, who is in a provincial jail (serving a one-year sentence for theft and assault). "No one messes with him," Tommy explained.

Tommy described his friends as being like "brothers." He tries his best to keep up friendships with boys he used to know in other places. He hopes that his mother will stay in one city, though her present partner is violent and an alcoholic and it appears unlikely she will stay with him long. The family has only welfare coming in, which means there is no money for Tommy to join a hockey or football team. He attends school sporadically, and hopes one day to become a mechanic, though at the moment takes no automotive classes.

Despite this bleak picture, Tommy did very well while in detention, maintaining his level of privileges and learning to control his anger. He felt good about the advances he made in his schoolwork and enjoyed the many sporting activities provided for the boys. Now out of custody, he spends most of his time hanging around with friends, intimidating other people, but not breaking the law.

Given the problems confronting him at home, Tommy's "solution" has been to construct the one powerful identity that is readily available to him: delinquent. In and out of custody, Tommy finds peers who accept him in this one way, and who reflect back to him his status as a troublemaker. Even when Tommy tries to be something other than a delinquent, he remains stuck with this label. Unable to construct another self-definition, he tries to sustain the image of a "tough guy" among his peers: "I want people to think I'm tough."

The Chameleon

Becoming unstuck is most often accomplished through the serendipitous discovery and acquisition of another label. The life histories of the participants show how chance encounters with new groups of peers and adults, though circumscribed by socioeconomic forces, offer opportunities to construct a new identity.

In their search for acceptance, high-risk teens may share their power of self-definition with others through superficial conformity. Conformity brings a measure of acceptance within the group, and allows the vulnerable youth to use group identity to appear more powerful than he or she feels otherwise. The chameleon-like coping strategies of Tanya (age 14) are typical.

Tanya is a pleasant young woman, plain in her features and not very popular with her peers. She and her four-year-old brother, Brian, live with their mother. Tanya sees her father every second weekend. The couple divorced three years ago. At first, the children lived with their father due to their mother's emotional instability (she was under psychiatric care for 18 months). During that time, Tanya took over the "mother role" with regard to her younger brother and acted "as a wife" for her father. She was responsible for all the housework while also attending school full-time.

Tanya has done well in school and has become involved in the politics of her low-income housing project. She is very proud of her recent appointment to the board of the recreation center. She makes a good impression on adults, though she has only a few close friends her own age. She tries desperately to fit in with her peers by adopting their mannerisms, but is seldom accepted as much by them as she is by adults.

Tanya has once been caught shoplifting, having sto-

410 len a few cosmetics that she said her family could not afford. Tanya spends most of her time away from home, involved in extracurricular activities.

Tanya's ability to fit in with adults, as well as her constant effort to make new friends with peers, helps her avoid feelings of alienation and depression. She has
415 created a large network of relationships that sustain many different identities, though she asserts little influence, especially with her peers, over the labels she is given in each setting. Tanya explained: "I change when I'm in a particular environment. How I'm talking here
420 is not how I talk anywhere else. I'm a totally different person here than I am with my mom or my dad. I'm never the totally same person in every spot. I don't want people to know me totally, just a little bit about me. Feels better that way."
425 This changeability is not simply a function of her age and the associated search for identity (McAdams, 1985). Tanya alters who she is with each group of peers and adults she encounters because she lacks influence over how the labels given to her are con-
430 structed. Playing the chameleon helps teens like Tanya learn and practice the social skills they need to develop a self-definition of their own choosing.

What, then, moves a teen forward to the next stage of development, in which he or she has the power to
435 create an identity? The 41 case studies gathered in this research indicate that teens progress when they must assert an identity that does not conform to the group into which they have integrated. This divergence may occur when the teen's morality is transgressed by
440 peers. For example, David, whose chaotic life includes being bounced back and forth between a verbally abusive and alcoholic father and a battered and depressed mother, reached his moral limit when he learned that some of his peers were planning to burglarize the home
445 of a close friend. He refused to participate. His individuation from the group is not a separation from his peers, but a more equitable sharing with them in the way the group defines itself.

Acceptance

In the third stage, the high-risk teen shares in the
450 construction of one or more identities. Several of the participants, such as Melissa, had achieved this level of power.

Melissa, age 15, and her mother, father, and older sister requested counseling to help Melissa cope with her
455 father's mental illness. Her father was diagnosed with manic-depression after spending thousands of dollars on a trip to the United States and then becoming violent during a confrontation with border guards when returning to Canada. Her mother has had to work long hours to get
460 the family out of debt, while her father has been at home where he fights with the children.

Although Melissa's father is now on medication and his behavior is under control, her mother is still very anxious and worried. Neither parent has had much time
465 for Melissa in the last two years. She has been expected to replace her mother around the home and keep it running well. Melissa says she only gets attention when she does not do what she is told.

Her parents say Melissa used to be a "good girl," al-
470 ways helping around the home, never upset, and pleasant to be around. At the time the family began counseling, Melissa was said to be suicidal, truant from school, sexually active, smoking, spending money "frivolously," and refusing to go to church. Melissa had just come back after
475 running away for two days, during which time she tried to harm herself. Melissa explained that she felt like she was being expected to be the "mother" while at home, and that she did not feel ready or able to do the job. She longed for things to be back to how they were before her
480 father's illness.

With her peers, Melissa is outgoing and assertive. She has a boyfriend, and insists that she maintains a great deal of say over how she expresses her sexuality. She feels comfortable being who she is when out of the home.
485 She also likes to break with the gender norms of her peers, and is very proud of her success in an automotive course.

Melissa's search for a positive self-definition has taken her out of her home, where she is seen as a "sub-
490 stitute mother." Her self-constructed identity within the peer group enhances how she feels about herself. With her peers, she is accepted both as a member of a group and as a unique individual. She stated: "I make all my own choices. Like being with a guy or not, and who my
495 friends are, and if I smoke or if I don't smoke."

Other high-risk teens demonstrated this capacity to exercise control over the labels assigned to them. Johnny, a former addict, organized a Narcotics Anonymous group for young people in his community.
500 He had used his time in custody to create a new identity for himself. Troy recently confronted his abusive father about the emotional and physical abuse he suffered as a child, changed peer groups, and nurtured other friendships. Beth, an ecologically minded young
505 woman, gained self-esteem from participation in social causes. This, in turn, helped her deal with the chaos in her family. These are just a few of the paths high-risk youths have followed in constructing identities that bring them acceptance and power.

Conclusion

510 The concept of peer pressure leads to the belief that the peer group demands conformity to its norms, which may include delinquency. The notion that adolescents experience anxiety or frustration when unable to follow "the dictums of their peers" (Brown et al., 1986) sup-
515 ports the idea that teens sacrifice personal agency. However, the high-risk youths in the present study provided a different perspective. The peer group was experienced as a forum in which to participate in the collective construction of both a group and individual iden-
520 tity. Arguably, both group and individual status reflect the ability to convince others of self-worth (Varenne, 1982).

525 By exploiting opportunities available to them through the peer group, high-risk youths challenge the stigmatizing labels assigned to them by their families and community. As they participate with peers in the creation of self-definitions, they move from feelings of worthlessness and disempowerment to confidence and well-being.

530 In sum, peer pressure was revealed to be a myth that enables adults to explain youths' troubling behaviors. Rather, the high-risk adolescents in the present study indicated that adoption of the behavior and appearance of peers was a consciously employed strategy 535 to enhance personal and social power.

References

Anthony, E. J., & Cohler, B. J. (Eds.). (1987). *The invulnerable child*. New York: Guilford Press.

Batcher, E. (1987). Building the barriers: Adolescent girls delimit the future. In G. H. Nemiroff (Ed.), *Women and men: Interdisciplinary readings on gender* (pp. 150-164). Montreal: Fitzhenny and Whiteside.

Bauman, K. E., & Ennett, S. T. (1996). On the importance of peer influence for adolescent drug use: Commonly neglected considerations. *Addiction, 91*(2), 185-198.

Berger P. L., & Luckmann, T. (1966). *The social construction of reality*. New York: Anchor.

Brown, B. B., Clasen, D. R., & Eicher, S. A. (1986). Perceptions of peer pressure, peer conformity dispositions, and self-reported behavior among adolescents. *Developmental Psychology, 22*(4), 521-530.

Brown, B. B., & Lohr, M. N. (1987). Peer-group affiliation and adolescent self-esteem: An integration of ego-identity and symbolic-interaction theories. *Journal of Personality and Social Psychology, 52*(1), 47-55.

Campbell, J. (1988). *The power of myth*. New York: Doubleday.

Clasen, D. R., & Brown, B. B. (1985). The multidimensionality of peer pressure in adolescence. *Journal of Youth and Adolescence, 14*(6), 451-468.

Cochran, M. M. (1988). Addressing youth and family vulnerability: Empowerment in an ecological context. *Canadian Journal of Public Health, 79* (Suppl. 2), 510-516.

Coleman, J. S. (1961). *The adolescent society*. New York: The Free Press.

Daly, K. (1992). The fit between qualitative research and characteristics of families. In J. F. Gilgun, K. Daly, & G. Handel (Eds.), *Qualitative methods in family research* (pp. 3-11). Newbury Park, CA: Sage.

Eagleton, T. (1983). *Literary theory: An introduction*. Minneapolis, MN: University of Minnesota Press.

Foucault, M. (1965). *Madness and civilization: A history of insanity in the age of reason* (R. Howard, Trans.). New York: Pantheon. (Original work published 1961).

Foucault, M. (1980). *Power/knowledge* (C. Gordon, L. Marshall, J. Mepham, & K. Soper, Trans.). New York: Pantheon Books. (Original work published 1972).

Furman, W., & Gavin, L. A. (1989). Peers' influence on adjustment and development. In T. J. Berndt & G. W. Ladd (Eds.), *Peer relationships in child development* (pp. 319-340). New York: John Wiley & Sons.

Garmezy, N. (1985). Stress-resistant children: The search for protective factors. In J. E. Stevenson (Ed.), *Recent research in developmental psychopathology* (pp. 213-233). New York: Pergamon.

Gergen, K. J., & Davis, K. (Eds.) (1985). *The social construction of the person*. New York: Springer-Verlag.

Glaser, B. G., & Strauss, A. L. (1967). *The discovery of grounded theory: Strategies for qualitative research*. New York: Aldine de Gruyter.

Goffman, E. (1961). *Asylums: Essays on the social situation of mental patients and other inmates*. Chicago: Aldine.

Gottfredson, G. D. (1987). Peer group interventions to reduce the risk of delinquent behavior: A selective review and a new evaluation. *Criminology, 25*(3), 671-714.

Handel, G. (1992). The qualitative tradition in family research. In J. F. Gilgun, K. Daly, & G. Handel (Eds.), *Qualitative methods in family research* (pp. 12-21). Newbury Park, CA: Sage.

Hurrelmann, K., & Engel, U. (1992). Delinquency as a symptom of adolescents' orientation toward status and success. *Journal of Youth and Adolescence, 21*(1), 119-138.

Hutchinson, R. L., Tess, D. E., Gleckman, A. D., & Spence, W. C. (1992). Psychosocial characteristics of institutionalized adolescents: Resilient or at risk? *Adolescence, 27*(106), 339-356.

Kramer, M. (1992). Barriers to the primary prevention of mental, neurological, and psychosocial disorders of children: A global perspective. In G. W. Albee, L. A. Bond, & T. V. Cook Monsey (Eds.), *Improving children's lives: Global perspectives on prevention* (pp. 3-36). Newbury Park, CA: Sage.

Kuchuck, S. (1993). Understanding and modifying identifications in an adolescent boys therapy group. *Journal of Child and Adolescent Group Therapy, 3*(4), 189-201.

Laing, R. D., & Esterson, A. (1964). *Sanity, madness, and the family*. Harmondsworth, England: Penguin.

Lincoln, Y. S., & Guba, E. G. (1985). *Naturalistic inquiry*. Newbury Park, CA: Sage.

Maturana, H. R., & Varela, F. J. (1987). *The tree of knowledge*. Boston: New Science Library/Shambhala.

Matza, D. (1964). *Delinquency and drift*. New York: John Wiley & Sons.

McAdams, D. P. (1985). *Power, intimacy, and the life story*. Homewood, IL: Dorsey.

McAdams, D. P. (1995). *The stories we live by*. New York: William Morrow.

Michell, L., & West, P. (1996). Peer pressure to smoke: The meaning depends on the method. *Health Education Research, 11*(1), 39-49.

Newman, P. R., & Newman, B. M. (1976). Early adolescence and its conflict: Group identity versus alienation. *Adolescence, 11*(42), 261-274.

Pearl, R., Bryan, T., & Herzog, A. (1990). Resisting or acquiescing to peer pressure to engage in misconduct: Adolescents' expectations of probable consequences. *Journal of Youth and Adolescence, 19*(1), 43-55.

Pombeni, M. L., Kirchler, E., & Palmonari, A. (1990). Identification with peers as a strategy to muddle through the troubles of the adolescent years. *Journal of Adolescence, 13,* 351-369.

Rich, J. (1968). *Interviewing children and adolescents*. London: MacMillan.

Rolf, J., Masten, A. S., Ciccetti, D., Nuechterlein, K. H., & Weintraub, S. (Eds.). (1990). *Risk and protective factors in the development of psychopathology*. Cambridge, MA: Cambridge University Press.

Rutter, M. (1987). Psychosocial resilience and protective mechanisms. *American Journal of Orthopsychiatry, 57*(3), 316-331.

Schatzman, L., & Strauss, A. L. (1973). *Field research*. Englewood Cliffs, NJ: Prentice-Hall.

Schein, E. H. (1987). *The clinical perspective in fieldwork*. Newbury Park, CA: Sage.

Selman, R. L., & Schultz, L. H. (1989). Children's strategies for interpersonal negotiation with peers. In T. J. Berndt & G. W. Ladd (Eds.), *Peer relationships in child development* (pp. 371-406). New York: John Wiley & Sons.

Simmons, C. H., & Parsons, R. J. (1983). Developing internality and perceived competence: The empowerment of adolescent girls. *Adolescence, 18*(72), 917-922.

Simon, T. R., Dent, C. W., & Sussman, S. (1997). Vulnerability to victimization, concurrent problem behaviors, and peer influence as predictors of in-school weapon carrying among high school students. *Violence and Victims, 12*(3), 277-289.

Snyder, S. U. (1992). Interviewing college students about their constructions of love. In J. F. Gilgun, K. Daly, & G. Handel (Eds.), *Qualitative methods in family research* (pp. 43-65). Newbury Park, CA: Sage.

Szasz, T. S. (1961). *The myth of mental illness*. New York: Hoeber-Harper.

Tyler, F. B., Tyler, S. L., Tommasello, A., & Connolly, M. R. (1992). Huckleberry Finn and street youth everywhere: An approach to primary prevention. In G. W. Albee, L. A. Bond, & T. V. Cook Monsey (Eds.), *Improving children's lives: Global perspectives on prevention* (pp. 200-212). Newbury Park, CA: Sage.

Ungar, M. (1995). *A naturalistic study of the relationship between the process of empowerment and mental health during adolescence*. Doctoral dissertation, Wilfrid Laurier University, Waterloo, Ontario, Canada.

Varenne, H. (1982). Jocks and freaks: The symbolic structure of the expression of social interaction among American senior high school students. In G. Spindler (Ed.), *Doing the ethnography of schooling* (pp. 210-235). New York: Holt, Rinehart and Winston.

Weedon, C. (1987). *Feminist practice and poststructuralist theory*. Cambridge, MA: Blackwell.

Ziervogel, C. F., Ahmed, N., Fisher, A. J., & Robertson, B. A. (1997). Alcohol misuse in South African male adolescents: A qualitative investigation. *International Quarterly of Community Health Education, 17*(1), 25-41.

Note: This study was supported by a grant from the Social Sciences and Humanities Research Council of Canada. Special thanks to Eli Teram, Geoffrey Nelson, Patricia Kelley, and Isaac Prilleltensky for their assistance in conducting this research.

Address correspondence to: Michael T. Ungar, School of Social Work, Memorial University of Newfoundland, St. John's, Newfoundland, Canada A1C 5S7.

Exercise for Article 16

Factual Questions

1. How did Clasen & Brown (1985) define peer pressure?

2. What biopsychosocial risk factors were present in the adolescents in this study?

3. What was the sample size for this study?

4. Each teen participated in how many interviews? How long did the interviews last?

5. The second interviews were used to ensure what?

6. According to the researcher, what is the *third* developmental stage?

7. The researcher concludes that adolescents in this study experienced the peer group as a forum in which to participate in the collective construction of what two things?

Questions for Discussion

8. In the table of contents of this book, this research article is classified as "qualitative." Do you agree that it is qualitative? Why? Why not?

9. Based on correlational studies, one could argue that peers influence friends to use drugs *or* that adolescents who are inclined to use drugs select similar friends. Do you think one of these possibilities is better than the other? Explain. (See lines 112–140.)

10. Most of the participants in this research were clients in the researcher's clinical practice. In your opinion, is this a strength or weakness of the study? Explain. (See lines 188–190.)

11. In your opinion, does this study provide strong evidence that peer pressure is a myth? Explain.

12. If you were to conduct another study on the same topic, what changes in the research methodology would you make, if any?

Quality Ratings

Directions: Indicate your level of agreement with each of the following statements by circling a number from 5 for strongly agree (SA) to 1 for strongly disagree (SD). If you believe an item is not applicable to this research article, leave it blank. Be prepared to explain your ratings.

A. The introduction establishes the importance of the study.

    SA   5   4   3   2   1   SD

B. The literature review establishes the context for the study.

    SA   5   4   3   2   1   SD

C. The research purpose, question, or hypothesis is clearly stated.

    SA   5   4   3   2   1   SD

D. The method of sampling is sound.

    SA   5   4   3   2   1   SD

E. Relevant demographics (for example, age, gender, and ethnicity) are described.

    SA   5   4   3   2   1   SD

F. Measurement procedures are adequate.

    SA   5   4   3   2   1   SD

G. All procedures have been described in sufficient detail to permit a replication of the study.

    SA   5   4   3   2   1   SD

H. The participants have been adequately protected from potential harm.

    SA   5   4   3   2   1   SD

I. The results are clearly described.

    SA   5   4   3   2   1   SD

J. The discussion/conclusion is appropriate.

    SA   5   4   3   2   1   SD

K. Despite any flaws, the report is worthy of publication.

    SA   5   4   3   2   1   SD

Article 17

Virtual Corporeality: Adolescent Girls and Their Bodies in Cyberspace

Kerrie Michelle Smyres
Arizona State University

ABSTRACT. This piece, framed in a critical feminist perspective, explores the relationship adolescent girls have with their bodies and how they share these experiences with their peers. Through qualitative analysis of the interactions of members of gURL, an online community for teenaged girls, themes of compulsory heterosexuality and the desire to attract boys are examined in relation to body dissatisfaction. Perhaps more significantly, issues surrounding ethnography and the Internet, including questions of the possible need for informed consent in a private public space, the reality of cyberspace experience, and the nature of the population of Internet users, are also explored and addressed.

From *Cybersociology*, (www.cybersociology.com) *6*, 1-18. Copyright © 1999 by Kerrie Michelle Smyres. Reprinted with permission.

Rationale

Please help me. I know i am on the way to anorexia, but i cant stop myself. I know I am fat, and i WANT to be annorexic. I know it is very harmful, but i cannot lose any weight. I need some more alternitives before really am in trouble. Please Please help me. — ScorpioSistah, anorexia, 3/17/99

This comment, obtained through my participant observation experience and uttered by a teenage girl, encapsulates the impetus for this project. Bodies are problematic for many, if not all, girls and women. As illustration of this point, Garner (1997) discovered that body dissatisfaction is increasing at a faster rate than ever before among both men and women; among the 3,452 female respondents in this study, 89% desired to lose weight (p. 34). These findings are especially problematic for women and are affecting them at younger and younger ages. A study of 36,000 students in Minnesota found that girls with negative body image were three times more likely than boys of the same age to say that they feel bad about themselves and were more likely to believe that others see them in a negative light. The study also found that negative body image is associated with suicide risk for girls, not for boys (American Association of University Women, 1990). As Wooley and Wooley (1984) discovered, girls are more influenced, and thus, more vulnerable to, cultural standards of ideal body images, than boys are. Recently, a national health study found that 40% of the 2,379 nine- and ten-year-old girls studied were trying to lose weight (Schreiber, Pike, Wilfley, & Rodin, 1995). Similarly, a study of almost five hundred schoolgirls reveals that 81% of the ten-year-olds had dieted at least once (Mellin, Scully & Irwin, 1986). It is disheartening to note that these studies are merely examples from the plethora of body image research that indicates that women and girls are dissatisfied with and worried about their bodies.

Even without the aforementioned studies, it is readily noticeable that adolescent girls are concerned about their bodies. Magazines targeted to this demographic (nearly all of which have a photograph of a beautiful, thin woman on the cover) consist of little except suggestions for looking great for that boy, how to get rid of pimples once and for all, and methods for minimizing the appearance of cellulite. The cultural ideal body size for women, as portrayed by models, is unattainable for most women and is likely to lead to feelings of self-devaluation, depression and helplessness (Rodin, Silberstein, & Striegel-Moore, 1984). Women and girls are also consistently taught from an early age that their self-worth is largely dependent on how they look. The fact that women earn more money than men in only two job categories, modeling and prostitution, serves to illustrate this point (Wolf, 1992).

Scholars are now generally aware of the internalized beliefs and lived consequences of the all-consuming desire for beauty, but few have discussed these experiences in women's own words. Those who do tend to describe women's experiences without overt discussion of the different experiences one encounters at different stages in life (see Spitzack, 1990a, 1990b; Hesse-Biber, 1996). Others focus on one specific activity of a variety of women (see Smythe, 1995). Interestingly, there are very few studies that enable adolescent girls, who are at the stage of entering into a woman's body, to discuss their experience. A large majority of those that do so rely primarily on interviews between adult researchers and adolescent respondents (Grogan & Wainwright, 1996; Guillen & Barr, 1994; Lerner & Brackney, 1978). Additionally, the lines between eating disorders and body image are often blurred, with a heavy focus usually on anorexia and bulimia (see Chernin, 1981, 1985; Pipher, 1995).

The turbulence of adolescence, filled with struggles and secrecy, causes one to question how much information teenage girls are willing to comfortably disclose to adults. Thus, it is necessary to examine the experience of adolescent girls in their own words and on their own terms without apparent adult intervention. Brumberg (1997) begins this exploration through examination of adolescent diaries throughout the twentieth century and discusses a wide range of the tribulations of teen years throughout history. In addition, it is important to examine how girls feel about particular topics in a limited space and time. In an attempt to provide a more narrow look at the lives of adolescent girls at the end of the twentieth century, I observed participants in what appears to be a safe space where I could be unobtrusive, a Web site devoted to teenage girls and adolescent struggles (www.gURL.com).

As a critical feminist with profoundly painful memories of my adolescent experience of my body, I am in a particularly vulnerable position. My primary desire is to begin to type furiously and share my new-found self-assurance with these girls. Of course, I realize that my acceptance of my body, while better than it was in high school, is still not altogether positive. More important, I know that my altered perspective came from years of struggle and self-education and that I cannot send a magic bullet that will soothe the strife of these girls. Also, I recognize, fundamentally, that the struggle has been beneficial for me and know that this is just one more aspect of uncovering enough of one's identity. This background is necessary to understand that I have a deep emotional investment in the topic and, consequently, a personal commitment to the participants. Additionally, this history has enabled me to become critical of the systemic and relational factors that influence how a woman learns and maintains her view of her body. It is important to recognize my position as it influences the way I view the world and the data. As such, discussion of my experiences with my body, the data, and the findings are threaded throughout this discussion.

Ethnography on the World Wide Web

The elusive nature of the Internet may raise questions regarding the site choice. Before these issues are addressed, it is important to recognize the numerous reasons that a Web site is an ideal place to begin research on such a sensitive topic. One of the most pressing concerns is that teenagers are a difficult population to approach as they are considered minors and, thus, parental consent is necessary. Although such consent is not as pressing for an observation-based study, ethical issues arise in doing so. Within these constraints, studying teenagers acting and interacting in a natural environment is nearly impossible. I considered eavesdropping in the dressing rooms of teen

clothing stores, but was concerned that bodies would be on the forefront of discussion in this instance. Furthermore, the history one has with a close friend, a likely shopping partner, might obscure the information I was trying to gain by only providing part of the story. I also wanted them to remain anonymous while discussing intimate life issues, for their sake and mine. As mentioned, one fear is that I would make judgments about the validity of complaints. Finally, and perhaps most important, I wanted them to be in a safe space, one that they had specifically chosen, and one where they felt comfortable to speak their minds.

It may be easy and appropriate to some to consider the Internet as simply another communication channel, and many Web-based studies have explored the Internet in just that fashion (Paccagnella, 1997). Those who have begun to research this vast, unknown world from the perspective of social constructivism reveal that the Internet is much more than a medium. Turkle (1996) examines anthropologist Ray Oldenberg's writings about "the 'great good place'—the local bar, the bistro, the coffee shop–where members of a community can gather for easy company, conversation, and a sense of belonging." Oldenberg considers these places to be the "heart of individual social integration and community vitality" (paragraph 1). Turkle comments that coffee-houses and cafes have experienced a resurgence in recent years, but "most of them do not serve, much less recreate, coherent communities and, as a result, the odor of nostalgia often seems as strong as the espresso" (paragraph 1). Where, then, does one go for this community? Many (see Masterson, 1997; Meyer, 1997; Nunes, 1995; Turkle, 1996) argue that people are creating a much-needed sense of community in the virtual world. Rheingold (1993) proffers a similar definition based on his extensive personal experience in the on-line world. He defines virtual communities as "social aggregations that emerge from the Net when enough people carry on those public discussions long enough, with sufficient human feeling, to form webs of personal relationships in cyberspace" (p. 5). While some may, at first, discount the Web as nothing more than an alternative medium, it is evident that others believe that the Internet contains an intricately woven web of complex relationships and communities. Furthermore, some studies show that online interactions can be even more social and rule-governed than more traditional media (see Spears and Lea, 1992, 1994).

The kinds of community found on the Internet are unique because they are not based on proximity, as so many relationships are, but on shared interests. These relations are what Haraway (1991) refers to as "affinity groups—related not by blood, but by choice" (p. 155). Rheingold (1993) agrees with this assertion and furthers it by claiming that virtual communities exist at "a specific place...and time" but it is "a cognitive and social [place], not a geographical one" (61).

185 The primary research published on computer mediated communication (CMC) focuses on multiuser dimensions (MUDs), virtual communities where users interact through typed commands as characters they have created who exist in an online society with typical
190 social ills and expectations. Although gURL does not include the diverse elements typically seen in a MUD or a physical community, this site still serves a crucial function in creating a sense of community for adolescent girls all over the world.

195 Another aspect of the Internet that is regarded positively is its role in locating a space for one's voice. Through the examination of stories of seasoned "MUDers," Turkle asserts that "These young people feel they have no political voice, and they look to cy-
200 berspace to help them find one" (1996, paragraph 21). Turkle invokes Radaway's argument that women often use romance novels not for "escaping but building realities less limited than their own. Romance reading becomes a form of resistance, a challenge to the stulti-
205 fying categories of everyday life" (1996, paragraph 33). According to Turkle, Radaway's perspective can allow us to regard online communities as places of resistance to a multitude of avenues of oppression. Similarly, I argue that the adolescent girls that frequent
210 gURL are searching for their own voices in a patriarchal culture that devalues the input of "kids."

One frequent objection to Web-based research is that there is no foolproof way to verify the identity of participants. As Deetz (lecture, 4/23/99) argues, iden-
215 tity is an ever-changing construction that is constantly created and recreated as a conglomeration of personal and social experiences. With this definition of identity, identities are never fixed and, as such, it is nearly impossible to know, with a capital K, identity no matter
220 how extensive the interaction is. Within this perspective, a more accurate way to address the objections of Web research is that a researcher can never be sure of the demographics of site users. This is absolutely correct; there is no possible way to obtain confirmation of
225 this information. Even though gURL states that only girls 13 and older are allowed to access the site and requires that users register with their names, email addresses, birthdate and birthplace, even the site owners cannot verify the age or sex of each user. Additionally,
230 although the vast majority of users are adolescents, gURL acknowledges that a fair number of users identify themselves as college age.

Beyond relying on a "gut feeling" about each posting, there are important considerations that can be
235 made to assuage one's fears about user demographics. To begin with, the researcher can participate in and/or examine a variety of Web sites to ascertain general interaction patterns and discussion topics based on the site's requested user demographics. Before choosing
240 gURL as the ethnographic site, I visited 14 other online communities where women's bodies were designated as important topics of conversation and, thus, had bul-

letin boards specifically for the topic. The requested users for different sites included only girls under 15,
245 girls and women age 13-35, teenage boys and girls, only girls and women, all men, boys, women and girls, only men and women over the age of 18, and all men, boys, women and girls under the age of 25. Becoming familiar with the type of information discussed and the
250 diverse methods of approaching and responding to topics on these different sites provided invaluable information about the demographics of site users. For example, on the sites that are specifically for girls and/or women, the topics typically revolve around their
255 dislike of their bodies, complaints about not getting dates, and assurances that their bodies "aren't that bad" or that "not all men are creeps." Furthermore, occasional announcements are made that a man or boy has entered the site and he provides his perspective. The
260 sites that attract men, boys, women and girls tend to contain postings that request the perspective of the "opposite" sex or adversarial debates on the enactment of social ideals. Obviously, the researcher cannot verify the demographics of the users, but different types of
265 conversations appear to occur when sexes are mixed, either by invitation or intrusion. Furthermore, users on "girl only" sites asked boys to leave the bulletin board or chat room and chastised girls who requested that boys join the conversation on the site.

270 Additionally, site users regulate those who do not fit the expectations of the site. An interesting discussion occurred on gURL right before I began data collection that highlights this process. The name brat_4_ever was found frequently in many of the "body
275 issue" forums, yet the questions asked were inconsistent. Many other users noted the discrepancies and brought them to the attention of brat_4_ever and every other user. An example of this is from piklegrl who posted,

280 Honey, STOP BULLSHITTING EVERY-ONE AND START TELLING THE TRUTH. YOU ARE WASTING OUR TIME WITH YOUR PEICE OF CRAP STORIES. YOU ARE 9 AT ONE TIME, THEN YOU ARE 12, AND YESTERDAY YOU WERE ASKING WHAT
285 SEX IS BECAUSE YOU AND YOUR GIRLFRIEND WERE GOING TO HAVE SEX. IF YOU ARE JUST GOING TO LIE OUT YOUR ASS, THEN GO SOMEWHERE ELSE, CAUSE I'M SURE NO ONE WANTS TO WASTE THEIR TIME WITH YOUR
290 BULLCRAP. Thank-you and please.....GO AWAY! (bras, 3/7/99)

At least nine other users posted similar responses to brat_4_ever, and every other one included requests for brat_4_ever to quit wasting their time because the site
295 users had "real problems" to attend to.

Methods

The Scene

The mission statement and description of gURL provide exquisite insight into the intentions of the site.

gURL is a different approach to the experience of being a teenage girl. We are committed to discussing issues that affect the lives of girls age 13 and up in a nonjudgmental, personal way. Through honest writing, visuals and liberal use of humor, we try to give girls a new way of looking at subjects that are crucial to their lives. Our content deals frankly with sexuality, emotions, body image, etc. If this is a problem for you, you might not like it here.

The gURL site was launched in April 1996 [as a class project of three college women at the Interactive Telecommunications Program at New York University]. At our readers' enthusiastic requests, we created the gURL connection a year later as a members-only area for communicating and exchanging ideas online. The site states that our community extends and extends from our content. We hope to provide connection and identification in a way that is not possible in other media. (http://www.gURL/hq/info/)

Clearly, the founders of gURL and those who support the site have discovered that the target audience flocks to the page, and it has gained an extraordinary amount of popularity among Web sites and popular press. A search on Infoseek, a popular Internet search engine, indicates more than 60 sites that have reviewed gURL. Of these sites, every one provides an overwhelmingly supportive and positive assessment of gURL. Furthermore, the site has gained attention in the popular press, including ABC, *Elle*, and the *New York Times* (see www.gurl.com/hq/info/). The number of monthly visitors is a sign that gURL has achieved its goal of creating an online community for girls experiencing that oh-so-lonely and awkward time of adolescence. Although the owners of gURL do not disclose the number of site visitors or members they have, they do acknowledge that they "experience a 40% growth in traffic every month" and the staff makes sure they update the site content frequently "to keep users coming back and spreading the word among their uninitiated friends" (McGinty 1998, paragraph 9).

The staff of gURL explains a portion of the site as "The gURL mag/zine is frequently updated and contains stories, games and interactive content. The gURL connection is our free membership area which provides a valuable community for teenage girls. The connection offers chat, the gURL palace (which enables visual based chat), posting boards, pen-pal lists and homepage listings."

Visiting the homepage of gURL begins to explain why the site is so popular among adolescent girls. With its black background, brightly colored text and off-beat fonts, the page is "funky" and inviting. The logo that appears on the homepage and throughout the site consists of the word "gURL" written over a drawn image of a girl's arm and her hand clenched in a fist. The site name is a clever combination of girl, the audience the site appeals to, and URL, which stands for universal relay protocol, more commonly referred to as the Web site address.

The content of the site is diverse, but targeted toward a specific age group of adolescent girls between the ages of 13 and 19. On this site, girls have the opportunity to visit secretadmirer@gURL to find out "does the person you like like you, too?" They may also set up shop on the site with free gURLmAIL (e-mail address) and gURLpages (individual homepages hosted by gURL) which are grouped into gURLnet, "all the best teen girl sites under one roof!"

Users may also browse gURL mag/zine, the online magazine on the site that addresses topics such as "ha! *the big 12; the piercing 2*," "looks aren't everything—*virtual makeover*," "where do I go from here? *palm reading may has an excellent sense of humor...,*" and "deal with it! *help me heather.*" These articles are an example from a recent visit; they change weekly and address various teen issues in a sometimes serious, sometimes silly manner. Other potential interests of users are addressed in areas such as "gURLmusic," "gURLmovies," and "shopping."

In addition to reading, girls are given voice in "mouthpiece" and "connection." In mouthpiece, users gain access to a teen girl's take on current news, are able to "dig or dis" new media offerings and can view the artwork of other adolescent girls in the gallery. The connection section requires users to register to enter and provide a username and password for future visits. Entrance into connection enables users to access "our free community with chat, pen-pal lists, poetry shoutouts and much more!!" It is in this section that my research is focused, particularly in the "shoutout for advice" section. Shoutouts enable users to post their opinions or ask questions on a variety of topics including school, dating, family, friends, and bodies.

Participants

As previously mentioned, it is not possible to confirm the demographics of the participants, but some important information can be obtained by recognizing that those who visit gURL all have Internet access and they have voluntarily visited and joined the gURL community. With computers still a luxury for many and Internet access as an additional expense, it is easy to assume that the majority of visitors are situated in middle-class families or higher on the socioeconomic hierarchy. In that they have all voluntarily joined the gURL community and are actively participating in discussions within it, one assumes that they are actively seeking other friends and/or another community outside the one in which they live and socialize. Considering that adolescence is a lonely, turbulent time, it almost seems intuitive that teenagers will seek out advice and support from others with the same experiences in a space where the risk of being ostracized or teased is fairly low.

Data Collection (Evaluation of the Site, Shoutouts, Articles About the Site)

410   Data for this study were collected from the shoutout for advice section on gURL.com. Over the course of a month and a half, I spent approximately 60 hours on the site exploring all areas of the Web site, reading posts from users on a daily basis and waiting (with

415 baited breath!) for responses or updates on their situations. In this time, I gained extensive knowledge of the sense of community the staff members of gURL attempt to foster and how adolescent girls interact within that context. Much of this information was obtained by

420 simply following links to see where they took me within the site. I also read reviews of the site from more than 60 Web site reviewers and examined newspaper articles about the site.

    I examined two bulletin boards in the shoutout for

425 advice under the body section. These were, "Do guys judge girls?" and "Exercise." I chose these two sites because they address issues other than those that have been the focus of previous research, namely breasts, menstruation and sexual activity. Additionally, the ti-

430 tles intrigued me. "Do guys judge girls?" is a vague topic that could invite conversations from a wide range of angles. I was interested in seeing what angles the users chose and what topics were touched upon. The title of "Exercise" provides more defined boundaries

435 for the discussion, but it is interesting to understand how the discussion deviates from these boundaries and what topics are addressed instead. Analyzing the discussions on the boards exposes very few differences between the two bulletin boards and those that do exist

440 are superficial at best.

    The literature review provided considerably more than a place to find gaps in research as it provided extensive insight into the role of the Internet in human communication, methods of data collection, and prob-

445 lems associated with ethnography on the Web. Interestingly, very little of this information was obtained from print sources, but a copious amount was found on the Internet itself.

    As I attempted to remain unobtrusive, I read only

450 the statements provided by site users and did not participate in any discussion or contact the users outside the bulletin boards. Furthermore, my research question sought to uncover the topics adolescent girls would discuss in their own space and without the intervention

455 of adults. Within this, I did not need to clarify information or probe into why the girls felt this way. Instead, the data found on the site were sufficient for this initial study.

    One benefit of this type of research was easy access

460 into the site. I simply added my name to the list of site subscribers, obtained a username and password, and was free to log onto the site at any time. Because this is not a real-time part of the site, it was easy to remain anonymous. Quite simply, no one even knew I was

465 there.

Locating the Researcher

    Fascinatingly, I found it difficult to remain on the outside of the site. I subscribe to the belief that communication and qualitative research are interactive, ongoing processes where meaning is developed be-

470 tween and among participants. Clearly, I was taking the words of the users and combining their shoutouts with my knowledge and experience to obtain an understanding of their beliefs about their bodies. In this sense, the process is co-creational, but I wonder about

475 the nature of co-creation when one is unaware that others are making meaning of their statements and, even if they realize that this is likely occurring, they do not know what meanings are constructed. An example of this occurring raises the concern that one must consider

480 who responds to whom, when the response occurs (if at all), and how others react to the response. A memo in my field notes speculates how zelda2000 will feel if her question is not answered. I worry that she has turned to the bulletin board as a chance to get an honest

485 opinion and assistance with a serious issue. Will she be hurt if no one answers, or will she justify as I have?

    Another unique aspect of an Internet-based ethnography is that this participant observation is conducted through a Web site, where I was not an active partici-

490 pant, nor was I observing more than text. As I have mentioned, a Web site is a necessary and significant site for observation to occur, but it is incongruent with my presuppositions regarding participant observation. With this in mind, there are several aspects of the expe-

495 rience to address that will explain my position and experience while indicating that I was truly acting as a participant observer in this context.

    Although I say that I was not a participant observer, the nature of such a Web site and bulletin boards re-

500 quired that I be a participant as well as an observer. The role of participant is gained through site registration with a username, password and e-mail address as well as simply reading the posted messages. I am unable to cite specific statistics, but the assumption in the

505 computer world is that the vast majority of site subscribers read the messages posted by others, but never post their own. In a similar fashion, Masterson (1997) discusses his experience of gaining a high-status position on a MUD. In this situation, he explains that:

510   ...there was some consideration of the possibility that the researcher's words and deeds might be altering or even creating the phenomena being observed. However, part of the position attained was the ability to make oneself completely invisible to all other participants. While in-

515 visible, no significant differences in the behavior of the other participants were noted. In addition, while this position was noteworthy on one of the three MUDs studied, the researcher held no such position on the other two; again, no significant differences in the behaviors of the

520 other participants were noted. The ease with which the author could define his own social status while assuming multiple identities was an affordance perhaps peculiar to MUDs and their ilk" (Masterson, paragraph 73).

Although the context of gURL precluded me from conducting this sort of "experiment," the findings of Masterson's study indicate that participation of a researcher may have little or no impact on the interaction among site visitors.

Analysis

The variety of data collected from the site consisted of more than 150 pages of text, which included a rich description of the appearance of the site itself, the statements of the site users and outside assessments of the site. Additionally, the researcher's interpretations of the site icons and bulletin board postings appeared in the data. I began with the intention of using the open coding strategies explicated by Strauss and Corbin (1998) to determine categories and their properties and dimensions. I expected to draw on Kvale's (1997) notion of meaning categorization to ameliorate the process. However, as I began to familiarize myself with the site and the data, I discovered that meaning condensation would be most beneficial in interpreting this data (Kvale, 1997). Through this method, I was able to allow meanings to emerge from the text and examine how these meanings were interrelated.

The "Holy Trinity"

Kvale (1997) argues that researchers in the realm of social science have elevated the concepts of generalizability, reliability and validity to the status of a "scientific holy trinity." As such, qualitative research in the social "sciences" is expected to conform to these values. It is problematic for many to attempt to conform the fluid nature of human interaction and identity into the constructs, but Kvale argues that a reconceptualization of the terms in relation to the fluidity of social existence is advantageous to qualitative research. In this reframing, he asserts that "The discussion represents a rather moderate postmodernism; although rejecting the notion of an objective, universal truth, it accepts the possibility of specific local, personal and community forms of truth, with a focus on daily life and local narrative" (Kvale, 1997, p. 231). In order to explore these concepts and bolster the perceived legitimacy of my arguments, I will explore my research in relation to the trinity.

Generalizability

If asked to explain my position on the generalizability of qualitative research, my immediate response would be that it cannot occur because human experience is based on a variety of interactive factors that cannot represent the experience of all members of a large population. In conducting this research, however, I find myself identifying wholeheartedly with the assertions of the site users and expect that their experiences hold true for the majority of adolescent girls. Had I approached this project with little knowledge of the role of women's bodies in western society and previous research findings, I expect that I would have

avoided generalizing their experiences. With this knowledge, it is nearly impossible for me to avoid generalizations because the experiences discussed by gURL subscribers resoundingly support previous research findings. Thus, in combining this qualitative piece with the results from a vast number of previous quantitative and qualitative studies, it is apparent that these findings coincide with others and, thus, are considered generalizable.

Reliability

One concern I had in approaching this site was that I would be unable to "read" the emotion of the interactants and would need verbal and nonverbal cues beyond the text that were inaccessible due to the nature of the study. I found doing so astonishingly simple, to the point that I fret and wonder if I ascribe emotions that participants may not have actually experienced or that are different from the emotions they were trying to convey. Since I never heard the voices of the interactants, I have, unwittingly, created a mental persona for each with unique vocal qualities and text-specific inflection. While this is useful in understanding the data, it is problematic to give participants the qualities the researcher expects them to have. If my original fear had come true, then I would not have so much concern about the reliability of my coding.

The deep involvement I have in this topic required me to pay close attention to the reliability of my analysis. The most powerful tool to assist in checking my interpretations was for me to code the data three separate times, each time printing a new copy to mark up, and letting approximately a week go between analysis periods. I also frequently turned to friends and colleagues to ask how they would interpret a phrase to see if our interpretations aligned. Although these techniques were efficacious, and the study has a relatively high degree of validity, member checking would have been another, and arguably better, mode of assessing reliability. I did not, however, wish to expose myself as a researcher at this time, so I chose to avoid asking site users if my interpretations corresponded with their experiences.

Validity

The validity of this study is also high when considered in relation to the seven stages of validation explicated by Kvale (p. 237). Previous research studies provided the theoretical presuppositions of the piece and contributed to the assumption that the design of the study would provide knowledge into the human condition. Additionally, the design was carefully assessed in relation to previous CMC research and ethical expectations of the field, the researcher, and the site. As Paccagnella asserts:

Field research conducted with unobtrusive techniques is inevitably doomed to create major ethical problems. Scholars generally do not agree on common ethical guidelines...All, though, are concerned with the privacy of the users and do take precautions such as changing names, pseudonyms, or addresses from the logs. Changing not only real names, but also aliases or pseudonyms (where used) proves the respect of the researchers for the social reality of cyberspace (paragraph 10).

Paccagnella invokes the following assertion of Sheizaf Rafaeli to further illustrate the position of a large number of CMC researchers, including mine:

We view public discourse on CMC as just that: public. Analysis of such content, where individuals,' institutions' and lists' identities are shielded, is not subject to 'Human Subject' restraints. Such study is more akin to the study of tombstone epitaphs, graffiti, or letters to the editor. Personal?—yes. Private? — no (paragraph 11).

The third technique for validation that Kvale describes requires *in situ* confirmation in the interview context, thus I was unable to employ this method. I was also unable to use his recommendations for transcribing from oral to written style as the data were already written.

Analyzing, the fifth step Kvale describes, considers "whether the questions put to an interview text are valid and whether the logic of interpretation is sound" (p. 237). While this is an abstract term to attempt to tie down in relation to these data, Kvale asserts that validation requires checking and questioning (pp. 242-243). In checking, I examined my expectations for and presuppositions of the study as well as explored my history with the topic. Each time I began analyzing, I reminded myself of the same aspects of my relationship with body image as I have shared with you. Additionally, I questioned my analysis to check for possible alternative explanations of the data. Questioning requires answering the "what" and the "why" before asking "how." Kvale invokes the work of Becker to illustrate that "to decide what a picture is telling us the truth about...we should ask ourselves what questions it might be answering" (p. 243). As previously discussed, the researcher who relies on CMC for data must accept that the narratives of participants may be false. Yet, those who accept, as I do, that the majority, if not all, of these postings are true representations of the users' experiences at that time, also accept that the "whys" of their expressions are also true at the given time. Combining this expectation with previous research on adolescent girls and body image, I was able to ask the data a variety of questions to ascertain a multitude of "whys."

Now that I have chosen the community with which to share my findings and have reported the findings in what I perceived to be a valid and accurate way, I am opening this piece for your interpretation of my ability to fully complete steps six and seven posited by Kvale, validating and reporting. As such, I seek your feedback and interpretation of the following findings.

Findings

You Can Never Be Too Thin...

With or without providing reasons why, many users indicate a desire to have a "better" body than they currently have. Often, the desire for a different body was couched in discussion of factors that provoked a desire to be thin, but the overwhelming concern on both bulletin boards was to be thinner. Lickity206 makes this very clear in her post, "i need to know how you would loose about 10 lbs. in 1 month I am chuuby and have big thighs i am not fat but want to be skinny" (exercise, 3/13/99). Although Lickity206 makes it very clear that she is not fat, she does assert that she is not skinny, but hopes to become so with the information she obtains from other gURLs.

From a feminist perspective, Lickity206 raises the concern that oppressive body ideals encourage women to be thin even if they are not fat to begin with. Other users confirm this, for example, QtPie2003 implores, "please help! i'll take any advice possible!! i eat healthy, am athletic, and like the only part of my body that is fat is my knees and my legs.... please help me... pleaseee! thanx!" (exercise, 3/13/99). Similar statements are also made in the following examples:

okay, let me get this straight. I am a VERY healthy gURL, i eat healthy, i am very athletic, i go to the gym a lot and play basket ball, raquetball, u know stuff like that. i go there about every weekend w/ my friends. But, the thing is, I think i have big thighs. i have a sort of big stomache when i sit down. I am 12 years old, and i weigh some where in the 90s. is that healthy?? Don't get me wrong, i am very pretty, healthy.. i am good in a lot of different ways. BUT I THINK I AM FAT!! I told my mom that and she just said NO! U R NOT FAT AT ALL!! my friends say the same thing. I don't know if i believe them though?? PLEASE HELP ME!!!!!!!!!!!!! (bippity_boppity_boop, exercise, 3/14/99)

HELP!!!!!! I am Fat!....i KNOW i am fat! im not just putting myself down cos i've had bad things in life. I exercise myself off.I train.I swim.i eat sooooooooo much good stuff.And after school i play soccer with my friends!...no matter what happens, i always GAIN weight. Any tips that would help me? Melissa if u can see this ring me up and tell me if u think im over weight or just average. Cos i feel real bad about myself cos everyl teases me and calls me fat and blob and stuff....it is REALLY hurting me!" (FriendShipMaker do guys judge, 4/11/99)

These three shoutouts exemplify beauty standards that cause healthy, muscular girls to question their appearance. Although these girls are active and likely within a "normal" weight range, they are concerned that their bodies are too big. Furthermore, although the ages of all the users are not known, bippity_boppity_boop's statement reveals that girls as young as 12 years old are concerned about weight even though their bodies have likely not yet begun to develop the additional body fat that comes with beauty.

...Or Can You?

As illustrated by the previous comments, a common assumption among those who feel they are fat is that their problems will disappear if their "excess" weight would disappear. In contrast, I maintain that even "perfect people" are often dissatisfied with their looks and their bodies. Many users of gURL confirmed this. Dream_Maker84 recognizes that her experience is "weird" as she states,

> This is really weird. I am 100lbs and I hate it! I know some poeple who weigh that much but at least they aren't flat! I really hate being like this because some guys are only nice to girls who look "good". It is kind of depressing to watch all of your friends go with someone (expecially a boy you like) and you are all alone. Does anyone know why guys judges girls based on how big their chest and hips are? Is there a way to get a guy to look past that? (do guys judge, 3/21/99)

The distress Dream_Maker84 experiences reveals that although she is thin, she is still not perfect because her breasts are also small. PSP offers an interesting contrast to this in her assertion that:

> Honestly I don't know why you girls are trying to loose weight. I'm 5'4 and weigh 120lbs. I'm trying to gain weight. Guys like girls with curves. If anything I am jealous of you!!! You should be glad that you have something. All I have is chest and that's it. I'm black and 16yrs. IN the black community they like girls with some meat on their bones and I eat anything and everything. I don't know what you girls are complaining about, you should be happy. Don't get me wrong I have boyfriends and guy friends but I would like to gain some weight in the hip and butt area. Someone respond to me please!!!!!!!!!!! (exercise, 4/11/99)

For PSP, the problem is not that she needs more weight in certain places, but that she needs more weight in general. Although this may be at odds with what some of the site users experience with their own bodies, no one offered a challenge to PSP's desire. Those who did respond did so with an offer of sympathy. Monirose claims that she identifies with PSP and that she is too thin, but cannot gain weight. For Monirose, some of the problems associated with being thin come from the perceptions of others. She states, "I've tried eating all the time but nothing helps. I hate how everyone thinks I'm anorexic just because I'm thin. Also there are some girls that will actually get mad at me for being like this. I want to gain weight but people don't understand. I just wanted you to know there are other people like you out there" (exercise, 4/12/99). These postings reveal that those who consider themselves thin, and thus are categorized as "beautiful people," still experience anxiety and self-disgust based on the notion that their bodies do not align with social ideals, or if they do, the girls do not perceive that they do.

And Make It Quick!

No matter if the user wanted to gain or lose weight, fast results were often requested. As demonstrated above, Lickity206 asks for advice on how to lose 10 pounds in a month (exercise, 3/13/99). Likewise, JsKa makes a plea for help in weight loss because "...it's like March already and I NEED to loose ALOT of weight before graduation in June..." (exercise, 3/18/99). Yet another example is the posting by saweet that reads, "hi.im like 100 lbs overweight but i dont look that fat and i still wear a size 16 . if you've lost lots of weight please share you tips with me email me at rose6891 i really appreciate it . i wanna be a size 4 before school next year" (exercise, 4/6/99). Likewise, in the following shoutout, QT_Precious requests a diet plan that will help her lose 10 to 20 pounds, preferably 20, in two weeks.

> Hey gURLS~~ I am 5' tall and weigh 125lbs. I feel very over weight, but I don't look it. I hold my weight very nicely, and also I am big boned. I would just like to lose around 10-20lbs. (My goal is 20lbs. to lose!) I am fixing to order tae-bo, and I play softball, fast-pitch softball, I cheerlead, I act, and so, I am always on the go. When I am home, I grab whatever I can get to eat. Any tips? I also need a good diet plan to help me get down a little smaller, bye April 21st. If anyone could help at all then please do!! Thanx alot!! You can post your message on here for me, (i am on here everyday) or you can email me at QT_Precious@gurlmail.com Thanx!! QT. (exercise, 4/7/99.

These are just a few examples of the concerns of girls to lose weight as soon as possible in order to meet goals of being a certain weight or size for "special events" like graduation, summer or the next school year. In these examples, health concerns are not addressed, nor are clear reasons delineated for why the user desires to lose weight. Yes, special events are mentioned, but no user expands on why these special events are important for them to lose weight for.

Attention From Boys Is Important

A theme that gURLs return to with an overwhelming frequency is that attention from boys is extremely important. It is even apparent that girls validate their self-worth through such attention and believe that they will not receive attention from boys if they are fat. In a request for assistance, zelda2000 proclaims, "...I don't get noticed by alot of the guys at school! Am I ugly is there something wrong with me?" (do guys judge, 3/15/99). Clearly, it is important to be noticed by boys and that being "ugly" or "having something wrong" is the cause for inattention. From this follows the belief that if a girl is ugly, then boys will pay no attention to her. Keylarg exemplifies this by stating, "I know I can be compatible with some of my guy friends romantically but it is hard to get over the fact that I am overweight" (do guys judge, 3/17/99).

It Is What Is on the Inside That Counts...or Does It?

An overwhelming number of users provide advice with some variation of assurance that affability and a good personality are more important than being physically attractive. Though it appears that participants have the belief and/or knowledge that fundamentally, what is inside is what matters, unfortunately, more emphasis is placed on outer appearances. While the reasons for this are vague and potentially numerous, the two explanations offered are that it takes time to meet a "decent guy" and that boys are not always able to look beyond appearance to see girls "for who they really are." In a different discussion area, one girl responds to such suggestions by saying, "Gee, thanks for the advice, but I am so tired of hearing that I just have to wait." As these girls are part of a society that preaches compulsory heterosexuality and pressures women to "have it all," it is not surprising that they feel obligated to be beautiful to attract boys. Although some argue that the focus of the third wave of feminism is to destroy unrealistic and harmful body ideals (Walker, 1998), it seems that message has not yet reached a large audience. Instead, girls appear to verbally embrace the advice of so many parents that what is on the inside is much more important than physical appearance, but they, like their mothers, aunts, grandmothers, etc., do not practice the message of this advice in everyday life.

Another facet of this theme is that if one is attractive, accepts this as reality, and shares this opinion with others, she is conceited. Chica732 very clearly tells cutegirly, and every reader, it is "arrogant and rude" to talk about "how cute you were." She continues the message with an obvious self-restraint by saying, "Aaaargh! I had better just finish here before I jusst [sic] totally blow up!" In the opinion of this participant and the assumption that others agree through their silence, it is evident that self-righteousness is definitely "uncool." Others also reprimand cutegirly as well as every other user who allows her "head to get too big."

And We Are All Heterosexual, Too...Aren't We?

Fascinatingly, the discussion in these data revolves around heterosexualized norms. Further exploration into the site exhibits a consistent conformity to these norms, except when the discussion topic is explicitly homosexuality (When Girls Like Girls..., for example). In these topics, the concern is not how to attract the attention of other girls, but if it is okay to have sexual desire for same-sex individuals or requests for cyber-experimentation into homosexuality via e-mail, chat rooms and masturbation. Perhaps this is in direct relation to the hatred of homosexuality in this culture, but it is interesting that girls do not worry about how to attract other girls, but rather if they are "normal" for having these feelings.

Someday Your Prince Will Come

In line with the expectation that all users are heterosexual, users seem to be sitting, waiting for the perfect man to sweep them off their feet. Perhaps one of the most disturbing themes for a feminist to read is the frequent reassurance that some day some guy will notice how pretty/cute/great/nice/etc. the girl is and will "come to his senses." This is problematic because although users often tell others that weight, size or looks should not matter, they reassure those who are concerned that boys will still notice them in spite of these "flaws."

...Guys dont usually judge that much and no not all guys like blonde blue eyes (no offense to blonde and blue eyed girls)The real question to ask ur self is there any guy u want to go out with or want to spend time with b/c thats a big part of it. I mean i use to call my self fat, ugly etc u name it i called my self that and my friends never said anything to help me feel better and that made me feel worst. Time is a big deal wit a b/f i mean i was single for 2 years b4 i went out wit this one guy and he is my true love we went out for 9 months and i still love him and i havent goin out wit any one else (KeeblerElf-99, do guys judge, 4/1/99)

Speaking from experience guys don't always want skinny girls..i am 5'9 and 120lbs, and i eat like you wouldn't believe, people say i'm pretty too, but do you see me walking around with a boyfriend? no so guys don't care how fat or skinny you are they're attracted to more than the outside, your attitude and personality makes up for alot of it, so quit putting yourself down and stand up high and have a more positive attitude towards yourself and a positive outlook towards life. (silver_angel, do guys judge, 4/12/99).

Even more frequent is the advice that boys are not truly attracted to extremely thin girls, but they prefer "chubby" girls. Examples of this include,

I agree totally with what u said about the meat stuff. most of the guys I know make fun of the girls that are super skinny. I'm not saying that they are all ugly or anything. But i know of 2 girls in my school who are barley even there. all the guys call them aneorixe. it's how your bodies are. if you r fat or chunky your supposed to be that way so don't fret. (peebles10, exercise, 3/23/99).

A fascinating approach to the idea that boys prefer girls "with some meat" is offered by piklegrl, who states,

Ok, this is for every girl. For all you girls whho are trying to look like the girls in magazines, or the models, so that guys will like you, or find you attractive, STOP! Cause guys DO NOT like those types of girls. The only reason guys look at girls who are that skinny, is because they thnk that those type of girls are the ones who will give it to them. But what they really like, is girls who have meat on them, and that doesn't especially mean muscle meat, but the fattier meat. They like girls with a bit more of a pudgy stomach, cause it's softer to touch, and looks better. They like the girls with legs that have some meat on them, not when it's skin and bones. So if

965 the reason you are going for that model-thin look, so that you can get guys' attention, I don't suggest you do it, cause the girls that they find the most attractive, are the ones with meat on them. The other girls are just sex objects to them. The only reason they go for model-thin girls, is because to them, the stereotype of a slut, is someone who is model-thin. So take my advice. I have plenty of guy friends who have explained this all to me.
970 B-4 I wanted the model thin look, but then they told me if I was to be that skinny, guys would look at me as a slut, so don't do it. (exercise, 3/23/99)

According to this user, as well as others who have replied in support of this concept, girls should not try to
975 be really thin to attract boys because then the only boys that will date them will be those that will pressure them into sexual activity.

How Advice Is Given

Considering how advice is given moves beyond simply hearing the voices of the site users, but is an
980 interesting look into interaction management. When advice is given, it always takes one of two forms. Either the person offering advice tells the person requesting advice that she has had a similar experience or that the problem is not as bad as the person requesting
985 advice thinks it is. Sometimes the two strategies are used in conjunction, but no other strategies are used as a means to provide advice.

Discussion and Conclusion

The use of qualitative methods in the context of the Internet proved considerably less troublesome than
990 anticipated. One of the most problematic aspects of this study was my perspective that objectivity cannot exist in social research. My experience in the field was imbued with the sense that objectivity does not exist, but that partiality is potentially destructive. As my reflec-
995 tions indicate, I could easily have joined in the conversation on gURL when I was 13, and may well have uttered the same statements these adolescents do. This is beneficial in that I feel I am attuned to their experience, but problematic in that I have a biased view that
1000 such thoughts are harmful. I know these beliefs are supported with scholarly research, but I also know I am more profoundly interested in body image than others, thus I examine it at a much deeper level than others. Perhaps more significantly, I remember nights of cry-
1005 ing myself to sleep wishing for a magic fairy to come and fix my thighs. Since these memories are so painful for me, I assume they represent the experience and, thus, agony of the majority of teenage girls. I assume that these girls may contemplate engaging in extraordi-
1010 narily harmful behavior because they believe they are so ugly that no boy will ever like them. Some postings indicate this may be the case (like the instance where the girl says that she wants to be anorexic), but I am afraid of overgeneralizing my experience.
1015 Considering these complications, it is evident that I approached the research from a perspective that could

easily taint the findings. In relation to my development as a researcher, my main goal in this project was test-
1020 ing my ability to interact with the data in a way that I was to co-create meaning with numerous adolescent girls without attempting to overlay my experience on theirs. Through careful analysis of the text and reliance on Kvale's explication of the social scientific trinity
1025 and modes of adhering to it, I was able to remove myself from the data enough to let it speak for itself, but not so much that I tried to reduce my experiences and previous research to a level of insignificance. Furthermore, this study was an exploration into the dubious
1030 online world that is filled with complications and contradictions. This venture was also successful in that I was able to access information I would likely be unable to access in any other medium. Additionally, this project increased my belief in the "realness" of the online
1035 world and the experiences of those who interact within it.

This study could be used as a starting point for a diverse path of future inquiries. It provides new insight into human experience and the role of the Internet in "real life" as well as the voices and struggles of adoles-
1040 cent girls. Future research could further the exploration of CMC and/or open new doors for enabling adolescent girls to find their voices in a complex, socially constrictive world.

References

American Association of University Women (1990). *Shortchanging girls: Shortchanging America: Full data report.* Washington, DC: American Association of University Women.
Brumberg, J. J. (1997). *The body project: An intimate history of American girls.* New York: Vintage.
Chernin, K. (1981). *The obsession: Reflections on the tyranny of slenderness.* New York: Harper & Row.
Chernin, K. (1985). *The hungry self: Women, eating and identity.* New York: Harper & Row.
Garner, D. M. (1997, January/February). The 1997 body image survey results. *Psychology Today,* pp. 31-44, 75-84.
Grogan, S. & Wainwright, N. (1996). Growing up in the culture of slenderness: Girls' experiences of body dissatisfaction. *Women's Studies International Forum,* 19, 665-673.
Guillen, E. & Barr, S. (1994). Nutrition, dieting, and fitness messages in a magazine for adolescent women, 1970-1990. *Journal of Adolescent Health,* 15, 464-472.
Haraway, D. J. (1991). *Simians, Cyborgs and women: The reinvention of nature.* New York: Routledge.
Hesse-Biber, S. (1996). *Am I thin enough yet: The cult of thinness and the commercialization of identity.* New York: Oxford University Press.
Lerner, R. & Brackney, B. (1978). The importance of inner and outer body parts attitudes in the self-concept of late adolescents. *Sex Roles,* 4 (2), 225-238.
Masterson, J. T. (1997). *Ethnography of a Virtual Society: How a gangling, wiry half-elf found a way to fit in* [268 paragraphs]. Retrieved May 2, 1999 from the World Wide Web: http://www.montana.com/john/thesis/.
McGinty, R. (1998). *Golden link: gURL* [9 paragraphs]. Retrieved April 28, 1999 from the World Wide Web: http://www.mediacentral.com/Magazines/MediaCentral/Gold/19980309.htm
Mellin, L. M., Scully, S., & Irwin, C. E. (1986). Disordered eating characteristics in preadolescent girls. Meeting of the American Dietetic Association, Las Vegas, (Abstract).
Meyer, C. (1997). Human Identity in the Age of Computers: Virtual Communities and Identity Deception. Retrieved May 2, 1999, from the World Wide Web: http://www.iac.net/ %7Elongshot/thesis/.
Nunes, M. (1995). Baudrillard in cyberspace: Internet, virtuality, and postmodernity. *Style,* 29, 314-327.
Paccagnella, L. (1997). Getting the Seats of Your Pants Dirty: Strategies for Ethnographic Research on Virtual Communities. *Journal of Computer-Mediated Communication* [On-line], 3 (1). Available: http://www.ascusc.org/jcmc/vol3/issue1/paccagnella.html#rcroft.

Pipher, M. B. (1995). *Reviving Ophelia : Saving the selves of adolescent girls.* New York: Ballantine.

Rheingold, H. (1993). *The virtual community.* New York: Harper.

Rodin, J., Silberstein, L. R., & Striegel-Moore, R. H. (1984). Women and weight: A normative discontent. In T. B. Sonderegger (Ed.), *Nebraska symposium on motivation, vol. 32: Psychology and gender* (pp. 267-307). Lincoln: University of Nebraska Press.

Schreiber, G. B., Pike, K. M., Wilfley, D. E., & Rodin, J. (1995). Drive for thinness in black and white preadolescent girls. *International Journal of Eating Disorders,* 18 (1), 59-69.

Smythe, M. J. (1995). Talking bodies: Body talk at Bodyworks. *Communication Studies,* 46, 245-260.

Spears, R. & Lea, M. (1992). Social influence and the influence of the social in computer-mediated communication. In M. Lea (Ed.) *Contexts of computer-mediated communication* (pp. 30-65). Hemel-Hempstead: Harvester Wheatsheaf.

Spears, R. & Lea, M. (1994). Panacea or panopticon? The hidden power in computer-mediated communication. *Communication Research,* 4, 427-459.

Spitzack, C. J. (1990a). *Confessing excess: Women and the politics of body reduction.* Albany: State University of New York Press.

Spitzack, C. J. (1990b). Body talk: The politics of weight loss and female identity. In B. Bates & A. Taylor (Eds.), *Women communicating: Studies of women's talk* (pp. 51-74). Norwalk, NJ: Ablex.

Strauss, A. L. & Corbin, J. M. (1998). *Basics of Qualitative Research: Techniques and Procedures for Developing Grounded Theory, 2nd ed.* Newbury Park, CA: Sage.

Turkle, S. (1996). Virtuality and its discontents: Searching for community in cyberspace [40 paragraphs] *The American Prospect* [Online serial].24.(4). Available http://epn.org/ prospect/24/24turk.html.

Wolf, N. (1992). *The beauty myth.* New York: Doubleday.

Wooley, S.C. & Wooley, O.W. (1984, February). Feeling fat in a thin society. *Glamour,* 198-252.

Address correspondence to:
Kerrie Michelle Smyres. E-mail: kerrie.smyres@asu.edu

Exercise for Article 17

Factual Questions

1. The researcher states that an earlier researcher reported that women earn more money than men in only two job categories. What are the categories?

2. According to Rheingold, what is the definition of "virtual communities"?

3. The researcher visited how many other online communities where women's bodies were designated as important topics of conversation before selecting gURL for this study?

4. The gURL site is *targeted* toward what age group?

5. Did the researcher participate in any discussions with site users?

6. How many separate times (with approximately a week between recodings) did the researcher code the data?

7. According to the researcher, what is probably one of the most "disturbing" themes for a feminist to read?

Questions for Discussion

8. The researcher notes that she has "a deep emotional investment" in the topic of her research. In your opinion, would it have been better if the research had been conducted by someone with less of a personal interest? Explain. (See lines 104–107.)

9. The researcher notes that a frequent objection to Web-based research is that there is no foolproof way to verify the identity of the participants. Do you think this problem invalidates this particular study? Why? Why not? (See lines 212–214.)

10. The researcher states that it is reasonable to assume that the majority of Internet users are middle-class or higher. Do you agree with this assumption? If yes, how might it affect the results and their interpretation? (See lines 396–400.)

11. In general, has this study convinced you that the Internet is a valid place to obtain research data? Explain.

Quality Ratings

Directions: Indicate your level of agreement with each of the following statements by circling a number from 5 for strongly agree (SA) to 1 for strongly disagree (SD). If you believe an item is not applicable to this research article, leave it blank. Be prepared to explain your ratings.

A. The introduction establishes the importance of the study.

    SA   5   4   3   2   1   SD

B. The literature review establishes the context for the study.

    SA   5   4   3   2   1   SD

C. The research purpose, question, or hypothesis is clearly stated.

    SA   5   4   3   2   1   SD

D. The method of sampling is sound.

    SA   5   4   3   2   1   SD

E. Relevant demographics (for example, age, gender, and ethnicity) are described.

    SA   5   4   3   2   1   SD

F. Measurement procedures are adequate.

    SA   5   4   3   2   1   SD

G. All procedures have been described in sufficient detail to permit a replication of the study.

    SA   5   4   3   2   1   SD

H. The participants have been adequately protected from potential harm.

    SA   5   4   3   2   1   SD

I. The results are clearly described.

SA   5   4   3   2   1   SD

J. The discussion/conclusion is appropriate.

SA   5   4   3   2   1   SD

K. Despite any flaws, the report is worthy of publication.

SA   5   4   3   2   1   SD

Article 18

Conflicting Bureaucracies, Conflicted Work: Dilemmas in Case Management for Homeless People with Mental Illness

Linda E. Francis
State University of New York at Stony Brook

ABSTRACT. This ethnographic study finds a case management agency torn between the rules of two conflicting bureaucracies. Funded by a federal grant, the agency is administered by the county, and the regulations of the two systems turn out to be incompatible. This conflict creates dilemmas in providing services to clients: meeting eligibility criteria for services from the federal grant meant the clients did not meet the eligibility criteria for many county services. Agency staff reacted to this dilemma by bending rules, finding loopholes, and investing extra time and emotional labor in each client. The role-conflict engendered by bureaucratic disjunction creates frustration, resentment, and burnout within the agency.

From *Journal of Sociology and Social Welfare, XXVII*, 97–112. Copyright © 2000 by Journal of Sociology and Social Welfare. Reprinted with permission.

Case Management in the Mental Health System

Prior to deinstitutionalization, institutions provided all needed services under one roof, including food, shelter, clothing, medical care, and psychiatric treatment. By contrast, outside of the institution, these
5   services were fragmented and spread across the medical and social service systems (Grob, 1994). For persons with mental illness such services were difficult to access. Even with symptoms under control with medication, many patients lacked the skills necessary to
10 negotiate these complex service systems, leaving many with no services at all (Freedman & Moran, 1984).

In 1977, the National Institute of Mental Health began the Community Support Program in an attempt to coordinate these diverse services in ways that were not
15 covered under the 1963 Community Mental Health Centers Act. This program created a federal and state partnership to develop community support programs. The program sought to increase the availability of housing, income support, psychiatric treatment, medi-
20 cal treatment, and other services by encouraging states to change their own mental health systems. Though the Community Support Program later refocused on evaluation, in its inception we see the roots of intensive

case management programs for persons with severe
25 mental illness (Grob, 1994).

Over the past decade case management has become one of the most widely used methods to deliver services to persons with severe mental illness. At the most basic level, the role of the case manager is to determine
30 the needs of clients, connect them to services, and help to ensure a reasonable quality of life in the community. Case managers in intensive service agencies provide services at a much higher level, including teaching skills of daily living, arranging transportation, and pro-
35 viding services outside of traditional locations and hours. The tasks of case managers vary widely depending on the environment in which they work, with some located in agencies that provide most services in-house, and others drawing primarily on resources in the
40 community (Robinson and Toff-Bergman, 1990). The common denominator is that case managers serve as liaison, advocate, and resource for persons with mental illness and their families (Rog, 1988).

Most of the research on case management for peo-
45 ple with severe mental illness has focused on measuring client outcomes as a determinant of efficacy, usually in terms of keeping people out of the hospital and living as independently as possible. However, the results of these studies are difficult to interpret because
50 the definitions of case management and the conditions under which case managers practice are variable (Solomon, 1992, Rubin, 1992; Chamberlain and Rapp, 1991). As a result, it is impossible to determine if cross-sectional client outcome variables are even
55 measuring the same things (Solomon, 1992, Spicer et al., 1994).

Addressing problems such as this is one of the greatest strengths of ethnography. Through naturalistic observation and unstructured interviews, the researcher
60 can illuminate the contents of the "black box" of interventions (Corbin & Strass, 1990) and determine what is really happening in the course of service delivery. The initial intent of this study was just that: to illuminate the crucial activities of case management and clarify
65 what those activities accomplish in the eyes of the

workers. However, as is often the case with qualitative research, the questions proved more complicated than anticipated. This case study demonstrates the extremely influential nature of the social work context, that is, the resources, bureaucratic rules, and politics of social systems in which the agency is embedded. The agency in this study was forced into a "Catch-22" situation, in which the rules regulating its operation prevented it from delivering the services it was being funded to provide. This vulnerability to vagaries of local conditions may give us a clue to why case management services are not only so difficult to measure, but frequently difficult to provide.

Despite the growing importance of case management, few have done ethnographic research of this part of the mental health care system. The experiences of people in other parts of health care have been well documented, some in extremely well-known studies. In *Asylums,* Goffman (1961) examines life in the mental hospital. In *Life in the Ward,* Coser (1959), tells the story of both patients and staff in a nonpsychiatric hospital, while Becker et al. in *Boys in White* do the same for physicians-in-training in medical school (1961). Estroff (1981), in *Making It Crazy,* brings to light the lives of clients of one of the first Assertive Community Treatment Programs. More recently, Hopper (1998) and Liebow (1993) have brought to life the once invisible experiences of homeless people, many of whom suffer mental illness.

Despite the contributions of each of these studies, none of them truly explores the delivery of *social* services in mental health. With the decline of the psychiatric institution, such services have become cornerstones of the community mental health system. Case management, with its growing role in this system, offers an ideal point of entry to study how mental health service delivery occurs. A qualitative approach allows for an assessment of this process without the imposition of preconceived hypotheses. That is, the providers themselves have the opportunity to tell the story of their own experiences on case management teams. As will become evident in the pages to follow, this allows the participants in the study to provide not only the answers, but the questions as well.

The research questions for this study developed in two stages. Initially I sought to uncover in more detail some of the crucial components of the social services intervention that is case management. However, the issues which emerged in the course of the fieldwork proved to be more interesting than the original question. The results reported in this paper thus address two concerns: 1) what activities constitute intensive case management, and 2) how does the system environment affect their implementation? The data presented in the following pages give at least one possible answer to the second question, and indirectly, to the first research question as well.

Data

Ethnography of an Intensive Case Management Agency

The Research Site. The research site for this study is an agency providing intensive case management services to homeless persons who suffer from mental disorder and substance abuse. This agency, called REACH (a pseudonym), is located in a moderately large city in the southeastern U.S. and is funded by a federal grant as part of an ongoing multisite national demonstration project. The purpose of the demonstration was to investigate means of integrating and defragmenting community mental health service systems. Despite federal funding, however, the administration of REACH was under the jurisdiction of the county community mental health system.

The organization and mission of REACH were nontraditional. The agency was made up of two teams of service providers rather than autonomous case managers. Each client was assigned to a team, rather than a single case manager, and worked with all members of each team. In addition, both teams were familiar with each others' clients. Morning staff meetings each day reviewed all new material, problems, or achievements, so that all staff of the agency were updated and capable of handling emergencies for any client of REACH. All staff members (teams and administration) shared revolving 24-hour on-call support duties.

The REACH teams had not only case managers, but consumer-staff members and nurses. At the time of the research, there was one consumer-staff person on each team, both with histories of addiction and homelessness or near homelessness. Ideally, each team was supposed to have five members, including a nurse on each team, but due to a budget freeze by the county, the teams were working only partially staffed, each with three members plus one shared nurse.

The mission of the agency was very client-directed, with active follow-ups of clients, an emphasis on client choice, and a requirement that clients be included in all formal discussions of their cases. Meetings with clients took place *in vivo,* that is, where the client was. This frequently required appointments at the clients' residences, on park benches, or at the local drop-in center, wherever the client was able to be. Clients who missed appointments were sought and rescheduled. Emphasis was on keeping clients in services, despite the formidable obstacles to achieving continuity with an inherently transient population. To maintain this intensive level of service, caseloads were very small, about 50 clients per team, or roughly 15 clients per team member.

Data Collection. As a study of process, this project was done ethnographically, with data coming primarily from participant observation of case management work and unstructured interviews with the team members. This includes an inventory and description of the daily activities that constitute case management for service recipients. Over a five-month period, I attended staff

meetings, participated in daily agency activities, and accompanied every team member on at least two days
180 when they provided services out of the office. I had opportunities to see my participants working both with clients in a variety of settings, and with staff from other parts of the social services system. On an average day, I arrived in time for the morning staff meeting and re-
185 view of clients. I then accompanied the team I was "shadowing" that week into their team room for their team meeting. I spent the rest of the day with a single team member, who would explain paperwork, relate phone calls, and take me along on visits to clients.

190 Over the course of the study, I also conducted detailed individual unstructured interviews with all ten staff members in the agency to gather insight into their views on the different constraints and resources under which staff members and teams operate. These staff
195 members constitute the ten subjects in this study, including six team members, a nurse, an outreach worker, the project manager, and the project director. In total, the data comprise five months of field notes, 10 interviews, and program documents. As with many
200 case studies, the sample size for this study is quite small due to the limited size of the agency; however, the detail and length of data collection lend credibility to the results. These data were transcribed as text onto a computer, and qualitatively coded and analyzed using
205 HyperResearch, a text analysis program.

Results

The Contradictions of the Case Management Role

I originally entered the field with a general question: *What is case management, and what, in their own eyes, do case managers do?* I soon found this question to be inadequate. My respondents all gave answers
210 couched in terms of what they would like to do as managers, what they intended to do, or what they were supposed to do by the terms of the agency's federal grant funding. However, nearly all then wanted to tell me in the next breath why it was very difficult to do the
215 activities they had just described to me. Indeed, they spent much more time telling me why they were not able to provide the services they wanted to or felt they were supposed to than they did telling me about what they did do. That is, what they really wanted to talk
220 about was their frustration.

This frustration has become the topic that has emerged from this analysis, and the main subject of this paper. My main question here is: *Why is it so difficult in this agency to deliver their intensive case man-*
225 *agement services to homeless persons with mental illness, and what are the consequences of this difficulty?* Such a question is tightly tied to the immediate circumstances of this particular agency, and as such appears to have little generalizability. However, the broader im-
230 plications of structural and bureaucratic conflict have repercussions for social workers throughout the field of human services.

REACH was a federally funded project that had been inserted into an already functioning county sys-
235 tem. This position of being juxtaposed between two systems created tensions from the day the agency opened its doors, and interfered with the agency's ability to serve their clients. REACH was designed and federally funded to develop nontraditional approaches
240 to engaging a difficult population, but they were stymied by more traditional expectations and structures at the local level. REACH staff often found themselves torn between the rules of the two systems—federal and county—and the needs of the clients. That is, they
245 could not meet all three points simultaneously.

An example of this was that the agency was funded by their grant to provide services for homeless people with mental illness, especially those with substance abuse problems as well. To provide these services,
250 REACH was supposed to draw on local resources. Homeless services in the county wanted only clients whose mental illness had been stabilized and who did not abuse substances. Yet the mental health treatment available to stabilize clients through Community Men-
255 tal Health Services assumed that the client had not only transportation, but an address and phone number—in other words, that they be housed. And many substance abuse services frequently had mental illness as an exclusion criterion from their residential programs, or
260 required that clients have housing and transportation to attend their outpatient programs. In other words, in order to get housing, you had to be already treated, but in order to get treated, you had to have housing. Thus the county system had services set up for people who
265 were homeless *or* mentally ill *or* substance abusers, but not all three. So the federal grant regulations and the county system in practice often had mutually exclusive targets: eligibility for the grant sometimes created automatic ineligibility for many county services. As
270 one case manager protested, they were often caught between the two government bureaucracies with which they had to deal:

The way [our program] is set up, we're caught in not just one bureaucracy but two. So it's like [we were funded
275 with] the understanding was that [we] were going to be able to do some creative things. But when we attempted the creativity, the county system was like: oh, no, you can't do that. . . And then we also have [federal] guidelines and their bureaucracy and criteria and you run
280 against some things with them. So in between here we are, and it's like we're being squished. And what's happening is that the client is getting lost in all this.

As a result, there was a pervasive sense among the case managers that neither of the two systems were
285 really concerned about whether their clients were actually getting any help.

This feeling was repeatedly reinforced by the contradictions between system rules and client needs. For instance, the eligibility criteria for many services ex-
290 cluded the very people most in need of the service. One

concern was that a grant that had been allocated to the county to provide housing for homeless people stipulated that clients be homeless when they applied, and that they remained homeless until they received the housing certificate. However, the process of sending an application through county bureaucracy often took three or four months. The case managers were simply not willing to leave their clients with no housing that long just so they would stay eligible for a particular source of housing. After all, housing was only the first step in a long road to improvement. According to one team member:

> We can't just leave them out there on the streets with wolves and not place them somewhere safe .... So while we're trying to get them to move forward, I've crossed the boundaries to the [housing] status now, and so I've jeopardized their housing. And so now I'm going to have to come up with another strategy on how I'm going to find you housing because you're not eligible for the certificate anymore.

A diagnosis of substance abuse could complicate matters even more by reducing the already small number of housing options available to the clients. Another team member described these difficulties:

> I set up two interviews for [supported housing]. But you have to have 6 mos. clean time . . . Some of these people are not going to meet these criteria. I mean, you can have the ideal drunk, and you can say stop drinking and he's going to get better. It doesn't work that way. Things don't fit like that.

Often the case managers resort to bending, or even breaking, the rules in order to do their jobs: that is, to provide services to their clients.

> The way everything's set up doesn't make sense. You can't do this because this person doesn't meet this criteria, so you almost have to make it fit. Be flexible and break some rules . . . you have to look at it and say, this didn't happen exactly like this, but if he's eligible for this, and then we start getting picky about things and find little loopholes and stuff. Sometimes the system doesn't work.

This working around the rules holds even for the federal requirements of REACH. For example, many of their clients suffer from severe addictions to the point that this problem overshadows everything else, even their mental illness. Indeed, this sometimes seems to be the norm for homeless people with severe mental illness, at least among the REACH participants. But substance abuse – or even related personality disorders – could not be their primary diagnosis, due to the eligibility criteria of the grant. So rather than disqualify someone in need of their help, they would find a way to make that person eligible.

> Interviewer: I'm thinking of this morning, when the assistant director said to the psychiatrist 'We need a different diagnosis in order to make him eligible.'

> Respondent: Yes, like I'm doing the medical records, and a lot of the people have substance abuse diagnoses. Well, this program is set up for homeless, severely and persistently mentally ill people . . . These people have mental illness, but we cannot put it as the substance abuse is what we're treating. We've got to put it that we're treating major depression, or something. And really . . . we are, even though they do need the substance abuse treatment too. [So] these people, either you change their diagnoses, or they don't meet the criteria. I mean, it's not like they don't have a mental illness, but the substance abuse is something that's coming up front moreso than the mental illness. The system says, 'We want it this way,' we'll get it this way.

So agency staff are often torn between their clients and the system. If they are unable to "make it fit," they lose clients and the ability to provide for their needs. Such an outcome goes against their mission and their funding. As a result, the agency is caught in sort of a case management "Catch-22" between system rules and client needs.

> You do feel powerless, because you promise to support someone who is mentally ill and who's without a home, and that's a big task. Because ... there's always administrative stuff that you have to adhere to; it's like, you really don't have any power. It's like a hierarchy, it's the administrators, it's [our agency] and it's the participants. And they look at you as the one with the power, and it's like, but I really don't have power. And they don't understand that. All they see is one system.

Another team member:

> [But] what's going to happen is, if you tell them 'I can help you,' and then as it turns out you can only help them for three months, you know, they're going to be like, 'You're not meeting my needs.'

The result is that the agency has difficulty keeping clients. With clients who are extremely hard to engage, and who can disappear if they feel no need to be visible, the lack of means to keep them engaged adds aggravation to the frustration the REACH teams already experience. To forestall client drop-outs, team members invest themselves personally through persuasion and emotional labor (Hochschild, 1983) to keep each client on board while the case managers struggle with the system. Such conditions are unsurprisingly a cause of burnout.

> I don't think that there are many elected representatives that will understand that Shawn going to an ice hockey game with friends from the Drop In Center is a better place for him to be than where he was. And the fact that he was there is going to make a difference, and it was money well spent. We don't know how to quantify those stories . . . and it's because [they're all unique and individual]. And we cherish individuality, and it's part of what our nation calls our own, but it's also something that we don't know how to support.

The service providers in this study were torn between three disjunctive sets of expectations: the rules

405 of the two systems, and the needs of their clients. They try to find a workable compromise and frequently do not succeed. One of the three sets is often left unmet. This is a constant source of frustration for the team members, especially when it is the client who loses out.

Discussion

410 The present research is a case study of a single agency located in a single county mental health system, which raises questions about its generalizability to social services. What can we learn from the case managers of REACH? While on the surface this analysis only
415 illuminates the personal agonies of the workers in one agency, the results have broader theoretical and practical implications. In terms of my first research question on the activities of case management, we see that case managers engage in more than the concrete services
420 identified in the literature, they invest emotional labor as well. The stress literature identifies both of these activities as forms of social support, instrumental and socioemotional (Thoits, 1986). Instrumental support includes all the basic services considered part of case
425 management: money, food, shelter, clothes, transportation, medical care, etc. Socioemotional support, on the other hand, includes more invisible aid in the form of talking about problems, listening, encouraging, and applauding success.

430 The staff in this study most likely provided more socioemotional support than most workers in their position, as they used it as a means of making up for shortcomings in the instrumental support they had to offer. Nonetheless, most social service providers en-
435 gage in this as a sort of "invisible service" to their clients. Empathy, rapport, and understanding are overtly part of social work training, and are highly valued skills in the profession. Their influence appears even in the accomplishment of more instrumental tasks. For
440 instance, the staff at REACH did not merely link their clients to other services, but negotiated barriers to services in a politically charged system. In addition, like all case managers, they were perpetually engaged in trying to tailor a general system to the unique needs
445 of individual clients. Such efforts entail diplomacy, sensitivity, and rapport, all of which have sizable emotional components. Intensive case management, then, entails service linkage, advocacy, *and* socioemotional support as crucial elements of service delivery.

450 Regarding my second research question, the results on the difficulty of delivering services illustrate possible consequences of bureaucratic conflict for any agency straddling two or more systems. Weber lists as the first characteristic of a bureaucracy that "[t]here is
455 the principle of fixed and official jurisdictional areas, which are generally ordered by rules, that is, by laws or administrative regulations" (Gerth and Mills, 1946). These rules and areas circumscribe the duties and powers of those working within the bureaucracy, main-
460 taining and supporting its authority. As Weber points out, in a well-ordered bureaucracy, these duties are routinized and well-regulated, and conflict seldom arises.

Yet, in this study, we see an example of two routi-
465 nized bureaucracies coming into conflict within a single agency. As a result, duties are no longer clear cut, and powers even less so. Merton captures this dilemma nicely in his conception of role-conflict within a role-set (1957, 1967). The case manager holds a social po-
470 sition – a role – within a social system, that is, the system of county mental health. To the degree that the case manager has incongruent expectations between the roles defined by each bureaucracy, the role occupant, the case manager, is conflicted.

475 Such a situation illustrates rather well a partial answer to a question raised by Merton himself:

"The assumed structural basis for potential disturbance of a role-set gives rise to a double question: Which social mechanisms, if any, operate to counteract the theoreti-
480 cally assumed instability of role-sets, and, correlatively, under which circumstances do these social mechanisms fail to operate, with resulting inefficiency, confusion, and conflict?"

This study provides a partial answer; the overlap of
485 bureaucracies, institutions, or social systems, more generally, sets up conditions under which expectations collide, and role-sets become unstable.

Such a notion adds a new dimension to existing work on the difficulty of providing services to persons
490 with severe mental illness. Previous research has focused on barriers to service delivery (e.g., as described by Boyer, 1987; Rog, 1988; and Morrissey et al., 1986), such as fragmentation in the system, or noncompliance and lack of resources among the service
495 population. The case managers in this study did not see their frustration in that light, however. To them, the source of the frustration was their perception of being caught between disparate federal and county systems. In particular, the case managers experienced a sense of
500 being bound in a web of bureaucratic contradictions, such that their own service system was itself preventing them from providing services. Under the rules of these two systems, they had contradictory work expectations. In other words, the case managers experi-
505 enced this conflict between two bureaucracies as conflict within their occupational role.

According to Merton's theory of the "role-set," each position in the social structure has not just one associated role, but a set of roles reflecting the various
510 obligations vis-a-vis relevant others. His own example of a teacher has one set of expectations regarding interactions with students, and entirely another set regarding her interactions with the school principal or superintendent (1957). This is roughly comparable to a case
515 manager who has three sets of role-expectations, one with each of two funding agencies, and one with clients. To the degree that these expectations are mutually incompatible, the case manager experiences conflict

520 between roles within a set, what Merton calls role con- flict. Thus role-set theory provides a vocabulary for discussing the process whereby the structural becomes personal, and the external conflict of systems becomes internalized.

525 Stryker (1980) describes how external conflict can have psychological and emotional effects through our roles. According to Stryker, roles are the materials we use to identify who we are. Engaging in actions that are in keeping with our role-identities reinforces our sense of self. Expanding on Stryker's work, Heise (1978,
530 1987) argues that if conflicts within established roles endure and cannot be argued away, these conflicts will lead to change in the role-identity. If the conflicts are comprised of negative or disempowering information, the change in the role-identity will be negative as well.
535 By this argument, the role conflict experienced by the case managers may have been more than frustrating, it may have been threatening to their sense of self. By preventing the case managers from doing what they wanted to do, the systemic contradiction could poten-
540 tially prevent them from being who they want to be. That is, by constraining their actions, the systems also prevented them from enacting their chosen occupa- tional role-identities in a positive way (Stryker, 1980). This bred a range of discontents, including anger, de-
545 fensiveness, bitterness, powerlessness, and apathy. If frustration was the short-term result of contradiction, its long-term consequence was occupational demorali- zation among the very people striving to ameliorate the despair of others.
550 Such a conflict between bureaucracies is hardly un- usual in the social services. Indeed, multiple funding sources and overlapping bureaucracies may be more the norm than the exception. If this is the case, then the role conflict illuminated in this study may be wide-
555 spread indeed. While such conflict may not consis- tently reach the same proportions as in this case – in- deed, exacerbating factors were rife in this site – the conflict appears quite likely to exist.

The lesson for program planners and policymakers,
560 then, is this: bureaucratic disjunctions may well be played out in occupational role conflict for program staff. Burnout is not merely personal, it is structural as well. When designing new programs, a hostile or con- flicted system can make the most well-planned pro-
565 gram go awry. To limit such disjunctions, planners must take into account flaws in the existing system and degrees to which the existing system may not match with the program to be implemented.

Conclusion

This agency's untenable position between two sys-
570 tems obviously makes a difference in the effectiveness of its services. The fact that the agency's targets are, by definition, extremely difficult clients to serve is a con- tributing factor to the dilemma as well. REACH found itself torn between the rules and resources of two con-
575 flicting bureaucracies. This conflict created dilemmas in providing services to clients: Meeting eligibility criteria for services from the federation grant meant the clients did not meet the eligibility criteria for many county services. REACH staff reacted to this dilemma
580 by bending rules, finding loopholes, and investing extra time and emotional labor in each client. Despite this, it remained very hard to provide desired services to their clients, and many slipped away. Aware of the bureau- cratic conflict, but unable to find recourse for their di-
585 lemmas, the REACH staff grew frustrated, angry, and resentful of the county system.

Epilogue

The agency's untenable situation between two in- compatible bureaucracies was, as evident in this paper, inherently unstable. It, combined with budgetary com-
590 plications in the system, led to increasing resentment between the county and REACH. Toward the end of my fieldwork, the county abruptly took advantage of a quiet offer from the state to take over administration of the program. REACH staff arrived at work one day to
595 find a letter informing them that they were suddenly state, rather than county, employees. Despite the shock and consternation produced by the change, it turned out to be an improvement for all concerned. A few months after my departure from the field, REACH had moved
600 into its new role at the outreach and community service arm of the local State Psychiatric Hospital. Oddly enough, despite the expected greater ideological con- flict between an in-patient hospital and an intensive community support program, the combination worked.
605 The reduction in bureaucratic conflict (largely due to the fact that the State had few pre-existing community service regulations to conflict with those of REACH) seemed to more than compensate for the surface dis- parities. REACH continued in this position through the
610 end of its federal funding, obtaining stability that it had been unable to achieve when dealing with the county, its apparent systemic peer.

References

Becker, Howard S., B. Geers, E. Hughes, and A. Strauss. 1961. *Boys in White: Student Culture in Medical School.* Chicago: University of Chicago Press.

Boyer, Carol A. 1987. "Obstacles in Urban Housing Policy for the Chronically Mentally Ill," pp. 71–81 in David Mechanic (Ed.), *Improving Mental Health Services: What the Social Sciences Can Tell Us.*

Chamberlain, R., MSW, and C. A. Rapp, Ph.D. 1991. "A Decade of Case Management: A Methodological Review of Outcome Research." *Community Mental Health Journal,* 27, 3:171–188.

Corbin, Juliet and Anselm Strass. 1990. *The Basics of Qualitative Research.* Thousand Oaks, CA: Sage.

Coser, Rose Laub. 1962. *Life in the Ward.* East Lansing: Michigan State Uni- versity Press.

Estroff, Sue E. 1981. *Making It Crazy: An Ethnography of Psychiatric Clients in an American Community.* Berkeley: University of California Press.

Freedman, Ruth I., and Ann Moran. 1984. *Wanderers in a Promised Land: The Chronically Mentally Ill and Deinstitutionalization.* Supplement of *Medical Care,* Vol. 22, No. 12.

Gerth, H.H. and C. Wright Mills, eds. 1946. *From Mar Weber: Essays in Sociology.* New York: Oxford University Press.

Goffman, Erving. 1961. *Asylums: Essays on the Social Situation of Mental Patients and Other Inmates.* New York: Anchor.

Goffman, Erving. 1974. *Asylums: Essays on the Social Situation of Mental Patients and Other Inmates.* Garden City, N.Y: Anchor.

Grob, Gerald N. 1994. *The Mad Among Us: A History of the Care of America's Mentally Ill.* NY: Free Press.

Heise, David R. 1979. *Understanding Events: Affect and the Construction of Social Action.* New York: Cambridge.

——— 1987. "Affect Control Theory: Concepts and Model." *Journal of Mathematical Sociology,* 13:1–33.

Hochschild, Arlie. 1983. *The Managed Heart: Commercialization of Human Feeling.* Berkeley: University of California Press.

Hopper, Kim. 1998. "Housing the Homeless." *Social Policy:* Spring, 1998.

Jencks, Christopher. 1994. "Housing the Homeless." *The New York Review,* May 12.

Liebow, Elliot. 1993. *Tell Them Who I Am: The Lives of Homeless Women.* New York: Free Press.

Merton, Robert K. 1967. *On Theoretical Sociology.* NY: The Free Press.

Merton, Robert K. 1957. "The Role-Set: Problems in Sociological Theory." *The British Journal of Sociology.* Volume VIII, June.

Morrissey, Joseph P., Kostas Guinis, Susan Barrow, Elmer L. Struening, and Steven E. Katz. 1986. "Organizational Barriers to Serving the Mentally Ill Homeless," pp. 93–108 in Billy E. Jones (Ed.), *Treating the Homeless: Urban Psychiatry's Challenge.*

Morse, Janice M. (ed.) 1994. *Critical Issues on Qualitative Research Methods.* Newbury Park: Sage.

Rog, Debra J. 1988. "Engaging Homeless Persons with Mental Illness into Treatment." Publication #PE-0501 of the National Mental Health Association. Prepared for the Division of Education and Service Systems Liaison of the National Institute of Mental Health.

Rubin, Allen. 1992. "Is Case Management Effective for People with Serious Mental Illness? A Research Review." *Health and Social Work,* 17, 2:138-150.

Solomon, Phyllis. 1992. "The Efficacy of Case Management Services for Severely Mentally Disabled Clients." *Community Mental Health Journal,* 28, 3:163–180.

Spicer, Paul, Mark Willenbring, Frank Miller, and Elgie Raymond. 1994. "Ethnographic Evaluation of Case Management for Homeless Alcoholics." *Practicing Anthropology,* 16, 4:23–26.

Strauss, Anselm, and Juliet Corbin. 1990. *Basics of Qualitative Research: Grounded Theory Procedures and Techniques.* Newbury Park: Sage.

Thoits, Peggy. 1986. "Social support as coping assistance." *Journal of Consulting and Clinical Psychology.* 54:416–423.

Exercise for Article 18

Factual Questions

1. What was the "initial intent" of this study?

2. REACH was under the jurisdiction of what level of government?

3. What was the size of the caseloads in this program?

4. On an average day, what would the researcher do after the morning staff meeting (including review of clients) and attending the team meeting?

5. According to the researcher, what lends credibility to the results despite the small sample size?

6. To provide services to homeless people with mental illness and substance abuse problems, the agency was supposed to draw on what?

Questions for Discussion

7. In the table of contents of this book, this study is classified as an example of qualitative research. Do you agree with this classification? Explain.

8. If you were conducting a study on this topic, would you select a qualitative or quantitative approach? Explain.

9. The researcher uses the term "participant observation." What do you think this term means? (See lines 171–174.)

10. Do you think the generalizability of the results of this study is limited? Explain. (See lines 227–232 and 410–417.)

Quality Ratings

Directions: Indicate your level of agreement with each of the following statements by circling a number from 5 for strongly agree (SA) to 1 for strongly disagree (SD). If you believe an item is not applicable to this research article, leave it blank. Be prepared to explain your ratings.

A. The introduction establishes the importance of the study.

SA   5   4   3   2   1   SD

B. The literature review establishes the context for the study.

SA   5   4   3   2   1   SD

C. The research purpose, question, or hypothesis is clearly stated.

SA   5   4   3   2   1   SD

D. The method of sampling is sound.

SA   5   4   3   2   1   SD

E. Relevant demographics (for example, age, gender, and ethnicity) are described.

SA   5   4   3   2   1   SD

F. Measurement procedures are adequate.

SA   5   4   3   2   1   SD

G. All procedures have been described in sufficient detail to permit a replication of the study.

SA   5   4   3   2   1   SD

H. The participants have been adequately protected from potential harm.

SA   5   4   3   2   1   SD

I. The results are clearly described.

SA   5   4   3   2   1   SD

J. The discussion/conclusion is appropriate.

SA   5   4   3   2   1   SD

K. Despite any flaws, the report is worthy of publication.

SA   5   4   3   2   1   SD

Article 19

High Hopes in a Grim World: Emerging Adults' Views of Their Futures and "Generation X"

Jeffrey Jensen Arnett
University of Maryland

ABSTRACT. Views of the future were explored among emerging adults (aged 21 through 28). In general, they viewed their personal futures optimistically and believed their lives would be as good or better than their parents' lives in aspects such as financial well-being, career achievements, personal relationships, and overall quality of life. Interview responses indicated that many participants emphasized personal relationships, especially marriage, as the foundation of their future happiness. However, regarding the future of their generation as a whole, they were pessimistic. A majority of them agreed with the "Generation X" characterization of their generation as cynical and pessimistic. Reasons for this cynicism and pessimism were diverse and included economic prospects as well as societal problems such as crime and environmental destruction. Nevertheless, the participants tended to believe they would succeed in their personal pursuit of happiness even amidst the difficult conditions facing their generation and the world.

From *Youth & Society, 31,* 267–286. Copyright © 2000 by Sage Publications, Inc. All rights reserved.

Dramatic demographic changes have taken place during the past 30 years for young people in their late teens and 20s in American society. As recently as 1970, the median age of marriage was 21 for females [5] and 23 for males; by 1996, it had risen to 25 for females and 27 for males (U.S. Bureau of the Census, 1997). Age of first childbirth followed a similar pattern. Also during this time, the proportion of young people obtaining higher education after high school [10] rose steeply from 48% in 1970 to 60% by 1993 (Arnett & Taber, 1994; Schulenberg, Bachman, Johnston, & O'Malley, 1995). Similar changes have taken place in other industrialized countries (Noble, Cover, & Yanagishita, 1996).

[15] In effect, a new period of life has opened up between adolescence and adulthood as a normative experience for young people in industrialized societies. The late teens and early 20s are no longer a period in which the typical pattern is to enter and settle into long-term [20] adult roles. On the contrary, it is a period of life characterized for many young people by a high degree of change, experimentation, and instability (Rindfuss, 1991) as they explore a variety of possibilities in love, work, and worldviews (Arnett, 1998, in press; Arnett, [25] Ramos, & Jensen, in press). The period was originally termed "youth" by Keniston (1971), but because of certain inadequacies in the term *youth*, it has more recently been called *emerging adulthood* (see Arnett, 1998, in press; Arnett & Taber, 1994). Emerging adult- [30] hood is conceptualized as beginning with the end of secondary education, usually age 18 in American society, and ending in the mid- to late 20s for most people as the experimentation of the period is succeeded by more enduring life choices (Arnett, 1998, in press).

[35] Emerging adulthood is distinct demographically and subjectively from adolescence (roughly from ages 10 through 17) and young adulthood (roughly from age 30 to the early 40s). Emerging adulthood is distinct demographically because it is a period characterized by [40] an exceptionally high level of demographic change and diversity. For example, residential mobility peaks in the mid-20s, and the 20s are also years of frequent change and transition in occupation, educational status, and personal relationships (Rindfuss, 1991). Emerging [45] adulthood is also distinct subjectively. The majority of adolescents do not believe they have reached adulthood, and the majority of people aged 30 and older believe they have, but most people in their 20s see themselves as somewhere in between adolescence and [50] adulthood: The majority answer "in some respects yes, in some respects no" when asked whether they feel they have reached adulthood (Arnett, 1997, 2000).

Despite the fact that a period of emerging adulthood has become normative in American society, little [55] research has focused on development during the 20s. Although studies of college students are abundant in social science research, research on young people who do not attend college and on young people beyond college age is scarce (William T. Grant Foundation [60] Commission on Work, Family and Citizenship, 1988). Keniston's (1971) conception of youth did not generate research attention to the period, and the concept of emerging adulthood has only been articulated very recently (Arnett, 1998, in press; Arnett & Taber, 1994).

65 One exception to this neglect is the long tradition of sociological and demographic research on the timing of transition events such as marriage and parenthood (e.g., Hogan & Astone, 1986; Marini, 1984; Rindfuss, 1991). Other than this area, however, there is little research on 70 this age period (Jessor, Donovan, & Costa, 1991).

In lieu of scholarly attention, a great deal of public attention has focused on this period in the past decade in works of fiction and in journalistic accounts. These works have tended to depict young people in their 20s 75 as pessimistic and uncertain as they approach the threshold of adulthood. Most notably, Coupland's (1991) novel *Generation X* portrayed three rootless young people in their mid- to late 20s and their reluctance to make the role transitions associated with the 80 transition to adulthood (e.g., marriage, a long-term occupation). The novel generated a remarkable amount of attention and commentary, and "Generation X" quickly became familiar as a term applied to the current generation of young people in their late teens and 85 20s.

Journalists have devoted considerable attention to Generation X. In journalistic accounts, Generation X has been described as materialistic, pessimistic, and cynical (Giles, 1994; Hornblower, 1997; Kinsley, 90 1994). Young people in their 20s are often depicted as daunted by the mixed economic prospects that face them in the workplace, by the personal debt they have accumulated by the time they leave higher education, and by the national debt that has been left to them by 95 previous generations (Roper Organization, 1993). At the same time, they are depicted as ambitious and eager to pursue their financial, occupational, and personal goals (Hornblower, 1997).

Most of the information used by journalists in de-100 picting Generation X in this way comes from polling data and marketing research, especially by Yankelovich Partners and the Roper Organization. For example, in a 1996 poll, Yankelovich Partners found that 64% of young people aged 18 to 24 agreed that "mate-105 rial things, like what I drive and the house I live in, are really important to me" (Hornblower, 1997, p. 65). About one-half believed that they would be better off financially than their parents. Nearly all—96%—agreed, "I am very sure that someday I will get to 110 where I want to be in life" (p. 62). In a 1992 poll, the Roper Organization found 18- to 29-year-olds to have higher material aspirations than 18- to 29-year-olds polled by the organization in 1978 (Roper Organization, 1993). Fifty-nine percent aspired to have a lot of 115 money (compared with 50% in 1978), 42% aspired to have a second car (28% in 1978), and 41% aspired to have a vacation home (25% in 1978). Sixty-nine percent included a job that pays a lot more than average as part of their definition of "the good life" (58% in 120 1978). However, an equal percentage included an interesting job as part of their definition. Many of the poll results on the views of emerging adults concern

economic issues, partly because these are believed to be issues that are especially salient to young people as 125 they enter the workforce, but also because the objective of pollsters such as Yankelovich Partners and the Roper Organization is to inform their corporate clients about the economic characteristics of their potential customers.

130 This study is an exploration of views of the future among emerging adults, including not only economic issues but also their views of their prospects in terms of career achievements, personal relationships, and overall quality of life. Views of the future are an important 135 topic with respect to emerging adults because for many of them, the nature and quality of their adult lives remain to be constructed. It is a time when, for many young people, few major life decisions have been settled and a wide range of options remains possible. For 140 this reason, questions about the future are especially relevant to their lives.

In addition to questions about their own futures, participants in the study were asked what they perceived to be the view of the future held by young peo-145 ple more generally. Specifically, they were asked whether they agreed with the depiction of their generation as pessimistic and cynical as reflected in the term *Generation X*. This question was asked in order to compare it with the questions on their personal futures 150 to get a sense of how they compared their own view of the future with the view of the future held by their generation. It was also asked to explore the validity of popular ideas about Generation X.

Method
Participants
The participants were 140 persons aged 21 to 28 155 years. General characteristics of the sample are shown in Table 1. The sample was evenly divided between 21- to 24-year-olds (50%) and 25- to 28-year-olds (50%) and between males and females. Close to half of the participants were married, and about one-fourth had 160 had at least one child. Two-thirds of the participants were employed full-time, and one-fourth part-time. 28% were in school full-time, and 8% were enrolled part-time. "Some college" was the modal level of education, indicated by 52% of the participants. There was 165 a broad range of variability in the social class of the participants' families of origin, as indicated by father's and mother's education.

Procedure
The data presented here were collected as part of a larger study on emerging adults in their 20s. The study 170 took place in a medium-sized city in the Midwest. Potential participants were identified through enrollment lists from the two local high schools for the previous 3 to 10 years. All persons on the enrollment lists who had current addresses in the area that could be identified 175 through phone book listings or by contacting their parents were sent a letter describing the study and then

contacted by phone. Of the persons contacted, 72% agreed to participate in the study. Data collection took place in the author's office or the participant's home, depending on the participant's preference. The study was conducted during 1994 and 1995.

Measures

The study included an interview and a questionnaire. Questionnaire items that pertained to participants' views of the future were as follows:

"Overall, do you think the quality of your life is likely to be better or worse than your parents' has been?"

"Overall, do you think your financial well-being in adulthood is likely to be better or worse than your parents' has been?"

"Overall, do you think your career achievements are likely to be better or worse than your parents' have been?"

"Overall, do you think your personal relationships in adulthood are likely to be better or worse than your parents' have been?"

For each of these questions, participants could answer "better," "worse," or "about the same."

From the interview, two questions were of interest for this article. One was similar to one of the items on the questionnaire and concerned participants' personal futures: "Do you think your life, overall, is likely to be better or worse than your parents' lives have been?" The second concerned their perceptions of their generation's views of the future: "Some people have called your generation *Generation X* and said that one of the distinctive characteristics of your generation is that you tend to be cynical and pessimistic about the future. Do you think this is true of your generation?" This question was added after the study had begun and was answered by 76 of the participants.

Results and Discussion

The results and the discussion are integrated in this section. This approach was taken because it was believed that the qualitative interview results, in particular, were better suited to discussion commentary at the time they were presented rather than in a separate section. With respect to the statistics on the quantitative data, analyses were conducted using chi-square tests. The four questionnaire items about participants' personal futures and the coded Generation X question from the interview were analyzed in relation to age (21 to 24 vs. 25 to 28), gender, marital status, parenthood (no children vs. one or more children), father's education, mother's education, and parental divorce. These are all variables that could conceivably be related to emerging adults' views of the future. Only analyses that were statistically significant are discussed below.

With respect to the qualitative data, for the interview question on overall quality of life in comparison to parents' lives, there was a nearly identical question on the questionnaire, so the interview data were used only for illustration of certain themes underlying their

responses to the questionnaire item. For the interview question about Generation X, responses were coded into three categories: agree, disagree, and ambiguous or uncodable. Responses were coded by the author, and 30% of the responses were coded by a second coder, a colleague of the author who was not otherwise involved in the study. The rate of agreement was more than 90%. The author then identified themes within participants' responses to the interview question and selected quotes for illustrating those themes.

Table 1
Background Characteristics of the Sample

Characteristic	%
Gender	
Male	53
Female	47
Employment	
Full	67
Part	24
None	9
Ethnicity	
White	94
Black	5
Other	1
Marital status	
Married	60
Single	40
Current educational status	
In school full-time	28
In school part-time	8
Not in school	65
Number of children	
None	73
One	14
Two or more	13
Mother's education	
Less than high school degree	8
High school degree	23
Some college	23
College degree	27
Some graduate school or graduate school degree	19
Father's education	
Less than high school degree	8
High school degree	24
Some college	15
College degree	24
Some graduate school or graduate school degree	30

Views of Their Personal Futures

The questionnaire results indicated that overwhelmingly, the emerging adults believed their lives would be as good or better than their parents' lives had been (see Table 2). This was true for overall quality of life, $\chi^2 (2, N = 138) = 41.2$, $p < .001$, as well as for the specific areas of financial well-being, $\chi^2 (2, N = 139) = 11.1$, $p < .01$; career achievements, $\chi^2 (2, N = 139) = 30.3$, $p < .001$; and personal relationships, $\chi^2 (2, N = 139) = 62.6$, $p < .001$. A majority believed that their overall quality of life (52%) and their personal relationships (58%) would be better than their parents' had been. 45% believed that their financial well-being would be better than their parents' had been, and 47% believed that their career achievements would be better. The finding that slightly less than half believed their financial well-being would be better than their parents was nearly identical to the results of a similar question in a national poll in 1996 by Yankelovich Partners (Hornblower, 1997).

Table 2
Emerging Adults' Comparisons of Their Future Lives in Relation to Their Parents' Lives (in percentages)

	Worse	Same	Better
Overall quality of life	9	39	52
Financial well-being	22	34	45
Career achievements	12	42	47
Personal relationships	4	39	58

Further insights into the meaning of their responses on the questionnaire were provided in their interview responses to the question, "Do you think your life, overall, is likely to be better or worse than your parents' lives have been?" Several themes emerged in the interviews. One theme was that when emerging adults indicated that they expected their lives were going to be the same as their parents' lives, this was typically a highly optimistic response because it was the response of emerging adults who viewed their parents' lives in highly favorable terms. In other words, "the same as parents" meant a happy and successful life. For example, a 24-year-old woman responded:

I would be very, very content if it was the same. I definitely don't want it to be worse, that's for sure. And I don't know if it could be any better. They have a great life.

Similarly, a 24-year-old man answered:

I think it will be about the same, actually. I want it to be. I think they've been a great example. I think they're wonderful people and they've given a lot to this world.

A second theme in the interviews was that financial well-being was secondary to other aspects of their hopes for the future, especially for emerging adults whose parents had been financially successful. For example, a 27-year-old man who was a singer in a rock band and whose father had been a biology professor indicated that he would probably not make as much money as his father but that it did not matter in terms of his future happiness:

I have meager needs. The things that I'm looking for in life aren't going to come with a bunch of money and a big house . . . I don't think I'll make as much money as him, but I don't need as much either.

A 25-year-old man believed the overall quality of his life would be better in comparison to that of his father, who was a successful and wealthy physician:

As I view it, yes, my quality of life will be better. I don't think my dad's happy. He thinks he's happy, but he's on a grind. He's on a rat race. The good side is he's in a profession that helps people.... But personally, all these career things that have to be done, I don't know. I think I'm able to step back, so I think I'll be able to be more happy, and that translates into a higher quality of life. I won't be anywhere as wealthy as they will; I've accepted that.... That's the whole point of most fathers' lives is to make their son's life better, and we're reaping the benefit of that. I'm able to choose not to be rich because I know what it's like. I know I can live without it.

However, this view depended to some extent on the economic status of the parents. Those whose parents were not as wealthy tended to place more value on the attainment of financial security, and were more likely to see their future lives as better financially and occupationally. In the quantitative analyses, those whose fathers' education was relatively lower were more likely to believe that their lives would be better than their parents' lives financially, χ^2 (8, $N = 118$) = 28.20, $p < .001$; in terms of career achievements, χ^2 (8, $N = 118$) = 30.28, $p < .001$; and overall, χ^2 (8, $N= 118$) = 30.21, $p < .001$. (A similar pattern was found with respect to mother's education.) For example, this 25-year-old woman saw her and her husband's financial success as part of a sequence of generational progress:

[My parents] both came from hard childhoods and they made a lot of their life. And I think their lives were better than their parents' lives, and I think it can only get better. I mean, they've brought us up to a stage higher than what they were, and I think that I can bring myself up higher than the stage that they were. I think with [my husband] and I both having all this education, we would be having jobs that will put us in a little higher bracket than them. So financially, I think we'll be a little better off.

Overall, however, the results of the interviews suggest that poll results indicating that emerging adults are materialistic and prize financial well-being may be misleading. It appears that although they like having material things and would prefer to be well-off financially, for many of them, that goal is secondary to their enjoyment of their work and to their more general pursuit of happiness. Similar results have been found in other studies of American's views of work (Colby, Sippola, & Phelps, in press; Jensen, 1998).

It should be added that the views of this sample on their financial futures may be different than the views of emerging adults from other parts of American society. The emerging adults in this study were predominantly White (94%), and the majority of them had at least one parent with a college degree. Would views of their personal futures be different, more pessimistic, among emerging adults who were from lower social classes and/or who were members of ethnic minorities? Perhaps. It is interesting to note that in this study, those from relatively low socioeconomic backgrounds were more optimistic than others about their personal futures (in relation to their parents' lives). Similar results were reported in a recent study of college students' views of their futures (Eskilson & Wiley, 1999).

It is possible that there are relations between social class and ethnicity in emerging adults' views of the future. Studies of young African Americans have shown that those from lower social classes are more optimistic about their prospects of succeeding in American society than those from the middle class, because those in the middle class are more likely to have had direct experience with racism from Whites as a result of having more daily contact with them (Hochschild, 1996). However, this study cannot speak to the experience of emerging adults in ethnic minorities except to suggest that their views of the future would be an intriguing topic for further investigation.

A third theme in the interviews was the preeminence of personal relationships as a basis for happiness. Of the four questions on the questionnaire comparing their future lives with their parents' lives, the emerging adults were most likely to think their lives would be better than their parents' lives in terms of personal relationships. (Binomial tests showed that only for the question on personal relationships were emerging adults more likely to answer "better" than "the same," $p < .05$.) In response to the interview question as well, this theme was prominent. Personal relationships, especially the marriage relationship, were seen as the ultimate source of happiness by many of them.

This was especially true for those who had come from a family in which the parents had divorced or had had frequent conflicts. They emphatically believed that their own marriages would be better. Samuel Johnson is often quoted as having said, "Remarriage is the triumph of hope over experience." For this generation of emerging adults, even a first marriage often represents such a triumph. On the questionnaire, participants whose parents had divorced were more likely than participants from nondivorced families to believe their personal relationships would be better than their parents' had been, χ^2 (2, $N=137$) = 9.90, $p < .01$. It was only with respect to personal relationships—and not with respect to financial well-being, career achievements, or their overall lives—that participants from divorced families were more likely than those from nondivorced families to believe their lives would be better than their parents' lives.

This view was also evident in interview responses. For example, a 24-year-old woman asserted: "I think [my life is] going to be better [than my parents']. I don't foresee a divorce in my future." Similarly, a 26-year-old man said he thought his life would be

> better.... I don't think about it so much financially. I think about it more from a personal standpoint. The fact that they got divorced, I consider that as not being successful and therefore I obviously hope that does not happen to me. So in that respect, I expect it to be better.

A 29-year-old man responded:

> Mentally, it will be better . . . I ain't going to divorce Chris. She'd have to kill me to get rid of me, you know, because she's a one of a kind woman, you know. I've never met anybody like her. Like I said, I can just see us staying together just like this, always getting along.

A 26-year-old woman hoped to succeed in this respect where her friends had failed:

> I think it's going to be better. I'm hoping to have a marriage that lasts forever. I know too many of my friends who have gotten married and gotten divorced already, and I don't want that to happen. I want to be one of those people that are married for 60 years or something.

In sum, the emerging adults in this study viewed their personal futures with high hopes. With few exceptions, they expected their lives to be as good or better than their parents' lives. When they talked about their occupational futures, they emphasized the importance of finding personal satisfaction in their work rather than seeking jobs that would provide financial well-being first and foremost. Personal relationships, especially marriage, were viewed by them as the most important component of their future happiness, and the majority of them believed that they would be more successful in this respect than their parents had been.

Views of Generation X

Overall, the questionnaire results in combination with the interview results indicated a considerable amount of optimism among the participants with respect to their personal lives. However, they tended to see their generation's prospects in much more pessimistic terms. The question was, "Some people have called your generation 'Generation X' and said that one of the distinctive characteristics of your generation is that you tend to be cynical and pessimistic about the future. Do you think this is true of your generation, or not?" Of the participants, 59% agreed with the characterization of their generation as cynical and pessimistic, whereas 22% disagreed (the other 19% gave ambiguous or uncodable responses). The difference in the proportion of "agree" and "disagree" responses was significant in a binomial test ($p < .001$). Chi-square analyses indicated that there were no differences among participants in their responses to this question with respect to age, gender, marital status, parenthood status, father's education, mother's education, parental divorce, or their responses to any of the four questions concerning their views of their personal futures.

The reasons many of them viewed their generation as cynical and pessimistic were varied, but common responses included limited economic opportunities and increased awareness of societal problems such as crime and environmental destruction. Although most of them viewed their personal financial and career prospects as bright (as we have seen), many of the participants viewed their generation's economic prospects as bleak. A 23-year-old woman stated,

I think we're kind of, in some ways, the lost generation. We all were brought up to think, "You finish high school, you go to college, you get a degree, and you go out to work," just like our parents did. Then when we get to college, we realize we don't know what we want, and we still don't know. We graduate with a degree we didn't want. I would say probably 7 out of 10 of my friends do that right now; they've already had their degrees and have jobs totally unrelated to their field.

A 27-year-old man had a similar view and gave it a political lineage:

I guess it comes from growing up during the 70s with Watergate and all the problems with Carter. Then you start college and you've got Reagan who's slashing everything in education, and you just kind of think, "Well, they're trying to do everything they can just to knock us down a little bit, to keep the haves and the have nots further apart," and it seems a lot now that you've got people with college degrees that work in McDonald's, you know. There's nowhere to go when you get out of school because all the jobs are already taken.

These views support the perspective of Cote and Allahar (1994), who attacked *credentialism*, the increased requirement for educational degrees simply for the sake of the credential, although the material learned in the course of obtaining the degree often has little relationship to the skills necessary for the jobs young people end up taking. Cote and Allahar (1994) also argued that more higher education graduates are produced than the economy demands, so that many graduates—in their analysis, close to half—end up underemployed after graduation with jobs that require lower levels of skill than their education has provided them.

A second common theme of pessimism was increased awareness of problems such as crime and the destruction of the environment. For example, a 28-year-old woman saw a variety of formidable problems in the world around her:

There's so many things going on in the world that are so horrible now that haven't always been going on.... Things from the ozone layer, to overcrowding, to natural disasters, to AIDS and hunger and poverty, all those things.

With respect to these sorts of problems too, the participants could see the world as grim even when they viewed their own lives optimistically. Another 28-year-old woman explicitly contrasted the conditions of her own life with the conditions of the world as a whole:

I feel like I work very hard to be positive about what I have firm control over, and that's my life and how I lead my life and how I behave toward people around me. But I have a lot of concerns about society as a whole. I mean, I guess you could say that I am, deep down, pessimistic about events happening in the world.... Crime and guns scare me to death.... I've always been careful, but I've never had an edge of fear on me, and I think I have that now. And that makes me real pessimistic that society has come to that and especially makes me scared about the

idea of ever having a family of my own, because if it's like this now, what will it be 10 or 20 years from now in terms of trying to raise a family?

Similarly, this 24-year-old man hoped to preserve his prospects and those of his family in the face of difficult conditions in the world:

I think the nation as a whole is really headed for some tough stuff.... Just picking up the paper or watching the news, it kind of gets you down on the future, you know. You hear about all these kids with their guns in school.... It doesn't leave you with too much hope, but I try not to get down about it.... I mean, it's going to affect everybody, all this stuff that's going on, but I think if I raise my kids the way that I was raised, in what I believe is the truth, then I think they'll have an advantage over the other kids.

However, participants sometimes stated that it was not so much that societal problems had actually become worse but that awareness of the problems had increased in their generation due to pervasive media coverage. A 24-year-old man found his optimism difficult to sustain in the face of the media:

I try to be pretty optimistic about things, but then I like to watch the news too, and sometimes you have to be pessimistic about some of that stuff you see. It's like it's never going to change, you know.

This view was echoed by a 24-year-old woman:

It seems like the world just isn't as safe a place anymore. There's more violence on TV, and everywhere you go, it's there. People are more on guard much of the time.

The views of this 25-year-old man were similar:

Overpopulation…crime, and all that stuff. Just the way governments are; just everything.... It's a big mess. And I think, just through media and stuff, it's in your face so much that I think that adds to it. I mean, I threw my TV out; I don't even watch TV.... I just try to deal with my little circle right in town here, and I'm having the time of my life, to tell you the truth.... As far as being happy, it doesn't take a lot to make me happy, but as far as the whole world picture goes, it's a lot more crazy.

These comments provide support for the cultivation hypothesis (Gerbner, Gross, Morgan, & Signorelli, 1994), which has proposed that television distorts the way people view the condition of the society around them. A variety of studies have demonstrated an aspect of the cultivation hypothesis known as the "Mean World Syndrome," which states that people who watch relatively large amounts of television are more likely than others to see the world as dangerous, violent, and crime ridden. This has been found to be true for both children (Singer, Singer, & Rapaczynski, 1984) and adults (Gerbner, Gross, Morgan, & Signorelli, 1980, 1986). The comments shown above indicate that in the views of some emerging adults, watching television contributes to a perception of the world as dangerous and filled with problems. However, it should be added that this was a theme that came up in response to a question that was not specifically about media or television. It would take further, more systematic investigation of this issue to determine how widespread this view is among emerging adults and to assess the contribution of television to their pessimism in relation to other factors.

There were also emerging adults who agreed that many in their generation were cynical and pessimistic, but who dissented from this view themselves, sometimes quite vehemently. As one 21-year-old man stated,

I recycle as much as the next guy, but I really don't see the world as just becoming covered with garbage or the ozone layer disappearing. I really think it may have been exaggerated. It just seems like a lot of my generation just likes to whine about the horrible world that they were left by the generation before, but I think the generation before had to worry about nuclear war and stuff like that a lot more than my generation does now. I think if anything the world's gotten better in the past 50 years than it had been before.

Some of those who dissented also believed implicitly in the cultivation hypothesis. For example, this 24-year-old man stated,

I think we're bombarded with a sense of helplessness. If it's not homosexuality, it's the great whales or the ozone layer....[The media] just bombard us with negatives. Violence, crime, everything. Guns, drugs, disease. [But the truth is that] we are not in trouble.... Life is not in the balance. We're all not going to fall off the face of the earth tomorrow like we would be made to believe. I think a lot of people my age buy into everything the media says.... Our generation was raised by the television. We weren't raised by our parents in a lot of instances.... I don't think that anybody realizes how affected they are.

Furthermore, although a majority of participants agreed with the Generation X description of their generation as cynical and pessimistic, a substantial proportion (22%) disagreed with this view, not just as applied to themselves but as applied to their generation as a whole. For example, this 28-year-old woman stated,

No. Not at all, because I think maybe the generation before us was pessimistic and that's why we're now having to be more optimistic and set our sights a little differently. This is the recycling generation, this is the plan-for-our-future generation.

Overall, however, participants agreed that their generation sees the world pessimistically and has good reason to see it that way.

Summary and Conclusion

Emerging adulthood is a time when, for many young people, questions about the future are paramount. Of course, ruminating about the future is part of the human condition, and people of all ages speculate about what their lives may be like 1 year, 5 years, and many years into the future. However, questions about the future are especially salient for emerging adults

because for many of them, major decisions in love, work, and worldviews have yet to be made (Arnett, in press). Even for those who have made these decisions and entered adult roles, as most of them have by their late 20s, the majority of their adult lives lie ahead of them, and the fate of their early aspirations has yet to be determined.

The results of this study show a sharp distinction between how they view their personal futures and how they view their generation's perspective on the future. The study provides some support for the Generation X view that there is a cynical and pessimistic generational identity among young Americans currently in their 20s. Many young people do believe that their generation is cynical and pessimistic. They hear this view articulated by their peers and in the media, and many of them share this view themselves. They realize that a college degree is by no means a guarantee of finding a satisfying, fulfilling occupation. They worry about crime and a variety of other societal problems, and they wonder if they will be able to protect their children from being harmed by those problems. Some of them believe that the media inflate the extent of the problems in American society and resent the way they believe the media "bombard us" with news about the problems. But they feel there is no escape from the bombardment and, ultimately, no escape from living with the fear that those problems may one day harm them and those close to them.

Even amidst what they see as a grim world, however, most emerging adults maintain high hopes for their personal futures. A large proportion of them believe that their lives will be better than their parents' lives have been, in a variety of respects. Even when they believe the quality of their lives is likely to be the same as their parents' lives, this tends to be an optimistic response because it is often stated by emerging adults who see their parents' lives in a favorable light. Having a life like their parents' lives means having a life of personal success and happiness.

Where their parents have succeeded in life, they generally believe they will do just as well. Where their parents have failed, especially for those with parents whose marriages have failed, they believe they will do better. None of them believe that their own marriages will be among some 60% of first marriages forecasted to end in divorce. Financially too, they are optimistic, even if they have grown up in a family of relatively low socioeconomic status. In fact, in this study, social class background was inversely related to their views of their personal futures: those from relatively low social class backgrounds were even more confident than those from relatively high social class backgrounds that their lives would be better than their parents, financially as well as in other respects.

The optimism of these emerging adults is, in part, a reflection of the optimistic bias that exists for most people in most aspects of life (Weinstein & Klein,

1996). In general, people of all ages tend to believe that unpleasant events are more likely to happen to other
700 people than to themselves. However, this view is perhaps especially easy to sustain in emerging adulthood when so many things about their lives remain to be determined and when so many possibilities have yet to harden into accomplished facts. Although their views
705 of their futures may be optimistic and may not accurately reflect the futures in store for them, their optimism arguably serves an important psychological function. The belief that they will ultimately prevail in their personal pursuit of happiness, that their personal
710 success is not only possible but inevitable, allows them to proceed with confidence through a world they regard as fraught with peril.

References

Arnett, J. J. (1997). Young people's conceptions of the transition to adulthood. *Youth & Society, 29*, 1–23.

Arnett, J. J. (1998). Learning to stand alone: The contemporary American transition to adulthood in cultural and historical context. *Human Development, 41*, 295–315.

Arnett, J. J. (2000). *Conceptions of the transition to adulthood from adolescence through midlife.* Manuscript submitted for publication.

Arnett, J. J. (in press). Emerging adulthood: A theory of development from the late teens to the late twenties. *American Psychologist.*

Arnett, J. J., Ramos, K. D., & Jensen, L. A. (in press). Ideological views in emerging adulthood: Balancing autonomy and community. *Journal of Adult Development.*

Arnett, J., & Taber, S. (1994). Adolescence terminable and interminable: When does adolescence end? *Journal of Youth & Adolescence, 23*, 517–537.

Colby, A., Sippola, L., & Phelps, E. (1999). Social responsibility and paid work in contemporary life. In A. Rossi (Ed.), *Caring and doing for others: Social responsibility in the domains of family, work, and community.* Chicago: University of Chicago Press.

Cote, J. E., & Allahar, A. L. (1994). *Generation on hold: Coming of age in the late twentieth century.* New York: New York University Press.

Coupland, D. (1991). *Generation X.* New York: St. Martin's.

Eskilson, A., & Wiley, M. G. (1999). Solving for the X: Aspirations and expectations of college students. *Journal of Youth & Adolescence, 28*, 51–70.

Gerbner, G., Gross, L., Morgan, M., & Signorelli, N. (1980). The "mainstreaming" of America: Violence profile no. 11. *Journal of Communication, 30*, 10–29.

Gerbner, G., Gross, L., Morgan, M., & Signorelli, N. (1986). The dynamics of the cultivation process. In J. Bryant & D. Zillman (Eds.), *Perspectives on media effects* (pp. 17–48). Hillsdale, NJ: Lawrence Erlbaum.

Gerbner, G., Gross, L., Morgan, M., & Signorelli, N. (1994). *Television violence profile no. 16.* Philadelphia: Annenberg School for Communication.

Giles, J. (1994, June 6). Generalizations X. *Newsweek*, pp. 64–72.

Hochschild, J. L. (1996). *Facing up to the American dream: Race, class, and the soul of the nation.* Princeton, NJ: Princeton University Press.

Hogan, D. P., & Astone, N. M. (1986). The transition to adulthood. *Annual Review of Sociology, 12*, 109–130.

Hornblower, M. (1997, June 9). Great Xpectations. *Time*, pp. 58–68.

Jensen, L. (1998). *The culture war and the American dream: Family and work.* Manuscript submitted for publication.

Jessor, R., Donovan, J. E., & Costa, F. M. (1991). *Beyond adolescence: Problem behavior and young adult development.* New York: Cambridge University Press.

Keniston, K. (1971). *Youth and dissent: The rise of a new opposition.* Orlando, FL: Harcourt Brace.

Kinsley, M. (1994, March 21). Back from the future. *The New Republic*, p. 6.

Marini, M. M. (1984). The order of events in the transition to adulthood. *Social Forces, 63*, 229–244.

Noble, J., Cover, J., & Yanagishita, M. (1996). *The world's youth.* Washington, DC: Population Reference Bureau.

Rindfuss, R. R. (1991). The young adult years: Diversity, structural change, and fertility. *Demography, 28*, 493–512.

Roper Organization. (1993, July). Twentysomething Americans. *The Public Pulse, 8*(7), 1–3.

Schulenberg, J., Bachman, J. G., Johnston, L. D., & O'Malley, P. M. (1995). American adolescents' views on family and work: Historical trends from 1976–1992. In P. Noack, M. Hofer, & J. Youniss (Eds.), *Psychological responses to social change: Human development in changing environments* (pp. 37–66). New York: de Gruyter.

Singer, D. G., Singer, J. L., & Rapaczynski, W. (1984). Family patterns and television viewing as predictors of children's beliefs and aggression. *Journal of Communication, 34*, 73–89.

U.S. Bureau of the Census (1997). *Statistical abstracts of the United States: 1997.* Washington, DC: Author.

Weinstein, N., & Klein, W. M. (1996). Unrealistic optimism: Present and future. *Journal of Social and Clinical Psychology, 15*, 1–8.

William T. Grant Foundation Commission on Work, Family, & Citizenship. (1988, February). *The forgotten half: Non-college-bound youth in America.* Washington, DC: William T. Grant Foundation.

Note: Jeffrey Jensen Arnett is a visiting associate professor in the Department of Human Development at the University of Maryland. His research interests include risk behavior and media use in adolescence and a wide variety of topics in emerging adulthood. He is the author of *Metalheads: Heavy Metal Music and Adolescent Alienation*, published in 1996 by Westview Press. Recent publications include "Adolescent Storm and Stress, Reconsidered," in the *American Psychologist*.

Exercise for Article 19

Factual Questions

1. "Emerging adulthood" is conceptualized as beginning with the end of what?

2. What was the age range of the participants in this study?

3. The second interview question (about Generation X tending to be cynical and pessimistic) was asked of how many participants?

4. What was the percentage rate of agreement for the coding by the researcher and the second coder?

5. Whites constituted what percentage of the sample?

6. What does the "cultivation hypothesis" propose?

7. The "optimistic bias" suggests that people of all ages tend to believe what?

Questions for Discussion

8. Of the persons contacted, 72% agreed to participate in the study. In your opinion, is this an adequate response rate? Explain. (See lines 177–178.)

9. The researcher used both a questionnaire and an interview. Does this make the study more interesting than if he had used only one of these methods to collect data? Explain.

10. Comment on the adequacy of the questions the researcher asked. Would you add any questions? Delete any? Modify any? Explain. (See lines 182–210.)

11. To what population(s), if any, would you be willing to generalize the results of this study?

12. If you were to conduct another study on the same topic, what changes in the research methodology, if any, would you make?

Quality Ratings

Directions: Indicate your level of agreement with each of the following statements by circling a number from 5 for strongly agree (SA) to 1 for strongly disagree (SD). If you believe an item is not applicable to this research article, leave it blank. Be prepared to explain your ratings.

A. The introduction establishes the importance of the study.

    SA   5   4   3   2   1   SD

B. The literature review establishes the context for the study.

    SA   5   4   3   2   1   SD

C. The research purpose, question, or hypothesis is clearly stated.

    SA   5   4   3   2   1   SD

D. The method of sampling is sound.

    SA   5   4   3   2   1   SD

E. Relevant demographics (for example, age, gender, and ethnicity) are described.

    SA   5   4   3   2   1   SD

F. Measurement procedures are adequate.

    SA   5   4   3   2   1   SD

G. All procedures have been described in sufficient detail to permit a replication of the study.

    SA   5   4   3   2   1   SD

H. The participants have been adequately protected from potential harm.

    SA   5   4   3   2   1   SD

I. The results are clearly described.

    SA   5   4   3   2   1   SD

J. The discussion/conclusion is appropriate.

    SA   5   4   3   2   1   SD

K. Despite any flaws, the report is worthy of publication.

    SA   5   4   3   2   1   SD

Article 20

Couples Watching Television:
Gender, Power, and the Remote Control

Alexis J. Walker
Oregon State University

ABSTRACT. I sought to confirm that partners in close relationships "do gender" (West & Zimmerman, 1987) and exercise power (Komter, 1989) even in their ordinary everyday behavior and specifically in their selection of television programming via a remote control device (RCD). Individuals in 36 couples (86% heterosexual, 14% gay or lesbian) were interviewed. Men in heterosexual couples use and control the RCD more than women, and their partners find RCD use more frustrating than they do. Heterosexual women also are less able than men to get their partners to watch a desired show. The results confirm that couples create and strengthen stereotypical notions of gender through the exercise of power, even in the mundane, joint, leisure activity of watching television.

From *Journal of Marriage and the Family*, *58*, 813–823. Copyright © 1996 by the National Council on Family Relations, 3989 Central Ave. NE, Suite 550, Minneapolis, MN 55421. Reprinted by permission. All rights reserved.

Five years ago, my parents bought a second television set because my mother refused to watch television with my father any longer. "I can't stand the way he flips through the channels," she said. Note that my fa- 5 ther actually has the use of the new television, and my mother has been relegated to the den with the older model. Nevertheless, mother now has her own set, and conflicts about the remote control device have been reduced considerably.

10 Several years ago, journalist Ellen Goodman (1993, p. 181) published an essay in which she described the RCD as "the most reactionary implement currently used to undermine equality in modern marriage." Because family scholars rarely study such mundane, ev- 15 eryday life experience, there is little research available to confirm Goodman's sentiments or to assess the prevalence of solutions to television-watching disagreements such as that employed by my parents. RCD use, however, presents a challenging arena in which to 20 examine gender and relationship issues in the experience of daily living.

Over the past 20 years, feminist scholars have shown that ordinary, routine, run-of-the-mill activities that take place inside homes every day bear an uncanny 25 resemblance to the social structure. For example, the distribution of household labor and of child care is gendered in the same way that paid work is gendered: The more boring and less desirable tasks are disproportionately performed by women, and status has a 30 way of reducing men's, but not women's, participation in these tasks. (See Thompson & Walker, 1989, for a review.) Examining television-watching behavior is a way to extend the feminist analysis to couples' leisure.

Despite the fact that television watching is the 35 dominant recreational activity in the United States today (Robinson, 1990), there is little research on this topic in the family studies literature. Indeed, there is little family research on leisure at all (but see Crawford, Geoffrey, & Crouter, 1986; Hill, 1988; Holman & 40 Jacquart, 1988), although scholars often mention that employed wives and mothers have very little of it (e.g., Coverman & Sheley, 1986; Hochschild, 1989; Mederer, 1993). Recently, Firestone and Shelton (1994), using data from the 1981 *Study of Time Use*, confirmed 45 that married women have less overall leisure time than married men. They also demonstrated gender-divergent patterns in the connection between paid work and both domestic (in-home) and out-of-home leisure time. Women who are employed have less out-of-home lei- 50 sure time than men do, but men who are employed have less domestic leisure time than employed women. Specifically, they found that employment hours do not affect the amount of leisure time that married women have at home. To explain this surprising finding, 55 Firestone and Shelton speculated that leisure at home appears to be the same for employed and nonemployed wives because leisure is compatible with household chores and with child care. In other words, women combine family work with leisure activities. For exam- 60 ple, they iron while watching television.

Although there is little research on leisure in family studies, there is considerable literature on gender and leisure in the field of leisure studies. For example, Henderson (1990), predating Firestone and Shelton 65 (1994), described women's leisure as fragmented because much of it takes place at home where it is mingled with domestic labor. In comparison with men, women say that leisure is less of a priority and that they do not deserve it. Some activities that are defined as 70 leisure pursuits, such as family picnics, are actually occasions for women's work, making leisure a possible source of internal conflict for women (Shank, 1986; Shaw, 1985). In fact, Henderson (1994) called for a deconstruction of leisure because the term embodies contradictions for women, contradictions that may be evident particularly in family leisure (Shaw, 1991).

To develop a way to measure couples' television-watching behavior, I sought guidance from the empirical research on television watching, which also is considerable. Here, studies describe various types of RCD use, sometimes referred to as (a) grazing (sometimes called surfing)—progressing through three or more channels with no more than 5 seconds on any one channel for the purpose of seeing what is available; (b) zapping—switching channels to avoid something, usually a commercial; and (c) zipping—fast-forwarding during a prerecorded program, mostly to avoid commercials (Cornwell et al., 1993; Walker & Bellamy, 1991).

Observational, survey, in-depth interview, and ethnographic data from communications researchers using a wide variety of sampling strategies revealed that when heterosexual families with children watch television together, fathers dominate in program selection and in the use of the RCD. Sons are active as well, using the RCD more than either their mothers or their sisters. That gender differences are smaller among younger persons, however, suggests a potential for women and men to be more similar in their remote control behavior in the future, when the RCD-using youth of today are adults (Copeland & Schweitzer, 1993; Cornwell et al., 1993; Eastman & Newton, 1995; Heeter & Greenberg, 1985; Krendl, Troiano, Dawson, & Clark, 1993; Lindlof, Shatzer, & Wilkinson, 1988; Morley, 1988; Perse & Ferguson, 1993). Note that the dominance in RCD use by men and boys in a family context is not evident when individuals are observed alone. In an experimental study, women were no less likely to use the RCD than were men (Bryant & Rockwell, 1993). The authors concluded that a social context is necessary to produce such gendered behavior.

Morley (1988) described fathers as using the RCD for unnegotiated channel switching—that is, changing channels when they want to—without explaining their behavior to or consulting other television watchers. Unemployed fathers, by the way, are less likely than employed fathers to use the RCD in this way, suggesting a possible connection between RCD use and the use of legitimate power—that is, power derived from and supported by societal norms and values (e.g., Farrington & Chertok, 1993).

Why so much channel switching? Men say they change channels to avoid commercials, to see if something better is on, to see what they are missing, to watch news reports, because they like variety, to avoid looking up the printed listings, to annoy others, and, my favorite reason, to watch more than one show at the same time (Perse & Ferguson, 1993). By contrast, women say they change channels to watch a specific program. A frightening finding is that the children of heavy RCD users are also heavy users, suggesting that parents pass on this behavior and that we can anticipate more grazing in the future (Heeter & Greenberg, 1985).

Copeland and Schweitzer (1993) concluded: "Men have usually been viewed as the persons who control program selection, and domination of the remote control seems to make visually explicit what may have previously been implicit" (p. 165). This notion of power, clearly stated in the language of the communications researchers, is missing from the family research on leisure. In their studies, however, the communications researchers have focused almost exclusively on parents watching television with their children. Rarely have they studied couples watching television. Furthermore, students of communication rarely have combined data about television watching and RCD use with questions of primary interest to those of us who study close relationships among adults. For example, are there any ways in which watching television with your partner is frustrating? Would you change the way that you watch television with your partner if you could? How do you influence your partner to watch something that you want to watch?

These questions address issues of power in relationships described by Aafke Komter (1989). She demonstrated that power is evident not only in the direct, observable resolution of conflict between partners, but also in covert or nonobservable events that reflect structural inequality. Direct expression of power reflects manifest power; covert expression reflects latent power. Examples of latent power are the ability to prevent issues from being raised, the anticipation of the desires of the more powerful partner, and resignation to an undesirable situation due to the fear of a negative reaction from the more powerful partner or worry that change might harm the relationship in some way (see also Huston, 1983; McDonald, 1980). In addition to other domains (e.g., family labor and sexual interaction), Komter included leisure in her study, but she focused only on hobbies and interaction with friends.

I chose to wed the focus of communications researchers on television-watching behavior with Komter's (1989) approach to studying power. I expected that heterosexual couples would "do gender" (West & Zimmerman, 1987) even in such a mundane activity as joint television watching. I anticipated that the creation and affirmation of gender would be evident in the (manifest and latent) power men have over their women partners in the domain of leisure activity. Furthermore, I sought to confirm the importance of gender in partner interaction by examining joint television watching behavior in lesbian and gay couples as well (see Kollock, Blumstein, & Schwartz, 1985).

Method

Participants

The sample for this study was characterized by its diversity. Participants were recruited primarily by students enrolled in an upper-division undergraduate course on gender and family relationships. In recruiting respondent pairs, students worked in groups of four to maximize diversity. Couples were chosen so that each group of four students would select a diverse set of pairs. All respondents were in a romantic (i.e., heterosexual married, heterosexual cohabiting, or cohabiting gay or lesbian) relationship in which both individuals were at least 18 years old. All couples had been living together for at least 1 year and had a television set with an RCD. Within each group, however, participants included (a) couples varying in relationship length, from shorter (1 year) to longer (15 years or more); (b) a lesbian or gay couple; (c) at least one married couple; (d) at least one heterosexual, cohabiting, or unmarried couple; (e) couples with and without children; (f) at least one couple in which at least one partner was Asian American, African American, Latino, or of mixed race; and (g) couples in which both partners were employed and couples in which only one partner was employed. Fourteen percent ($n = 5$ pairs) of the 36 couples (72 individuals) were gay or lesbian. Here, and for much of this report, I focus attention on the 31 heterosexual pairs.

Women and men in these heterosexual couples did not differ significantly on sociodemographic characteristics. (Table 1 shows these characteristics for all couples.) The typical respondent was 34 years old ($SD = 12.69$) and had completed 2 years of academic work beyond high school. Most (77%, $n = 48$) were White, although nearly one-quarter were either African American, Hispanic, or of mixed race. Nearly three-quarters (74%, $n = 48$) were married; one-quarter was cohabiting. On average, their relationships had been in existence for 10 years. Most (77%, $n = 48$) respondents were employed, and just over 30% ($n = 19$) were students; only 16% ($n = 10$) of the sample, however, were nonemployed, nonretired students. Heterosexual respondents represented three income groups. Just over one-third earned less than $20,000 annually, one-third reported an annual household income between $20,000 and $39,999, and just under one-third earned $40,000 or more. One-third had children living at home.

Measures

A semistructured interview was administered to each member of the couple. In addition to sociodemographic questions, respondents were asked about the number and location of television sets and videocassette recorders in the home, the frequency with which they and their partners watched television, and other activities they engage in while watching television. They were asked about use of the RCD, in general, while watching with their partner and during the program most recently watched with the partner. They were also asked if their most recent experience was typical of their joint television watching. These questions were quantitative in nature and are similar to the types of questions asked of participants by communications researchers. Additional single-item, quantitative questions were derived from the family studies literature; that is, questions about relationship happiness, happiness with the way things are regarding watching television with the partner, and how much partners enjoy the time they spend together.

Other questions focused on issues of power à la Komter (1989). These questions were open-ended and concerned changed expectations about watching television with the partner over the history of the relationship, how the couple decides on a program to watch together, how partners get each other to watch programs that they want to watch, and their frustrations with watching television with their partner. Respondents were asked if they would like to change anything about the way they watch television together, if they thought they would be successful at making these changes, whether it would be worth it for them to make the changes, and how their partner would react to the changes. In addition, any changes they had already made in their joint television-watching behavior were described.

Procedures

A coin toss was used to determine which partner to interview first. Partners were interviewed separately, usually in their own homes, by trained student interviewers. Interviews were audiotaped and transcribed. SAS was used to analyze the quantitative data, and transcriptions were read and reread for analysis of the open-ended data.

Results

On average, the heterosexual couples had 1.81 television sets ($SD = 0.99$), but some had only 1, and a few had as many as 5. They had 1.30 videocassette recorders ($SD = 0.53$), with a range from 1 to 3. They also had 1.30 RCDs ($SD = 0.68$), with a range from 1 to 3. The typical home had basic cable television (with no extra channels) or a satellite dish.

These individuals watched television quite often—on average almost daily for nearly 3 hours per day ($M = 2.77$, $SD = 1.48$). During the week prior to the interview, they had, on average, watched television together on 4.87 days ($SD = 2.09$). Nearly all, 94% ($n = 29$), of the women and 87% ($n = 27$) of the men reported that, regarding watching television with their partners, they were happy with the way things are. Yet two-thirds of the women and three-fifths of the men reported that there were things about their joint television watching that were frustrating to them. The interview transcripts were revealing about these frustrations. Women complained about their partners' grazing behavior, both during a show and when they first turned on the televi-

Table 1
Characteristics of Respondents in the Sample

Characteristic	Heterosexual Partners ($n = 62$)		Lesbian or Gay Partners ($n = 10$)	
	M or %	*SD* or *n*	*M* or %	*SD* or *n*
Age	34.1	12.69	36.4	7.52
Education level[a]	3.1	1.70	4.1	1.52
Race (% White)	77.4	48	100.0	10
Relationship status (%)				
Cohabiting	25.8	16	100.0	10
First marriage	58.1	36		
Previous marriage	16.1	10	10.0	1
Years in relationship	10.2	11.22	8.1	3.51
Children at home (%)	32.3	20	0.0	0
Employed (%)	77.4	48	90.0	9
Employment hours[b]	2.8	1.41	3.1	0.38
Income[c]	2.2	1.26	2.4	1.13

Note: Within heterosexual couples, there were no significant differences by gender for any of these variables.
[a]Education measured from 0 (*less than high school*) to 6 (*graduate degree*).
[b]Employment hours measured from 0 (*0 to 10 hours per week*) to 4 (*more than 40 hours per week*).
[c]Income measured from 1 (*less than $20,000*) to 5 (*more than $80,000*).

sion set. One woman in a 3-year cohabiting relationship said:

I would say that the only thing that's frustrating for me is when we first turn on the TV and he just flips through the channels. It drives me crazy because you can't tell what's on, because he just goes through and goes through and goes through.

Another woman, in the 17th year of a first marriage, reported, "[I get frustrated] only if I get hooked into one show and then he flips it to another one. As soon as I get hooked into something else, he flips it to something else." Such reports from women were common. A married man spontaneously agreed: "We don't watch TV a lot together; I would rather do other activities with my wife. Channel switching wasn't a problem until...the remote control." Indeed, many men indicated that their women partners were bothered by this behavior.

In contrast, men reported being frustrated with the quality of the programming or the circumstances of watching, rather than with RCD activity. For example, one husband said, "I wish we had a VCR.... I wish we had one of those TVs where you could watch two things on the screen at once." Another said, "It's sort of frustrating when I want to watch something she doesn't, and she goes into the other room and gets sort of pouty about it." A third reported, "No, [nothing is frustrating], but she does talk a little."

I looked specifically at the RCD; for example, where is the RCD usually located? Men were more likely than women to say that they usually hold the RCD or have it near them, $\chi^2(1, n = 62) = 7.38, p < .01$, and they were less likely than women to say that their partner usually holds it or has it near them, $\chi^2(1, n = 62) = 14.47, p < .001$. In half the couples ($n = 16$), according to both women and men, men have the RCD. In over 80% ($n = 25$) of the couples, according to both

the women and the men, the women do not have control of it solely. According to 16% ($n = 5$) of the women and 10% ($n = 3$) of the men, women control the remote. In roughly one-third of the couples, the RCD is in a neutral location, or both take turns holding it. The pattern was the same when respondents were asked about the RCD's location during the most recent television show that they watched together. The RCD was more likely to be located near men than near women or near both members of the couple, $\chi^2(2, n = 59) = 13.12$, $p < .001$. The transcriptions support this general pattern of RCD location, as well. A husband reported, "I usually use the remote because I know how to use it, and it usually sits right in front of me while I am on the couch." A young married woman said, "I had the baby [the RCD] this time. This was a rare occasion." Roger (all names are pseudonyms), a married man, reported:

I frequently have the remote at my side. I won't change the channel until we are ready to look for something else. If there is someone who wants to change the channel at a commercial, it will be Sally [his wife]. I will hand the remote to her, and she will change it to another favorite show, and then back. And that is very typical.

Sally agreed. The last time they watched television together, the RCD was in "Roger's pocket! Either in his shirt pocket or bathrobe pocket." A young, married man reported:

I don't hold [the RCD], but I pretty much have control of it, and if I don't care what's on, then I let her have it. Sometimes we fight over it. Not like fight, but, I mean, it's like, "You always have the remote control."

Women were significantly more likely than men to say that RCD use was frustrating to them, $\chi^2(1, n = 62) = 8.42, p < .01$. Only 10% ($n = 3$) of the men, but 42% ($n = 13$) of the women evidenced such frustration. Furthermore, women ($M = 0.61$, $SD = 0.79$) reported that significantly more RCD behaviors were frustrating to them than men reported ($M = 0.15$, $SD = 0.37$) $t(48)$ = -2.70, $p < .01$. Yet 30% ($n = 9$) of the women in the sample and 16% ($n = 5$) of the frustrated men reported that they would like to change how the RCD is used during their joint television watching. This difference was not significant.

What was frustrating about RCD use? Respondents reported being frustrated by the amount of grazing, the speed of grazing, heavy use of the RCD, and the partner taking too long to go back to a channel after switching from it during a commercial. A few respondents actually indicated concern about their own frequent RCD use. Women and men, however, reported similar percentages of other television-watching behaviors that were frustrating (e.g., too much time watching television; bothersome behaviors of the partner, such as making fun of a program); 58% ($n = 18$) of the women and 48% ($n = 15$) of the men were frustrated by these other behaviors.

Thus far, I have shown that men control the RCD more than women and that women are more frustrated by RCD behaviors than men are. I also asked about the other activities engaged in while watching television. Two types of activities were mentioned: family work (e.g., child care, cooking, laundry) and pleasurable activities, such as doing nothing (i.e., relaxing), eating, drinking, playing computer games, and so on. When activities within each type were summed, the findings were revealing. When asked about their most recent joint television-watching episode, men ($M = 1.00$, $SD = 0.52$) responded that they were significantly more likely than women ($M = 0.74$, $SD = 0.44$) to engage in pleasurable behaviors while watching television, $t(62)$ = 2.11, $p < .04$. Women ($M = 0.36$, $SD = 0.71$) were not more likely than men ($M = 0.13$, $SD = 0.34$) to do family work while they watched television, although the data suggested a trend in this regard, $t(62) = -1.60$, $p < .12$. The small proportion of households with children (32%, $n = 10$) may have contributed to this finding. At least 80% of both women and men described this most recent experience as typical of their joint television watching and of their RCD use. Interestingly, women ($M = 2.84$, $SD = 0.74$) tended more than men ($M = 3.16$, $SD = 0.69$) to describe the particular show they watched as their partner's preference rather than their own, $t(60) = 1.78$, $p < .08$.

Recall that 30% of the women said they would change the use of the RCD during their joint television watching if they could. Only half as many men would make such a change. The open-ended data support these results. For example, a young married woman described her technique of standing in front of the television to interrupt the signal from the RCD. Another young married woman said that her partner used the RCD to watch more than one program at a time. "I should get him one of those TVs with all the little windows so he can watch them all," she said sarcastically. A middle-aged married woman said that she would like

to change their television watching so that she would have "control of the remote for half of our viewing time." Of those who would like to make any changes in their television watching, one in five women expected that they would *not* be successful.

Men typically admitted their heavier RCD use. For example, a middle-aged married man said that he switched channels to avoid commercials. "I'm the guilty party," he said. "My [family members] would leave it there and watch the commercial. I just change it because I'd rather not be insulted by commercials."

One of the most provocative questions asked of respondents was "How do you get your partner to watch a show that you want to watch?" The results were enlightening. A cohabiting woman said, "I tell him that would be a good one to watch, and he says, 'No,' and keeps changing [channels]. I whine, and then usually I don't get [my way]." A middle-aged married woman said:

> Let me think here, when does that occur? [Laughing.] If I really want to watch, I'll say, "I want to watch this one."... I'll say, "Come in here and watch this" if he's not in the room, but pretty much we watch the same things a lot, whether or not that's because I let him. He, a lot of the time, turns it on, and I'll come in and join him. But, if it's something I really want to watch, I'll say, "Don't flip the channel; I want to see this."

In contrast, a young married man said that he gets his partner to watch a show he wants to watch in this way:

> I just sneak the remote away from her if she has it, or, if I'm there first, then.... I mean, if there's sports on, that's usually what we watch unless there's something else on. I mean, usually if there's...some kind of sports game on, we usually watch that, but unless there's...another show on that, you know, she can talk me into, deter my interest, or something....

When asked how his partner gets him to watch something that she wants to watch, he reported:

> Oh, I guess, if there's not anything that I'm...real big on watching then I'll let her choose, or if she, you know, she's interested in something.... A bunch of times, we watch TV, and it's like, well, we'll go back, and, well, that's kind of interesting, we go back and forth.

His wife agreed:

> I usually don't have to beg him. I don't know. [Laughing.] I tie him down, and say, "You're watching this." I don't know. He usually just comes over, and if it's not what he wants, then he'll take the remote and try to find sports.

In other words, this couple watches sports when it is available. If there is no sports program on television and if the husband does not have something else he really wants to watch, then the wife may choose a show, but her husband will be looking for a sports program while her show is on, or at least he will go back and forth between her show and others.

A woman who has been married for 18 years was

deliberate in her efforts to watch a particular show:

> I usually start a couple of days ahead of time when I see them advertised, and it is something that I am going to want to watch. I tell him to "get prepared!" I have to be relatively adamant about it. When the time comes up, I have to remind him ahead of time that I told him earlier that I want to watch the program.

When her husband wants to watch a program, however, she said, "He just watches what he wants. He doesn't ask." Finally, a married man reported, "I just say I want to watch something, and if she wants to watch something really bad, I will let her watch what she wants to watch." Ultimately, the authority is his.

The data are much the same when people report on changes they would like to see in the way they watch television together. One man who has been cohabiting with his partner for one year said, "I should probably let her 'drive' sometimes, but [it] would bug me too much not to be able to do it." A woman who has been married for 37 years painted a brighter picture. When asked, "How do you feel about watching TV with your husband? Are you happy with the way things are?" she responded:

> Yes, right now. But see, without the VCR we'd be in trouble because I just tape anything I want to see. Without that, there'd be more conflict.... Buying a second TV has changed the way we watch TV. It's made it easier—less stress, less conflict.

A young married man also was more positive. When asked, "Have you changed the way you watch television together?" he replied, "We take turns watching our programs, and I let her hold the remote during her programs."

Earlier, I mentioned that 14% ($n = 5$) of the couples in this study were gay or lesbian. In these couples, too, one partner usually is more likely than the other to use the RCD. In a gay male couple, one nearly always used the RCD, and the other almost never used it. When the RCD user was asked why they have this typical pattern, he responded: "Why? I don't know. I just like using the remote. I think I'm better at it than he is." In answer to a question regarding whether he used the RCD at all, his partner indicated: "He doesn't let me." In a second gay male couple, one partner again was far more likely to use the remote than the other partner, but both reported using controlling strategies to get their partner to watch a show they wanted to watch. Greg said, "I just tell him I want to watch it, and we do." Rob said, "I just turn it on, and that is what we watch." When asked, "How does your partner get you to watch a program he wants to watch?" Greg replied: "I usually don't watch programs I don't want to watch. If he asked me to watch it with him for a purpose, I would."

In contrast, one partner in a lesbian pair reported, "If we are both here, we try to make sure it's something that we both like." In fact, this couple limited their television viewing to avoid potential problems resulting from their different styles of RCD use. They also made it a practice to talk to each other during the commercials, in part, so that the one partner who tended to do so, would not graze. A second lesbian pair reported similar behavior. When asked, "Think back to the beginning of your relationship with [your partner]. Have your expectations about watching television with her changed over time?" she responded:

> In the beginning,...TV watching was something we could do when we didn't know each other very well yet. You know, it was kind of like a sort of a neutral or a little bit less personal activity that we could sit and watch TV together as a shared activity. And it's still a shared activity.... We don't use it to tune each other out, and if someone wants to talk, we just click the mute button or turn it off.

Becky's partner, Mary, used the RCD much more often than Becky did. According to Becky, however, when Mary grazes, "she's perfectly willing, if I say, 'This looks really good,' she'll stop. She doesn't dominate that way." In fact, when Mary grazes, "she'll just say, 'Is this bothering you?'" Mary agreed that she was the one who usually held the RCD, but that they shared, too. "If Becky has a show she really likes, then I give her the remote so I'm sure I don't play with the TV while she's watching her show." Mary does not "let" her partner hold the RCD; she asks her to hold it to keep her own behavior in check. Indeed, Mary's frustration with their joint television watching comes from her own behavior: "Well, I feel self-conscious about how much I change the channels because I know that she doesn't like to change as often or as fast as I do." Although based on a very modest sample, these findings are intriguing and illustrate how couples successfully develop and maintain egalitarian or peer relationships.

Discussion

These data confirm that for women in heterosexual pairs leisure is a source of conflict—conflict between their own enjoyment and the enjoyment of their partners (Shank, 1986; Shaw, 1985, 1991). The data expose the contradictions between the goal and the reality of leisure for women. Support also comes from the findings that men, more than women, combine other pleasurable pursuits with television watching. Others (Coverman & Sheley, 1986; Firestone & Shelton, 1994; Hochschild, 1989; Mederer, 1993) have shown that women more than men dovetail family labor with their leisure activity.

The data also support previous work suggesting that when heterosexual couples watch television together, men dominate in program selection and in the use of the RCD (Copeland & Schweitzer, 1993; Cornwell et al., 1993; Eastman & Newton, 1995; Heeter & Greenberg, 1985; Krendl et al., 1993; Lindlof et al., 1988; Morley, 1988; Perse & Ferguson, 1993). Indeed, unnegotiated channel switching by male partners was a fre-

595 quent occurrence in this sample. Men use the RCD to avoid commercials, to watch more than one show at a time, and to check what else is on (Perse & Ferguson, 1993). And they do so even when their partners are frustrated by these behaviors.

600 The data reveal that men have power over women in heterosexual relationships (Komter, 1989). Men are more likely than women to watch what they want on television and to do so without considering their partner's wishes. Men control the RCD, which gives them 605 the means to watch what they want, when they want, in the way that they want. Men also persist in RCD use that is frustrating to their women partners. These are examples of manifest power. Men make overt attempts to get their way and are successful at doing so. Men's 610 power is evident, as well, in the lesser power of their women partners. For example, women struggle to get their male partners to watch a program they want to watch and are less able than men to do so. Furthermore, women watch a preferred show on a different 615 television set or videotape it so that they can watch it later. These options do not prevent a husband or male partner from watching a show that he wants to watch when he wants to watch it.

Men's latent power over women is evident as well. 620 Even though women rarely control the RCD, fewer than half report that RCD use is frustrating to them, and only 30% say they would like to change their partner's RCD behavior. According to Komter (1989), resignation to the way things are is evidence of latent 625 power. Another illustration of the effect of latent power is anticipation of a negative reaction. Only four women feel they would be successful if they attempted to change the way their partners use the RCD. In the heterosexual sample, women seem less able than men to 630 raise issues of concern to them, they anticipate the struggles they will encounter when and if their own preferences are made known, and they predict a negative reaction to their wishes from their male partners.

Confirmation of men's latent power over their 635 women partners also was demonstrated by a series of auxiliary analyses. I was unable to explain the dependent variables of respondent's relationship happiness or respondent's enjoyment of the time the couple spends together with independent variables such as frustration 640 with remote control use, dominance of the remote control, or desire to change frustrating remote control use. As Komter (1989) suggested, both lesser power and resignation on the part of women contribute to the appearance of balance in these pairs.

645 Joint television watching in heterosexual couples is hardly an egalitarian experience. As is true for my mother, some women use a second television or a videocassette recorder to level the playing field (i.e., so that they are able to watch the shows they want to 650 watch). A second television set, however, reduces joint leisure time among those couples who can afford it, and a VCR means that a woman may have to wait to watch her show. Even these solutions to conflict around joint television watching demonstrate that cou- 655 ples watching television are not simply passive couch potatoes. They are doing gender, that is, acting in ways consistent with social structures and helping to create and maintain them at the same time.

Everyday couple interaction is hardly mundane and 660 run-of-the-mill. It is a systematic recreation and reinforcement of social patterns. Couples' leisure behavior is gendered in the same way that household labor is gendered: Social status enhances men's leisure activity relative to women's. Thus, leisure activity has gen- 665 dered meanings (Ferree, 1990). Through it, women and men are creating and affirming themselves and each other as separate and unequal (Ferree, 1990; Thompson, 1993). In other words, leisure activity is both an occasion for relaxation and an occasion for doing gen- 670 der (Fenstermaker, West, & Zimmerman, 1991; Shaw, 1991).

As Osmond and Thorne (1993) point out, "Gender relations are basically power relations" (p. 593). Because the power of men in families is legitimate—that 675 is, backed by structural and cultural supports—it constrains the less powerful to act to maintain the social order and the stability of their relationship (Farrington & Chertok, 1993). Few women make demands of their heterosexual partners so that their patterns of television 680 watching change. Instead, they say they are "happy" with their joint television watching. This same pattern is evident when we examine family labor. Most women describe the objectively uneven distribution of household work as fair (Thompson, 1991).

685 Hochschild (1989) argued that women give up leisure as an indirect strategy to bolster a myth of equality. Rather than resenting her male partner's leisure time, a woman uses the time when he is pursuing his own leisure or interests to engage in what she describes 690 as her interests: housework and child care. Overall, she defines their level of involvement at home as equal, a view that can be sustained only if she ignores her own lack of leisure time, as well as the amount of leisure time her partner has. Hochschild also suggested that a 695 woman sees her male partner's leisure time as more valuable than her own because she feels that more of his identity and time than hers are committed to paid work. She concludes, therefore, that he deserves extra relaxation. In Hochschild's view, and in Komter's 700 (1989), women cannot afford to feel resentment in their close relationships.

In a review of the literature, Szinovacz (1987) wrote that there were few studies of how people in families exercise power. She argued that such studies 705 are needed, as are studies on strategies of resisting power. The data reported here suggest that the exercise of power around couples' television watching behavior can be overt and relentless. Men's strategies to control the content and style of viewing are ways in which they 710 do gender. Women's resistance strategies (e.g., getting

119

a second television set, using the VCR) are also ways of doing gender. They do little to upset the intracouple power dynamics. Indeed, most women whose male partners are excessive grazers do not describe resis-
715 tance strategies at all. Instead, they maintain the status quo (Komter, 1989).

Of interest is that in lesbian and gay couples one person was more likely to be the heavier RCD user, as well. Yet these couples had some unique patterns. The
720 behavior of the lesbian couples, in particular, is suggestive for those of us wishing to establish and maintain egalitarian partnerships. One lesbian woman demonstrated a solution to the conflict between partners when one is distressed by the other's RCD behavior.
725 Asked, "Is there anything else you'd like to tell us?" she responded:

Well, I think that the most important thing for me is to remember to be sensitive to the fact that she doesn't have the same tastes as me, and I try to think about that. And,
730 if she mentions that she likes something, then I ask her before I change the channel if she's done watching it, or if she's not interested, if I could change the channel.

In this act, she elevates the importance of her partner's wishes to the level of her own. She demonstrates the
735 consideration that her partner desires and deserves (Hochschild, 1989; Thompson, 1991). When asked if it would be important for them to make changes in the way they watch television together, her partner expressed insight into her own behavior. Mary, the RCD
740 user, likes to "veg out" and watch TV, but Becky likes to:

pretend I'm not going to watch, I'm going to get a magazine or the newspaper,...or I'll bring some desk paper work over to do.... I think, well, I'll just sit there in the
745 living room while Mary watches TV. I'll work on our bills or something.... Then, what happens is I'll look around and think that looks kind of interesting. Although usually by the time I've looked around, she's changed the channel.... I think what happens is that she's more up
750 front about saying, "Hey, I'm going to veg out here and watch some TV," and I pretend I'm going to do more worthwhile things, and I end up just watching TV anyway.

Perhaps these two women, with their honesty to
755 themselves, their sensitivity to each other, and their concern about the ways in which their own behavior is or could be a problem in their relationship, are doing gender, too. They are concerned with the relationship, rather than with getting their own way. This is how
760 women are said to make connection and to demonstrate care, to give what Hochschild (1989) described as a gift of gratitude. Using these strategies, they maximize joint enjoyment of leisure and minimize power imbalances. Rather then reproducing structural hierarchies,
765 they create a bond of equality and provide a different course for the resolution of inherent conflict within couples.

The results from this study are hardly definitive.

They are based on a small, volunteer sample, albeit one
770 sufficiently diverse to include different types of close, romantic relationships. Additionally, the very small number of lesbian and gay couples suggests a need to exercise caution when generalizing from these findings. Further study with larger, representative samples
775 will be required to extend these findings beyond the couples interviewed here.

Nevertheless, the patterns I identified are similar to those found in other studies of television watching in families and of the intersection of gender and power in
780 close relationships. Mundane activities are important for understanding the intersection of gender and power in close relationships. Indeed, as Lull (1988) noted:

Television is not only a technological medium that transmits bits of information from impersonal institutions
785 to anonymous audiences, [but] it is a social medium, too—a means by which audience members communicate and construct strategies to achieve a wide range of personal and social objectives. (p. 258)

Others (Morley, 1988; Spigel, 1992) have pointed out
790 that the way men engage with television programming and women watch more distractedly are illustrations of cultural power. Daytime television programming in the 1950s, for example, was designed to be repetitive and fragmented to facilitate joint housework and television
795 watching for women (Spigel, 1992), thus helping to create and reinforce the view that leisure at home is problematic for women. The availability of the RCD does not change the fact that women's leisure is fragmented.
800 Recently, I toured an area of Portland, Oregon, billed as "The Street of Dreams," where there are a half dozen homes costing nearly a million dollars apiece. Each year, such homes are opened temporarily to members of a curious public who will never be able to
805 afford them. Inside one was a theater room with three television sets mounted side-by-side along the back wall. A moment after we arrived, a middle-aged heterosexual couple entered the room. The woman smiled and said to the man, "Look, Dan, you could get rid of
810 the remote!" If three television sets in one room is a solution to the problem of being able to watch only one show at a time, gendered struggles inherent in such mundane, everyday activity as watching television are destined to continue. They will do so until women and
815 men are equal in both their microlevel interactions and in the broader social structure.

References

Bryant. J., & Rockwell, S. C. (1993). Remote control devices in television program selection: Experimental evidence. In J. R. Walker & R. V. Bellamy, Jr. (Eds.), *The remote control in the new age of television* (pp. 73–85). Westport, CT: Praeger.

Copeland, G. A., & Schweitzer, K. (1993). Domination of the remote control during family viewing. In J. R. Walker & R. V. Bellamy, Jr. (Eds.), *The remote control in the new age of television* (pp. 155–168). Westport, CT: Praeger.

Cornwell, N. C., Everett, S., Everett, S. E., Moriarty, S., Russomanno, J. A., Tracey, M., & Trager, R. (1993). Measuring RCD use: Method matters. In J. R. Walker & R. V. Bellamy, Jr. (Eds.), *The remote control in the new age of television* (pp. 43–55). Westport, CT: Praeger.

Coverman, S., & Sheley, J. F. (1986). Change in men's housework and child-care time, 1965–1975. *Journal of Marriage and the Family, 48,* 413–422.

Crawford, D. W., Geoffrey, G., & Crouter, A. C. (1986). The stability of leisure preferences. *Journal of Leisure Research, 18,* 96–115.

Eastman, S. T., & Newton, G. D. (1995). Delineating grazing: Observations of remote control use. *Journal of Communication, 45,* 77–95.

Farrington, K., & Chertok, E. (1993). Social conflict theories of the family. In P. G. Boss, W. J. Doherty, R. LaRossa, W. R. Schumm, & S. K. Steinmetz (Eds.), *Sourcebook of family theories and methods: A contextual approach* (pp. 357–381). New York: Plenum.

Fenstermaker, S., West, C., & Zimmerman, D. H. (1991). Gender inequality: New conceptual terrain. In R. L. Blumberg (Ed.), *Gender, family, and economy: The triple overlap* (pp. 289–307). Newbury Park, CA: Sage.

Ferree, M. M. (1990). Beyond separate spheres: Feminism and family research. *Journal of Marriage and the Family, 52,* 866–884.

Firestone, J., & Shelton, B. A. (1994). A comparison of women's and men's leisure time: Subtle effects of the double day. *Leisure Sciences, 16,* 45–60.

Goodman, E. (1993). Click. In *Value judgments* (pp. 180–182). New York: Farrar, Strauss, & Giroux.

Heeter, C., & Greenberg, B. S. (1985). Profiling the zappers. *Journal of Advertising Research, 25,* 15–19.

Henderson, K. A. (1990). The meaning of leisure for women: An integrative review of the research. *Journal of Leisure Research, 22,* 228–243.

Henderson, K. A. (1994). Perspectives on analyzing gender, women, and leisure. *Journal of Leisure Research, 26,* 119–137.

Hill, M. S. (1988). Marital stability and spouses' shared time. *Journal of Family Issues, 9,* 427–451.

Hochschild, A. (with Machung, A.) (1989). *The second shift: Working parents and the revolution at home.* New York: Viking.

Holman, T. B., & Jacquart, M. (1988). Leisure-activity patterns and marital satisfaction: A further test. *Journal of Marriage and the Family, 50,* 69–77.

Huston, T. L. (1983). Power. In H. H. Kelley, E. Berscheid, A. Christensen, J. H. Harvey, T. L. Huston, G. Levinger, E. McClintock, L. A. Peplau, & D. R. Patterson (Eds.), *Close relationships* (pp. 169–219). New York: W. H. Freeman.

Kollock, P., Blumstein, P., & Schwartz, P. (1985). Sex and power in interaction: Conversational privilege and duties. *American Sociological Review, 50,* 34–46.

Komter, A. (1989). Hidden power in marriage. *Gender and Society, 3,* 187–216.

Krendl, K. A., Troiano, C., Dawson, R., & Clark, G. (1993). "OK, where's the remote?" Children, families, and remote control devices. In J. R. Walker & R. V. Bellamy, Jr. (Eds.), *The remote control in the new age of television* (pp. 137–153). Westport, CT: Praeger.

Lindlof, T. R., Shatzer, M. J., & Wilkinson, D. (1988). Accommodation of video and television in the American family. In J. Lull (Ed.), *World families watch television* (pp. 158–192). Newbury Park, CA: Sage.

Lull, J. (1988). Constructing rituals of extension through family television viewing. In J. Lull (Ed.), *World families watch television* (pp. 237–259). Newbury Park, CA: Sage.

McDonald, G. W. (1980). Family power: The assessment of a decade of theory and research, 1970–1979. *Journal of Marriage and the Family, 42,* 841–854.

Mederer, H. (1993). Division of labor in two-earner homes: Task accomplishment versus household management as critical variables in perceptions about family work. *Journal of Marriage and the Family, 55,* 133–145.

Morley, D. (1988). Domestic relations: The framework of family viewing in Great Britain. In J. Lull (Ed.), *World families watch television* (pp. 22–48). Newbury Park, CA: Sage.

Osmond, M. W., & Thorne, B. (1993). Feminist theories: The social construction of gender in families and society. In P. G. Boss, W. J. Doherty, R. LaRossa, W. R. Schumm, & S. K. Steinmetz (Eds.), *Sourcebook of family theories and methods: A contextual approach* (pp. 591–623). New York: Plenum.

Perse, E. M., & Ferguson, D. A. (1993). Gender differences in remote control use. In J. R. Walker & R. V. Bellamy, Jr. (Eds.), *The remote control in the new age of television* (pp. 169–186). Westport, CT: Praeger.

Robinson, J. P. (1990, September). I love my TV. *American Demographics, 12,* 24–27.

Shank, J. W. (1986). An exploration of leisure in the lives of dual-career women. *Journal of Leisure Research, 18,* 300–319.

Shaw, S. M. (1985). Gender and leisure: Inequality in the distribution of leisure time. *Journal of Leisure Research, 17,* 266–282.

Shaw, S. M. (1991). Gender, leisure, and constraint: Towards a framework for the analysis of women's leisure. *Journal of Leisure Research, 26,* 8–22.

Spigel, L. (1992). *Make room for TV: Television and the family idea in postwar America.* Chicago: University of Chicago.

Szinovacz, M. E. (1987). Family power. In M. B. Sussman & S. K. Steinmetz (Eds.), *Handbook of marriage and the family* (pp. 651–693). New York: Plenum.

Thompson, L. (1991). Family work: Women's sense of fairness. *Journal of Family Issues, 12,* 181–196.

Thompson, L. (1993). Conceptualizing gender in marriage: The case of marital care. *Journal of Marriage and the Family, 55,* 557–569.

Thompson, L., & Walker, A. J. (1989). Gender in families: Women and men in marriage, work, and parenthood. *Journal of Marriage and the Family, 51,* 845–871.

Walker, J. R., & Bellamy, R. V., Jr. (1991). Gratifications of grazing: An exploratory study of remote control use. *Journalism Quarterly, 68,* 422–431.

West, C., & Zimmerman, D. H. (1987). Doing gender. *Gender and Society, 1,* 125–151.

Note: This is an expanded version of the presidential address presented at the 1995 annual meeting of the National Council on Family Relations, Portland, Oregon. I thank the following individuals for their help: Kinsey Green, for providing funds to support a graduate research assistant for this project; Alan Acock, for releasing me from a course during academic year 1994–1995; Janet Lee and Rebecca Warner, for their assistance with measurement; Linda Eddy and the students enrolled in HDFS 442 in the spring of 1994, for their role in data collection; Lori Schreiner, for coding the quantitative data; and Sally Bowman, Alan Acock, Fuzhong Li, John Bratten, and, especially, Takashi Yamamoto, for their help with data analysis. I am grateful also to Katherine Allen, Mark Fine, and two anonymous reviewers for their careful and thoughtful reading of an earlier draft of this article.

Exercise for Article 20

Factual Questions

1. According to feminist scholars, what bears an "uncanny resemblance" to the social structure?

2. According to the literature review, what reason(s) do women give for changing channels? Do they give the same reason(s) men give?

3. Who was "primarily" responsible for recruiting participants?

4. What was the mean age of the heterosexual partners?

5. Why was a coin tossed?

6. What was the mean number of hours that television was watched each day by the participants?

7. What percentage of the men reported that RCD use was frustrating to them?

Questions for Discussion

8. The author begins her research article with a personal anecdote. (See lines 1–9.) In your opinion, does this strengthen or weaken the article?

9. In your opinion, did the inclusion of lesbian/gay couples strengthen this study? Weaken it? Explain.

10. The interviews were audiotaped. Are there advantages and disadvantages of doing this? Explain.

11. Are the quantitative results or the qualitative results more convincing to you? Do the two types of results complement each other? Explain.

12. If you were to conduct another study on the same topic, what changes in the research methodology would you make, if any?

Quality Ratings

Directions: Indicate your level of agreement with each of the following statements by circling a number from 5 for strongly agree (SA) to 1 for strongly disagree (SD). If you believe an item is not applicable to this research article, leave it blank. Be prepared to explain your ratings.

A. The introduction establishes the importance of the study.

    SA   5   4   3   2   1   SD

B. The literature review establishes the context for the study.

    SA   5   4   3   2   1   SD

C. The research purpose, question, or hypothesis is clearly stated.

    SA   5   4   3   2   1   SD

D. The method of sampling is sound.

    SA   5   4   3   2   1   SD

E. Relevant demographics (for example, age, gender, and ethnicity) are described.

    SA   5   4   3   2   1   SD

F. Measurement procedures are adequate.

    SA   5   4   3   2   1   SD

G. All procedures have been described in sufficient detail to permit a replication of the study.

    SA   5   4   3   2   1   SD

H. The participants have been adequately protected from potential harm.

    SA   5   4   3   2   1   SD

I. The results are clearly described.

    SA   5   4   3   2   1   SD

J. The discussion/conclusion is appropriate.

    SA   5   4   3   2   1   SD

K. Despite any flaws, the report is worthy of publication.

    SA   5   4   3   2   1   SD

Article 21

The Influence of a Big Brothers Program on the Adjustment of Boys in Single-Parent Families

Douglas A. Abbott
University of Nebraska-Lincoln

William H. Meredith
University of Nebraska-Lincoln

Rolee Self-Kelly
Big Brothers-Big Sisters of the Midlands

M. Elizabeth Davis
University of Nebraska at Omaha

ABSTRACT. This study is an evaluation of the self-competence, academic performance, behavioral problems, and parent-child relations of boys who had been raised in single-parent families headed by their mothers and who had weekly contact with an adult friend or companion through a midwestern affiliate of the Big Brothers/Big Sisters of America. Results indicated that participation in such a program was not related to changes in the areas investigated. These findings are not consistent with the social support literature suggesting that an adult companion or friend may benefit children in single-parent families. Further study with a larger sample, over a longer time frame, is recommended.

From *The Journal of Psychology, 131,* 143–156. Copyright © 1997 by Heldref Publications, 1319 Eighteenth St., N.W., Washington, DC 20036-1802. Reprinted with permission from the Helen Dwight Reid Educational Foundation.

Professionals in the field of marriage and the family are increasingly concerned about the fragmentation of the American family and its effects on children (Children's Defense Fund, 1988). The divorce rate remains
5   high, and it is estimated that over 50% of the marriages of those now in their 20s will end in divorce (Norton & Moorman, 1987). Over 1,000,000 children will experience the trauma of their parents' divorce or separation each year (Spanier, 1989). The rate of out-of-wedlock
10   pregnancy also continues to increase, and currently 27% of all live births are to unwed women, which leaves another 1,000,000 children per year in single-parent families (Edwards, 1987).

Children in single-parent families may be at greater
15   risk than children of two-parent families (Amato & Keith, 1991a, 1991b; Bahr, 1989; Bilge & Kaufman, 1983; Booth, Brinkerhoff, & White, 1984; Booth & Edwards, 1989; Bumpass, 1990; McLanahan & Booth, 1989; Glenn & Kramer, 1985, 1987; Krein, 1986;
20   Lauer & Lauer, 1991; Mackinnon, Brody, & Stoneman, 1982; Mueller & Cooper, 1986). Amato (1993) suggested that single parenthood is problematic for children's socialization because many children with one parent receive less economic and emotional support,
25   practical assistance, information, guidance, and supervision, and less role modeling for adult interpersonal interaction than children in two-parent families.

Wallerstein has studied children from families disrupted by divorce across three generations and con-
30   cluded that such children "lose something fundamental to their development—family structure, the scaffolding upon which children mount successive developmental stages, which supports their psychological, physical and emotional ascent into maturity" (Wallerstein &
35   Blakeslee, 1990, p. 64). Lamb (1987) concluded: "Suffice it to say the boys growing up without fathers seemed to have problems in the areas of sex-role and gender-identity development, school performance, psychological adjustment, and perhaps, in the control of
40   aggression" (p. 14).

As a result of the increasing numbers of children in single-parent families, programs have been established that pair an adult volunteer with a child who may benefit from adult companionship. The largest and most
45   prominent of these programs in America is the Big Brothers/Big Sisters organization. The purpose of this study was to evaluate the influence of a Big Brothers program on the academic, psychological, and social development of boys. Knowledge acquired from this
50   type of research may improve the effectiveness of intervention programs that seek to support children in single-parent families.

Potential Benefits of Social Support for Children of Single Parents

If we accept the premise that, on average, children in single-parent families are more likely to experience
55   difficulties, then the question becomes, what can we do to assist and support these children? Amato (1993) presents some evidence that such children may experience a higher level of well-being if another adult is available to provide the role functions of the absent
60   parent (see also Dornbusch et al., 1985). Santrock and Warshak (1979) found that contact with adult caretakers other than the custodial mother was associated with positive behavior among children of divorced parents. Cochran, Larner, Riley, Gunnarsson, and Henderson
65   (1990) reported that among boys in families with only

the mother as the parent, school success was associated with the amount of task-orientated interaction with adult male relatives.

70   Guidubaldi, Cleminshaw, Perry, and McLaughlin (1983) found that a child's positive relationships with adult caretakers predicted positive social adjustment. Sandler, Miller, Short, and Wolchik (1989) suggested that positive interaction with caring adults can enhance the self-esteem of children experiencing stressful life
75   events like divorce (see also Sandler, Wolchik, & Brower, 1987). These studies suggest that an adult friend or companion who provides some caretaking functions may have a beneficial impact on a child in a single-parent family. Thus, one therapeutic option is to
80   provide the child with regular contact with an adult friend who shows a consistent interest and concern in the child's welfare.

Child-adult companion programs such as Big Brothers/Big Sisters are one type of intervention that
85   may help to support a child in a single-parent family. The Big Brothers/Big Sisters program is a national, nonprofit organization that recruits adults who volunteer to spend some time each week with a child from a single-parent family whose custodial parent has re-
90   quested this service. The organization was started in 1907 and now has 502 affiliate programs distributed in all 50 states. There are approximately 50,000 boys and girls being served by Big Brothers/Big Sisters. Volunteers are carefully screened and then matched with a
95   same-sex child. The volunteer meets with the child each week for a visit and/or activity.

In spite of the growing number of volunteer programs, we found no published studies on the value of or effectiveness of adult companions on the emotional
100   or social development of children from single-parent families. There is some research on how contact and involvement by the noncustodial father influences a child's adjustment to divorce, but these studies were not considered equivalent to the influence of a nonre-
105   lative adult companion on a child's development (Guidubaldi, 1986).

Theory and Hypothesis

An adult companion program such as Big Brothers/Big Sisters may provide a positive influence on a child's development. This assumption rests on two the-
110   oretical foundations: modeling theory and social support theory (Bandura, 1977; Lee, 1979; Wolchik, Ruehlman, Braver, & Sandler, 1989). Modeling theory stresses the importance of the relationship between the observer (e.g., the child) and the model (e.g., the Big
115   Brother) in eliciting imitative behavior. The child is more likely to model adult action and personality if the adult is seen as important, powerful, warm and nurturant (Bandura & Walters, 1963). The Big Brother or Big Sister volunteer serves as a positive role model for
120   the child in a variety of vocational, psychological and social ways.

One aspect of social support theory suggests that an individual or family is more likely to cope with stressful or difficult life circumstances (e.g., low-income
125   single parenting) if supported by family, friends, and helping professionals or organizations (Boss, 1988; Milardo, 1988; Perlman & Rook, 1987; Unger & Powell, 1980). The Big Brothers/Big Sisters agency personnel provide institutional support to the single parent
130   through frequent interviews (every 2 to 3 months), counseling, and referral to other community resources. This type of social support may buffer the child against the stressful life events so often experienced by poor children in single-parent families (Cohen & Willis,
135   1985).

Supported by these theoretical assumptions, our program evaluation was guided by the major goals of the local Big Brothers/Big Sisters program, which were to (a) improve the child's feelings of self-competence,
140   (b) encourage the child's achievement in school, (c) monitor the child's psychosocial problems, and (d) encourage a positive parent-child relationship. Given these goals, we posited that regular adult companionship over many months could have many beneficial
145   general effects on a child's development. A child's feelings of self-competence may be enhanced by regular, long-term contact with an adult companion. The special attention and the weekly activities with an attentive and interested adult may help the child feel
150   better about himself or herself.

In addition, an adult volunteer who frequently shares facts and feelings about work and careers and helps the child with homework and school projects may encourage the child's school performance. Ideally,
155   with enhanced self-competence and improved school performance, the child may be less likely to display behavioral problems. Finally, the parent-child relationship may be indirectly affected by the combined effect of all these factors. A child who is more self-
160   competent, who is doing better in school, and who displays fewer behavior problems, may engender more positive relations with his mother. The Big Brother or Big Sister may also directly encourage the child to work out conflicts and problems with his mother.
165   Our major purpose in this study was to evaluate whether a child's participation in a companionship program was related to changes in the child's (a) self-competence, (b) school performance, (c) emotional and social problems, and (d) parent-child relationship.
170   Based on the previous rationale, we hypothesized that boys with a Big Brother would evidence greater improvement over time in self-competence, in school performance, in reducing emotional and social problems, and in the quality of the parent-child relationship
175   than boys without a Big Brother.

Method

Participants

We selected the children from single-parent families and the adult companions from a midwestern affiliate of the Big Brothers/Big Sisters of America, a nationally known and well-respected adult-companion program. Because the great majority of clients at this chapter of Big Brothers/Big Sisters were boys, only boys 8-14 years of age were selected for the study. All children came from mother-headed, single-parent households. None of the boys had been diagnosed with any mental or physical disabilities.

About 120 boys began the study, approximately 40 in the intervention group (those who received a Big Brother) and 80 in the comparison group (those on the waiting list who had not yet received a Big Brother). Out of the comparison group (at the end of the study), those boys who matched most closely the demographics of the intervention groups were selected for the final sample. Over the 2-year span of the study, about 60% of the boys dropped out of the program because of relocation or loss of contact with the organization.

The final sample consisted of 44 boys: 22 in the intervention group, who had had at least weekly contact with a Big Brother for 12-18 months, and 22 in comparison group, who had been on the waiting list for 12-18 months and had not yet received an adult companion. The boys were matched on several variables such as age, race, number of siblings, mother's education and income, reason for single-parent status (e.g., divorced/separated, widowed, or unwed motherhood), the child's age when the father left home, and the extent of the child's contact with the noncustodial father. No significant differences were found between the intervention and comparison groups on any of these variables (see Table 1).

Design and Procedure

A pretest-posttest longitudinal design was used. Boys with Big Brothers were compared with boys on the waiting list on the outcome measures at the beginning of the study and then 12-18 months later. We obtained permission from both parents and children by using adult and child consent forms. Big Brothers case managers administered the self-report questionnaires to the parents and children during a regularly scheduled visit required by the program. The surveys were administered to the intervention group when the children were matched with an adult volunteer and then 12-18 months after the match. The comparison group was surveyed when they were put on the waiting list and then 12-18 months later if they had not yet been assigned a Big Brother.

Instruments and Measures

To measure the child's level of self-competence and personal competence, we administered Harter's (1985) Self-Perception Profile. This scale measures six domains of competence: scholastic, social, athletic, physical, behavioral conduct, and global self-competence. Harter's scale is generally accepted as a valid and reliable measure of various components of self-competence (Stigler, Smith, & Mao, 1985).

The Harter instrument uses a structured alternative format. The child is first asked to decide which kind of child is most like him or her, and then whether this is *sort of true* or *really true* for him or her. Items are scored from 1 to 4, with 1 indicating low perceived competence. Each of the six subscales contained six items. Reliabilities for all subscales based on Cronbach's alpha ranged from .71 to .86 on four samples as reported by Harter (1985). Two test-retest evaluations were completed after 3 months and correlated at .80 and .83 (Harter, 1985). Cronbach's alpha reliability for this study was .85.

The children's school performance was evaluated by obtaining the child's school grades after receiving written permission from the parents. Grades were based on a 5-point scale with a 1 indicating superior performance or a grade of A.

To measure the child's relationship with his mother, we developed the Family Feelings scales, consisting of two forms, one for the child to complete and one for the mother to complete. The items on both scales were similar in content but worded for a child to evaluate his relationship with his mother (e.g., "Mom and I fight about the same things over and over"), or for the mother to evaluate her relationship with her son (e.g., "My son and I fight about the same things over and over"). We developed the scales after a review of items from the Parent-Adolescent Communication Scale (Barnes & Olson, 1985), the Family Satisfaction Scale (Olson & Wilson, 1985), the Family Environment Scale (Moos & Moos, 1981), and the Inventory of Family Feelings (Lowman, 1981).

Our scale was evaluated for content validity and age appropriateness by 15 family professionals in child development, social work, psychology, and sociology. Two professors in teacher education determined that the reading level of the scale was suitable for young children. The scale was composed of 28 items. A high score on the Family Feelings Scale indicates more positive parent-child relations. For this study, the mean on the child version of family feelings was 63.4 ($SD = 8.0$) and Cronbach's alpha was .78. For the parent version, the mean was 63.3 ($SD = 7.9$) and Cronbach's alpha was .85.

To measure the child's social and emotional problems, we had the mothers complete the Revised Behavior Problem Checklist (Quay & Peterson, 1987). The RBPC consists of 89 items scored on a 3-point scale: *no problem* (0), *mild problem* (1), *severe problem* (2). It is appropriate to use the total score of all 89 items and/or the individual subscale scores.

The checklist is divided into six subscales: Conduct

Table 1
Demographic Characteristics of Boys with and without a Big Brother

Characteristic	With a Big Brother (n = 22)		Without a Big Brother (n = 22)	
	M	SD	M	SD
Child's age	9.7	3.5	10.7	1.6
Mother's age	36.3	4.5	36.1	5.1
Mother's education	14 yrs	3.5	13 yrs	3.1
Siblings	1.3	0.7	1.6	1.2
Age when father left home	4.5	3.7	3.6	3.3
Mother's average income	$11,000–$20,000		$11,000–$20,000	
Father living	75%		76%	
Reason for single parent				
Divorce	71%		80%	
Unmarried	19%		10%	
Widowed	10%		10%	
Father visitation	Once a year or less		Once a year or less	

Disorder (e.g., gets into fights); Socialized Aggression (e.g. belongs to a gang); Immaturity (e.g., is irresponsible and undependable); Anxiety-Withdrawal (e.g., feels inferior); Psychotic Behavior (e.g., expresses strange
290 ideas); Motor Excess (e.g., is restless, unable to sit still). The instrument is rated at the fifth-grade reading level and takes approximately 15 minutes to complete. Quay and Peterson (1987) provide substantial reliability and validity information, including 2-month
295 test-retest correlations of .61–.83 with various samples of children. The RBPC has strong correlations with measures of similar content including the Child Behavior Checklist (Achenbach & Edelbrock, 1983) and Conner's Revised Parent Rating Scale (Conners, 1970).
300 For this sample, the mean score for behavior problems was 46.6 (SD = 29.9) and Cronbach's alpha was .96.

Results

Significant correlations among dependent variables would indicate that multivariate statistics should be used, whereas a lack of significant associations would
305 indicate multiple ANOVAs should be computed (Huberty & Morris, 1989). Because there were no significant correlations between grade point average or quality of parent-child relationship as perceived by the parent and the child, we computed three 2 (group: boys
310 with Big Brothers vs. boys without) x 2 (time: Time 1, Time 2) repeated measures ANOVAs on each of these three dependent variables.

The other two dependent measures were Harter's Self-Competence subscales and Quay's Behavior
315 Problem subscales. Because the Harter subscales are interrelated, and Quay's subscales are interrelated, two 2 (group) x 2 (time) MANOVAs were done to assess differences on these measures between boys with and without Big Brothers. Because of the exploratory na-
320 ture of these analyses, an alpha level of p < .10 was used.

The major research question of this study was whether the boys, who over a sustained period of time,

had regular companionship of a Big Brother differed
325 from a matched sample of boys without a Big Brother in the areas of self-concept, school grades, emotional relationships with their mothers, and frequency of behavioral problems. The t tests revealed no pretest group differences between the boys with Big Brothers and the
330 boys without Big Brothers on any dependent measures.

The results of the overall MANOVA revealed no significant Group x Time interaction and no group or time main effects on the set of self-competence subscales between boys with and without Big Brothers.
335 There were no significant Group x Time interactions and no group or time main effects on any of the behavior problem subscales between boys with and without Big Brothers.

There was a significant Group x Time interaction
340 related to grade point average, $F(1, 39)$ = 3.6, p < .07; contrary to our hypothesis, analysis of simple effects indicated that performance in school of boys with a Big Brother *decreased* from Time 1 (M = 2.13) to Time 2 (M = 2.43), $F(1, 39)$ = 3.0, p < .09 (1 = high GPA, 5 =
345 low GPA). The boys *without* a Big Brother showed no significant change in grade point average from Time 1 (M = 2.71) to Time 2 (M = 2.56).

There was a significant Group x Time interaction on parents' perceptions of the parent-child relationship,
350 $F(1, 42)$ = 3.3, p < .08. Analysis of simple effects indicated that the mothers of boys without a Big Brother reported improvement in the parent-child relationship from Time 1 (M = 62.5) to Time 2 (M = 67.1), $F(1, 42)$ = 5.53, p < .02. Mothers of boys with Big Brothers
355 reported no significant change in their parent-child relationship from Time 1 (M = 64.0) to Time 2 (M = 63.5).

With regard to the children's perceptions of the parent-child relationship, there was no Group x Time
360 interaction, and there was no group main effect. A time main effect, $F(1, 42)$ = 2.7, p < .06, indicated that all the boys in both groups reported improved parent-child

126

Table 2
A Comparison of Boys with and without a Big Brother on Major Dependent Variables

| | With a Big Brother (*n* = 22) | | | | Without a Big Brother (*n* = 22) | | | |
| | Pretest | | Posttest | | Pretest | | Posttest | |
Variable	*M*	*SD*	*M*	*SD*	*M*	*SD*	*M*	*SD*
Child feeling	64.7	8.2	65.5	5.6	62.0	8.2	65.6	5.6
Parent feeling	64.0	7.6	63.5	9.4	62.5	8.1	67.1	9.7
Grade point average	2.13	1.0	2.43	1.1	2.71	1.1	2.56	1.2
Self-perceived competence								
Scholastic	18.5	3.8	17.6	4.2	16.5	4.9	16.4	3.0
Social	16.4	4.5	17.5	4.1	16.7	5.1	17.1	4.1
Athletic	16.4	4.4	18.5	3.8	17.1	5.7	16.9	3.9
Appearance	17.6	4.3	17.5	3.2	16.2	3.8	16.1	5.4
Behavior	18.5	2.6	17.8	5.4	16.9	5.1	15.9	3.9
Global	19.3	3.7	18.7	4.3	18.1	4.3	18.3	3.1
Behavior problems								
Conduct	16.7	11.0	17.3	11.1	21.0	11.6	20.4	11.8
Aggression	3.2	3.7	2.6	3.6	3.6	4.3	3.2	5.0
Immaturity	8.6	5.9	8.5	6.2	10.6	7.3	11.0	9.6
Anxiety	8.5	4.4	7.4	4.6	9.1	5.0	8.0	5.1
Psychotic	1.5	1.9	2.0	2.8	1.6	2.3	1.8	2.6
Motor	2.0	2.1	2.1	2.5	3.5	3.1	2.8	2.9

relationships from Time 1 (*M* = 63.3) to Time 2 (*M* = 65.6).

365   Table 2 contains the statistics related to a comparison of boys with and without a Big Brother on the major dependent variables.

Discussion

In general, the results of this research indicate that the weekly companionship of an adult volunteer was 370 not related to positive changes in certain developmental outcomes for boys participating in the Big Brothers program. These findings are not consistent with the social support literature that suggests that children in nonnuclear families often benefit from the companion- 375 ship and active involvement of an adult friend (Cochran et al., 1990; Ihinger-Tallman, 1986; Lamb, 1982). Other researchers have also suggested that adult companions/friends may help children buffer stressful life events, enhance their self-esteem, and reduce deviant 380 behaviors (Dornbush et al., 1985; Sandler et al., 1989).

Our results, however, should be viewed with caution. One year may not be long enough to register changes in our particular dependent measures, especially with our small sample. Our measures (grade 385 point average, behavioral problems, self-competence, and the quality of parent-child relations) may have shown changes if the study had been extended over a longer period of time.

We were surprised that the school grades of boys 390 with a Big Brother showed no improvement over the boys without a Big Brother. This result was unexpected because the case workers at Big Brothers told us re-

peatedly that an adult companion frequently asks questions about the child's school performance and 395 encourages the child's attendance and achievement in school. Many volunteers help with the child's homework and school projects. Some Big Brothers go to the child's school open house, or may accompany the child's parent to parent-teacher conferences. Further- 400 more, the Big Brother, who is usually college educated and employed, may serve as a school/work role model for the male child, thus indirectly encouraging the child to succeed in school.

There were no significant changes in behavioral 405 problems for the boys with and without a Big Brother across the time period of this study. One explanation for this may be that their scores at the beginning and end of this study were already high. The subscale means on conduct disorder, socialized aggression, and 410 anxiety withdrawal for boys with *and* without Big Brothers were one to two standard deviations above Quay's norms for normal children, and similar to Quay's norms for his clinical samples of inpatients and outpatients at psychiatric facilities (Quay & Peterson, 415 1983).

Modest gains in the quality of the parent-child relationship, as reported by all the boys, are difficult to explain. Improvement may be the natural result of time and the continued adjustment of the child and parent to 420 a single-parent family situation. On the other hand, gains may be related to the mother and child's involvement in the Big Brothers organization.

Again, caution is warranted in evaluating these

findings. The results could be an artifact of the small
sample. In addition, the magnitude of the differences
on the dependent measures between the boys with and
without a Big Brother are small. This may indicate that
the intervention of a volunteer companion, in and of
itself, has only a limited impact on the development of
boys in single-parent households. On the other hand, it
may also indicate that the mothers of the control boys,
motivated to have their sons placed with a Big Brother,
may have attempted to accomplish this goal in other
ways, that is, by giving more personal attention to their
sons or finding other adult friends for them. A third
explanation for these findings may suggest that the
variables we studied and the method of measuring
these concepts were less than adequate to identify
change in development over a 1-year period.

Given these limitations, suggestions for improvements of this study are warranted. The impact of such a
program might have been more readily assessed if a
larger pool of boys had been evaluated. Multisite samples could be pooled together from several cities across
the country. Also, the time frame of the project could
have been extended to 2 or 3 years if more resources
had been available. However, given the mobility of Big
Brothers/Big Sisters clients and volunteers, the evaluation of a larger sample over a longer time period may
be difficult to accomplish. One solution might be to use
different developmental measures that are more sensitive to change over a shorter period of time. In addition, any child on a waiting list may need more regular
contact with the organization to prevent dropouts. Program staff could provide occasional activities, such as a
field trip, a swimming party, or a parent-child activity
for the families on the waiting list.

Arrangements with the various Big Brothers/Big
Sisters programs could be worked out so that the researchers have more direct access to the participants.
For this study, we were not allowed to contact the participants directly. We could only remind the case managers of when to do the assessments and hope they
would follow through and collect the data on time. On
several occasions, however, because of staff turnover
or work overload, data were not collected or were obtained too late to be of use in the study.

Implications for Practice

In this study, program goals were not clearly and
concisely articulated and we (the research team) may
have missed some of the important outcomes or benefits of this program. Thus, the first implication of this
study is a pragmatic one. When doing program evaluation, program staff and the external evaluation team if
one is used, should make a concerted effort to identify
and specify as concretely as possible the program goals
and expected behavioral outcomes (Posavac & Carey,
1985; Rutman, 1977). Research methods could then be
more easily designed and used to evaluate performance
objectives. For example, if the goal of the program is
improved parent-child communication, then specific
assessments of communication, using a variety of instruments, can be done.

A second advantage to ongoing evaluation is that it
may remind program staff of program goals, and this
may encourage accomplishment of those goals. Ongoing evaluation may also serve to motivate program
staff to carry out their responsibilities by providing
them with periodic progress reports on the children and
adults they serve (Theobald, 1985).

Another suggestion for improving program evaluation would be the use of some qualitative measures in
the evaluation (Gilgun, 1992; Rossi & Freeman, 1989).
The results of our quantitative study may have limited
our understanding of how such programs benefit children. In this study, structured interviews with mothers
and sons, asking them directly to talk about any perceived effects of participation in the program, may
have yielded relevant data that are not easily obtained
through quantitative global variables such as our measures of self-competence or grade point average.

In programs like Big Brothers/Big Sisters, where an
adult has direct and intensive interaction with a child,
the quality of that child-adult relationship may be a key
variable in predicting improvement in child outcomes.
This relationship variable should be evaluated and
monitored closely. If practitioners examined specific
aspects of the child-adult relationship and the processes
of relationship development, it may be possible to understand how or why the relationship flourishes or fails
and how this is related to program goals.

Another implication of this study is that children
who have chosen to participate in such adult-helper
programs may be at high risk for social and emotional
difficulties. Program staff may want to administer more
thorough intake evaluations of these children to gain a
better understanding of the nature of their clients. If
some children are rated as high risk, then more selective matching with adult helpers could be done. An
adult volunteer could be chosen (or recruited) who has
the knowledge and skills to deal with a more disturbed
or difficult child. These adults could also be provided
with special training by the sponsoring organization.

Although this study does not provide evidence that
a volunteer program like Big Brothers/Big Sisters has a
significant positive influence on the development of
male children in homes headed by the mother, this does
not mean that such programs are not effective. Additional research is needed in order to understand how
such a program may benefit a child and what can be
done to improve the effectiveness of such programs. If
current trends in divorce and unwed parenthood continue, the numbers of children from single-parent
homes will only increase, and understanding their
challenges and developing strategies to assist them
should be a high priority for social service professionals.

References

Achenbach, T. M., & Edelbrock, C. (1983). *Manual for the Child Behavior Checklist.* Burlington, VT: Dept. of Psychiatry, University of Vermont.

Amato, P. R. (1993). Children's adjustment to divorce: Theories, hypotheses, and empirical support. *Journal of Marriage and the Family, 55,* 23-38.

Amato, P., & Keith, B. (1991a). Parental divorce and adult well-being: A meta-analysis. *Journal of Marriage and the Family, 53,* 43-58.

Amato, P., & Keith, B. (1991b). Parental divorce and the well-being of children: A meta-analysis. *Psychological Bulletin, 110,* 26-46.

Bahr, S. (1989). *Family interaction* (pp. 178-180). New York: Macmillan.

Bandura, A. (1977). *Social learning theory.* Englewood Cliffs, NJ: Prentice-Hall.

Bandura, A., & Walters, R. (1963). *Social learning and personality development.* New York: Holt, Rinehart & Winston.

Barnes, H., & Olson, D. H. (1985). Parent-adolescent communication. In D. H. Olson & Associates (Eds.), *Family inventories.* St. Paul, MN: Family Social Science, University of Minnesota.

Bilge, B., & Kaufman, G. (1983). Children of divorce and one-parent families: Cross-cultural perspectives. *Family Relations, 32,* 59-71.

Booth, A., Brinkerhoff, D., & White, L. (1984). The impact of parental divorce on courtship. *Journal of Marriage and the Family, 46,* 85-94.

Booth, A., & Edwards, J. (1989). Transmission of marital and family quality over the generations: The effect of parental divorce and unhappiness. *Journal of Divorce, 14,* 41-58.

Boss, P. (1988). *Family stress management.* Newbury Park, CA: Sage.

Bumpass, L. (1990). Children's experience in single-parent families: Implications of cohabitation and marital transitions. *Family Planning Perspectives, 21,* 256-260.

Children's Defense Fund. (1988). *A briefing book on the status of American children in 1988.* Washington, DC: Author.

Cochran, M., Larner, M., Riley, D., Gunnarsson, L., & Henderson, C. (1990). *Extending families: The social networks of parents and their children.* Cambridge, MA: Cambridge University Press.

Cohen, S., & Willis, T. (1985). Stress, social support, and the buffering hypothesis. *Psychological Bulletin, 98,* 310-317.

Conners, C. (1970). Symptom patterns in hyperkinetic, neurotic, and normal children. *Child Development, 41,* 667-682.

Dornbush, S., Carlsmith, J., Bushwall, S., Ritter, P., Leiderman, H., Hastort, A. H., & Gross, R. T. (1985). Single parents, extended households, and the control of adolescents. *Child Development, 56,* 326-341.

Edwards, J. N. (1987). Changing family structure and youthful well-being: Assessing the future. *Journal of Family Issues, 8,* 355-371.

Gilgun, J. (1992). *Qualitative methods in family research.* Newbury Park, CA: Sage.

Glenn, N. D., & Kramer, K. (1985). The psychological well-being of adult children of divorce. *Journal of Marriage and the Family, 47,* 905-912.

Glenn, N. D., & Kramer, K. B. (1987). The marriages and divorces of the children of divorce. *Journal of Marriage and the Family, 49,* 811-825.

Guidubaldi, J. (1986). The role of selected family environmental factors in children's post-divorce adjustment. *Family Relations, 35,* 141-142.

Guidubaldi, J., Cleminshaw, H., Perry, J., & McLaughlin, K. (1983). The impact of parental divorce on children: Report of a national NAP study. *School Psychology Review, 12,* 300-323.

Harter, S. (1985). *Manual for the Self-Perception Profile for Children.* Denver, CO: University of Denver Press.

Huberty, C. J., & Morris, J. D. (1989). Multivariate analysis versus multiple univariate analyses. *Psychological Bulletin, 105,* 302-308.

Ihinger-Tallman, M. (1986). Member adjustment in single-parent families: Theory building. *Family Relations, 35,* 215-222.

Krein, S. F. (1986). Growing up in a single-parent family: The effect of education and earnings on young men. *Family Relations, 35,* 161-168.

Lamb, M. E. (1982). *Nontraditional families: Parenting and child development.* Hillsdale, NJ: Erlbaum.

Lamb, M. E. (1987). *The father's role in child development: Cross-cultural perspectives.* Hillsdale, NJ: Erlbaum.

Lauer, R., & Lauer, J. (1991). The long-term relational consequences of problematic family backgrounds. *Family Relations, 40,* 286-290.

Lee, G. R. (1979). Effects of social networks on the family. In W. Burr, R. Hill, F. Nye, & I. Reiss (Eds.), *Contemporary theories about the family* (pp. 27-56). New York: The Free Press.

Lowman, J. (1981). Love, hate, and the family: Measures of emotion. In E. E. Filsinger & R. Lewis (Eds.), *Assessing marriage: New behavioral approaches* (pp. 55-73). Beverly Hills, CA: Sage.

Mackinnon, C. E., Brody, G. H., & Stoneman, Z. (1982). The effects of divorce and maternal employment on the home environment of preschool children. *Child Development, 53,* 1392-1399.

McLanahan, S., & Booth, K. (1989). Mother-only families: Problems, prospects and politics. *Journal of Marriage and the Family, 51,* 557-588.

Milardo, R. (1988). *Families and social networks.* Newbury Park, CA: Sage.

Moos, R. H., & Moos, B. S. (1981). *Family Environment Scale manual.* Palo Alto, CA: Consulting Psychologists Press.

Mueller, D. P., & Cooper. P. W. (1986). Children of single-parent families: How they fare as young adults. *Family Relations, 35,* 169-176.

Norton, A. J., & Moorman. J. E. (1987). Current trends in marriage and divorce among American women. *Journal of Marriage and the Family, 49,* 3-14.

Olson, D. H., & Wilson, M. (1985). In D. H. Olson & Associates (Eds.), *Family inventories.* St. Paul, MN: Family Social Science, University of Minnesota.

Perlman, D., & Rook, K. (1987). Social support, social deficits, and the family. In S. Oskamp (Ed.), *Family process and problems: Social psychological aspects.* Newbury Park. CA: Sage.

Posavac, E., & Carey, R. (1985). *Program evaluation: Methods and case studies.* Englewood Cliffs, NJ: Prentice-Hall.

Quay, H. C., & Peterson, D. (1983). A dimensional approach to behavior disorder: The Revised Behavior Problem Checklist. *School Psychology Review, 12,* 244-249.

Quay, H. C., & Peterson, D. (1987). *Manual for the Revised Behavior Problem Checklist.* Coral Gables, FL: Herbert C. Quay.

Rossi, P., & Freeman, H. (1989). *Evaluation: A systematic approach.* Newbury Park. CA: Sage.

Rutman, L. (1977). *Evaluation research methods: A basic guide.* Beverly Hills, CA: Sage.

Sandler, I., Miller, P., Short, J., & Wolchik, W. (1989). Social support as a protective factor for children in stress. In D. Belle (Ed.), *Children's social networks and social support* (pp. 277-307). New York: Wiley.

Sandler, I., Wolchik, S., & Brower, S. (1987). Social support and children of divorce. In I. G. Sarason (Ed.), *Social support: Theory, research and application* (pp. 371-391). New York: Wiley.

Santrock, J., & Warshak, R. (1979). Father custody and social development in boys and girls. *Journal of Social Issues, 35,* 112-125.

Spanier, G. B. (1989). Bequeathing family continuity. *Journal of Marriage and the Family, 51,* 3-13.

Stigler, J., Smith, S., & Mao, L. (1985). The self-perception of competence by Chinese children. *Child Development, 56,* 1259-1270.

Theobald, W. (1985). *The evaluation of human service programs.* Champaign, IL: Management Learning Laboratories.

Unger, D., & Powell, D. (1980). Supporting families under stress: The role of social networks. *Family Relations, 29,* 566-574.

Wallerstein, J. S., & Blakeslee, S. (1990). *Second chances: Men, women and children a decade after divorce.* New York: Ticknor & Fields.

Wolchik, S., Ruehlman, L., Braver, S., & Sandler, I. (1989). Social support of children of divorce: Direct and stress-buffering effects. *American Journal of Community Psychology, 17,* 485-501.

Address correspondence to: William H. Meredith, University of Nebraska-Lincoln, Arts and Sciences Hall 108, Omaha Campus, 60th and Dodge, Omaha, NE 68182-0214.

Exercise for Article 21

Factual Questions

1. What is the specific hypothesis for this study?

2. The boys in the intervention group were matched with the boys in the comparison group on a number of demographic variables. Were any of the differences between the two groups on these variables statistically significant?

3. How was the content validity of the Family Feelings Scales determined?

4. What value of p was used as the cutting point to determine statistical significance?

5. On the pretest, which group had a higher GPA?

6. Which result "surprised" the researchers?

7. Do the researchers think that the time frame for this study was adequate? Explain.

Questions for Discussion

8. Do you think that a sample of 44 is adequate for a study of this type? Explain. (See lines 197–202.)

9. The boys were *not* randomly assigned to the intervention and comparison groups. Does this affect the validity of the evaluation? Explain. (See lines 197–210.)

10. The researchers provide a sample item from the boys' version of the Family Feelings scale. Does this sample item help you understand what the scale measures? Would you like to see more of the items? Explain. (See lines 251–260.)

11. The researchers suggest that a longer period of time might have yielded different results. Do you agree? If yes, what period of time would you suggest using? Explain. (See lines 381–388 and 445–447.)

12. The researchers suggest that a study with a multisite sample might improve the study. Do you agree? Explain. (See lines 440–445.)

Quality Ratings

Directions: Indicate your level of agreement with each of the following statements by circling a number from 5 for strongly agree (SA) to 1 for strongly disagree (SD). If you believe an item is not applicable to this research article, leave it blank. Be prepared to explain your ratings.

A. The introduction establishes the importance of the study.

SA   5   4   3   2   1   SD

B. The literature review establishes the context for the study.

SA   5   4   3   2   1   SD

C. The research purpose, question, or hypothesis is clearly stated.

SA   5   4   3   2   1   SD

D. The method of sampling is sound.

SA   5   4   3   2   1   SD

E. Relevant demographics (for example, age, gender, and ethnicity) are described.

SA   5   4   3   2   1   SD

F. Measurement procedures are adequate.

SA   5   4   3   2   1   SD

G. All procedures have been described in sufficient detail to permit a replication of the study.

SA   5   4   3   2   1   SD

H. The participants have been adequately protected from potential harm.

SA   5   4   3   2   1   SD

I. The results are clearly described.

SA   5   4   3   2   1   SD

J. The discussion/conclusion is appropriate.

SA   5   4   3   2   1   SD

K. Despite any flaws, the report is worthy of publication.

SA   5   4   3   2   1   SD

Article 22

A Consumer View of Teen Living Programs: Teen Parents' Satisfaction with Program Components and Services

Mary Elizabeth Collins
Boston University

Cristi Lemon
Boston University

Elizabeth Street
Boston University

ABSTRACT. This paper reports on the program satisfaction of teen parents who resided in residential programs developed as part of welfare reform in Massachusetts. These teen living programs (TLPs) provide an alternative living situation for teen-parent welfare recipients who cannot live with a parent or guardian, but who must live in an approved setting to receive assistance. One hundred ninety-nine interviews were conducted with teen parents, 72 with those who were currently living in the program and 127 with those who had left the program. Both quantitative and qualitative data were collected to assess global satisfaction with services, satisfaction with specific program components, and other open-ended feedback about the program. The measurement of program satisfaction is particularly important for programs serving young people, as they typically have few opportunities to voice their views. Consequently, implications for further program practice are identified.

From *Families in Society: The Journal of Contemporary Human Services*, *81*, 284–293. Copyright © 2000 by Families International, Inc. Reprinted with permission.

If programs are designed to be dynamic, adaptive, and responsive, the measurement of client satisfaction with services is a necessary component of program evaluation. In two circumstances, the measurement of

5 satisfaction is particularly crucial. First, new program models can benefit from the collection of data on client satisfaction because they are typically in a developmental stage and most able to incorporate client feedback into program change. Second, measurement

10 of satisfaction is also particularly appropriate when the consumers of services are those with limited power such as youth in residential programs. For these populations, collection of data about consumer satisfaction provides a voice to program clients.

15 In Massachusetts, a new program model has been developed to serve teen mothers and their children affected by welfare reform. In response to legislation that requires teen parents receiving welfare to live with their parent, adult relative, or guardian, the

20 Massachusetts legislature has funded teen living programs (TLPs), which provide an alternative setting

for those unable to meet the living requirement (due to abuse, neglect, or other family circumstances). As a new program, the State of Massachusetts Department

25 of Transitional Assistance (DTA) supported an evaluation to assess the extent to which key outcomes of the program were attained. Earlier reports have described clients' attainment of outcomes (Collins, Stevens, & Lane, 2000) and the key issues in service

30 delivery (Collins, Lane, & Stevens, 1999). The current study examines data collected from the teen parents regarding their satisfaction with program components, satisfaction with other program elements (e.g., staff relationships), and suggestions for further program

35 development.

Background

Several authors have noted the importance of measuring satisfaction. Speaking primarily about client satisfaction with treatment services, Heflinger, Sonnichsen, and Brannan (1996) write that satisfaction

40 provides a viewpoint that is necessary for evaluation concerned with multiple stakeholders, that it is a primary domain necessary for examining program effectiveness, that it furnishes administrators and policy makers with the feedback needed to improve service

45 delivery, and that it offers a measure of "acceptability" of treatment that may be related to compliance and success. Corrigan (1990), in discussing satisfaction with mental-health settings, suggests that in addition to overall satisfaction, the identification of the elements

50 that consumers find satisfying is necessary for developing user-friendly services. Moreover, LaSala (1997) has suggested that client satisfaction is an appealing outcome measure because it has strong face validity, is consistent with social-work values, and can

55 be an inexpensive method of data collection.

Program satisfaction is particularly important in youth services because young people typically lack the power to express dissatisfaction in meaningful ways and generally cannot display dissatisfaction by

60 terminating services. Specifically, in residentially based programs, young people typically must follow many program rules but have little input into program

131

structure. Despite its importance, the measurement of satisfaction has been particularly lacking in services for children and youth (Stüntzner-Gibson, Koren, & DeChillo, 1995; Shapiro, Walker, & Jacobson, 1997).

Stüntzner-Gibson, Koren, and DeChillo (1995) reviewed several studies aimed at measuring children's satisfaction with services and concluded that child satisfaction can be measured in a manner that is reliable and sensitive to program differences, although most studies have been limited by a focus on medical services. Previous studies have also been positively biased by an over-reliance on quantitative measures, which are less likely than qualitative methods to elicit responses that reflect dissatisfaction (Perreault, Leichner, Sabourin, & Gendreau, 1993). Moreover, Godley, Fiedler, and Funk (1998) found qualitative questions to be particularly important in identifying specific aspects of service that might be improved.

Attempting to respond to some of the concerns regarding the measurement of youth satisfaction, Stüntzner-Gibson, Koren, and DeChillo (1995) developed the Youth Satisfaction Questionnaire to gather information about children's opinions of the range of services and activities in which they were involved. The questionnaire included five general satisfaction questions and several questions related to the specific services and activities in which the child participated (e.g., counseling, special education). They concluded that "asking children what they think of the services and activities in which they are involved appears to be both meaningful and potentially useful as an approach to evaluating services" (p. 622).

Using a qualitative approach and studying a population similar to the one described in the current study, McMillen, Rideout, Fisher, and Tucker (1997) examined the views of former consumers of independent-living programs for youth in out-of-home care. They note that while there have been recent evaluations of independent-living services, few studies have attempted to identify the components of the program that are most beneficial to those leaving care. In focus-group interviews, former youth were asked to describe the services that were most helpful in teaching them how to live independently and to identify who was most helpful in their transition to independent living. Through the interviews, several prominent themes were identified including specific program components that were viewed as helpful and not helpful; perceptions of the helpfulness of the foster home, caseworkers, and independent-living specialists; and the difficulty of the transition in leaving care.

Despite the important reasons for collecting satisfaction data, several potential problems with the measurement of satisfaction have been noted. Criticisms have most commonly included the lack of variability in quantitative scores and the tendency for clients to consistently report moderate to high levels of satisfaction (Heflinger, Sonnichsen, & Brannan, 1996;

Larson, Attkisson, Hargreaves, & Nguyen, 1979; Lebow, 1983). Other criticisms have included a lack of specificity in measures, lack of standard scales, sampling bias, and inconsistency in format (Lebow, 1982; Nguyen, Attkisson, & Stegner, 1983).

In the current study, the measurement of adolescents' feedback regarding the strengths and weaknesses of the program used both quantitative and qualitative data collection and analysis. There were several additional strengths to our method of measuring satisfaction. First, several dimensions of the program were assessed, including overall satisfaction, specific program components, and less tangible elements such as emotional support. Second, data were collected by an independent team, rather than by program personnel, which is likely to elicit more objective answers, thereby reducing the tendency of positive response bias. Third, data were collected during face-to-face interviews, a method with a higher completion rate than mailed questionnaires. Finally, data were collected from both those in the program and those having left the program; therefore, any bias related to perception between those currently in and those out of the program can be documented.

Program Description

At the time of the evaluation, the TLP network had 22 sites throughout the state and a total of 110 beds. Individual program sites are operated by several private social-service agencies through contracts with the Department of Social Services. The program settings include congregate care facilities, small group homes, and supervised apartments. A comprehensive approach to services is intended. Thus, programs must include 24-hour skilled staffing and supervision of residents and their children; access to licensed child care (preferably on-site); access to educational, counseling, and health services; case management; and a curriculum of parenting and independent-living skills.

Entry into the program begins when a teen parent applies for welfare benefits. If the teen states that she is unable to live at home or with an adult relative or legal guardian, she is referred for an assessment conducted by the Department of Social Services. If the teen does not accept the recommendation (to either return to her parents' or guardians' home or to enter a TLP), she is no longer eligible for welfare assistance; the case is closed after 30 days and referred to an outreach program.

Method

Only those who had been in the program for at least one month were included in the study. At the time of the study, a total of 288 teens had been served by the program for at least one month. Interviewers were able to locate and contact 201 teens. Only two refused to participate, resulting in 199 completed interviews; 127 were former TLP residents and 72 were current

175 program residents. The total response rate was 69% overall.

In-person interviews were conducted during a two-month field period from mid-April to mid-June of 1998. The interviews were conducted by masters' stu-
180 dents from the Boston University School of Social Work in a setting chosen by the teen parent, usually in her home. The survey instrument inquired about experiences both while the teen parent was in the program and after she left the program. Data on satisfac-
185 tion was collected in two ways: by asking participants to rate services according to how helpful they were and by asking the young women three open-ended questions: (1) What do/did you find helpful about being in the TLP? (2) What do/did you find not helpful
190 about being in the TLP? and (3) What other types of assistance do you think might have been/might be helpful? Finally, the interviewer asked each participant if she had any other thoughts or comments about how TLPs might better serve teen parents.
195 Two measures of global satisfaction were developed. One measure, global components, was based on an average of ratings for each of the program components. These were calculated separately for each client and were based on the client's perception of
200 receipt of services (i.e., if a client reported not receiving a service, that component was not included in the average score). The second measure, global-qualitative components, was derived from a review of the open-ended responses and the assignment of a
205 subjective code on a five-point scale (very unsatisfied to very satisfied) based on the types of comments that the teen parent made about the program. Those expressing no sentiments were coded as "3" (neither satisfied nor dissatisfied). Inter-rater reliability of the
210 global-qualitative score was calculated and found to be good ($r = .77$, $p < .001$). Although a discussion of program components is sometimes included in the qualitative data, teen responses in these sections also reflected their feelings about relationships with
215 program staff and with the other teen parents, the physical setting, and other less tangible elements of the program that are not captured by the ratings of program components. Thus, the global-qualitative rating was found to correlate moderately with the global-
220 components score ($r = .42$, $p < .001$), as would be expected.

Results

Our results are presented in four sections: description of participants, program components, global satisfaction, and qualitative feedback.

Participants

225 Table 1 shows a description of clients, and information about those who were current clients in the program and those who were past clients is provided separately. All clients were female. The average age at entry into the program was approximately 18 years.

230 Latinas were the largest racial group served by the program, followed by African Americans, Caucasians, and "other" (generally biracial). The primary language of clients was English, followed by Spanish, with a few whose primary language was Haitian Creole or "other."
235 Most teens were already parenting at the time of intake into the TLP.

Table 1
Client Characteristics at Intake (N = 199)

	In Program (N = 72)	Follow up (N = 127)
Demographics		
Age at entry	*M* = 18.09	*M* = 17.83
Race		
Latina	36%	37%
African American	26%	30%
Caucasian	22%	24%
Other	15%	9%
Language		
English	75%	78%
Spanish	21%	19%
Haitian Creole	1%	3%
Other	3%	1%
Parenting Status (at intake)		
Parenting	57%	67%
Pregnant	25%	19%
Pregnant and parenting	18%	15%
Living Situation		
Permanent	56%	57%
Temporary (friends/family)	29%	27%
Temporary (other)	15%	16%
Reason for entering TLP		
Couldn't get along w/family	41%	35%
Parents not available	24%	12%
Parents' home too small	17%	16%
Kicked out due to pregnancy	13%	15%
Drugs in home	9%	5%
Abuse	4%	10%
Wanted own apartment	3%	7%
Other	6%	19%
Previous work experience (yes)	81%	77%
Previous education		
In school	51%	42%
In GED program	21%	26%
Sources of social support		
No one	8%	13%
Mother	42%	39%
Father of baby	49%	36%
Friends	26%	28%
Relatives	8%	27%
Siblings	21%	20%
Father of baby's family	22%	17%

In terms of their living situations prior to entering the TLP, most young women had lived with their families in a self-described "permanent" living
240 situation, whereas less than half lived in a "temporary" situation. Because the new living-arrangement requirement allows teens the option of living with their parents, adult family member, or guardian, teens were asked why they were unable to live with their parents
245 or guardian (and therefore required placement in a TLP). The most common reasons reported were that they could not get along with their parents, their parents' homes were too small, they had been kicked

out due to pregnancy, or their parents were unavailable
250 (e.g., deceased, out of state, incarcerated).

Regarding previous schooling, approximately half reported that they had been attending school at entry into the TLP. An additional quarter were in a general equivalency diploma (GED) program. Most of the
255 young women reported having worked at some time. Typical of teenage employment, these jobs were in the areas of retail, fast food, office work, and other low-skilled occupations.

Program Components

Tables 2 and 3 provide information about clients'
260 perceptions of receiving services and their rating of services as either "pretty helpful" or "very helpful." For many program components, it was not expected that 100% of teens would receive the service. This is the case for child care, prenatal care, early intervention
265 service, school/GED, employment services, and counseling. Child care and early intervention service would only be relevant for those teens who were parenting, and prenatal care would only be appropriate for those who were pregnant. Similarly, the
270 school/GED component would only be needed by those who had not attained a high-school diploma, and employment services would only be needed by those who had a diploma or GED. Thus, those components with higher percentages of participants receiving a
275 service were those that serve most clients; parenting skills, life skills, and health services are targeted towards all teens, regardless of parenting or educational status, and, thus, these components have the highest percentages receiving the service. Columns
280 four and five examine the satisfaction with services received for those who reported receiving the service. These findings are described more fully below.

Table 2
Assessment of Program Components by Current TLP Residents
(N = 72)

	Receiving service		Receiving service, view it as pretty or very helpful	
	No.	%	No.	%
Life-skills classes	61	84.7	35	57.4
Parenting-skills classes	67	93.1	47	70.1
Child care	54	75.0	45	83.3
Prenatal care	20	27.8	17	85.0
Early intervention services	35	48.6	28	80.0
Health services	57	79.2	45	78.9
Health and safety classes	50	69.4	36	72.0
Housing-search assistance	52	72.2	19	36.5
School/GED	51	70.8	41	80.4
Employment services	33	45.8	15	45.5
Counseling	49	69.0	34	69.4

Current Residents. When asked to rate services according to how helpful they were, more than 80% of
285 current clients reported ratings of pretty helpful or very helpful on four components: child care, prenatal care,

early intervention services, and school/GED. Two services, housing search assistance and employment services, had percentages of less than 50% reporting
290 that they were pretty helpful or very helpful.

Former Residents. Responses of former residents were similar to those of current residents. Former residents rated child care (91%), school/GED (81%), and follow-up services (80%) as most helpful. Less
295 than 50% of former residents found three components to be pretty helpful or very helpful: life-skills classes (40%), housing-search assistance (40%), and employment services (48%).

In comparing current and former residents, the
300 tables show that those former residents who received child care, housing-search assistance, school or GED programs, and employment services found them slightly more helpful than current residents. Conversely, former residents rated services such as life-skills
305 classes, parenting-skills classes, prenatal care, early intervention services, health and safety classes, and counseling as less helpful than did current residents. Follow-up services are available post-program and were, therefore, only reported by former TLP residents.
310 It is unfortunate that less than half (47%) reported receiving such services, because they were frequently rated as helpful.

Table 3
Assessment of Program Components by Former TLP Residents
(N = 127)

	Receiving Service		Receiving service, view it as pretty of very helpful	
	No.	%	No.	%
Life-skills classes	96	76.8	38	39.6
Parenting-skills classes	112	88.9	69	61.6
Child care	91	71.7	83	91.0
Prenatal care	26	20.5	17	65.0
Early intervention services	75	59.1	51	68.0
Health services	87	69.0	61	70.0
Health and safety classes	82	64.6	55	67.0
Housing-search assistance	85	66.9	34	40.0
School/GED	93	73.2	75	81.0
Employment services	50	39.4	24	48.0
Counseling	89	70.1	52	58.0
Follow-up services	60	47.2	48	80.0

Global Satisfaction

Two measures of global satisfaction were developed. The global-components measure of satisfaction
315 was a summary score based on ratings of individual program components (four-point scale with 1 = not at all helpful and 4 = very helpful). The mean satisfaction score was 2.87 (SD = .68). The global-qualitative satisfaction score was based on a five-point scale (with 1
320 = very unsatisfied and 5 = very satisfied). The mean satisfaction score was 3.12 (SD = 1.06). For both measures, a series of analyses involving t tests, one-way analysis of variance (ANOVA), and correlation was conducted to examine client and program
325 characteristics related to both measures of satisfaction.

Global Components. No demographic characteristics of the clients were found to be related to satisfaction (the characteristics examined included parenting status [pregnant, parenting, or pregnant and parenting], race, age, primary language [English versus non-English], and citizenship [U.S. versus non-U.S.]). Program characteristics that were tested included number of full-time staff as percentage of total staff, number of college-educated staff as percentage of total staff, staff turnover (average loss of staff in months), and capacity of the TLP. One relationship was found to be significant; capacity of the TLP was negatively correlated with program satisfaction ($r = -.22, p < .01$).

Neither teen's length of stay in the program nor (for those who had exited) length of time since leaving the program was related to program satisfaction. However, whether the teen was in or out of the program at the time of interview was related to her satisfaction; those who were in the program had higher mean satisfaction scores (3.01) compared with those who were out (2.79; $t = 2.27, p < .05$).

Also examined were variables that examined the teens' personal situation at entry: housing situation, educational status, employment, and reason for entering the TLP. Those who attended a GED program prior to entering the TLP were more satisfied than those who had not (3.03 vs. 2.81; $t = 1.98; p < .05$). Also, those who reported a history of abuse were less satisfied than those who did not (2.60 vs. 2.93; $t = 2.70, p < .01$).

Table 4
Assessment of TLP by Current and Former TLP Residents: What Is/Was Helpful about the Teen Living Program?
(N = 404)

	No. of Responses	% of Total Response
Programming	97	24.0
Emotional support from staff and/or residents	79	19.6
Met basic needs	58	14.4
Access to school/GED	31	7.7
Child care	21	5.2
Budgeting	21	5.2
Housing search	17	4.2
Taught me how to be responsible	17	4.2
Nothing is/was helpful	34	8.4
Other	29	7.2

Global-Qualitative Components. When the analysis used the measure of satisfaction based on subjective reading of client comments, similar, but not identical, patterns were found. The capacity of the TLP again was negatively correlated ($r = -.14, p < .05$) with satisfaction. Also, those who had attended a GED program prior to the TLP were more satisfied (3.40 vs. 3.01; $t = 2.29, p < .05$), and those who were placed because of abuse were less satisfied at a marginal level (2.77 vs. 3.16; $t = 1.94, p < .10$). Unlike the previous analysis, satisfaction level was not related to whether the teen was currently in the program or had left.

In addition, the subjective method of measuring satisfaction uncovered some additional relationships. Length of stay in the TLP was positively correlated with satisfaction ($r = .14, p < .05$). Additionally, two marginal relationships were found. Those who attended school prior to entering the TLP were less satisfied than those who had not attended school (2.96 vs. 3.23; $t = 1.76, p < .10$). An interesting finding was that those who left their previous living situations specifically because of the new living requirement reported higher satisfaction than those who did not state this as a reason for leaving their previous situations (3.59 vs. 3.08; $t = 1.93, p < .10$); other possible reasons included couldn't get along with other household members, kicked out due to pregnancy, evicted, displaced by domestic violence, unsafe/unsanitary, too expensive, and program requirement (e.g., time limit on length of stay).

Qualitative Feedback

Open-ended data were coded into categories based on a content analysis. The research team coded responses for the following questions: (1) What is/was helpful about the TLP? (2) What is/was not helpful about the TLP? and (3) Do you have any additional thoughts or comments about the TLP? Tables 4 and 5 list the teens' responses to the first two questions and the frequency with which the responses were given. Because the questions were asked in an open-ended format, teens often gave more than one response for each question. For example, when asked what was helpful about the TLP, one respondent replied, "A roof over our heads, family environment, counseling, schooling and child care." This particular response received five different codes. Thus, the total number of responses for these open-ended questions is greater than the number of teens interviewed.

What Is/Was Helpful. When asked what is/was helpful about the TLP, most responses (24%) were regarding programming. Frequently mentioned components included parenting classes, counseling, and early intervention services. In teens' own words, specific responses in this category included "I learned how to act with kids, discipline without hitting, how to talk to kids, about cooking and eating balanced meals" and "money management, help with stress, understanding and dealing with children of all ages."

Emotional support from staff and/or residents was the second most frequently mentioned (20%) helpful aspect of the TLP. Examples of these responses included "I was confident talking to them about anything"; "Living here is the biggest support I've had"; "They ask how you're doing every day. If you have a problem, they're there for you"; "They help you figure out your goal, help you know when you might get into trouble and tell you to make the choice. They help you to be mature"; and "You could see other people in your situation. There was support among teens."

Fourteen percent of the responses emphasized the program's ability to meet their basic needs. Included in this category were comments related to food, shelter, and transportation. Illustrative comments that describe the helpfulness of meeting basic needs include "I'd probably be living on the streets otherwise" and "They help us with transportation and to do our errands."

What Is/Was Not Helpful. When asked what was not helpful about the TLP, 26% of the responses mentioned rules, curfews, and lack of privacy. Teen comments included the following: "It's supposed to be independent living, but it feels like they're babysitting us"; "The rules change every month and the staff doesn't follow through with rules or commitments"; "It took so much to get to the next level that I rarely got to earn more privileges"; and "They're always watching you; having to raise my kid to their requirements; treating everyone the same despite maturity."

Another area of dissatisfaction was the report of conflicts with staff or other residents (20% of responses). Specific comments include "Bad communication between staff and residents. They didn't listen to our point of view" and "The other people who live here are very difficult to live with."

Fourteen percent of the comments were related to a specific piece of programming that respondents did not like. Additionally, 8% of the comments stated that the TLPs had a lack of services. Other comments focused on the physical facility or the program environment (e.g., "Chaos— too many people and babies").

Additional Comments. When asked for additional comments about the TLP, some respondents elaborated on previous statements while others described the changes that they would make to improve the TLP. The most common responses included giving residents more independence and privacy (19% of responses), expanding programming (13% of responses), and increasing consistency and organization in the TLP (11% of responses). For example, "Don't give us so many consequences for the littlest things we do wrong"; "Loosen up on rules for those over 18. It feels like incarceration. It's not right when you're paying rent"; and "Programs seem like a punishment for having children rather than helping."

When asked about additional services that might be helpful to TLP residents, the majority of teens responded that they needed help finding housing so that they could move into independent-living situations. Other suggestions included better transportation, more staff, neighborhood information for new residents, financial planning for the future, workshops on domestic violence, and help getting a driver's license.

Although the question asked specifically for improvement suggestions and, thus, the comments tended to focus on problems, some teens reiterated their positive comments (e.g., "I really like the program. It's

a good place because it would be harder on my own. It helps you plan for being a parent and your future").

Discussion

Both the quantitative and qualitative data provide evidence that the teen parents' experiences in the program and feelings about the program varied in important ways. Some teens reported great experiences (e.g., "living here is the biggest support I've had"), and others reported poor experiences (e.g., "programs seem like a punishment for having children rather than helping"). The majority of teens report a mixed experience and perceive some aspects of the program as helpful and some as not helpful. The data suggest some areas of program strength and other areas in which efforts aimed at program improvement can be directed.

Table 5
Assessment of TLP by Current and Former TLP Residents:
What Is/Was NOT Helpful about the Teen Living Program?
(N = 321)

	No. of Responses	% of Total Response
Lack of independence	82	25.5
Conflicts with staff and/or residents	65	20.2
Programming	45	14.0
Lack of services	25	7.8
Facilities	14	4.4
Lack of support	14	4.4
Overcrowded	7	2.2
Lack of case-by-case assessment	6	1.9
Lack of transportation	6	1.9
Lack of diversity/cultural awareness	5	1.6
Nothing is/was not helpful	28	8.7
Other	24	7.5

Although component ratings demonstrated variability, several components were rated particularly high. Child care and school/GED services were received by the majority of teens and were rated highly by both current and former program participants. This suggests that the teens are well aware of major barriers to self-sufficiency (lack of child care, lack of diploma) and are appreciative of these services when made available. The three program components demonstrating the lowest satisfaction ratings were life-skills classes, housing-search services, and employment assistance. Both housing-search services and employment assistance are concrete types of assistance that are critical to the teen's continued development beyond the TLP. Although both can be limited by factors outside of the program's control (e.g., the housing market and the labor market), a primary intent of the program is to strengthen the teen's ability to lead a self-sufficient lifestyle. Thus, both program- and system-level efforts appear to be needed. In particular, housing-search services and employment services might be linked to the program's follow-up services. This would help to ensure the young family remained in safe housing and that the young woman could take steps to increase her

520 employability and earning potential. Follow-up services were rated highly by those who had left, but, unfortunately, this was a program component that lacked wide coverage. Sites have reported that with limited staff time, particularly when programs are full,
525 they are restricted in their ability to sufficiently follow up with clients; however, they are also aware of this program weakness and are developing means to strengthen this component (Collins, Lane, & Stevens, 1999). Allocation of specific funds and staff resources,
530 as well as definition of the concrete steps to engage in follow up (e.g., timing and methods of contacts), appear needed. At the same time, system-level advocacy is warranted at the local and state levels to increase the supply of affordable housing within the
535 community, create access to nontraditional and well-paying jobs, and enhance a variety of transitional housing and employment services.

Certain characteristics of the programs and the clients themselves were related to satisfaction. Level of
540 satisfaction was higher for those in smaller programs, for those who were currently in the program versus those who had left, for those who had attended a GED program prior to entry into the TLP, and for those who had not been placed for reasons of abuse. Several
545 explanations can be proposed for these identified relationships. Smaller programs offer more individualized attention, engender a more homelike atmosphere, and restrict the likelihood of "chaos." It is interesting that those respondents currently in the program re-
550 ported higher satisfaction; staff commonly stated that teens are more grateful for the program after they have left than while they are in, but the data suggest otherwise. This relationship only held for the satisfaction measure that was based on program
555 components; however, it was not observed for the satisfaction measure based on open-ended comments. Thus, while teens are receiving services, they appear to recognize the utility of those services to a greater degree than after they leave.
560 We suspect that the reason those who have attended a GED program prior to entry are more satisfied is because the program facilitated the completion of the GED (a goal in which they had already demonstrated some interest) and possibly assisted them in attaining
565 further education. Those who had not previously attended a GED program may have been more resentful than appreciative of the education requirement. Finally, satisfaction was lower for those who had been placed for reasons of abuse. These
570 young women are likely to be dealing with a variety of feelings associated with victimization experiences that may not be directly addressed by the programs. One nonsignificant, but important, finding is the lack of a relationship between demographic characteristics and
575 satisfaction; this suggests the program provides generally equitable treatment.

The second satisfaction measure was based on open-ended responses and was not limited to measuring satisfaction with program components. Length of
580 stay was related to this second measure but not the first. It may be that a longer length of stay is needed to develop the type of relationships within the program that result in a higher level of satisfaction, or it may be that those who stay are more satisfied with the
585 program. Also noteworthy is that those who entered because of the new DTA requirement were found to be more satisfied. At first this seems surprising, because teens who had been living on their own might be expected to be more resentful of moving into a group liv-
590 ing situation. It may suggest, however, that these teens had few other problems (e.g., no history of abuse or victimization, no previous eviction) and, therefore, were not dealing with serious personal issues and could appreciate the program to a greater extent than those
595 who had other issues with which they were coping. Teens who have lived on their own may also be highly cognizant of how difficult it can be, and thus may be more grateful for support provided, as opposed to those who have not been on their own and have idealized
600 visions of what it would be like.

Some teen comments speak to the feelings of support within the group (e.g., "You could see other people in your situation. There was support among teens.") and others speak to dissatisfaction with the group (e.g.,
605 "The other people who live here are very difficult to live with"). Although the program model is not treatment-oriented and, therefore, does not use the group-living experience to provide a therapeutic environment, development of supportive relationships
610 is encouraged both among the teens and with staff. Given the challenges the young women face after leaving the program, and thus the need for ongoing encouragement and support, more explicit attention to the initiation, maintenance, and termination of various
615 social networks and support mechanisms might be an additional means of adding to the teens' repertoire of life skills. Similar issues are raised and addressed by the program in terms of the support provided to the young women by the fathers of their children as well as
620 other family members. Program sites vary in the extent to which the fathers and other family members are included in programming. Such variation is, in part, due to the individualized circumstances of the teens; some are virtually alone in the world, and others have
625 ongoing and positive contact with the father of their children and their family members. Programs attempt to include fathers when appropriate (e.g., in parenting and life-skills classes), but sites also acknowledge that this is another area where programming could be
630 improved and extended.

Based on client statements, the main dissatisfactions with the program are lack of independence and too many rules. This is not a surprising finding; group living is not easy, and adolescence is a stage of life

635 during which the struggle for increased independence is critical. As in any group-living situation (whether a formal program, a chosen informal arrangement, or a family), all individuals must adjust and respect each other for a satisfactory experience. To limit dissatis-
640 faction in this area, the program can aim to find ways to allow as much independence and as few rules as possible. For example, most of the programs pool the adolescents' food stamps and conduct joint menu planning, shopping, and meal preparation. One site,
645 however, did not do this, stating that by allowing each teen to make these decisions herself, it is "one less thing the program is controlling." Moreover, the type of house rules must be responsive to this particular population. These teens are adolescent mothers who
650 receive welfare. Their needs are not the same as those of runaways or homeless or abused adolescents (although some may have suffered these circumstances). Workers in programs with a history of serving these other populations need to be especially sensitive to the
655 difference in population and be certain that they do not transfer program philosophy and rules to this new population without reflection and justification.

Some comments of teens suggest a misunderstanding of the program intent. The program is not an
660 independent-living program, although some teens view it as such. Furthermore, although a portion of their welfare benefit is used to pay program fees, it is not "rent" and the relationship is not one of landlord to tenant. While it is not unusual for program participants
665 to have different ideas of the nature of the program than either program designers or program staff, clearer communication about the nature of the program is needed to help with this aspect of program dissatisfaction.

670 In conclusion, we comment briefly on two broader issues: the utilization of client-satisfaction data and the relationship of client-satisfaction data to outcomes. For the most part, the feedback provided by the teen mothers appears appropriate and a reflection of reality,
675 thus providing important information about program operations. Ways to institutionalize client feedback are needed in this program model, as well as in other programs serving youth. Although house meetings occur at most program sites to provide a forum for
680 discussion of house issues, no formal mechanism exists to consistently gather data about client satisfaction or to use such information for program improvement. Ongoing data collection is needed and is relatively easy and inexpensive. Individual program sites can use such
685 data primarily regarding issues related to staff relationships and the nature of the individual house rules. This data can also be used as part of the contract monitoring process for individual sites. Additionally, data regarding program components and the larger
690 issues of program philosophy (e.g., the careful balance between a group model and encouragement of

independence) should be used to guide the ongoing development of the program model.

Finally, although the relationship between client
695 satisfaction and client outcome is an important one, our focus here was not on outcome but on satisfaction and the improvement of programs. Like Godley, Fiedler, and Funk (1998), we believe that consumer satisfaction need not be directly related to outcome to be an
700 important goal for policymakers and practitioners. Consumers of services have a right to be treated in ways that they view with satisfaction. Programs cannot successfully affect outcomes unless program participants remain in the program for a sufficient period.
705 We suspect, therefore, that attention to increasing program satisfaction will result in more teens staying with the program for longer periods, which may, in turn, lead to attainment of important outcomes.

References

Collins, M. E., Lane, T S., & Stevens, J. W (1999). Teen parents and welfare reform: Findings from a survey of teens affected by living requirements. Unpublished manuscript available from first author.

Collins, M. E., Stevens, J. W., & Lane, T S. (in press). Teen living programs: A description of program components and issues in service delivery. *Social Work.*

Corrigan, P. W. (1990). Consumer satisfaction with institutional and community care. *Community Mental Health Journal, 26*(2), 151–165.

Godley, S. H., Fiedler, E. M., & Funk, R. R. (1998). Consumer satisfaction of parents and their children with child/adolescent mental health services. *Evaluation and Program Planning, 21,* 31–45.

Heflinger, C. A., Sonnichsen, S. E., & Brannan, A. M. (1996). Parent satisfaction with children's mental health services in a children's mental health managed care demonstration. *The Journal of Mental Health Administration, 23*(1), 69–79.

Larson, D., Attkisson, C., Hargreaves, W., & Nguyen, T. (1979). Assessment of patient satisfaction: Development of a general scale. *Evaluation and Program Planning, 2,* 197–207.

LaSala, M. C. (1997). Client satisfaction: Consideration of correlates and response bias. *Families in Society, 78*(1), 54–64.

Lebow, J. (1982). Consumer satisfaction with mental health treatment. *Psychological Bulletin, 91,* 244–259.

Lebow, J. (1983). Research assessing consumer satisfaction with mental health treatment: A review of findings. *Evaluation and Program Planning, 5,* 211–236.

McMillen, J. C., Rideout, G. B., Fisher R. H., & Tucker, J. (1997). Independent-living services: The views of former foster youth. *Families in Society, 78*(5), 471–479.

Nguyen, T. D., Attkisson, C. C., & Stegner, B. L. (1983). Assessment of patient satisfaction: Development and refinement of a service evaluation questionnaire. *Evaluation and Program Planning, 6,* 299–314.

Perreault, M., Leichner, P., Sabourin, S., & Gendreau, P. (1993). Patient satisfaction with outpatient psychiatric services: Qualitative and quantitative assessments. *Evaluation and Program Planning, 16,* 109–118.

Shapiro, J. P., Walker, C. J., & Jacobson, B. J. (1997). The youth client satisfaction questionnaire: Development, construct validation, and factor structure. *Journal of Clinical Psychology, 26*(1), 87–98.

Stüntzner-Gibson, D., Koren, P E., & DeChillo, N. (1995). The youth satisfaction questionnaire: What kids think of services. *Families in Society, 76*(10), 616–624. .

About the authors: Mary Elizabeth Collins is assistant professor at Boston University School of Social Work. Cristi Lemon and Elizabeth Street are former graduate students of Boston University School of Social Work.

Note: This study was completed under contract to the Massachusetts Department of Transitional Assistance.

Address correspondence to: Mary Elizabeth Collins, Boston University, School of Social Work, 264 Bay State Road, Boston, MA 02215.

Exercise for Article 22

Factual Questions

1. According to LaSala (1977), why is client satisfaction an appealing outcome measure?

2. What is the value of the inter-rater reliability coefficient for the global-qualitative scores?

3. Among current residents, which two services had percentages of less than 50% reporting that they were pretty helpful or very helpful?

4. At intake, what percentage of those in the program reported that the father of the baby was a source of social support?

5. Based on the qualitative feedback, what was the second most frequently mentioned helpful aspect of the TLP?

6. What percentage of former TLP residents viewed child care as pretty helpful or very helpful?

7. When current and former residents were asked about what is/was *not* helpful, what percentage cited lack of independence?

8. Does the fact that a portion of the teen's benefit is used to pay program fees constitute "rent"? Accordingly, is the program designed to create a tenant-landlord relationship?

Questions for Discussion

9. Have the researchers convinced you that it is important to examine clients' satisfaction with programs (in contrast with examining clients' attainment of outcomes)? Do you think that satisfaction or attainment of outcomes is more important in a program such as the TLP? Explain.

10. Was Table 1 useful in helping you "see" the clients? Explain.

11. Do you agree that it was better to have an independent team (rather than program personnel) collect the data? Explain. (See lines 134–138.)

12. Do you agree with the researchers' decision to use both current and former residents in this evaluation? Explain.

13. Did the quantitative (Global Satisfaction) data and the qualitative (Global-Qualitative) data contribute equally to understanding the clients' satisfaction? Explain.

14. Based on the information in this research article, would you strongly support the continuance of teen living programs (TLPs) in Massachusetts? Do the results convince you that they should be used in additional states? Explain.

15. If you were to plan an evaluation of clients' satisfaction with TLPs, would you use the same methodology described in this research article? Would you make changes? Be specific in the explanation of your answers.

Quality Ratings

Directions: Indicate your level of agreement with each of the following statements by circling a number from 5 for strongly agree (SA) to 1 for strongly disagree (SD). If you believe an item is not applicable to this research article, leave it blank. Be prepared to explain your ratings.

A. The introduction establishes the importance of the study.

SA   5   4   3   2   1   SD

B. The literature review establishes the context for the study.

SA   5   4   3   2   1   SD

C. The research purpose, question, or hypothesis is clearly stated.

SA   5   4   3   2   1   SD

D. The method of sampling is sound.

SA   5   4   3   2   1   SD

E. Relevant demographics (for example, age, gender, and ethnicity) are described.

SA   5   4   3   2   1   SD

F. Measurement procedures are adequate.

SA   5   4   3   2   1   SD

G. All procedures have been described in sufficient detail to permit a replication of the study.

SA   5   4   3   2   1   SD

H. The participants have been adequately protected from potential harm.

SA   5   4   3   2   1   SD

I. The results are clearly described.

SA   5   4   3   2   1   SD

J. The discussion/conclusion is appropriate.

       SA   5   4   3   2   1   SD

K. Despite any flaws, the report is worthy of publication.

       SA   5   4   3   2   1   SD

Article 23

The Effectiveness of CASAs in Achieving Positive Outcomes for Children

Pat Litzelfelner
University of Kentucky

ABSTRACT. Using a quasi-experimental design, this study evaluated the effectiveness of CASAs [court-appointed special advocates] in achieving positive outcomes for children, and examined the process variables believed to lead to permanency for children. Data were collected from court and CASA program files over a two-year period on 200 children, who were compared to children without CASA volunteers on outcome and process variables. Findings indicate that CASAs may have helped reduce the number of placements and court continuances children experienced, and that more services were provided to children with CASAs than to those without. Additional research is needed to further evaluate the impact of CASA services on children.

From *Child Welfare*, LXXIX, 179–193. Copyright © 2000 by the Child Welfare League of America, Inc. Reprinted with permission.

The Child Abuse Prevention and Treatment Act of 1976 mandated that children involved in judicial proceedings due to abuse or neglect have a *guardian ad litem* (GAL) appointed to advocate for their best inter-
5   ests. In 1977, dissatisfied with the effort and cost of using attorneys as GALs, juvenile court judges in King County, Washington, began using citizen volunteers as GALs, calling them court-appointed special advocates (CASA). By 1998, 843 CASA and CASA-affiliated
10 programs were established nationwide, with more than 47,000 volunteers representing 183,339 children (National CASA Association 1998).

CASAs provide a voice for children in judicial proceedings and advocate for the placement of children in
15 safe homes intended to be permanent. They are trained community volunteers who are asked to make a commitment for the duration of a child's involvement with the court and child welfare systems. Because CASA volunteers are usually assigned to only one case at a
20 time, they typically can give more time and attention to it than can attorneys and/or child welfare workers. Additionally, children can benefit from having an advocate who is outside the court system, child welfare system, and parent-child relationship.
25 CASA programs may follow one of four models: (1) *the GAL model*—the CASA is the child's GAL; (2) *the "friend of the court" model*—the CASA serves as

an impartial observer, conducts investigations with key people, and makes recommendations to the court
30 (Children assigned a CASA under this model also have attorney GALs.); (3) *the "team" model*—the CASA and attorney are appointed by the court to perform the functions of the GAL, and the CASA works "for" the attorney by providing the attorney with needed infor-
35 mation to represent the child in judicial proceedings; and (4) *the "monitor" model*—the CASA monitors court orders for compliance and alerts the court about failures to comply, but has little, if any, contact with the children and families (Miller & Wolf Survey, in
40 Condelli 1988).

This study adds to the small body of literature presently available regarding the effectiveness of CASAs in helping achieve permanency for children who have been abused or neglected and are involved with the
45 court system.

Literature Review

Since the inception of the CASA program in 1977, only a handful of quantitative studies have been conducted regarding the impact CASA volunteers have on the lives of the children they serve, with inconclusive,
50 yet promising results. Utilizing a true experimental design, Abramson (1991) demonstrated that children assigned a CASA were less likely to re-enter out-of-home care once discharged than were children without CASAs. That study also showed that children with
55 CASAs were more likely to have case goals that reflected permanency than those not served by CASAs.

Three studies have demonstrated that children with CASA volunteers are more likely to be adopted than those who do not have CASA volunteers (Abramson
60 1991; Poertner & Press 1990; Smith 1992). Two other studies have demonstrated that children with CASAs experienced shorter stays in out-of-home care than children without CASAs (Oregon Governor's Task Force 1995; Leung 1996). Other research involving
65 CASAs suggests that children and families served by CASAs have more services provided to them by child welfare agencies than do children without such volunteers (CSR, Inc. 1990; Condelli 1988, Duquette & Ramsey 1987; Poertner & Press 1990).
70 Although most studies have found few differences between children with CASAs and those without on

many variables related to permanency, the findings of "no difference" suggest that children with CASAs do at least as well as children with attorney GALs on certain
75 outcome and process variables. Previous researchers (Leung 1996; Poertner & Press 1990) report that CASA is a cost-effective way to provide representation for children involved in judicial proceedings due to abuse or neglect.

Method
Variables
80 This study used a quasi-experimental group design to evaluate the effectiveness of CASA volunteers in achieving positive outcomes for children involved in the child welfare system. Child outcomes were defined as: (1) case closure rates, (2) the length of time children
85 were under court jurisdiction, and (3) the number of children adopted. In addition, the study examined court and out-of-home care process variables that are believed to help lead to permanency for children. The process variables examined were: (1) type of place-
90 ments children were in while in care, (2) number of court continuances, and (3) number of services provided to children and their families. Children with CASAs were compared to children without CASAs on child outcome and process variables. It was hypothe-
95 sized that children with CASA would perform better than children without CASAs on these measures.

Study Sites
The study took place in Kansas, where state legislation outlines the roles and responsibilities of CASA volunteers:

100   It shall be the primary duty of a CASA to personally investigate and become acquainted with the facts, conditions, and circumstances affecting the welfare of the child for whom appointed, to advocate the best interest of the child, and (to) assist the court in obtaining for the child
105   the most permanent, safe, and homelike placement possible. (Kansas Supreme Court 1995)

In Kansas, CASAs follow the "friend of the court" model and are primarily responsible for investigating and becoming familiar with the facts through inter-
110 views with children, family members, and other interested parties, and for making written recommendations to the court regarding child placement and services. Children in Kansas are also assigned attorneys as GALs to represent them in judicial proceedings.
115 Two sites were chosen for inclusion in the study, representing a medium and a large CASA program. The large CASA program was located in an urban area with a county population of 421,000. In 1994, the year the study began, there were 509 confirmed cases of
120 child abuse or neglect and approximately 1,175 children in out-of-home placements in the county; the program had 70 active CASA volunteers who served 186 children. The medium-size CASA program began in 1991. The county population was 84,000 and, at the

125 time the study began, the program had 45 active CASAs representing 90 children. There were 192 confirmed cases of child abuse or neglect and 211 children placed in out-of-home care in the study county.

Sample Selection
All children who were adjudicated to be "children
130 in need of care" at both sites during an 18-month period and who were assigned a CASA were included in the study (the treatment group). A comparison sample of children who entered the system at the same time but were not assigned CASAs was chosen from court
135 records. Because age, race, and type of maltreatment (i.e., physical abuse, sexual abuse, neglect) have been demonstrated to be related to child outcomes, comparison cases were matched to CASA cases on those variables. Children who were adjudicated juvenile offend-
140 ers were not included in the study.
The final study sample included 119 CASA and 81 comparison cases. More CASA than comparison cases were included because judges would often refer cases to the CASA program when volunteers were available
145 for appointment (usually following a training class). At times, no comparison cases were available that entered the system at the same time as those assigned to CASA.

Data Collection
The study used current information from juvenile
150 court and CASA program records for data collection. A data collection form was developed that included demographic information and the variables under study. Data were collected on each child in the study every six months for a two-year period. This type of
155 data collection allowed the researcher to "follow" the children and track their movements and the services provided to them as they proceeded through the court process. Using this longitudinal and prospective data collection process also helped assure the data's accu-
160 racy. The six-month follow-ups allowed for comparisons to be made between the groups at different points in time on certain variables.

Sample Characteristics
The sample characteristics for each group (CASA and comparison) are presented in Table 1. Bivariate
165 statistical analyses using t tests and chi squares were performed to determine if the CASA and comparison groups differed in terms of these case characteristics. The analysis revealed three case characteristic variables with statistically significant differences between
170 the CASA and comparison groups at the .05 level of significance: (1) severity of abuse, (2) caregiver substance abuse, and (3) number of siblings in care.
Children with CASA volunteers were more likely to be in care because of physical and/or sexual abuse
175 combined with neglect than were those in the comparison group. The CASA cases were also more likely to be involved with the courts due to neglect only. Com-

142

Table 1
Characteristics of the Study Sample

Characteristic	CASA (N = 119)	Comparison (N = 81)
Child's Age	M = 8.01	M = 8.86
Child's Race		
Caucasian	66 (55.4%)	39 (48.1%)
African American	26 (21.8%)	17 (20.9%)
Other	27 (22.6%)	25 (30.8%)
Child's Gender		
Male	62 (52.1%)	36 (44.4%)
Female	57 (47.8%)	45 (56.5%)
Type of Maltreatment***		
Physical and/or sexual abuse and neglect	25%	11%*
Physical or sexual abuse only	14%	27%*
Neglect only	38%	26%*
Parent request	10%	13%
Other or unknown	12%	14%
Caregiver substance abuse	53%	35%*
Number of Siblings in Care	M = 1.79	M = .85**
	SD = 1.8	SD = .96
Child is from a Single-Parent Home	73 (61.3%)	48 (59.2%)

* $p < .05$; **$p < .01$
***Note: More than one type of maltreatment may have occurred.

parison cases were more likely than CASA cases to have experienced physical or sexual abuse only and to
180 be involved with the courts by parents' request [x^2 (1, 4) = 15.20, p = .0043]. Caregiver substance abuse was found more frequently in the CASA cases than the comparison cases (53% compared to 35%, [χ^2 (1, 200) = 6.18, p = .0128]. Children with CASA volunteers
185 had, on the average, more siblings who were in out-of-home care than did the children in the comparison group (1.7 compared to .8) [t (189) = –4.76, p = .000].

Based on the differences between the CASA and
190 comparison groups, it might appear that the CASA cases are "more difficult" than the comparison cases. These case characteristics were entered as covariates in the analysis to statistically control for the influence they may have had on the dependent variables. Analy-
195 ses were also conducted to examine the effects of site differences on the case characteristics. These analyses suggested that there were no differences between the large and medium program sites on the characteristics of the children and families in the study.

Results

Case Closure Rates
200 During the two-year data collection period, 71 cases (35%) (Table 2) in the study sample experienced case closure with the courts (32% of the CASA cases and 41% of the comparison cases). Although this finding indicates that a higher percentage of comparison

205 cases reached closure, it is not statistically significant [χ^2 (1, 200) = 1.63, p = .2013].

Length of Time under Court Jurisdiction
The length of time children were under court jurisdiction was examined for group differences. The child's court adjudication date was used as the date of
210 entry into the system, and the last day of data collection or court case closure date was used as the end date. There were no statistically significant differences found between children with CASAs and those without CASAs on the average length of time under court ju-
215 risdiction. The average length of time for CASA cases was 29.9 months; for comparison cases, it was 29.4 months.

A second analysis examined the length of time under court jurisdiction for the 71 cases that had reached
220 case closure during the study period (38 CASA cases and 33 comparison cases) (Table 3). Of those cases that had reached closure, CASA cases averaged 26.12 months and comparison cases averaged 23.64 months under court jurisdiction. This difference was also not
225 statistically significant [t = –.82 (70), p = .416].

Adoptions
Of the 71 cases that had reached court closure, only eight (11.3% of the closed cases) had a completed adoption. During the course of the study, three children with CASAs (7.8% of the closed cases) and five com-
230 parison case children (15.1% of the closed cases) were adopted. Although a higher percentage of comparison

Table 2
Analysis of CASA and comparison cases on outcome and process variables considering all study cases (N = 200)

	CASA	Comparison
Outcome Variables	(N = 119)	(N = 81)
Case Closure Rate	38 (31.9%)	33 (40.7%)
Time in the System (all cases)	M = 29.95 mo.	M = 29.40 mo.
	SD = 13.73	SD = 15.07
Adoptions	3 (7.8%)	5 (15.1%)
Number of Placements	M = 3.9	M = 6.62**
Placement at the End of Study***		
Home/relative/adoptive home	39 (48.1%)	20 (41.6%)
Foster homes	24 (29.6%)	15 (31.2%)
Group homes/shelters	13 (16.0%)	5 (10.4%)
Institutions	5 (6.1%)	8 (16.6%)
Type of Moves		
Positive	23 (19.3%)	18 (22.2%)
Negative	22 (18.4%)	17 (20.9%)
Same level	74 (62.1%)	46 (56.7%)
Number of Court Continuances	M = 2.0	M = 2.5
	SD = 2.5	SD = 2.9
Number of Services Provided	M = 8.5	M = 6.35**
	SD = 5.0	SD = 3.9

*$p < .05$; **$p < .01$
***Represents children still in care at the end of the study ($n = 129$).

Number of Placements

In examining all cases in the study, children with CASA volunteers statistically had on average significantly fewer placements than children without CASA volunteers (3.9 compared to 6.6) [t (104) = 2.86, p = .005]. When considering the cases that reached closure, children with CASAs also averaged fewer placements than children without CASAs (2.5 compared to 5.2) [t (42) =1.98, p = .042].

Child's Placement at the End of the Study

For the purpose of analysis, placements were categorized from least to most restrictive: (1) home, relative home, adoptive home, and independent living; (2) family foster home; (3) emergency shelter or group home; and (4) residential treatment, hospitals, and institutions. Cases that had not yet experienced court case closure ($n = 129$) were examined for the type of placements children were in at the end of the study period. Findings indicated there were no differences between the percentage of children with CASA volunteers and

group children were adopted during the course of the study than children with CASAs, the small number of cases means that statistical analysis to assess these differences could not be performed. Information regarding the number of children in the study with adoptions pending or planned could not be obtained.

the percentage of children without volunteers in each placement category at the end of the study.

Child's Placement at Each Data Collection Period

The next analyses included all study cases and examined the child's placement at each data collection period (initial entry; 6, 12, 18, and 24 months postentry) to determine differences between the two groups on the percentage of children placed in each level of placement. No statistically significant differences were found in the percentage of CASA and comparison cases for each of the placement categories upon entry or at 6, 12, or 18 months after entry into the system. Because of the small number of cases still in the system and being tracked for the study after 24 months (38 cases), statistical analysis could not be performed at this data collection period. An examination of the number of children in each placement category at the 24-month data collection period, however, showed a higher percent of children with CASAs in placement with their parents or relatives, or in adoptive homes, than comparison cases (62% compared to 33%). In addition, a higher percent of children without CASAs were placed in institutions compared to children with CASAs (25% compared to 0%).

Types of Moves

Cases were examined for the types of moves experienced (positive, negative, same level) by the children during the course of the study. As suggested by Leung (1996), moves by children from more restrictive (i.e., group homes and institutions) to less restrictive (i.e., parent, relative, family foster home) placements are considered positive. Moves by children from less restrictive to more restrictive placements are considered negative. In comparing CASA cases and comparison cases, no significant differences were found in the number of children who experienced positive or negative moves while in care or the number that remained at the same level of placement.

Number of Court Continuances

On average, children with CASAs had 2.0 court continuances and comparison cases had 2.6 court continuances during the course of the study. The difference was not statistically significant. When considering the closed cases only ($n = 71$), statistically CASA cases experienced significantly fewer court continuances while under court jurisdiction than comparison cases (1.07 compared to 2.93) [$t (41) = 3.10, p = .004$].

Services

More services were provided to families with a CASA than to those without one (8.52 compared to 6.39) when considering all study cases. This difference was statistically significant [$t (195) = -3.34, p = .002$]. When examining the closed cases, no differences were found for the number of services provided to children with CASAs (6.2) compared to children and families without (5.4).

Table 3
Analysis of CASA and Comparison Cases Considering Only Cases That Experienced Closure (N = 71)

Process Variables	CASA ($N = 38$)	Comparison ($N = 33$)
Time in the System (months)	$M = 26.12$	$M = 23.64$
	$SD = 13.67$	$SD = 11.67$
Number of Placements	$M = 2.56$	$M = 5.25*$
	$SD = 3.2$	$SD = 2.0$
Number of Continuances	$M = 1.07$	$M = 2.93**$
	$SD = 1.3$	$SD = 3.23$
Number of Services Provided	$M = 6.2$	$M = 5.48$
	$SD = 4.5$	$SD = 3.8$

$*p < .05; **p < .01$

Summary

Results from this study indicate that the presence of a CASA on a case did not influence permanency outcomes for children as the outcomes were defined in this study. Children who were assigned a CASA and children who made up the comparison group achieved about the same outcomes. Findings from this study do suggest, however, that the presence of a CASA on a case may have some influence on the process variables

believed to influence child outcomes. Specifically, the findings indicate that children with CASAs had statistically fewer placements while in care and fewer court continuances than children without CASAs. Findings from the study also suggest that children with CASAs had more services provided during the course of the study than children without CASAs. Results indicated no statistically significant differences between children with CASAs and children without CASAs with regard to the level of placement restrictiveness or the type of moves the children experienced during the course of the study.

Analyses were also performed to determine whether there were group differences on outcome and process variables based on individual program sites. No differences between the treatment and control groups could be attributed to the study sites, thus ruling out site differences as an alternative explanation for the findings.

Study Limitations

The researcher was unable to gain permission for random assignment of cases to the CASA programs from the juvenile court personnel and judges. The quasi-experimental design used matched comparison cases with "like" characteristics of the CASA cases. Due to the lack of random assignment, however, there is no way to know if the groups (CASA and comparison) are equal on other characteristics that may influence the findings. For example, judges reportedly assign CASAs to the more "difficult" cases, which suggests that in the absence of the CASA intervention, these cases may have less positive outcomes than the comparison cases. Because of this selection bias, there is no way to know if the findings of the study can be attributed to the CASA intervention. Random assignment would assure that the groups are equal on other variables, except for "chance differences," which may influence the outcomes, such as case severity. This assumption cannot be made for quasi-experimental designs.

Another potential study limitation was the sample size. The sample may not have been large enough to find statistically significant group differences when they did exist. The sample size calculation estimated a sample of 600 (300 in each group) would be needed to detect group differences on the dependent variables if they existed. Therefore, the sample of 200 may not have detected group differences when they did exist.

Discussion

Although this study's findings must be considered sample specific in that they apply only to the programs under study, other CASA programs will likely find the information helpful.

Findings from this study indicate that CASAs may have an influence on the process activities (i.e., number of placement changes, number of court continuances, and number of services provided to children and fami-

lies) that are believed to lead to permanency for children. There has been little consistency among previous
CASA studies regarding which child outcomes and
process activities are impacted by CASA volunteers.
Perhaps one reason for the inconsistent findings across
studies is study site differences. CASA programs
throughout the country follow different program models (as previously described) with volunteers performing various roles and functions and perhaps working
toward different outcomes for children.

The absence of additional positive findings from
the present study may also suggest that the CASA programs studied are not focused on these child outcomes
and process activities. Outcome and process variables
not examined in this study that might be considered for
future studies include re-entry or recidivism rates, frequency of court and child welfare case reviews, number of planned versus unplanned moves for children,
number of sibling groups placed together, and length of
time from petition to adjudication hearings.

The 1996 reauthorization of P. L. 93-247 (allowing
volunteer CASAs to serve as GALs), federal funding
increases to CASA programs through the Office of
Juvenile Justice and Delinquency Prevention, and the
increase in the number of participants at the national
CASA conferences are all indications that the CASA
movement is continuing to gain momentum. As CASA
programs grow and develop, training programs should
have a strong emphasis on child outcomes, permanency, and least restrictive placement concepts, as well
as on aggressive advocacy strategies. To track the
status of the children they are serving, CASA programs
need to implement a child tracking database system. It
may also prove beneficial for future CASA research to
examine exactly what CASA volunteers do on behalf
of children that may influence permanency outcomes.
Given the cost-effectiveness of CASA and the over-
burdened child welfare and juvenile court system, the
use of citizen volunteers sanctioned by CASA programs remains a viable option to provide a voice for
children who have been abused or neglected and who
might otherwise become lost in the system.

References

Abramson, S. (1991). Use of court-appointed advocates to assist in perma-
nency planning for minority children. *Child Welfare, 70*, 477–487.
Child Abuse Prevention and Treatment Act of 1976. 42 U.S.C.§ 5103(b)(2)(G).
CSR, Incorporated. (1990). *Effective advocacy for dependent children: A
systems approach.* Governor's Task Force on juvenile justice, Washington,
DC: Author (unpublished report).
CSR, Incorporated. (1990). *National study of guardian ad litem representation.*
Washington, DC: Author (unpublished report).
Condelli, L. (1988). *National evaluation of the impact of guardian ad litem in
child abuse and neglect judicial proceedings.* National Center of Child
Abuse and Neglect, Administration of Children, Youth and Families,
Washington, DC: CSR, Inc.
Duquette, D. N., & Ramsey, S. H. (1987). Representation of children in child
abuse and neglect cases: An empirical look at what constitutes effective rep-
resentation. *Journal of Law Review, 20*, 341-408.
Kansas Supreme Court. (1995). *Code for the care of children: Statute on
guardian ad litem requirements,* Rule #110.
Leung, P. (1996). Is the court-appointed special advocate program effective? A
longitudinal analysis of time involvement and case outcomes. *Child Welfare,
75*, 269-84.
National CASA Association. (1998). *Annual program survey.* Seattle, WA:
Author.
Oregon Governor's Task Force on Juvenile Justice. (1995). *Effective advocacy
for dependent children: A systems approach.* Salem, OR: Author (unpublished report).
Poertner, J., & Press, A. (1990). Representation of children in child abuse and
neglect cases: A comparison of court appointed special advocates with staff
attorney models: Who best represents the interest of child in court? *Child
Welfare, 69*, 537-549.
Smith, S. (1992). *The effects of CASA volunteers on case duration and outcomes.* Texas Department of Protection and Regulatory Services (unpublished report).

About the author: Pat Litzelfelner, Ph.D., is assistant professor,
College of Social Work, University of Kentucky, Lexington, KY.

Acknowledgments: Funding for this research was provided by the
United Methodist Health Ministries Fund of Hutchinson, KS. The
author acknowledges Dennis Saleebey, Ph.D., Thomas McDonald,
Ph.D., John Poertner, Ph.D., and Mary Ann Jennings, Ph.D. for their
contributions to this research.

Address correspondence to: Pat Litzelfelner, College of Social
Work, 629 Patterson Office Tower, University of Kentucky, Lexington, KY 40506-0027.

About the copyright holder: Child Welfare League of America,
Inc. Phone: (202) 638-2952; e-mail: jounral@cwla.org; Web site:
http://www.cwla.org or contact PMDS at phone: (800) 407-6273;
e-mail: cwla@pmds.com

Exercise for Article 23

Factual Questions

1. At the time the study began, the 45 active CASAs represented how many children?

2. What percentage of the CASA group was reported to have caregiver substance abuse? What was the corresponding percentage for the comparison group?

3. Considering only cases that experienced closure, what was the mean number of months in the system for children with CASAs?

4. In Table 3, was the difference between the two means for number of continuances statistically significant? What is the basis for your answer?

5. Do judges reportedly assign "more difficult" *or* "less difficult" cases to CASAs?

6. Does the researcher regard this study's findings as "sample specific"?

Questions for Discussion

7. The researcher points out that it was not possible to assign children to the two conditions (CASA and Comparison) at random. In your opinion, does this seriously affect the validity of the evaluation of this program?

8. The researcher suggests that in future studies, it would be beneficial to examine "exactly what CASA volunteers do on behalf of children that may influence permanency outcomes." Do you agree? (See lines 404–407.)

9. Has this research convinced you that the assignment of CASAs is valuable? Has it convinced you to become a strong advocate for the continuation of CASAs? Why? Why not? If you are not sure, what additional types of information would you need to help you decide?

10. Are you convinced that social service programs such as CASA should be formally evaluated? Would the money for evaluation be better-spent providing services to clients? Explain.

Quality Ratings

Directions: Indicate your level of agreement with each of the following statements by circling a number from 5 for strongly agree (SA) to 1 for strongly disagree (SD). If you believe an item is not applicable to this research article, leave it blank. Be prepared to explain your ratings.

A. The introduction establishes the importance of the study.

SA   5   4   3   2   1   SD

B. The literature review establishes the context for the study.

SA   5   4   3   2   1   SD

C. The research purpose, question, or hypothesis is clearly stated.

SA   5   4   3   2   1   SD

D. The method of sampling is sound.

SA   5   4   3   2   1   SD

E. Relevant demographics (for example, age, gender, and ethnicity) are described.

SA   5   4   3   2   1   SD

F. Measurement procedures are adequate.

SA   5   4   3   2   1   SD

G. All procedures have been described in sufficient detail to permit a replication of the study.

SA   5   4   3   2   1   SD

H. The participants have been adequately protected from potential harm.

SA   5   4   3   2   1   SD

I. The results are clearly described.

SA   5   4   3   2   1   SD

J. The discussion/conclusion is appropriate.

SA   5   4   3   2   1   SD

K. Despite any flaws, the report is worthy of publication.

SA   5   4   3   2   1   SD

Article 24

Research on Religion-Accommodative Counseling: Review and Meta-Analysis

Michael E. McCullough
National Institute for Healthcare Research

ABSTRACT. The present meta-analysis examined data from 5 studies ($N = 111$) that compared the efficacy of standard approaches to counseling for depression with religion-accommodative approaches. There was no evidence that the religion-accommodative approaches were more or less efficacious than the standard approaches. Findings suggest that the choice to use religious approaches with religious clients is probably more a matter of client preference than a matter of differential efficacy. However, additional research is needed to examine whether religion-accommodative approaches yield differential treatment satisfaction or differential improvements in spiritual well-being or facilitate relapse prevention. Given the importance of religion to many potential consumers of psychological services, counseling psychologists should devote greater attention to religion-accommodative counseling in future studies.

From *Journal of Counseling Psychology*, 46, 92–98. Copyright © 1999 by the American Psychological Association, Inc. Reprinted with permission.

The United States is a highly religious country; 92% of its population are affiliated with a religion (Kosmin & Lachman, 1993). According to a 1995 survey, 96% of Americans believe in God or a universal spirit, 42% indicate that they attend a religious worship service weekly or almost weekly, 67% indicate that they are members of a church or synagogue, and 60% indicate that religion is "important" or "very important" in their lives (Gallup, 1995).

In addition, many scholars acknowledge that certain forms of religious involvement are associated with better functioning on a variety of measures of mental health. Reviews of this research (e.g., Bergin, 1991; Bergin, Masters, & Richards, 1987; Larson et al., 1992; Pargament, 1997; Schumaker, 1992; Worthington, Kurusu, McCullough, & Sandage, 1996) suggested that several forms of religious involvement (including intrinsic religious motivation, attendance at religious worship, receiving coping support from one's religious faith or religious congregation, and positive religious attributions for life events) are positively associated with a variety of measures of mental health. For example, various measures of religious involvement appear to be related to lower degrees of depressive symptoms in adults (Bienenfeld, Koenig, Larson, & Sherrill, 1997; Ellison, 1995; Kendler, Gardner, & Prescott, 1997) and children (Miller, Warner, Wickramaratne, & Weissman, 1997) and less suicide (e.g., Comstock & Partridge, 1972; Kark et al., 1996; Wandrei, 1985).

Koenig, George, and Peterson (1998) reported that depressed people scoring high on measures of intrinsic religiousness were significantly more likely to experience a remission of depression during nearly a 1-year follow-up than were depressed people with lower intrinsic religiousness, even after controlling for 30 potential demographic, psychosocial, and medical confounds. Other studies have shown that religious involvement, as gauged through single-item measures of frequency of religious worship and private prayer as well as more complex measures of religious coping, is related to positive psychological outcomes after major life events (e.g., Pargament et al., 1990; Pargament et al., 1994; Pargament, Smith, & Brant, 1995). This is the case even though several patterns of religious belief and religious coping (e.g., the belief that one's misfortunes are a punishment from God) are associated with greater psychological distress (Pargament, 1997).

Religion in Counseling and Psychotherapy

Some scholars (e.g., Bergin, 1991; Payne, Bergin, & Loftus, 1992; Richards & Bergin, 1997; Shafranske, 1996; Worthington et al., 1996) posited that considering clients' religiousness while designing treatment plans might have an important effect on the efficacy of treatment. Surveys of psychiatrists (Neeleman & King, 1993), psychologists (Bergin & Jensen, 1988; Shafranske & Malony, 1990), and mental health counselors (Kelly, 1995) also indicate that many mental health professionals believe that religious and spiritual values can and should be thoughtfully addressed in the course of mental health treatment. Moreover, a variety of analogue and clinical studies (e.g., Houts & Graham, 1986; T. A. Kelly & Strupp, 1992; Lewis & Lewis, 1985; McCullough & Worthington, 1995; McCullough, Worthington, Maxey, & Rachal, 1997; Morrow, Worthington, & McCullough, 1993) indicate that clients' religious beliefs can influence both (a) the conclusions of clinicians' structured psychological assessments and (b) the process of psychotherapy (cf. Luborsky et al., 1980).

Evidence from Comparative Efficacy Studies

Given the existing research on religion and mental health, an important question for counseling psychologists is whether supporting clients' religious beliefs and values in a structured treatment package yield clinical benefits that are equal to or greater than standard methods of psychological practice. Several empirical studies have addressed this issue. Although the findings of studies that have examined such questions have been reviewed in narrative fashion elsewhere (e.g., W. B. Johnson, 1993; Matthews et al., 1998; Worthington et al., 1996), no researchers have used meta-analytic methods to estimate quantitatively the differential efficacy of such treatments. Meta-analytic reviews that compare religious approaches to counseling with standard approaches to counseling are one of three meta-analytic strategies that can be used to examine whether a given therapeutic approach has therapeutic efficacy (Wampold, 1997).

In the present article, I review the existing research on such religious approaches to counseling using quantitative methods of research synthesis (e.g., Cooper & Hedges, 1994; Hunter & Schmidt, 1990) to estimate the differential efficacy of religious approaches in comparison to standard forms of counseling for depressed religious clients.

Method

Literature Search

The PsycLIT, PsycINFO, Medline, ERIC, and Dissertation Abstracts electronic databases were searched through August 1998 for published and unpublished studies that examined the differential efficacy of a religion-accommodative approach to counseling in comparison to a standard approach to counseling. The reference sections of relevant articles were searched for other studies that would be relevant to this review. This search process continued until no new studies were revealed. In addition, several experts in the field of religion and mental health were contacted to identify unpublished studies.

Studies had to meet four criteria to be included in the meta-analytic sample: They had to (a) compare a religion-accommodative approach to counseling to a standard approach to counseling; (b) randomly assign patients to treatments; (c) involve patients who were suffering from a specific set of psychological symptoms (e.g., anxiety or depression); and (d) offer equal amounts of treatment to clients in the religion-accommodative and standard treatments. Five published studies and one unpublished dissertation (W. B. Johnson, 1991), which was later reported in W. B. Johnson, DeVries, Ridley, Pettorini, and Peterson (1994), met these inclusion criteria. Several studies that investigated religious approaches to psychological treatment (e.g., Azhar & Varma, 1995a, 1995b; Azhar, Varma, & Dharap, 1994; Carlson, Bacaseta, & Simanton, 1988; Richards, Owen, & Stein, 1993; Rye & Par-

gament, 1997; Toh & Tan, 1997) were obtained, but these studies failed to meet all four inclusion criteria. Thus, they were omitted from the meta-analytic sample. A single rater determined which studies met inclusion criteria. This rater's decisions were made without reference to the results or discussion sections of the articles.

The resulting meta-analytic sample included five studies representing data from 111 counseling clients. Descriptions of study populations, measures used, and effect size estimates (with 95% confidence intervals) are given in Table 1.

The Studies

Researchers interested in accommodative forms of religious counseling have taken standard cognitive–behavioral protocols or specific techniques, such as cognitive restructuring (Beck, Rush, Shaw, & Emery, 1979), cognitive coping skills (Meichenbaum, 1985), and appeals to rational thinking (e.g., Ellis & Grieger, 1977), and have developed religion-friendly rationales for and versions of such protocols or techniques (W. B. Johnson & Ridley, 1992b). These adapted protocols or techniques are thought to be theoretically equivalent to standard cognitive–behavioral techniques (Propst, 1996), but more amenable to the religious world view and religious language that religious clients use to understand their lives and their problems. The five studies are described in greater detail next.

Propst (1980). Propst (1980) examined the differential efficacy of a manualized, religion-accommodative approach to cognitive restructuring and imagery modification. Volunteers who scored in the mild or moderate range of depression on the Beck Depression Inventory (BDI; Beck, Ward, Mendelson, Mock, & Erbaugh, 1961) and in at least the moderate range on the King and Hunt (1972) religion scales were randomly assigned to one of two treatments. The standard treatment was an integration of Beck's (1976) cognitive therapy for depression and Meichenbaum's (1973) cognitive–behavior modification. During eight 1-hr sessions conducted over 4 weeks, clients were trained to observe their cognitions and imagery during depressed moods. After clients were convinced of the links between their moods, thoughts, and images, they practiced cognitive restructuring skills for modifying their thoughts and images using imagery and positive self-statements (e.g., "I can see myself in the future coping with that particular situation"). Ten of eleven clients assigned to this condition completed it.

In the religion-accommodative treatment, clients completed the same therapeutic protocol as that used in the standard treatment. The only difference is that participants were trained to replace their negative cognitions and imagery with religious images (e.g., "I can visualize Christ going with me into that difficult situation in the future as I try to cope"). Seven of 9 clients assigned to this condition completed the treatment.

Table 1
Sample Sizes, Effect Sizes, and 95% Confidence Intervals (CI) for the Studies Included in the Meta-Analysis

Study	Religion-accommodative treatment n	Standard treatment n	Effect size (d_+)	95% CI
Propst (1980)	7	10	+0.41	−0.56/+1.39
Pecheur & Edwards (1984)	7	7	+0.53	−0.53/+1.60
Propst et al. (1992)	19	19	+0.51	−0.14/+1.15
W. B. Johnson & Ridley (1992a)	5	5	+0.29	−0.96/+1.53
W. B. Johnson et al. (1994)	16	16	−0.51	−1.22/+0.19

Pecheur and Edwards (1984). Pecheur and Edwards (1984) assessed the differential efficacy of Beck et al.'s (1979) cognitive therapy for depression and a religion-accommodative version of the same therapy. Clients were students from a Christian college who met research diagnostic criteria for major depressive disorder. They also scored in the depressed range on the BDI, the Hamilton Rating Scale for Depression (HRSD; Hamilton, 1960), and a single-item visual analogue scale. In the standard treatment, clients completed eight 50-min sessions of cognitive behavior modification. All 7 clients who were assigned to this treatment completed it.

In the religion-accommodative treatment, clients completed the standard cognitive therapy tasks specified in Beck et al. (1979); however, challenges to negative cognitions were placed in a religious context. For example, rather than replacing negative views of self with statements such as "Our self-acceptance and self-worth are not lost or lessened when we fail," the religion-accommodative approach trained clients to use self-statements such as, "God loves, accepts, and values us just as we are." This treatment was also administered according to a manual, which appears in Pecheur (1980).

Propst, Ostrom, Watkins, Dean, and Mashburn (1992). Propst et al. (1992) compared the efficacy of Beck et al.'s (1979) cognitive therapy for depression with a manualized, religion-accommodative version of the same therapy (see Propst, 1988). Clients were recruited from the community and scored at least 14 on the 28-item version of the HRSD. They also scored at least in the moderate range on standard measures of religious commitment (e.g., Allport & Ross, 1967; King & Hunt, 1972). Clients in the standard treatment completed 18 sessions of individual cognitive therapy for depression. All 19 clients enrolled in this condition completed it.

In the religion-accommodative treatment, clients completed 18 sessions of cognitive therapy that challenged negative cognitions and images by replacing them with positive thoughts and imagery of a religious nature, as in Propst (1980). All 19 clients enrolled in this condition completed it.

W. B. Johnson & Ridley (1992a). Johnson and Ridley (1992) compared the efficacy of rational-emotive therapy (RET), using Walen, DiGiuseppe, and Wessler's (1980) treatment manual, with a manualized, religion-accommodative version of the same therapy. Clients were theology students and local church members who scored in at least the mildly depressed range on the BDI. They also scored in the "intrinsic" range on a standard measure of religious motivation (Allport & Ross, 1967), suggesting that their religious faith was highly internalized. In the standard RET condition, clients completed six 50-min sessions in 3 weeks, including homework sessions and in-session rehearsal of rational-emotive techniques. All 5 clients assigned to this condition completed it.

In the religion-accommodative treatment, three explicitly Christian treatment components were added. First, clients were directed to dispute irrational beliefs using explicitly Christian beliefs, as in Propst (1980). Second, clients were encouraged to use Christian prayer, thoughts, and imagery in their homework assignments. Third, counselors used brief prayers at the end of each session. All 5 clients assigned to this condition completed it.

W. B. Johnson et al. (1994). W. B. Johnson et al. (1994) compared the efficacy of standard RET and a religion-accommodative form of RET, as in W. B. Johnson and Ridley (1992a). Selection criteria were almost identical to those reported in W. B. Johnson and Ridley (1992a). The standard RET condition was an eight-session protocol delivered over 8 weeks, and was based on two popular RET treatment manuals (Ellis & Dryden, 1987; Walen et al., 1980). All 16 clients assigned to this condition completed it.

The religion-accommodative treatment was based on two treatment manuals discussing Christian versions of RET (Backus, 1985; Thurman, 1989). Although the basic structure of RET was kept intact, clients were encouraged to dispute irrational beliefs based on scriptural beliefs and biblical examples. Homework assignments also used biblical examples and beliefs. All 16 clients assigned to this condition completed it.

Effect Size Estimates

Effect sizes and homogeneity statistics were calculated from means and standard deviations using the DSTAT statistical software, Version 1.10 (B. T. Johnson, 1989), using the formulas prescribed by Hedges and Olkin (1985). Effect sizes were based on the dif-

270 ference between the mean of clients in the standard counseling condition and the mean of clients in the religion-accommodative conditions. This difference was divided by the pooled standard deviation of clients in both conditions. All effect size estimates, expressed
275 as d_+ values, are corrected for the bias that is present in uncorrected g values, as recommended by Hedges and Olkin (1985). Effect sizes can be interpreted as the increased amount of symptom reduction afforded to participants in the religion-accommodative condition,
280 expressed in standard deviation units. In calculating aggregate effect size estimates, individual effect sizes were weighted by the inverse of their sampling error variance, so that studies with larger samples were given greater weight in the calculation of d_+ (Hedges & Ol-
285 kin, 1985).

The Q statistic was also used to estimate the degree of variability among the effect sizes. The Q statistic is basically a goodness-of-fit statistic with a roughly χ^2 distribution that enables a test of the hypothesis that all
290 observed effect sizes were drawn from the same population. Significant Q values imply a heterogeneous set of effect sizes (Hunter & Schmidt, 1990).

Handling Multiple Dependent Measures

All five studies used the BDI as a dependent measure of depression. Although two of the studies also
295 used the HRSD or a single-item visual analogue measure of depression, or both (Pecheur & Edwards, 1984; Propst et al., 1992), effect size estimates were based exclusively on the BDI for three reasons. First, the BDI has been shown to produce conservative effect size
300 estimates in comparison to rating scales that are completed by clinicians, such as the HRSD (Lambert, Hatch, Kingston, & Edwards, 1986). Second, single-item visual analogue measures of depression (e.g., Aitken, 1969) appear to contain remarkably little true
305 score variance (Faravelli, Albanesi, & Poli, 1986). Third, the aggregation of data across multiple dependent measures requires knowing their intercorrelations, which were not available for all five studies. Thus, the individual and mean effect size estimates reported here
310 can be considered to be somewhat conservative.

Handling Data from Multiple Follow-Up Periods

All five studies collected follow-up data within 1 week of the termination of the trial. Although three of the studies (W. B. Johnson et al., 1994; Pecheur & Edwards, 1984; Propst et al., 1992) also reported follow-
315 up data collected between 1 and 3 months after the termination of the trial, and one study (Propst et al., 1992) reported an effect size for a 24-month follow-up, we based our effect size estimates only on the data from the 1-week follow-up.

Other Problems with Coding Effect Sizes

320 Some studies reported data on additional experimental conditions, including self-monitoring and therapist contact conditions (Propst, 1980), waiting list

control conditions (Pecheur & Edwards, 1984; Propst et al., 1992), and pastoral counseling conditions (Propst
325 et al., 1992). Because none of these conditions were relevant to the central goal of this study, these data were neither coded nor included in the present meta-analytic study.

Two other problems arose in coding effect sizes.
330 First, although Propst (1980) reported posttreatment means on the BDI for both conditions, standard deviations were not reported. On the basis of the assumption that the other four studies in the present meta-analysis would yield similar pooled standard deviations for the
335 BDI, a mean standard deviation for posttest scores on the BDI from these studies (5.81) was used as an imputed standard deviation for Propst (1980). This imputed standard deviation produced a nonsignificant test statistic for the comparison of the religious and stan-
340 dard counseling conditions, as Propst (1980) reported, giving us confidence that our imputed standard deviation was not wholly inaccurate.

Second, Propst et al.'s (1992) results reported treatment effects separately for religious and nonrelig-
345 ious therapists, which was an independent factor in their experimental design. To collapse treatment effects across levels of the therapist religiousness factor, means and standard deviations obtained for religious and nonreligious therapists within each of the two re-
350 ligious counseling conditions were pooled before calculating an effect size for the treatments.

Corrections of Findings for Unreliability in Dependent Measures

Scholars in meta-analysis advise that effect size estimates be corrected for biases (Hunter & Schmidt, 1990, 1994). One of the easiest biases to correct is at-
355 tenuation resulting from unreliability in the dependent variable. This bias can be corrected by dividing observed effect sizes and standard errors by the square root of the internal consistency of the dependent variable. Because meta-analytic estimates of the BDI's
360 internal consistency were readily available (Beck, Steer, & Garbin, 1988, estimated its internal consistency at $\alpha = .86$), the observed mean effect size and its confidence interval (CI) were divided by the square root of .86, or .927. Corrections for attenuation result-
365 ing from unreliability of the dependent variable produce increased effect size estimates but also a proportionate increase in confidence intervals; thus, a nonsignificant effect size will not become significant as a result of this correction (Hunter & Schmidt, 1994).

Estimating Clinical Significance

370 We were also interested in whether religion-accommodative and standard approaches to counseling yielded clinically significant differences in efficacy (Jacobson & Revenstorf, 1988; Jacobson & Truax, 1991). Thus, we calculated meta-analytic summaries of
375 clinical significance for two studies that reported clinical significance data (using BDI > 9 as a cutoff for

"mild clinical depression"; Kendall, Hollon, Beck, Hammen, & Ingram, 1987).

Results

Observed Mean Effect Size and Attenuation-Corrected Effect Size

The mean effect size for the difference between religious and standard counseling during the 1-week follow-up period (number of effect sizes = 5, $N = 111$) was $d_+ = +0.18$ (95% CI: $-.20/+0.56$), indicating that clients in religion-accommodative counseling had slightly lower BDI scores at 1-week follow-up than did clients in standard counseling conditions. This effect size was not reliably different from zero ($p = .34$). The five effect sizes that contributed to this mean effect size were homogeneous, $Q(4) = 5.38$, $p > .10$. The mean effect size after correcting the effects for attenuation resulting from unreliability was $d_+ = +0.20$ (95% CI: $-0.19/+0.61$).

Differences in Clinical Significance

Two studies (W. B. Johnson & C. R. Ridley, 1992a; Propst, 1980) reported the percentage of participants in the religious and standard psychotherapy conditions who manifested evidence of at least mild clinical depression (BDI scores > 9) during the 1-week follow-up period. Aggregation of these data indicated that, among the 20 religion-accommodative counseling clients in the two studies, 4 (20%) were still at least mildly depressed at the end of treatment. Among the 26 standard counseling clients in the two studies, 9 (34.6%) were at least mildly depressed when treatment ended. This difference in clinical significance was not statistically significant, $\chi^2(1, N = 46) = 1.19, p > .10$.

Discussion

The goal of the present study was to review the existing empirical evidence regarding the comparative efficacy of religion-accommodative approaches to counseling depressed religious clients. These data suggest that, in the immediate period after completion of counseling, religious approaches to counseling do not have any significant superiority to standard approaches to counseling. Given that the differences in efficacy of most bonafide treatments are surprisingly small (e.g., Lambert & Bergin, 1994; Wampold, 1997), the existing literature on psychotherapy outcomes would have portended the present meta-analytic results. These findings corroborate some narrative reviews that claim equal efficacy for religion-accommodative and standard approaches to counseling (e.g., Worthington et al., 1996), and help to resolve the inconsistencies that others have observed among these studies (e.g., W. B. Johnson, 1993; Matthews et al., 1998).

Although it is true that the religious approaches to counseling were no more effective than the standard approaches to counseling, it is equally true that they were no less effective than the standard approaches to counseling. Thus, the decision to use religion-accommodative approaches might be most wisely based not on the results of comparative clinical trials, which tend to find no differences among well-manualized treatments, but rather on the basis of patient choice (see Wampold, 1997). Not every religious client would prefer or respond favorably to a religion-accommodative approach to counseling. Indeed, the available evidence suggests that all but the most highly religious clients would prefer an approach to counseling that deals with religious issues only peripherally rather than focally (Wyatt & Johnson, 1990; see Worthington et al., 1996, for review).

On the other hand, many religious clients—especially very conservative Christian clients—would indeed be attracted to a counseling approach (or counselor) precisely because the counseling approach (or the counselor) maintained that the clients' system of religious values were at the core of effective psychological change (Worthington et al., 1996). The research reviewed herein indicates that no empirical basis exists for withholding such religion-accommodative treatment from depressed religious clients who desire such a treatment approach.

The Last Word?

There is inherent danger in publishing meta-analytic results. Because of their ability to provide precise-looking point estimates and short CIs (especially when the observed effect size estimates are relatively heterogeneous), meta-analytic summaries can be perceived to be the last word in evaluating research questions. It would be unfortunate if the present results were interpreted as the last word in evaluating the efficacy of religious approaches to counseling, however, because interesting and important questions remain.

For example, although religion-accommodative approaches to counseling do not appear to be differentially efficacious in reducing symptoms (at least depressive symptoms), they might produce differential treatment satisfaction among some religious clients. Also, comparative studies of religion-accommodative therapy are needed with longer follow-up periods. It is possible that religion-accommodative approaches might prove to be superior to standard treatments in longer term follow-up periods, particularly in helping clients from relapsing, for example, back into depressive episodes. The differential effects of religion-accommodative and standard approaches to treatment also need to be investigated for a wider variety of disorders, including anxiety, anger, alcohol and drug problems, and marital and family problems. As well, although religion-accommodative and standard approaches to counseling do not appear to influence clients' religiousness or religious values differentially (Worthington et al., 1996), it is possible that religion-accommodative counseling yields differential improvements in religious clients' spiritual well-being.

Finally, on a technical note, it should be noted that

the studies in this body of literature currently have been seriously underpowered (i.e., in all cases fewer than 20 clients per treatment). This literature would benefit enormously from as few as three or four very high-quality, large-sample (i.e., 30 or more clients per condition) studies that investigated these questions in greater detail. W. B. Johnson (1993) provided other helpful methodological recommendations to which research on religion-accommodative counseling should adhere.

Limitations

The stability of meta-analytic findings comes from the number of studies included in the meta-analysis as well as the number of participants in the constituent studies. Thus, the findings from meta-analyses with small numbers of studies, such as the present study, are more easily overturned than meta-analyses that include larger numbers of studies. Although meta-analytic methods can be used to synthesize the results of as few as two studies (for examples of small-*k* meta-analyses, see Allison & Faith, 1996; Benschop et al., 1998; Kirsch, Montgomery, & Sapirstein, 1995; Uchino, Cacioppo, & Kiecolt-Glaser, 1996), our findings would obviously be considered more trustworthy if more studies had been available.

A second limitation of the present findings relates to the nature of the meta-analytic sample. The five studies reviewed herein all investigated religion-accommodative counseling with depressed Christian clients. We can only speculate whether the present pattern of results would generalize to different religious populations or to people with different sets of presenting problems. Obviously, research is needed to fill in such gaps.

Conclusion

A variety of empirical data now suggest that certain forms of religious involvement can help prevent the onset of psychological difficulties and enhance effective coping with stressors. In addition, the majority of mental health professionals and the general public believe that patients' religious beliefs should be adequately assessed and taken into consideration in mental health treatment. Moreover, data indicate that patients' religious commitments can play a substantial role in counseling processes (Worthington et al., 1996). Data from the present study also indicate that religious approaches to counseling can be as effective as standard approaches to counseling depressed persons. Thus, for some clients, particularly very religious Christian clients, religion-accommodative approaches to counseling could be, quite literally, the treatment of choice. It is hoped that the present study will encourage counseling psychologists to examine whether religion-accommodative approaches yield similar or even superior benefits on other important metrics of therapeutic change and with other common difficulties in living.

References

Aitken, R. C. B. (1969). Measurement of feeling using visual analogue scales. *Proceedings of the Royal Society of Medicine, 62*, 989–993.

Allison, D. B. & Faith, M. S. (1996). Hypnosis as an adjunct to cognitive-behavioral psychotherapy for obesity: A meta-analytic reappraisal. *Journal of Consulting and Clinical Psychology, 64*, 513–516.

Allport, G. W. & Ross, J. M. (1967). Personal religious orientation and prejudice. *Journal of Personality and Social Psychology, 5*, 432–443.

Azhar, M. Z. & Varma, S. L. (1995a). Religious psychotherapy in depressive patients. *Psychotherapy and Psychosomatics, 63*, 165–168.

Azhar, M. Z. & Varma, S. L. (1995b). Religious psychotherapy as management of bereavement. *Acta Psychiatrica Scandinavica, 91*, 233–235.

Azhar, M. Z., Varma, S. L. & Dharap, A. S. (1994). Religious psychotherapy in anxiety disorder patients. *Acta Psychiatrica Scandinavica, 90*, 1–3.

Backus, W. (1985). *Telling the truth to troubled people.* Minneapolis, MN: Bethany House.

Beck, A. T. (1976). *Cognitive therapy and the emotional disorders.* New York: International University Press.

Beck, A. T., Rush, A. J., Shaw, B. F. & Emery, G. (1979). *Cognitive therapy of depression.* New York: Guilford Press.

Beck, A. T., Steer, R. A. & Garbin, M. G. (1988). Psychometric properties of the Beck Depression Inventory: Twenty-five years of evaluation. *Clinical Psychology Review, 8*, 77–100.

Beck, A. T., Ward, C. H., Mendelson, M., Mock, J. E. & Erbaugh, J. K. (1961). An inventory for measuring depression. *Archives of General Psychiatry, 4*, 561–571.

Benschop, R. J., Geenen, R., Mills, P. J., Naliboff, B. D., Kiecolt-Glaser, J. K., Herbert, T. B., van der Pompe, G., Miller, G., Matthews, K. A., Godaert, G. L. R., Gilmore, S. L., Glaser, R., Heijnen, C. J., Dopp, J. M., Bijlsma, J. W. J., Solomon, G. F. & Cacioppo, J. T. (1998). Cardiovascular and immune responses to acute psychological stress in young and old women: A meta-analysis. *Psychosomatic Medicine, 60*, 290–296.

Bergin, A. E. (1991). Values and religious issues in psychotherapy and mental health. *American Psychologist, 46*, 394–403.

Bergin, A. E. & Jensen, J. P. (1988). Mental health values of professional therapists: A national interdisciplinary survey. *Professional Psychology: Research and Practice, 19*, 290–297.

Bergin, A. E., Masters, K. S. & Richards, P. S. (1987). Religiousness and mental health reconsidered: A study of an intrinsically religious sample. *Journal of Counseling Psychology, 34*, 197–204.

Bienenfeld, D., Koenig, H. G., Larson, D. B. & Sherrill, K. A. (1997). Psychosocial predictors of mental health in a population of elderly women. *American Journal of Geriatric Psychiatry, 5*, 43–53.

Carlson, C. R., Bacaseta, P. E. & Simanton, D. A. (1988). A controlled evaluation of devotional meditation and progressive relaxation. *Journal of Psychology and Theology, 16*, 362–368.

Comstock, G. W. & Partridge, K. B. (1972). Church attendance and health. *Journal of Chronic Disease, 25*, 665–672.

Cooper, H. & Hedges, L. V. (1994). *Handbook of research synthesis.* New York: Russell Sage Foundation.

DeVries, R., Ridley, C. R., Pettorini, D. & Peterson, D. R. (1994). The comparative efficacy of Christian and secular rational-emotive therapy with Christian clients. *Journal of Psychology and Theology, 22*, 130–140.

Edwards, K. J. (1984). A comparison of secular and religious versions of cognitive therapy with depressed Christian college students. *Journal of Psychology and Theology, 12*, 45–54.

Ellis, A. & Dryden, W. (1987). *The practice of rational-emotive therapy.* New York: Springer.

Ellis, A. & Grieger, R. (1977). *Handbook of rational-emotive therapy.* New York: Springer.

Ellison, C. G. (1995). Race, religious involvement, and depressive symptomatology in a southeastern U.S. community. *Social Science and Medicine, 40*, 1561–1572.

Faravelli, C., Albanesi, G. & Poli, E. (1986). Assessment of depression: A comparison of rating scales. *Journal of Affective Disorders, 11*, 245–253.

Gallup, G. (1995). *The Gallup poll: Public opinion 1995.* Wilmington, DE: Scholarly Resources.

Hamilton, M. (1960). A rating scale for depression. *Journal of Neurology, Neurosurgery, and Psychiatry, 23*, 56–62.

Hedges, L. V. & Olkin, I. (1985). *Statistical methods for meta-analysis.* Orlando, FL: Academic Press.

Houts, A. C. & Graham, K. (1986). Can religion make you crazy? Impact of client and therapist religious values on clinical judgments. *Journal of Consulting and Clinical Psychology, 54*, 267–271.

Hunter, J. E. & Schmidt, F. L. (1990). *Methods of meta-analysis: Correcting error and bias in research findings.* Newbury Park, CA: Sage.

Hunter, J. E. & Schmidt, F. L. (1994). Correcting for sources of artificial variation across studies. In H. Cooper & L. V. Hedges (Eds.), *Handbook of research synthesis* (pp. 323–336). New York: Russell Sage Foundation.

Jacobson, N. S. & Revenstorf, D. (1988). Statistics for assessing the clinical significance of psychotherapy techniques: Issues, problems, and new developments. *Behavioral Assessment, 10*, 133–145.

Jacobson, N. S. & Truax, P. (1991). Clinical significance: A statistical approach to defining meaningful change in psychotherapy research. *Journal of Consulting and Clinical Psychology, 59,* 12–19.

Johnson, B. T. (1989). *DSTAT: Software for the meta-analytic review of research literatures.* Hillsdale, NJ: Erlbaum.

Johnson, W. B. (1991). *The comparative efficacy of religious and nonreligious rational-emotive therapy with religious clients.* Unpublished doctoral dissertation, Fuller Graduate School of Psychology, Pasadena, CA.

Johnson, W. B. (1993). Outcome research and religious psychotherapies: Where are we and where are we going? *Journal of Psychology and Theology, 21,* 297–308.

Johnson, W. B. & Ridley, C. R. (1992b). Sources of gain in Christian counseling and psychotherapy. *The Counseling Psychologist, 20,* 159–175.

Kark, J. D., Shemi, G., Friedlander, Y., Martin, O., Manor, O. & Blondheim, S. H. (1996). Does religious observance promote health? Mortality in secular vs. religious kibbutzim in Israel. *American Journal of Public Health, 86,* 341–346.

Kelly, E. W. (1995). Counselor values: A national survey. *Journal of Counseling and Development, 73,* 648–653.

Kelly, T. A. & Strupp, H. H. (1992). Patient and therapist values in psychotherapy: Perceived changes, assimilation, similarity, and outcome. *Journal of Consulting and Clinical Psychology, 60,* 34–40.

Kendall, P. C., Hollon, S. D., Beck, A. T., Hammen, C. L. & Ingram, R. E. (1987). Issues and recommendations regarding use of the Beck Depression Inventory. *Cognitive Therapy and Research, 11,* 289–299.

Kendler, K. S., Gardner, C. O. & Prescott, C. A. (1997). Religion, psychopathology, and substance use and abuse: A multimeasure, genetic-epidemiologic study. *American Journal of Psychiatry, 154,* 322–329.

King, M. A. & Hunt, R. A. (1972). Measuring the religious variable: A replication. *Journal for the Scientific Study of Religion, 11,* 240–251.

Kirsch, I., Montgomery, G. & Sapirstein, G. (1995). Hypnosis as an adjunct to cognitive-behavioral psychotherapy: A meta-analysis. *Journal of Consulting and Clinical Psychology, 63,* 214–220.

Koenig, H. G., George, L. K. & Peterson, B. L. (1998). Religiosity and remission of depression in medically ill older patients. *American Journal of Psychiatry, 155,* 536–542.

Kosmin, B. A. & Lachman, S. P. (1993). *One nation under God: Religion in contemporary American society.* New York: Harmony.

Lambert, M. J. & Bergin, A. E. (1994). The effectiveness of psychotherapy. In A. E. Bergin & S. L. Garfield (Eds.), *Handbook of psychotherapy and behavior change* (4th ed., pp. 143–189). New York: Wiley.

Lambert, M. J., Hatch, D. R., Kingston, M. D. & Edwards, B. C. (1986). Zung, Beck, and Hamilton rating scales as measures of treatment outcome: A meta-analytic comparison. *Journal of Consulting and Clinical Psychology, 54,* 54–59.

Larson, D. B., Sherrill, K. A., Lyons, J. S., Craigie, F. C., Thielman, S. B., Greenwold, M. A. & Larson, S. S. (1992). Associations between dimensions of religious commitment and mental health reported in the *American Journal of Psychiatry* and *Archives of General Psychiatry:* 1978–1989. *American Journal of Psychiatry, 149,* 557–559.

Lewis, K. N. & Lewis, D. A. (1985). Impact of religious affiliation on therapists' judgments of patients. *Journal of Consulting and Clinical Psychology, 53,* 926–932.

Luborsky, L., Mintz, J., Auerbach, A., Cristoph, P., Bachrach, H., Todd, T., Johnson, M., Cohen, M. & O'Brien, C. P. (1980). Predicting the outcome of psychotherapy: Findings of the Penn Psychotherapy Project. *Archives of General Psychiatry, 37,* 471–481.

Matthews, D. A., McCullough, M. E., Larson, D. B., Koenig, H. G., Swyers, J. P. & Milano, M. G. (1998). Religious commitment and health: A review of the research and implications for family medicine. *Archives of Family Medicine, 7,* 118–124.

McCullough, M. E. & Worthington, E. L. (1995). College students' perceptions of a psychotherapist's treatment of a religious issue: Partial replication and extension. *Journal of Counseling and Development, 73,* 626–634.

McCullough, M. E., Worthington, E. L., Maxey, J. & Rachal, K. C. (1997). Gender in the context of supportive and challenging religious counseling interventions. *Journal of Counseling Psychology, 44,* 80–88.

Meichenbaum, D. (1973). *Therapist manual for cognitive behavior modification.* Unpublished manuscript, University of Waterloo, Ontario, Canada.

Meichenbaum, D. (1985). *Stress inoculation training.* New York: Pergamon Press.

Miller, L., Warner, V., Wickramaratne, P. & Weissman, M. (1997). Religiosity and depression: Ten-year follow-up of depressed mothers and offspring. *Journal of the American Academy of Child and Adolescent Psychiatry, 36,* 1416–1425.

Morrow, D., Worthington, E. L. & McCullough, M. E. (1993). Observers' perceptions of a psychotherapist's treatment of a religious issue. *Journal of Counseling and Development, 71,* 452–456.

Neeleman, J. & King, M. B. (1993). Psychiatrists' religious attitudes in relation to their clinical practice: A survey of 231 psychiatrists. *Acta Psychiatrica Scandinavica, 88,* 420–424.

Ostrom, R., Watkins, P., Dean, T. & Mashburn, D. (1992). Comparative efficacy of religious and nonreligious cognitive-behavioral therapy for the treatment of clinical depression in religious individuals. *Journal of Consulting and Clinical Psychology, 60,* 94–103.

Pargament, K. I. (1997). *The psychology of religion and coping.* New York: Guilford Press.

Pargament, K. I., Ensing, D. S., Falgout, K., Olsen, H., Reilly, B., Van Haitsma, K. & Warren, R. (1990). God help me: I. Religious coping efforts as predictors of the outcomes to significant life events. *American Journal of Community Psychology, 18,* 793–824.

Pargament, K. I., Ishler, K., Dubow, E., Stanik, P., Rouiller, R., Crowe, P., Cullman, E., Albert, M. & Royster, B. J. (1994). Methods of religious coping with the Gulf War: Cross-sectional and longitudinal analyses. *Journal for the Scientific Study of Religion, 33,* 347–361.

Pargament, K. I., Smith, B. & Brant, C. (1995, November). *Religious and nonreligious coping methods with the 1993 Midwest flood.* Paper presented at the meeting of the Society for the Scientific Study of Religion, St. Louis, MO.

Payne, I. R., Bergin, A. E. & Loftus, P. E. (1992). A review of attempts to integrate spiritual and standard psychotherapy techniques. *Journal of Psychotherapy Integration, 2,* 171–192.

Pecheur, D. (1980). *A comparison of the efficacy of secular and religious cognitive behavior modification in the treatment of depressed Christian college students.* Unpublished doctoral dissertation, Rosemead School of Psychology, La Mirada, CA.

Propst, R. L. (1980). The comparative efficacy of religious and nonreligious imagery for the treatment of mild depression in religious individuals. *Cognitive Therapy and Research, 4,* 167–178.

Propst, R. L. (1988). *Psychotherapy in a religious framework.* New York: Human Sciences Press.

Propst, R. L. (1996). Cognitive-behavioral therapy and the religious person. In E. P. Shafranske (Ed.), *Religion in the clinical practice of psychology* (pp. 391–408). Washington, DC: American Psychological Association.

Richards, P. S. & Bergin, A. E. (1997). *A spiritual strategy for counseling and psychotherapy.* Washington, DC: American Psychological Association.

Richards, P. S., Owen, L. & Stein, S. (1993). A religiously oriented group counseling intervention for self-defeating perfectionism: A pilot study. *Counseling and Values, 37,* 96–104.

Ridley, C. R. (1992a). Brief Christian and non-Christian rational-emotive therapy with depressed Christian clients: An exploratory study. *Counseling and Values, 36,* 220–229.

Rye, M. S. & Pargament, K. I. (1997, August). *Forgiveness and romantic relationships in college.* Paper presented at the 105th Annual Convention of the American Psychological Association, Chicago.

Schumaker, J. F. (1992). *Religion and mental health.* New York: Oxford University Press.

Shafranske, E. P. (1996). *Religion and the clinical practice of psychology.* Washington, DC: American Psychological Association.

Shafranske, E. P. & Malony, H. N. (1990). Clinical psychologists' religious and spiritual orientations and their practice of psychotherapy. *Psychotherapy, 27,* 72–78.

Thurman, C. (1989). *The lies we believe.* Nashville, TN: Thomas Nelson.

Toh, Y. & Tan, S. Y. (1997). The effectiveness of church-based lay counselors: A controlled outcome study. *Journal of Psychology and Christianity, 16,* 260–267.

Uchino, B. N., Cacioppo, J. T. & Kiecolt-Glaser, J. K. (1996). The relationship between social support and physiological processes: A review with emphasis on underlying mechanisms and implications for health. *Psychological Bulletin, 119,* 488–531.

Walen, S. R., DiGiuseppe, R. & Wessler, R. (1980). *A practitioner's guide to rational emotive therapy.* New York: Oxford University Press.

Wampold, B. E. (1997). Methodological problems in identifying efficacious psychotherapies. *Psychotherapy Research, 7,* 21–43.

Wandrei, K. E. (1985). Identifying potential suicides among high-risk women. *Social Work, 30,* 511–517.

Worthington, E. L., Kurusu, T. A., McCullough, M. E. & Sandage, S. J. (1996). Empirical research on religion and psychotherapeutic processes and outcomes: A ten-year review and research prospectus. *Psychological Bulletin, 119,* 448–487.

Wyatt, S. C. & Johnson, R. W. (1990). The influence of counselors' religious values on clients' perceptions of the counselor. *Journal of Psychology and Theology, 18,* 158–165.

Address correspondence to: Michael E. McCullough, National Institute for Healthcare Research, 6110 Executive Boulevard, Suite 908, Rockville, MD 20852. Electronic mail may be sent to Mike@nihr.org

Exercise for Article 24

Factual Questions

1. In the previous study by Koenig, George, and Peterson, how many potentially confounding variables were controlled for?

2. Which electronic databases were searched to locate relevant studies?

3. How many dissertations met the criteria for being included in the sample for the meta-analysis?

4. To determine effect sizes, the difference between the two means was divided by what?

5. Which of the five studies had the largest sample size?

6. What did the mean effect size (i.e., the mean for all five studies) indicate?

7. Was the mean effect size statistically significant (i.e., was it reliably different from zero)?

Questions for Discussion

8. Only studies in which patients were assigned to treatments at random were included in the meta-analytic sample. Was this a good idea? Explain. (See lines 106–110.)

9. What is your opinion on the researcher's decision to use data on only a one-week follow-up period? (See lines 311–319.)

10. The researcher notes that the five studies analyzed here were "seriously underpowered." Do you regard this as a serious limitation? Explain. (See lines 483–490.)

11. In your opinion, how important are the limitations the researcher discusses in lines 494–516?

12. Are the 95% confidence intervals (CIs) in Table 1 helpful? Explain.

13. In light of this review, what recommendations would you make to a future researcher who plans to conduct a single study (not a meta-analysis of other studies) on this topic?

Quality Ratings

Directions: Indicate your level of agreement with each of the following statements by circling a number from 5 for strongly agree (SA) to 1 for strongly disagree (SD). If you believe an item is not applicable to this research article, leave it blank. Be prepared to explain your ratings.

A. The introduction establishes the importance of the study.

SA 5 4 3 2 1 SD

B. The literature review establishes the context for the study.

SA 5 4 3 2 1 SD

C. The research purpose, question, or hypothesis is clearly stated.

SA 5 4 3 2 1 SD

D. The method of sampling is sound.

SA 5 4 3 2 1 SD

E. Relevant demographics (for example, age, gender, and ethnicity) are described.

SA 5 4 3 2 1 SD

F. Measurement procedures are adequate.

SA 5 4 3 2 1 SD

G. All procedures have been described in sufficient detail to permit a replication of the study.

SA 5 4 3 2 1 SD

H. The participants have been adequately protected from potential harm.

SA 5 4 3 2 1 SD

I. The results are clearly described.

SA 5 4 3 2 1 SD

J. The discussion/conclusion is appropriate.

SA 5 4 3 2 1 SD

K. Despite any flaws, the report is worthy of publication.

SA 5 4 3 2 1 SD

Article 25

In Search of Hopeful Glimpses: A Critique of Research Strategies in Current Boot Camp Evaluations

Sheldon X. Zhang
California State University, San Marcos

ABSTRACT. This article presents a comprehensive review of research strategies in recently published boot camp evaluations, points out areas where changes are needed, and suggests alternatives for future research efforts. In particular, it calls for wider use of self-report data and sample matching techniques to augment current measures of program effectiveness. It also emphasizes the inclusion of measures on offenders' community reintegration and the involvement of their social networks during and after treatment. More important, future studies should also examine how nonprogrammatic factors (i.e., staff commitment, staff/client interactions, and community setting) may affect the outcomes. An integrated evaluation paradigm is suggested.

From *Crime & Delinquency*, *44* (2), 314–334. Copyright © 1998 by Sage Publications, Inc. Reprinted with permission of Sage Publications, Inc. All rights reserved.

Overview and Purpose

The rapid growth of boot camps in recent years, together with other forms of intermediate sanctions, is largely the result of overcrowding in correctional agencies (Byrne, Lurigio, and Petersilia 1992). As early as
5 1983, criminal justice administrators identified prison and jail crowding as the most important issue facing them (Gettinger 1983). From 1970 to 1990, jail and prison populations increased by nearly four times their original populations (National Council on Crime and
10 Delinquency 1992). By 1995, there were 1.6 million offenders in jails and prisons, or 600 inmates per 100,000 residents (U.S. Bureau of Justice Statistics 1996). Many state prisons are under court order to reduce their inmate populations (Cronin 1994).
15 Since its appearance in Georgia and Oklahoma in 1983 (Parent 1989),[1] the idea of "shocking" criminal offenders into conformity through activities resembling those of military basic training has been embraced by an increasing number of both politicians and criminal
20 justice practitioners across the nation (Cronin 1994; MacKenzie, Brame, McDowall, and Souryal 1995; Morash and Rucker 1990; Hunter, Burton, Marquart, and Cuvelier 1992). Despite the disappointing findings

from most evaluations, the number of boot camps con-
25 tinues to grow (for detailed overviews and updates on the latest development in boot camps nationwide, see Cronin 1994; MacKenzie 1993; Bourque, Cronin, Pearson, Felker, Han, and Hill 1996).

Most boot camps appear to share similar sys-
30 tem-level goals, such as rehabilitating offenders, providing alternatives to long-term incarceration, and reducing prison/jail crowding. In a recent survey of boot camp administrators (MacKenzie and Souryal 1991), rehabilitation, recidivism reduction, and drug education
35 were ranked most highly as program goals, followed by reduction of crowding, development of work skills, and provision of a safe prison environment. The goals of deterrence, education (GED), and drug treatments were judged as somewhat less important, whereas the least
40 important were punishment and vocational training.

Despite these ambitious goals, the results have not been promising. Although some have found positive changes in participants' attitudes (MacKenzie and Shaw 1990; MacKenzie and Souryal 1995; Ransom
45 and Mastrorilli 1993; Hunter et al. 1992), few program evaluations have provided "hard" evidence of the effectiveness of these camps in terms of rehabilitation or reducing recidivism. According to the most comprehensive study to date (MacKenzie et al. 1995), based
50 on a comparative analysis of programs in eight states, no clear-cut statements can be made about the effectiveness of boot camps. In general, boot camp graduates do not fare better or worse after release than their counterparts in the conventional correctional system.
55 Boot camp programs have to be examined individually in terms of specific program components and characteristics to look for possible explanations for their different outcomes (MacKenzie et al. 1995). Empirical efforts have also failed to produce consistent findings
60 on other program effectiveness indicators such as increased prosocial behavior, reduction of technical violations, or reduced drug involvement of camp graduates (MacKenzie and Shaw 1993; MacKenzie and Brame 1995; Shaw and MacKenzie 1992). At present,
65 the only summarizing statement one can make about boot camps is the lack of any consistent effect, either

positive or negative.

However, it may be premature to declare boot camps useless as designed and implemented thus far, in that these findings, however mixed or disappointing, have largely been generated by studies using a limited range of techniques and methods. Cronin (1994) pointed out in her overview that it is unlikely that researchers will learn much more about the impact of boot camps on recidivism without better measures and research designs to ascertain the meaning and effects of the camp experience on subsequent behavior. As a first step in this effort, it seems appropriate to carry out a systematic overview of current boot camp research to assess critically what has been learned.

Methods and Procedures

To accomplish this goal, a comprehensive literature review of current boot camp evaluations was conducted. However, the review was by no means exhaustive. The numerous internal studies conducted by boot camp administering agencies were not included here because it would be difficult to select a representative range of these publications. Therefore, readers need to take into account the limited scope of this literature search, which focused on published studies involving primary data collections.

A mapping scheme was developed, as shown in Table 1, to identify four major areas of boot camp evaluations. This scheme included (1) program types (i.e., boot camp administering agency), (2) evaluation strategies, (3) data gathering methods, and (4) outcome measures.

This study identified the governmental agency responsible for operating the boot camp, and the identification of boot camp administering agencies was fairly straightforward. This review also identified the primary methodological approaches employed among the various evaluation design strategies. Although boot camps vary significantly in program designs and camp characteristics, they in general share similar goals at both the system and the individual levels. The outcome measures were selected on the basis of the extensive survey work done by MacKenzie and her colleagues (MacKenzie 1993; Souryal and MacKenzie 1995).

Patterns and Issues in Current Boot Camp Evaluations

There are several clear patterns in current boot camp research efforts, as shown in Table 1. First, most of the studies examine programs that are operated by state agencies and designed for adults. Second, most studies are quantitative with designs involving eligible subjects or a pre- and postdesign. Third, most evaluations rely on official records only and, finally, most studies have only examined individual outcomes (e.g., recidivism and prosocial attitudes), rather than system impacts (e.g., reduction in overcrowding and cost-effectiveness).

Boot Camps Operated by Federal/State Agencies Versus Local Jurisdictions

Although the Federal Bureau of Prisons also operates boot camps (MacKenzie 1993), no studies on any of its programs were located. This review found only four studies on two county-operated adult boot camps. A study by Freeman (1993) failed to find any significant change in the moral and maturational development among participants in a boot camp in Travis County, Texas, whereas the other three studies, all on the same program in Harris County, Texas, produced mixed findings (Hunter et al. 1992; Jones 1996; Anderson and Dyson 1996).

Because most of our knowledge on boot camps comes from state-operated programs, which presumably deal with different criminal populations from those of local jurisdictions, we know little about how county-level programs affect the local correctional population. An increasing number of counties have become interested in boot camps and for much the same reasons as the states. As of 1992, at least 10 states had county-level boot camp programs (Austin, Jones, and Bolyard 1993). However, these local programs tend to be more financially precarious and often short lived, which makes them less feasible for systematic evaluation. For instance, before the National Council on Crime and Delinquency could complete its evaluation, the Los Angeles County Sheriff's adult boot camp was forced to shut down prematurely because of funding problems (Austin et al. 1993).

Still, because jails house significant numbers of prison-bound offenders and serving time in them is often used in lieu of a prison sentence, boot camps could be a preferable option for local criminal justice jurisdictions (Austin et al. 1993). Additionally, evaluating boot camps in the local correctional environment with different populations will add to our understanding of the functions of this intermediate sanction.

Most boot camps have been designed for young adults convicted of nonviolent crimes (MacKenzie 1993). However, many local jurisdictions have also started boot camps for juvenile delinquents (Bourque et al. 1996). After all, the juvenile justice system also faces crowding problems as the number of delinquents in custody increased by 35 percent from 1978 to 1989, even though the nation's youth population actually declined by 11 percent (Office of Juvenile Justice and Delinquency Prevention 1992).

The most visible juvenile boot camps were the three demonstration projects funded in 1991 by the Office of Juvenile Justice and Delinquency Prevention (OJJDP) in Mobile, Alabama; Cleveland, Ohio; and Denver, Colorado. All published studies on juvenile boot camps identified in this review were on these three projects. Two of them found positive changes in participants' attitudes and behavior during the program (Bourque et al. 1996; Polsky and Fast 1993). But the positive changes were only observed among those who

Table 1
Boot Camp Evaluation Component Assessment

	1	2	3	4	5	6	7	8	9	10	11	12	13	14	15	16	17	18	19	20	21	22
Program type																						
Federal							X										X	X	X	X		
State	X	X		X	X	X		X		X	X	X	X	X	X	X						
County			X						X												X	X
Adult	X	X	X	X	X	X		X	X	X	X	X	X	X	X	X					X	X
Juvenile								X									X	X	X	X	X	
Evaluation Strategies																						
Quantitative																						
Random assignment																		X	X	X		
Eligible subjects	X			X	X	X							X	X							X	
Pre-post test			X							X	X						X					
Other		X										X				X						X
Qualitative								X	X							X						
Data gathering method																						
Official records	X	X	X	X	X	X				X	X	X	X	X	X	X	X	X	X	X	X	X
Field observations							X															
Self-reports																	X	X				
Case study								X														
Outcome measures																						
Individual level																						
Attitude change	X		X					X	X					X	X		X					
Positive behavior			X				X	X				X			X		X	X	X	X		
Recidivism					X	X							X			X		X	X	X	X	X
Drug education					X																	
Education											X						X	X	X	X		
System level																						
Reducing crowding		X									X											
Cost saving																		X	X	X		

1: MacKenzie and Shaw 1990; 2: MacKenzie and Parent 1991; 3: Hunter, Burton, Marquart and Cuvelier 1992; 4: MacKenzie, Shaw, and Souryal 1992; 5: Shaw and MacKenzie 1992; 6: MacKenzie and Shaw 1993; 7: Polsky and Fast 1993; 8: Ransom and Mastrorilli 1993; 9: Freeman 1993; 10: Christenberry, Burns, and Dickinson 1994; 11: MacKenzie and Piquero 1994; 12: MacKenzie and Brame 1995; 13: MacKenzie, Brame, McDowall, and Souryal 1995; 14: MacKenzie and Souryal 1995; 15: Mackenzie and Donaldson 1996; 16: Benda, Toombs, and Whiteside 1996; 17: Bourque, Cronin, Pearson, Felker, Han, and Hill 1996; 18: Peters 1996a (OJJDP-Mobile); 19: Peters 1996b (OJJDP-Denver); 20: Thomas and Peters 1996 (OJJDP-Cleveland); 21: Jones 1996; 22: Anderson and Dyson 1996.

completed the program and stayed in the aftercare. Had these studies included those who dropped out of either the boot camps or the aftercare programs, the positive changes might have been less pronounced. Attrition rates were high in all three locations, ranging from 41 to 76 percent (Bourque et al. 1996), and were attributed to new arrests for criminal offenses, going AWOL, and failure to comply.

In the recently published interim reports, serious operational and organizational problems were noted in all three demonstration projects, including high staff turnover, lack of understanding of the project among participating staff, unclear division of roles and responsibilities, reduction in funding, and extensive program changes at all levels in both the residential and aftercare phases. In fact, all three boot camp programs were considered only partially implemented (for details, see Peters 1996a, 1996b; Thomas and Peters 1996). As for recidivism, boot camp participants did not differ much from their control group counterparts, or worse, as in the case of Cleveland, youngsters in the experimental group recidivated at a higher rate than that of the control subjects. In Denver and Cleveland, it cost less to operate the boot camp programs than the traditional institutions, whereas in Mobile, the boot camp was more expensive than the control setting.[2]

These studies have provided valuable information on how well boot camps can be adapted to the needs of juvenile correction systems, particularly those operated by local jurisdictions. One obvious question for the three counties is, Will these boot camps, some of which have produced promising results, continue in operation once the federal money runs out?[3] This has been a problem for many treatment programs that have been launched by federal or state agencies and then terminated before enough information about their effectiveness could be accumulated. Even with these problems, the three OJJDP demonstration projects represent the only published evaluations of the efficacy of boot camps employing experimental designs.[4]

Selection of "Eligible" Subjects for Comparison

True experimental designs are rarely employed in criminal justice research, where judicial officers usually oppose the "randomized administration of justice." Evaluation strategies often must be modified to accommodate the target program or be restricted because of inadequate funding. But the most serious threat to a research project is the inability of the administering agency to implement the program as originally designed or planned, thus compromising the integrity of the research design and opening the results to alternative interpretations. The three OJJDP demonstration boot camp evaluations offer apt examples of these problems.

Most of the evaluations in this review employed quasi-experimental designs involving the use of comparison subjects in lieu of control groups or statistical techniques to control for possible confounding variables. A large number of these studies, especially those by MacKenzie and her colleagues, typically used so-called eligible candidates (defined by the researchers) for comparison purposes. In a study on the characteristics associated with successful adjustment to supervision after boot camp treatment, MacKenzie, Shaw, and Souryal (1992) used three groups of offenders who were compared to the boot camp graduates: (1) parolees who had served time in a regular prison, (2) probationers, and (3) dropouts from the boot camp program. The justification for the inclusion of the first two types of offenders was that they met legal eligibility, suitability, and acceptability criteria set up by the correctional agency. An obvious question is, Why then were these "eligible" candidates not selected for the boot camp? A possible explanation is the discrepancy between the official criteria and the actual screening process, which was not examined in their study. The very fact that these individuals had not been selected implies that they were considered less eligible than those who had been, irrespective of the "official criteria." Not surprisingly, MacKenzie et al. (1992) reported major discrepancies between the boot camp participants and their comparison subjects in terms of age, age at first arrest, and criminal history. These same factors were later found to be associated with higher levels of recidivism and poorer behavior during community supervision, thus the true effect of the boot camp experience remains unclear.[5]

The inclusion of boot camp dropouts for comparison purposes (see MacKenzie et al. 1992; MacKenzie et al. 1995) is particularly troublesome. In most cases (except for medical reasons), these dropouts either terminated their participation due to personal objections to the militaristic structure and chose to serve their sentences in prison or were dismissed for disciplinary problems and therefore can hardly be considered comparable to those who finished the boot camp program.

Individual Outcome Measures—Official Data Versus Self-Reports

Nearly all evaluations reviewed here relied solely on official records or information gathered by correctional agencies to measure recidivism, the most commonly used indicator of program effectiveness. With the exception of a few ethnographic studies, not a single study was found in which program participants were interviewed by independent researchers using self-report instruments. MacKenzie and Brame (1995, p. 114) acknowledged the limitation of relying exclusively on official records in current boot camp research and the importance of including self-report measures. However, it is not the case that boot camp participants have never responded to questions pertaining to their postprogram activities or attitudes. Several studies employed testing instruments administered by program officials to gather information on attitude changes and educational attainment during and/or after boot camp (Bourque et al. 1996; Shaw and MacKenzie 1992).

Self-report instruments to measure program effectiveness were used by MacKenzie et al. (1992) in their study of characteristics associated with successful adjustment to supervision in a Louisiana boot camp, and by MacKenzie and Brame (1995) in their analysis of community adjustment by boot camp participants in five states. In both studies, adjustment scales were constructed to measure employment, education, residential and financial stability, participation in treatment programs for drug abuse, and compliance with probation/parole conditions. However, rather than asking the offenders the questions directly, the researchers went to the community supervision (probation or parole) officers for the answers. In other words, the supervising officers were asked to report on their clients' performance. Although some measures were built into the instrument to assess the supervising officers' knowledge of the offenders' activities, these "self-reports" were in reality an extension of official records.

In short, our current knowledge of the impact of boot camps on recidivism comes from official sources. It is widely recognized that most criminal activities are neither detected nor acted upon by anyone in authority. The small fraction of crimes ever recorded may well contribute to the lack of significant findings about shock incarceration. Additionally, most evaluations track offenders for no longer than one year after the boot camp. Given the lag between the time of arrest and the time it is registered in the computer database, the actual observation period of these studies could be even shorter.

The point here is not to discredit the use of official data, but to illustrate the importance of including self-report measures to complement official statistics. Official data are easily accessible and inexpensive to compile, but they mainly reflect police activities. Self-report data, on the other hand, can provide much richer information on the issues of prevalence and incidence of criminal behavior. Although not as systematic as official records, self-reports have been found to be a reliable source of information with a remarkable degree of consistency between self-reported answers and official data (Erickson and Empey 1963; Gibson, Morrison, and West 1970; Blackmore 1974; Reuter, MacCoun, and Murphy 1990).

Many useful self-report instruments are readily available. The International Self-Report Delinquency questionnaire (ISRD) is one example. This instrument, originally created by criminologists from 15 Western countries, has gone through a series of empirical tests and is now considered methodologically sound (for a detailed discussion of it, see Junger-Tas, Terlouw, and Klein 1994). In addition, it has been used in Los Angeles and Omaha where its validity and applicability to U.S. populations was demonstrated (Junger-Tas, Klein, and Zhang 1992). The instrument contains well-constructed items to measure (1) the types of delinquent acts committed during a specified time frame, (2) the frequency of these acts, (3) the onset of admitted offenses, (4) the circumstances of the incidents, and (5) sociodemographic variables, including attitudes toward school and work, living arrangements, and circle of friends. Data uncovered by instruments such as this would be a valuable addition to official records.

System Impact and Individual Measures

Very few evaluations have examined the system goals that boot camp programs set out to accomplish. Shock incarceration emerged primarily as a response to prison crowding; but most published evaluations thus far have focused only on *individual* outcomes (i.e., recidivism, attitude, and behavior change). Although recidivism patterns invariably may affect prison crowding, the effect is usually indirect and requires long-term evaluation (MacKenzie and Parent 1991).

Part of the methodological problem here may be due to the small size of most programs. To ease current prison crowding, boot camps must be large enough to have institutional impact. Except for the boot camps in New York State with a total average camp population of about 1,500, few states operate programs that can be considered influential. In addition, many other factors also affect the impact of a boot camp on prison crowding: (1) the probability that participants would otherwise have been imprisoned, (2) the rate of program completion, (3) the difference between actual time served in prison and in boot camp, and (4) the rate of return to prison among inmates released from each type of program (Cronin 1994). Needless to say, collection of relevant data on these factors is a formidable task in program evaluation.

According to the U.S. General Accounting Office (1993), 11 out of 26 states operating boot camps in 1992 considered their programs helpful in reducing prison crowding. Although the cost of running boot camps rivaled that of traditional prisons in most states, New York, Georgia, Florida, and Louisiana reported significant savings from the use of boot camps. It is difficult to make meaningful comparisons among these agencies because of their different ways of accounting for savings and estimating prison crowding (Cronin 1994).

Due to the lack of computerized prison data from the past for comparison purposes, few independent studies have examined the direct impact on the correctional system of boot camps as currently designed and implemented. MacKenzie and Parent (1991) used a mathematical model to estimate the impact of the boot camp program on the Louisiana prison system and found modest bed-space savings. The same method was later repeated in a five-state evaluation (MacKenzie and Piquero 1994). Both studies affirmed that if boot camps were to reduce prison crowding, they must be carefully designed and administered with that purpose in mind. Furthermore, both studies raised the troublesome issue of "net widening"—extending shock incarceration to offenders who would otherwise

have received a lesser punitive sentence. Depending on who has the authority over placement (i.e., the sentencing judge or the correctional agency), boot camp programs vary significantly from state to state in the process of entry and exit decision making. Sentencing judges tend to use intermediate sanctions as an alternative to regular probation, but where correctional agencies control placement, more prison-bound offenders are likely to enter the program (Morris and Tonry 1990; MacKenzie and Souryal 1991). If program administrators cannot address the issue of enrolling participants who are truly prison bound, then whatever system impact they claim is open to question.

Besides alleviating prison crowding and reducing costs, boot camps have also been established to offer safe but punitive alternatives to long-term incarceration. Currently, all boot camps have mechanisms to discharge participants deemed unsuitable or to allow for voluntary exit (back to prison); thus they are safe to the extent that they are not releasing offenders into the community. However, the safety of program participants is a less clearly defined issue. Although physical dangers have not been reported in any study, some researchers have criticized the military drills as a potential source of abuse and as possibly detrimental to the offender's psychological well-being (Mathlas and Mathews 1991; Henggeler and Schoenwald 1994; MacKenzie and Donaldson 1996). Others have accused current boot camps of promoting misplaced masculinity and misogynistic attitudes (Morash and Rucker 1990). However, this critical rhetoric has not been supported by hard data. Obviously, more research attention should be directed at these system-level practices and goals in future studies.

Measuring Failure or Success

Definitive findings of success or failure as a result of shock incarceration are not likely to be produced. Mixed results often frustrate practitioners and policy makers who tend to discard equivocal findings as meaningless or irrelevant and retreat to their "gut feelings" or ideological convictions. To bridge the distance between researchers and practitioners, future studies should provide concrete guidance as to what can be reasonably expected from boot camps and what can be improved in the current intake and selection criteria, based on the characteristics associated with successful (not failed) program participants. In other words, instead of simply telling justice practitioners whether a boot camp works as a whole, researchers should produce specific suggestions as to where improvements can be made and what type of candidates are most likely to benefit from the program.

To identify these characteristics requires the use of both official records and self-report data. In each program, there are always participants who do not recidivate and who move on to become productive members of the society. Few efforts have been made to examine

460 the characteristics of these individuals or to provide profile information about the types of persons who are likely to succeed in a boot camp. Research focusing on such characteristics can generate far more useful in-formation to practitioners to guide future program im-
465 plementation. Such information would enable correc-tional officials to develop realistic expectations about their programs and their screening processes.

Program "effectiveness" should mean more than merely reducing recidivism, measured by most studies
470 as arrests or parole revocations. Most current studies do not examine prosocial activities such as employment, schooling, drug treatment, or vocational training, thus leaving readers with the impression that the success or failure of a program is solely a matter of how many
475 offenders continue to commit crimes. Also, little in-formation is available about how varied use of one's social support network may lead to different levels of community reintegration. The involvement of offend-ers' family members in their correctional activities may
480 prove to be more influential to their postprogram be-havior than any official interventions. This possibility is particularly likely in that most program participants are young adults. No studies thus far have included measures on the involvement of family members in
485 boot camp treatment.

There are many factors to consider in the search for characteristics associated with successful graduates. They include the offender's sociodemographic back-ground (e.g., age, race, education, living arrangement,
490 education, general attitudes toward school and work, social network, employment, and income), prior crimi-nal history (e.g., the number of prior arrests, the nature of the incident offense, prior contacts with welfare agencies for dependent or neglect status), correctional
495 history (e.g., the number of prior probation terms, jail/prison sentences, lengths, and any violations). These factors can provide far more specific profile characteristics of program participants than the current reliance on loosely conceived eligibility criteria, in
500 which offenders are mainly distinguished from each other in terms of risk level (nature of incident offense and prior criminal history). These factors may enable us to better understand the type of youths for whom the boot camp structure is likely to be effective.

Treatment Components and Nonprogrammatic Factors

505 Closely related to the task of identifying character-istics associated with successful and unsuccessful camp graduates is the delineation of the impact of different programmatic and nonprogrammatic components of boot camps on the outcomes. Many correctional inter-
510 vention programs appear to share identical or similar treatment strategies; however, few researchers have been able to explain why some programs were effec-tive while others were not (Palmer 1995). No one ge-neric intervention approach is likely to be found to be
515 very successful or unsuccessful because confounding

factors external to the treatment usually have a signifi-cant impact on the outcome. In other words, the effect of any treatment program is determined by the interac-tion of programmatic elements such as behavioral
520 modification, education/counseling, and life skills with nonprogrammatic factors such as staff/client interac-tions, setting, and flexible programming (Palmer 1995, p. 104).

Thus far, very few studies have attempted to sketch
525 out the connections between different components of a boot camp program and their outcomes, and even fewer have considered the relevance of nonprogrammatic factors. Most boot camp programs contain components that are not much different from traditional interven-
530 tions—group/individual counseling, education, and vocational training. Successful examples of these tra-ditional treatment models do exist. For instance, in his literature review covering more than 400 experimental studies from 1975 to 1989, Palmer (1991) found that,
535 using a $p < .05$ criterion, experimental programs out-performed control programs in 25 to 35 percent of all studies, whereas control programs led in less than 10 percent. Clearly, some interventions under some cir-cumstances have worked; the central question in
540 evaluation research is *which* ones have produced posi-tive effects (Palmer 1995).

It is also important to conduct systematic examina-tion of nonprogrammatic factors and conditions that are capable of influencing program outcomes irrespective
545 of the particular generic treatment approach (Palmer 1995). For example, using the same self-report index developed by MacKenzie and Shaw (1990), McCorkle (1995) found that both boot camp participants and their prison comparison inmates became more prosocial,
550 raising doubts about the necessity of the military at-mosphere to improve behavior and suggesting that the attitudinal improvement was likely due to factors extra-neous to the boot camp program (e.g., staff competence and commitment, program integrity, and the timing of
555 intervention).

External factors may help explain why some pro-grams had a positive influence on certain offenders whereas others did not. Palmer (1995) classified these factors into four categories: (1) staff characteristics
560 (e.g., personal styles, volunteers/professionals, com-mitment, and competence), (2) quality of staff/client interactions (e.g., surveillance, control, and self-ex-pression), (3) individual differences among offenders (personalities and maturity levels), and (4) program
565 settings (e.g., institutional, noninstitutional, and direct parole). For instance, Jesness (1975) found that posi-tive changes occurred more often when the delinquents felt positive toward staff, whereas Kelly and Baer (1971) found that delinquents reacting to situational
570 stress associated with their developmental stage (e.g., identity crisis) were more responsive to a wilderness program than those who were immature and/or emo-tionally disturbed.

Clearly, it is not enough to study program compo-
575 nents alone and examine how they might produce certain outcomes. Palmer's review (1995) offered an excellent guide for future studies on specific programmatic and nonprogrammatic factors to be included in a
systematic manner. The task of identifying effective
580 combinations of treatment components and nonprogrammatic factors may appear formidable. Aside from
the many treatment strategies, the four areas of nonprogrammatic factors each consist of numerous features or variables. The complexities involved in the
585 search for successful combinations require researchers
to develop clear and precise conceptual frameworks on
which systematic data items and assessment strategies
can be plotted.

This review suggests a conceptual framework that
590 views a boot camp program as a multifaceted intervention process composed of operational goals and treatments that are implemented by a staff with varying
personalities and professional qualifications. The program goals and strategies, as well as nonprogrammatic
595 factors, all interact with the characteristics of the delinquents. In this conceptual framework, the effectiveness
of boot camp treatment is mediated by two main variables—individual differences and nonprogrammatic
factors. On one hand, it is likely that boot camp pro-
600 grams are more likely to produce successful outcomes
when there is a high level of program integrity (consistency in treatment activities) and when involved
staff are well trained and motivated, and when the
staff-client interactions are positive. The nonprogram-
605 matic factors are further divided into two phases—
in-camp and aftercare. The aftercare phase involves nonprogrammatic factors that are slightly different from
the in-camp ones, in which family interactions, social
support network, and community environment may
610 play an important role in treatment effectiveness. On
the other hand, individual factors such as prior history,
substance abuse, and the age of onset may combine to
influence the effectiveness of boot camp treatment.
However, neither set of variables (individual and non-
615 programmatic) function independently of the other; instead, they are expected to have interactive effects on
program outcomes.

Discussion

Findings of current boot camp studies are complicated and difficult to interpret. Much more research
620 needs to be undertaken with greater use of different
methodological approaches and analytical strategies to
firm up our understanding of boot camps as compared
to traditional incarceration. These approaches and
strategies include the use of both official records and
625 self-reports that can examine both programmatic and
nonprogrammatic factors as related to different aspects
of the boot camps. The search for information to expli-
cate the functions of different program components and
explain why some offenders succeed whereas others

630 fail requires researchers to resist the temptation to address the simple question: "Do boot camps work?"
Such a blanket question increases the chances of
drawing misleading and simplistic conclusions, which
will in turn lead either to summarily dismissing or to
635 unduly extolling boot camps as a treatment option.

It is hoped that future studies can generate a set of
guidelines for administrators as to what type of participants to look for and what can be reasonably accomplished. To this end, they will not only contribute to
640 our currently scarce knowledge on boot camps in general but also provide practical and policy relevant information to correctional agencies.

This article has focused mainly on methodological
issues in current boot camp research but has *not*
645 claimed that boot camp outcomes will somehow drasti-
cally change if we include the alternative strategies as
discussed earlier; nor has it suggested that the current
lack of consistent findings results solely from inade-
quate research designs. It is possible that the lack of
650 clear findings (positive or negative) may result from
the fact that boot camps as currently designed and implemented are indeed not consistently effective. The
discussion here only called attention to the aspects and
strategies that have largely been neglected thus far in
655 boot camp research, and claimed that informed conclusions about the effectiveness of boot camp programs
should only be made by taking a more holistic approach in evaluation research designs.

Another issue, which is beyond the scope of this
660 study but which deserves serious attention from researchers, is the relative absence of theoretical guidance behind most current boot camp research. None of
the studies reviewed here set out to measure any the-
ory-based outcomes.[6] The question is not why boot
665 camps, as evaluated thus far, have failed to produce
successful outcomes, but rather why we should expect
them to be effective in the first place. Lacking a clear
conceptualization of what effects different components
of boot camp programs are supposed to produce and
670 how they are supposed to produce them, most evaluation studies thus far have relied on "common-sense"
criteria for outcome measures.

Theory-guided research that illuminates the logical
connection between the deployment of certain treat-
675 ment strategies and their expected outcomes is required. All criminological theories have some implications for criminal justice policy, and conversely, most
correctional practices are based on, either explicitly or
implicitly, some understanding of human behavior.
680 Unfortunately, as Ronald Akers poignantly pointed out
(1996, p. 11), "in most public discourse about criminal
justice policy, the underlying theoretical notions are
ill-stated and vaguely understood. A policy may be
adopted for political, economic, or bureaucratic rea-
685 sons, then a theoretical rationale is formulated or
adopted to justify the policy." As a consequence, a
program may be driven by no single coherent theory

but instead by an admixture of several or even con-flicting theoretical positions.

690   All of the boot camp programs surveyed by MacKenzie and Souryal (1991) had multiple goals at both system and individual levels. Obviously it would require a very comprehensive theory to accommodate or explain goal compatibility across the system and
695   individual levels. For instance, the top three goals in these surveyed boot camp programs were rehabilita-tion, recidivism reduction, and drug education, which were not much different from the goals of most correc-tional efforts in the past few decades, the only differ-
700   ence being in the delivery mechanism—the paramili-tary environment. Without theory-guided evaluations, our understanding of boot camps as a treatment model will probably remain limited and our conclusions questionable, because we cannot divine why the many
705   components of the program are placed together and how they interact to produce the results we have found.

At a philosophical level, boot camps as now oper-ated run counter to the current climate of opinion about criminal justice practices. Because politicians advocate
710   "tough" treatment for criminals, and correctional offi-cials want to "straighten out" offenders in a regimented environment, one would expect the deterrence doctrine to be the theoretical pillar of current boot camp treat-ment. In reality, the deterrent effect, if any, must be
715   minimal in that most programs allow voluntary exit for participants and the rest simply expel problematic par-ticipants. If politicians and practitioners expect boot camps to be effective, then the experience of a boot camp must be unpleasant so that offenders will not
720   want to recidivate.

On the other hand, most descriptions of boot camp programs suggest that they are driven by one or both of two criminological theories: (1) control theory (Gottfredson and Hirschi 1990), which centers on weak
725   self-control over deviant impulses as a result of inade-quate or poor training in early childhood, and (2) social learning theory, which focuses on differential identifi-cation and reinforcement, which fosters conformity (Akers 1996). Most program administrators would
730   agree that the military environment and its regimented activities are designed to instill discipline and respect for authority in offenders and reinforce self-control over criminal impulses and that the social learning pro-cess, with its drills and emphasis on group success over
735   individual needs, prepares participants for the transition toward a more prosocial lifestyle after graduation.

The argument for theory-guided research may not resonate with practitioners, in that utility and pragma-tism, not theoretical relevancy, are their focal concerns.
740   There may also be practical or ethical obstacles against carrying out the actions that testing a theory may re-quire (Akers 1996). There may be political or eco-nomic factors that come into play to enhance or retard the efforts needed to change criminal behavior, reduce
745   recidivism, or make the system operate better. Still,

these issues should not reduce the importance of ap-plying theoretical guidance to the designs of boot camp research, and a holistic approach in assessing boot camps should also include theoretical constructs. As
750   Palmer (1995) pointed out, a holistic approach in an evaluation strategy would require long-term, multi-study research projects focusing on nonprogrammatic as well as programmatic factors in an effort to deter-mine the specific combinations of treatment modalities
755   that lead to the most successful outcomes.

Notes

1. The militaristic approach to corrections is not new; similar tac-tics were used in the 19th century (Morash and Rucker 1990; Smith 1988).

2. It should be noted that the cost of the three programs cannot be compared across the sites because they each had a different imple-mentation plan. For instance, the savings of the boot camp in Cleve-land was primarily due to the shorter periods of confinement among members of the control group.

3. The Denver project was already closed in 1994, which limited the project evaluation at that site.

4. The only other study involving an experimental design was an internal report by Jean Bottcher (1995) of the California Youth Authority. However, the original random assignment design was compromised when few control subjects were paroled to enter the aftercare phase and when arrest records were unavailable at the time of data collection.

5. These variables (such as age, race, and prior records) could have been controlled through the use of sample matching. Selection crite-ria could have been set by the researchers on the basis of prior knowledge. Case (or sample) matching could have controlled for important background factors. However, case matching requires a large pool of potential candidates. Statistical techniques may be used to control for background variables. However, as the list of exoge-nous variables increases, the clarity of an analytical model as well as its conceptual parsimony decreases.

6. The only evaluation study that made a fleeting discussion on the theoretical relevance in boot camp programs was by Benda, Toombs, and Whiteside (1996).

References

Akers, Ronald L. 1996. *Criminological Theories: Introduction and Evaluation.* Los Angeles: Roxbury.

Anderson, James F., and Laronistine Dyson. 1996. "A Tracking Investigation to Determine Boot Camp Success and Offender Risk Assessment for CRIPP Participants." *Journal of Crime and Justice* 19:170-90.

Austin, James, Michael Jones, and Melissa Bolyard. 1993. "The Growing Use of Jail Boot Camps: The Current State of the Art." *National Institute of Jus-tice—Research in Brief* (October). Washington, DC: U.S. Department of Justice.

Benda, Brent B., Nancy J. Toombs, and Leanne Whiteside. 1996. "Recidivism Among Boot Camp Graduates: A Comparison of Drug Offenders to Other Offenders." *Journal of Criminal Justice* 24: 241-53.

Blackmore, John. 1974. "The Relationship Between Self-Reported Delin-quency and Official Convictions Amongst Adolescent Boys." *British Jour-nal of Criminology* 14:172-6.

Bottcher, Jean. 1995. *LEAD: A Boot Camp and Intensive Parole Program—A Summary of Preliminary Evaluation Findings.* Sacramento: California Youth Authority.

Bourque, Blair B., Roberta C. Cronin, Frank R. Pearson, Daniel B. Felker, Mei Han, and Sarah M. Hill. 1996. *Boot Camps for Juvenile Offenders: An Im-plementation Evaluation of Three Demonstration Programs.* Washington, DC: National Institute of Justice.

Byrne, James M., Arthur J. Lurigio, and Joan Petersilia, eds. 1992. *Smart Sentencing: The Emergence of Intermediate Sanctions.* Newbury Park, CA: Sage.

Christenberry, Nola J., John L. Burns, and Gerald B. Dickinson. 1994. "Gains in Educational Achievement by Inmates During the Arkansas Prison Boot Camp Program." *Journal of Correctional Education* 45:128-132.

Cronin, Roberta C. 1994. *Boot Camps for Adult and Juvenile Offenders: Over-view and Update.* Washington, DC: National Institute of Justice.

Erickson, Maynard L., and LaMar T. Empey, 1963. "Court Records, Unde-tected Delinquency, and Decision-Making." *Journal of Criminal Law,*

Criminology and Police Science 54:456-69.

Freeman, Loyal W. 1993. "Boot Camp and Inmate Moral Development: No Significant Effect." *Journal of Offender Rehabilitation* 19:123-7.

Gettinger, Stephen. 1983. "Assessing Criminal Justice Needs." *National Institute of Justice—Research in Brief.* Rockville, MD: National Criminal Justice Reference Service.

Gibson, H. B., Sylvia Morrison, and D. J. West. 1970. "The Confession of Known Offenses in Response to a Self-Reported Delinquency Schedule." *British Journal of Criminology* 10:277-80.

Gottfredson, Michael R. and Travis Hirschi. 1990. A *General Theory of Crime.* Palo Alto, CA: Stanford University Press.

Henggeler, Scott W. and Songja K. Schoenwald. 1994. "Boot Camps for Juvenile Offenders: Just Say No." *Journal of Child and Family Studies* 3:243-8.

Hunter, Robert J., Velmer S. Burton, James W. Marquart, and Steven J. Cuvelier. 1992. "Measuring Attitudinal Change of Boot Camp Participants." *Journal of Contemporary Criminal Justice* 8:283-98.

Jesness, Carl F. 1975. "Comparative Effectiveness of Behavior Modification and Transactional Analysis Programs for Delinquents." *Journal of Consulting and Clinical Psychology* 43:758-79.

Jones, Mark. 1996. "Do Boot Camp Graduates Make Better Probationers?" *Journal of Crime and Justice* 19:1-14.

Junger-Tas, Josine, Malcolm W. Klein, and Xiaodong Zhang. 1992. "Problems and Dilemmas in Comparative Self-Report Delinquency Research." Pp. 83-103 in *Offenders and Victims: Theory and Policy,* edited by D. P. Farrington and S. Walklate. London: British Society of Criminology and the Institute for the Study and Treatment of Delinquency.

Junger-Tas, Josine, Gert-Jan Terlouw, and Malcolm W. Klein. 1994. *Delinquent Behavior Among Youngsters in the Western World.* Amsterdam: Kugler.

Kelly, Francis J. and Daniel J. Baer. 1971. "Physical Challenge as a Treatment for Delinquency." *Crime & Delinquency* 17:437-47.

MacKenzie, Doris Layton. 1993. "Boot Camp Prisons in 1993." *National Institute of Justice Journal* November, pp. 21-8.

MacKenzie, Doris Layton and Robert Brame. 1995. "Shock Incarceration and Positive Adjustment During Community Supervision." *Journal of Quantitative Criminology* 11:111-41.

MacKenzie, Doris Layton, Robert Brame, David McDowall, and Claire Souryal. 1995. "Boot Camp Prisons and Recidivism in Eight States." *Criminology* 33:327-57.

MacKenzie, Doris Layton and Heidi Donaldson. 1996. "Boot Camp for Women Offenders." *Criminal Justice Review* 21:21-43.

MacKenzie, Doris Layton and Dale Parent. 1991. "Shock Incarceration and Prison Crowding in Louisiana." *Journal of Criminal Justice* 19:225-37.

MacKenzie, Doris Layton and Alex Piquero. 1994. "The Impact of Shock Incarceration Programs on Prison Crowding." *Crime & Delinquency* 40:222-49.

MacKenzie, Doris Layton and James W. Shaw. 1990. "Inmate Adjustment and Change During Shock Incarceration: The Impact of Correctional Boot Camp Programs." *Justice Quarterly* 7:125-49.

—. 1993. "The Impact of Shock Incarceration on Technical Violations and New Criminal Activities." *Justice Quarterly* 10:463-87.

MacKenzie, Doris Layton and Claire Souryal. 1994. *Multisite Evaluation of Shock Incarceration.* Washington, D.C.: National Institute of Justice.

MacKenzie, Doris Layton, James W. Shaw, and Claire Souryal. 1992. "Characteristics Associated with Successful Adjustment to Supervision—A Comparison of Parolees, Probationers, Shock Participants, and Shock Dropouts." *Criminal Justice and Behavior* 19:437-54.

MacKenzie, Doris Layton, and Claire Souryal. 1991. "Boot Camp Survey—Rehabilitation, Recidivism Reduction Outrank Punishment as Main Goals." *Corrections Today,* October, pp. 90-6.

___ 1995. "Inmates' Attitude Change During Incarceration: A Comparison of Boot Camp with Traditional Prison." *Justice Quarterly* 12:325-53.

Mathlas, Rudolf E. S. and James W. Mathews. 1991. "The Boot Camp Program for Offenders: Does the Shoe Fit?" *International Journal of Offender Therapy and Comparative Criminology* 35:322-6.

McCorkle, Richard C. 1995. "Correctional Boot Camps and Change in Attitude: Is All This Shouting Necessary? A Research Note." *Justice Quarterly* 12:365-75.

Morash, Merry and Lila Rucker. 1990. "A Critical Look at the Idea of Boot Camp as a Correctional Reform." *Crime & Delinquency* 36:204-22.

Morris, Norval and Michael Tonry. 1990. *Between Prison and Probation—Intermediate Punishments in a Rational Sentencing System.* New York: Oxford University Press.

National Council on Crime and Delinquency. 1992. *Criminal Justice Sentencing Policy Statement.* San Francisco: Author.

Office of Juvenile Justice and Delinquency Prevention. 1992. *National Juvenile Custody Trends, 1978-1989.* Washington, DC: U.S. Department of Justice.

Palmer, Ted. 1991. "The Effectiveness of Intervention: Recent Trends and Current Issues." *Crime & Delinquency* 37:330-46.

___.1995. "Programmatic and Nonprogrammatic Aspects of Successful Intervention: New Directions for Research." *Crime & Delinquency* 41: 100-31.

Parent, Dale. 1989. *Shock Incarceration: An Overview of Existing Programs.* Washington, DC: U.S. Department of Justice.

Peters, Michael. 1996a. *Evaluation of the Impact of Boot Camps for Juvenile Offenders—Mobile Interim Report.* Washington, DC: U.S. Department of Justice, Office of Juvenile Justice and Delinquency Prevention.

___.1996b. *Evaluation of the Impact of Boot Camps for Juvenile Offenders–Denver Interim Report.* Washington, DC: U.S. Department of Justice, Office of Juvenile Justice and Delinquency Prevention.

Polsky, Howard and Jonathan Fast. 1993. "Boot Camps, Juvenile Offenders, and Culture Shock." *Child and Youth Care Forum* 22:403-15.

Ransom, George and Mary Ellen Mastrorilli 1993. "The Massachusetts Boot Camp: Inmate Anecdotes." *The Prison Journal* 73:307-18.

Reuter, Peter, Robert MacCoun, and Patrick Murphy. 1990. *Money from Crime: A Study of the Economics of Drug Dealing in Washington, D.C.* Santa Monica, CA: RAND.

Shaw, James W. and Doris Layton MacKenzie. 1992. "The One-Year Community Supervision Performance of Drug Offenders and Louisiana DOC-Identified Substance Abusers Graduating from Shock Incarceration." *Journal of Criminal Justice* 20:501-16.

Smith, Beverly A. 1988. "Military Training at New York's Elmira Reformatory, 1888-1920. *Federal Probation* 54:33-40.

Souryal, Claire and Doris Layton MacKenzie. 1995. "Shock Incarceration and Recidivism: An Examination of Boot Camp Programs in Four States." Pp. 57-88 in *Intermediate Sanctions: Sentencing in the 1990s,* edited by J. Smykla and W. Selke. Cincinnati: Anderson.

Thomas, David and Michael Peters. 1996. *Evaluation of the Impact of Boot Camps for Juvenile Offenders–Cleveland Interim Report.* Washington, DC: U.S. Department of Justice, Office of Juvenile Justice and Delinquency Prevention.

U.S. Bureau of Justice Statistics. 1996. *Prison and Jail Inmates, 1995.* Washington, DC: U.S. Government Printing Office.

U.S. General Accounting Office. 1993. *Prison Boot Camps: Short-Term Prison Costs Reduced, but Long-Term Impact Uncertain.* Washington, DC: Author.

About the author: Sheldon X. Zhang is an associate professor of sociology at California State University, San Marcos.

Acknowledgments: This study was supported in part by a grant from the National Institute of Justice (96-SC-VX-0003). The author is solely responsible for the opinions expressed in this article. The author would like to acknowledge the helpful comments from Daniel Glaser, Therese Baker, and Don Gibbons on earlier drafts of this article.

Exercise for Article 25

Factual Questions

1. According to the literature review, boot camp administrators ranked which three program goals most highly?

2. Were most studies on boot camps qualitative *or* quantitative?

3. This review identified published studies on how many boot camp projects for juveniles?

4. Are "true experimental designs" common in criminal justice research? Why? Why not?

5. What does the author mean by "net widening"?

6. Have researchers made major efforts to identify the types of individuals who are likely to succeed in boot camp?

7. How does the author define "program integrity"?

Questions for Discussion

8. The reviewer states, "Despite the disappointing findings from most evaluations, the number of boot camps continues to grow." Speculate on the reasons for this apparent contradiction between policy and research. (See lines 23–25.)

9. The reviewer limited his review to published evaluations, excluding internal ones. Are there advantages to doing this? Disadvantages? Explain.

10. Table 1 shows that only three of the evaluations employed random assignment. Is this important to know? Why? Why not?

11. The reviewer states that *recidivism* was the most commonly used indicator of program effectiveness. Do you think that this is a good indicator? Explain. (See lines 271–274.)

12. Have your opinions on boot camps changed as a result of reading this review? Explain.

Quality Ratings

Directions: Indicate your level of agreement with each of the following statements by circling a number from 5 for strongly agree (SA) to 1 for strongly disagree (SD). If you believe an item is not applicable to this research article, leave it blank. Be prepared to explain your ratings.

A. The introduction establishes the importance of the study.

SA   5   4   3   2   1   SD

B. The literature review establishes the context for the study.

SA   5   4   3   2   1   SD

C. The research purpose, question, or hypothesis is clearly stated.

SA   5   4   3   2   1   SD

D. The method of sampling is sound.

SA   5   4   3   2   1   SD

E. Relevant demographics (for example, age, gender, and ethnicity) are described.

SA   5   4   3   2   1   SD

F. Measurement procedures are adequate.

SA   5   4   3   2   1   SD

G. All procedures have been described in sufficient detail to permit a replication of the study.

SA   5   4   3   2   1   SD

H. The participants have been adequately protected from potential harm.

SA   5   4   3   2   1   SD

I. The results are clearly described.

SA   5   4   3   2   1   SD

J. The discussion/conclusion is appropriate.

SA   5   4   3   2   1   SD

K. Despite any flaws, the report is worthy of publication.

SA   5   4   3   2   1   SD

Appendix A

Reading Research Reports: A Brief Introduction

David A. Schroeder   David E. Johnson   Thomas D. Jensen

To many students, the prospect of reading a research report in a professional journal elicits so much fear that no information is, in fact, transmitted. Such apprehension on the part of the reader is not necessary,
5 and we hope that this article will help students understand more clearly what such reports are all about and will teach them how to use these resources more effectively. Let us assure you that there is nothing mystical or magical about research reports, although they
10 may be somewhat more technical and precise in style, more intimidating in vocabulary, and more likely to refer to specific sources of information than are everyday mass media sources. However, once you get beyond these intimidating features, you will find that the
15 vast majority of research reports do a good job of guiding you through a project and informing you of important points of which you should be aware.

A scientific research report has but one purpose: to communicate to others the results of one's scientific
20 investigations. To ensure that readers will be able to appreciate fully the import and implications of the research, the author of the report will make every effort to describe the project so comprehensively that even a naive reader will be able to follow the logic as he or
25 she traces the author's thinking through the project.

A standardized format has been developed by editors and authors to facilitate effective communication. The format is subject to some modification, according to the specific needs and goals of a particular author for
30 a particular article, but, in general, most articles possess a number of features in common. We will briefly discuss the six major sections of research articles and the purpose of each. We hope that this selection will help you take full advantage of the subsequent articles
35 and to appreciate their content as informed "consumers" of social psychological research.

Heading

The heading of an article consists of the title, the name of the author or authors, and their institutional affiliations. Typically the title provides a brief descrip-
40 tion of the primary independent and dependent vari-
ables that have been investigated in the study. This information should help you begin to categorize the study into some implicit organizational framework that will help you keep track of the social psychological
45 material. For example, if the title includes the word *persuasion*, you should immediately recognize that the article will be related to the attitude-change literature, and you should prepare yourself to identify the similarities and differences between the present study and
50 the previous literature.

The names of the authors may also be important to you for at least two reasons. First, it is quite common for social psychologists to use the names of authors as a shorthand notation in referring among themselves to
55 critical articles. Rather than asking, "Have you read 'Videotape and the attribution process: Reversing actors' and observers' points of view'?", it is much easier to say, "Have you read the Storms (1973) article?" In addition, this strategy gives the author(s) credit for the
60 material contained in the article. Second, you will find that most researchers actively pursue programs of research that are specific to a particular area of interest. For example, you will eventually be able to recognize that an article written by Albert Bandura is likely to be
65 about social learning processes, while an article by Leonard Berkowitz is probably going to discuss aggression and violence. Once you begin to identify the major researchers in each area, you will find that you will be able to go beyond the information presented
70 within an article and understand not only how a piece of research fits into a well-defined body of literature but also how it may be related to other less obvious topics.

Abstract

The Abstract is a short (often less than 150 words)
75 preview of the contents of the article. The Abstract should be totally self-contained and intelligible without any reference to the article proper. It should briefly convey a statement of the problem explored, the methods used, the major results of the study, and the con-
80 clusions reached. The Abstract helps to set the stage and to prepare you for the article itself. Just as the title helps you place the article in a particular area of investigation, the Abstract helps pinpoint the exact question or questions to be addressed in the study.

Introduction

85 The Introduction provides the foundation for the

study itself and therefore for the remainder of the article. Thus, it serves several critical functions for the reader. First, it provides a context for the article and the study by discussing past literature that is relevant to and has implications for the present research. Second, it permits a thorough discussion of the rationale for the research that was conducted and a full description of the independent and dependent variables that were employed. Third, it allows the hypotheses that were tested to be stated explicitly, and the arguments on which these predictions were based to be elucidated. Each of these functions will be considered in detail.

The literature review that is typically the initial portion of the Introduction is not intended to provide a comprehensive restatement of all the published articles that are tangentially relevant to the present research. Normally, a selective review is presented—one that carefully sets up the rationale of the study and identifies deficiencies in our understanding of the phenomena being investigated. In taking this approach, the author is attempting to provide insights into the thought processes that preceded the actual conducting of the study. Usually, the literature review will begin by discussing rather broad conceptual issues (e.g., major theories, recognized areas of investigation) and will then gradually narrow its focus to more specific concerns (e.g., specific findings from previous research, methods that have been employed). It may be helpful to think of the Introduction as a funnel, gradually drawing one's attention to a central point that represents the critical feature of the article.

Following the review of the past literature, the author typically presents the rationale for his or her own research. A research study may have one of several goals as its primary aim: (1) It may be designed to answer a question specifically raised by the previous literature but left unanswered. (2) It may attempt to correct methodological flaws that have plagued previous research and threaten the validity of the conclusions reached. (3) It may seek to reconcile conflicting findings that have been reported in the literature, typically by identifying and/or eliminating confounding variables by exerting greater experimental control. (4) It may be designed to assess the validity of a scientific theory by testing one or more hypotheses that have been deduced or derived from that theory. (5) It may begin a novel line of research that has not been previously pursued or discussed in the literature. Research pursuing any of these five goals may yield significant contributions to a particular field of inquiry.

After providing the rationale for the study, the author properly continues to narrow the focus of the article from broad conceptual issues to the particular variables that are to be employed in the study. Ideally, in experimental studies, the author clearly identifies the independent and dependent variables to be used; in correlational studies, the predictor and criterion variables are specified. For those readers who do not have an extensive background in research methodology, a brief explanation of experimental and correlational studies may be in order.

Experimental studies. An experimental study is designed to identify cause-effect relationships between independent variables that the experimenter systematically manipulates and the dependent variable that is used to measure the behavior of interest. In such a study, the researcher controls the situation to eliminate or neutralize the effects of all extraneous factors that may affect the behavior of interest in order to assess more precisely the impact of the independent variables alone. In most instances, only the tightly controlled experimental method permits valid inferences of cause-effect relationships to be made.

Correlational studies. In some circumstances, the researcher cannot exert the degree of control over the situation that is necessary for a true experimental study. Rather than giving up the project, the researcher may explore alternative methods that may still permit an assessment of his or her hypotheses and predictions. One such alternative is the correlational approach. In a correlational study, the researcher specifies a set of measures that should be related conceptually to the display of a target behavior. The measure that is used to assess the target behavior is called the criterion variable; the measure from which the researcher expects to be able to make predictions about the criterion variable is called the predictor variable. Correlational studies permit the researcher to assess the degree of relationship between the predictor variable(s) and the criterion variable(s), but inferences of cause and effect cannot be validly made because the effects of extraneous variables have not been adequately controlled. Correlational studies are most frequently used in naturalistic or applied situations in which researchers must either tolerate the lack of control and do the best they can under the circumstances or give up any hope of testing their hypotheses.

After the discussion of these critical components of the study, the author explicitly states the exact predictions that the study is designed to test. The previous material should have set the stage sufficiently well for you as a reader to anticipate what these hypotheses will be, but it is incumbent on the author to present them nonetheless. The wording of the hypotheses may vary, some authors preferring to state the predictions in conceptual terms (e.g., "The arousal of cognitive dissonance due to counterattitudinal advocacy is expected to lead to greater attitude change than the presentation of an attitude-consistent argument.") and others preferring to state their predictions in terms of the actual operationalizations that they employed (e.g., "Subjects who received a $1 incentive to say that an objectively boring task was fun are expected to subsequently evaluate the task as being more enjoyable than subjects who were offered a $20 incentive to say that the task was interesting.").

In reading a research report, it is imperative that you pay attention to the relationship between the initial literature review, the rationale for the study, and the statement of the hypotheses. In a well-conceived and well-designed investigation, each section will flow logically from the preceding one; the internal consistency of the author's arguments will make for smooth transitions as the presentation advances. If there appear to be discontinuities or inconsistencies throughout the author's presentation, it would be wise to take a more critical view of the study—particularly if the predictions do not seem to follow logically from the earlier material. In such cases, the author may be trying to present as a prediction a description of the findings that were unexpectedly uncovered when the study was being conducted. Although there is nothing wrong with reporting unexpected findings in a journal article, the author should be honest enough to identify them as what they really are. As a reader, you should have much more confidence in the reliability of predictions that obtain than you do in data that can be described by postdictions only.

Method

To this point, the author has dealt with the study in relatively abstract terms, and has given little attention to the actual procedures used in conducting it. In the Method section, the author at last describes the operationalizations and procedures that were employed in the investigation. There are at least two reasons for the detailed presentation of this information. First, such a presentation allows interested readers to reconstruct the methodology used, so that a replication of the study can be undertaken. By conducting a replication using different subject populations and slightly different operationalizations of the same conceptual variables, more information can be gained about the validity of the conclusions that the original investigator reached. Second, even if a replication is not conducted, the careful description of the method used will permit you to evaluate the adequacy of the procedures employed.

The Method section typically comprises two or more subsections, each of which has a specific function to fulfill. Almost without exception, the Method section begins with a subject subsection, consisting of a complete description of the subjects who participated in the study.[1] The number of subjects should be indicated, and there should be a summary of important demographic information (e.g., numbers of male and female subjects, age) so that you can know to what populations the findings can be reasonably generalized. Sampling techniques that were used to recruit subjects and incentives used to induce volunteering should also be clearly specified. To the extent that subject characteristics are of primary importance to the goals of the research, greater detail is presented in this subsection, and more attention should be directed to it.

A procedures subsection is also almost always included in the Method section. This subsection presents a detailed account of the subjects' experiences in the experiment. Although other formats may also be effective, the most common presentation style is to describe the subjects' activities in chronological order. A thorough description of all questionnaires administered or tasks completed is given, as well as any other features that might be reasonably expected to affect the behavior of the subjects in the study.

After the procedures have been discussed, a full description of the independent variables in an experimental study, or predictor variables in a correlational study, is typically provided. Verbatim description of each of the different levels of each independent variable is presented, and similar detail is used to describe each predictor variable. This information may be included either in the procedures subsection or, if the description of these variables is quite lengthy, in a separate subsection.

After thoroughly describing these variables, the author usually describes the dependent variables in an experimental study, and the criterion variables in a correlational study. The description of the dependent and/or criterion variables also requires a verbatim specification of the exact operationalizations that were employed. When appropriate and available, information about the reliability and validity of these measures is also presented. In addition, if the investigator has included any questions that were intended to allow the effectiveness of the independent variable manipulation to be assessed, these manipulation checks are described at this point. All of this information may be incorporated in the procedures subsection or in a separate subsection.

After you have read the Method section, there should be no question about what has been done to the subjects who participated in the study. You should try to evaluate how representative the methods that were used were of the conceptual variables discussed in the Introduction. Manipulation checks may help to allay one's concerns, but poorly conceived manipulation checks are of little or no value. Therefore, it is important for you as a reader to remember that you are ultimately responsible for the critical evaluation of any research report.

Results

Once the full methodology of the study has been described for the reader, the author proceeds to report the results of the statistical analyses that were conducted on the data. The Results section is probably the most intimidating section for students to read, and often the most difficult section for researchers to write. You are typically confronted with terminology and analytical techniques with which you are at best unfa-

---

[1] *Editor's note:* Many researchers prefer the terms *participants* or *respondents* to the term *subjects*.

miliar, or at worst totally ignorant. There is no reason for you to feel bad about this state of affairs; as a neophyte in the world of research, you cannot expect mastery of all phases of research from the start. Even experienced researchers are often exposed to statistical techniques with which they are unfamiliar, requiring them either to learn the techniques or to rely on others to assess the appropriateness of the procedure. For the student researcher, a little experience and a conscientious effort to learn the basics will lead to mastery of the statistical skills necessary.

The author's task is similarly difficult. He or she is attempting to present the findings of the study in a straightforward and easily understood manner, but the presentation of statistical findings does not always lend itself readily to this task. The author must decide whether to present the results strictly within the text of the article or to use tables, graphs, and figures to help to convey the information effectively. Although the implications of the data may be clear to the researcher, trying to present the data clearly and concisely so that the reader will also be able to discern the implications is not necessarily assured. In addition, the author is obligated to present all the significant results obtained in the statistical analyses, not just the results that support the hypotheses being tested. Although this may clutter the presentation and detract from the simplicity of the interpretation, it must be remembered that the researcher's primary goal is to seek the truth, not to espouse a particular point of view that may not be supported by the data.

Discussion

The Discussion section is the part of the manuscript in which the author offers an evaluation and interpretation of the findings of the study, particularly as they relate to the hypotheses that were proposed in the Introduction. Typically the author will begin this section with a brief review of the major findings of the study and a clear statement of whether the data were consistent or inconsistent with the hypotheses. The discussion will then address any discrepancies between the predictions and the data, trying to resolve these inconsistencies and offering plausible reasons for their occurrence. In general, the first portion of the Discussion is devoted to an evaluation of the hypotheses that were originally set forth in the Introduction, given the data that were obtained in the research.

The Discussion may be seen as the inverse of the Introduction, paralleling the issues raised in that section in the opposite order of presentation. Therefore, after discussing the relationship of the data with the hypotheses, the author often attempts to integrate the new findings into the body of research that provided the background for the study. Just as this literature initially provided the context within which you can understand the rationale for the study, it subsequently provides the context within which the data can be understood and interpreted. The author's responsibility at this point is to help you recognize the potential import of the research, without relying on hype or gimmicks to make the point.

The Discussion continues to expand in terms of the breadth of ideas discussed until it reaches the broad, conceptual issues that are addressed by the superordinate theoretical work that originally stimulated the past research literature. If a particular piece of research is to make a significant contribution to the field, its findings must either clarify some past discrepancy in the literature, identify boundary conditions for the applicability of the critical theoretical work, reconcile differences of opinion among the researchers in the field, or otherwise contribute to a more complete understanding of the mechanisms and mediators of important social phenomena.

Once the author has reached the goals that are common to most journal articles, attention may be turned to less rigorous ideas. Depending on a particular journal's editorial policy and the availability of additional space, the author may finish the article with a brief section about possible applications of the present work, implications for future work in the area, and with some restraint, speculations about what lies ahead for the line of research. Scientists tend to have relatively little tolerance for conclusions without foundation and off-the-cuff comments made without full consideration. Therefore, authors must be careful not to overstep the bounds of propriety in making speculations about the future. But such exercises can be useful and can serve a heuristic function for other researchers if the notions stated are well conceived.

Finally, particularly if the article has been relatively long or complex, the author may decide to end it with a short Conclusion. The Conclusion usually simply restates the major arguments that have been made throughout the article, reminding the reader one last time of the value of the work.

As we suggested earlier, not all articles will follow the format exactly. Some latitude is allowed to accommodate the particular needs of the author and the quirks of the research being described. Given that the goal is effective communication of information, it would not be reasonable for the format to dictate what could and could not be included in a manuscript. We hope that this introduction will help to demystify research articles and provide you with some insights into what an author is trying to accomplish at various points in the report. Let us end with a word of encouragement: Your enjoyment of social psychology will be enhanced by your fuller appreciation of the sources of the information to which you are being exposed, and, to the extent that you are able to read and understand these original sources for yourself, your appreciation of this work will be maximized.

Reference

Storms, M. D. (1973). Videotape and the attribution process: Reversing actors' and observers' points of view. *Journal of Personality and Social Psychology, 27*, 165-175.

Exercise for Appendix A

Factual Questions

1. What four elements should the Abstract convey?

2. Which part of a report provides the "foundation" for the study and the remainder of the article?

3. Normally, should the literature review be selective *or* comprehensive?

4. If there is a research hypothesis, should it be explicitly stated in the Introduction?

5. Are experimental *or* correlational studies better for making inferences about cause-and-effect?

6. What is a *criterion variable* in a correlational study?

7. Which part of a report describes the operationalizations and procedures employed in the study?

8. The Method section usually begins with a description of what?

9. According to the authors, what is probably the most intimidating section of a research report for students?

10. Should experienced researchers expect to find statistical techniques with which they are unfamiliar when they read research reports?

11. How should the Discussion section of a research report typically begin?

12. Which part of a report usually simply restates the major arguments that have been made throughout the article?